Abnormal and clinical psychology

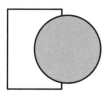

Abnormal and clinical psychology

An introductory textbook

Paul Bennett

Open University Press
Maidenhead · Philadelphia

Open University Press
McGraw-Hill Education
McGraw-Hill House
Shoppenhangers Road
Maidenhead
Berkshire
England
SL6 2QL

email: enquiries@openup.co.uk
world wide web: www.openup.co.uk

and
325 Chestnut Street
Philadelphia, PA 19106, USA

First Published 2003

A catalogue record of this book is available from the British Library

ISBN   0 335 21236 0 (pb)   0 335 21237 9 (hb)

Library of Congress Cataloging-in-Publication Data
   Bennett, Paul, 1955–
      Abnormal and clinical psychology : an introductory textbook/
   Paul Bennett.
         p. cm.
      Includes bibliographical references and index.
      ISBN 0-335-21237-9 – ISBN 0-335-21236-0 (pbk.)
      1. Psychology, Pathological.   2. Clinical psychology.   I. Title.
   RC454 .B446 2003
   616.89–dc21   2002035467

Typeset by Graphicraft Limited, Hong Kong
Printed in Great Britain by Biddles Ltd, www.biddles.co.uk

Contents

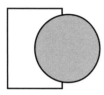

Illustrations

Figures

Tables

Boxes

 # Acknowledgements

I am grateful to the following people for their help, feedback and encouragement in writing this book, in particular: Mandy Iles, Ceri Phelps, John Baird, Lucy Johnstone, Graham Turpin, Peter Kinderman, Stu Brooke, Gill Bennett, Lucie Byrne, Ian Sutherland, Mary Birchall, and of course the unknown people who have kindly allowed me to tell their stories.

Part I
Background and methods

Introduction

This chapter introduces a number of issues relevant to abnormal psychology, many of which are returned to in more detail later in the book. It starts by considering what is meant by abnormal psychology and how this relates to mental health. It looks at how these ideas have changed over time, before considering ways in which mental health problems can be conceptualized. The chapter next examines a number of factors that contribute to the development of mental health disorders, focusing on genetic, biological, psychological, social and familial explanations. Finally, it introduces the biopsychosocial approach, which attempts to integrate these various factors into one holistic model. By the end of the chapter, you should have an understanding of:

- Modern concepts of abnormality
- Historical concepts and treatments of abnormality
- Issues of diagnosis: the key diagnostic classification systems and their alternatives
- Models of the **aetiology** of mental health problems: genetic, biological, psychological, socio-cultural and systemic or familial
- The biopsychosocial approach.

Modern concepts of abnormality

This book focuses on factors that contribute to mental health problems and their treatment. Despite its name, it actually excludes many individuals who would be considered 'abnormal', if one were to define abnormal as 'to differ from the norm'. Indeed, a number of simple definitions of abnormality may be proposed, none of which capture the essence of what is meant by the term abnormal in the context of mental health problems:

- *Statistical abnormality* implies that people who are statistically different from the norm are 'abnormal': the further from the norm one is, the greater the abnormality. While this may be true, it does not necessarily imply the presence of a mental disorder. People who are rich or highly attractive, those who engage in dangerous sports or who significantly achieve in their career, all differ significantly from the norm. But none of these would be seen as having a mental health problem.
- *Psychometric abnormality* implicates abnormality as a deviation from a statistically determined norm, such as the population average IQ of 100. In this case, an IQ score less than about 70–75 may define someone as having learning difficulties and suggests they will have some difficulties coping with life. However, the problems associated with a low IQ differ significantly across individuals depending on their life circumstances. So, even when an individual is defined as psychometrically 'abnormal', this tells us little about their actual condition or problems. Furthermore, if one takes the other end of the IQ spectrum, a deviation of 30 points above the mean is generally not considered to be abnormal nor to indicate the presence of mental health problems.
- *The Utopian model* suggests that only those who achieve their maximum potential within their lives are free of mental health problems. However, even those who propose this model (e.g. Rogers 1961: see Chapter 3 in this volume) accept that only relatively few people truly achieve their maximum potential. Accordingly, this model assumes that the majority of the population deviate from their optimal mental state and experience some degree of mental health problems. Poor mental health may be considered the norm, not the exception.
- *The presence of abnormal or deviant behaviour* is perhaps the closest of the simple models to provide an understanding of abnormality as it relates to mental health problems, because it implies a deviation from normal behaviour in some 'negative' way. But as a single criterion it is inadequate. Not all people with mental health problems engage in deviant behaviour, and not all deviant behaviours are a sign of mental health problems: stealing a car and 'joy riding', which places many people in danger, may be considered deviant abnormal behaviour by most people, but it is not a sign of a mental health problem.

More complex models of abnormality in the context of mental health consider abnormal behaviour to be a sign of a mental health problem when

- it is the result of distorted psychological processes
- it causes or is the result of distress and/or is dysfunctional
- it is an out-of-the ordinary response to particular circumstances.

A fourth criterion is that the individual may place themselves in danger as a result of a distorted view of the world, although this is relatively infrequent even among those who may be thought of as having a mental health problem. These criteria can perhaps be summarized as the 'four Ds': deviance (from the norm), distress, dysfunctional and dangerous. They generally hold true, but there are important exceptions. Paedophilia, for example, is not necessarily associated with personal distress, nor do people who engage in psychopathic behaviour experience remorse as a result of their actions.

Despite these criteria, which suggest some universality about what is and what is not a mental disorder, such judgements differ across social groups, societies and time. Definitions of mental disorders, deviance or abnormality are societally defined, not absolute. In some societies people who see visions and speak to themselves are considered wise and to have special powers. In others, they are considered to have a **psychotic** illness and to require treatment. In Puerto Rico, for example, a belief that one is surrounded by spirits is common; in the UK, such beliefs would probably result in hospitalization and being treated for schizophrenia. It is noteworthy that the activity of joy riding provided earlier as an example of abnormal behaviour will be considered so only by some groups in society; others may consider this to be acceptable, even admirable behaviour.

In some cases, odd behaviour may result in an individual being labelled eccentric – a more benign label than 'mad' or 'mentally ill'. What label is assigned may vary according to the degree to which the individual differs from the norm, how many of their behaviours are abnormal, and the implications of these behaviours to others. However, the nature of the label assigned has powerful implications for the individual. Perhaps the most extreme example of this can be found in a classic study reported by Rosenhan (1973). In it, he taught a number of students to act as if they were psychotic – by stating that they heard one-word **hallucinations** – in an attempt to study the processes of diagnosis and hospitalization. As Rosenhan predicted, most students were admitted into the hospital and assigned a diagnosis of schizophrenia. What was perhaps more surprising was that when the students broke their disguise and admitted to the hoax, many of their psychiatrists took this to be further evidence of their 'illness'. It took some weeks before some students were discharged from hospital, some with a diagnosis of 'schizophrenia in remission'.

Historical overview

Explanations of 'madness' have existed for much of our history, and have varied markedly over time. Early Chinese, Hebrew and Egyptian writings ascribed bizarre behaviours to demonic possession. By the first century BC, more biological explanations were predominant. Hippocrates, for example, considered abnormal behaviour to result from an imbalance between four fluids, or humours, within the body: yellow and black bile, blood and phlegm. Excess yellow bile, for example, resulted in mania; excess black bile resulted in melancholia. Treatment involved reducing levels of the relevant fluids through a variety of means. Levels of black bile, for example, could be reduced by a quiet life, a vegetarian diet, temperance, exercise and celibacy. Although radical treatment approaches such as bleeding or restraint by mechanical devices were evident at this time, the first-line treatment of both ancient Greeks and Romans was generally humane, and included providing comfort and a supportive atmosphere.

By the Middle Ages, the dominance of religious thinking and the clergy resulted in abnormal behaviour once more being considered the result of demonic possession. Treatment was provided by priests, and involved attempts to rid the individual of the demon through prayer, chanting and administration of holy water or bitter drinks. More radical approaches included insulting the devil, starving, whipping or stretching the affected individual. Perhaps the most dramatic treatment of people supposedly possessed by demons was the Catholic church's *Malleus Malforum* (witches' hammer) which provided a guide to the identification and treatment of witches, who were considered to blame for any ills that occurred within society. The manual stated that a sudden loss of reason was the result of demonic possession, and that burning was the one way to expel the devil.

Towards the end of the Middle Ages, power again shifted to the secular authorities and, as a result, biological theories of mental health problems once more became dominant. Institutions for the humane care of people with mental health problems were established. However, the initial success of these asylums led to them becoming over-crowded. As a result, the quality of care they provided deteriorated and become increasingly inhumane. One of the most famous of these institutions was Bethlem Hospital in London. Here, patients were bound by chains and, in certain phases of the moon, some were chained and whipped to prevent violence. Restraints were cruel and inhumane. The hospital became one of the most popular tourist attractions in London, with people paying to see the crazed inmates: hence the term, Bedlam.

The care of mentally disturbed people changed once more in the eighteenth century. William Tuke in Britain and Phillipe Pinel in France established more humane treatments; although asylums remained, their inmates were able to move around them freely. Treatments included working closely with inmates, reading and talking to them and taking them on regular walks. Many people were released from hospital as a result of their improved condition. This 'moral approach' to the treatment of the insane was based on the assumption that if all those with mental health problems were treated with care, they would improve sufficiently not to need further care. However, as success rates did not achieve this optimistic level and it became clear that not all those treated in this way would be cured, prejudice against people with mental health problems increased. Long-term incarceration once more became the norm.

Somatogenic and psychogenic perspectives

In the early twentieth century, theories and treatments of mental disorders diverged into two approaches: the somatogenic and psychogenic perspectives. The *somatogenic approach* considered mental abnormalities to result from biological disorders of the brain. A highly influential advocate of this approach, Emil Kraepelin, constructed the first modern typology of abnormal behaviour (Kraepelin [1883] 1981). He identified various clusters of symptoms, gave them a diagnostic label, and reported on their course. He measured the effects of various drugs on abnormal behaviour. Despite the rapid adoption of this approach, many of the interventions it led to, including remedies as diverse as tonsillectomy and **lobotomy** (see Chapter 3), proved ineffective. More recently, the biological approach has led to the development of powerful drugs used in the treatment of conditions as varied as depression, schizophrenia and anxiety disorders.

The *psychogenic approach* considered the primary causes of mental disorders to be psychological. It was initially led by an Austrian physician, Friedrich Mesmer. In 1778, he established a clinic in Paris to treat people with **hysterical disorders**. The treatment he provided, called mesmerism, involved the patient sitting in a darkened room filled with music. Mesmer then appeared dressed in a flamboyant costume and touched the troubled area of the individual's body with a special rod, a treatment that proved effective in a number of cases. Despite this, he was considered a charlatan and eventually banned from holding his clinics in Paris. Other leading advocates of the psychogenic approach, Jean Charcot and then Sigmund Freud, used hypnotism in the treatment of hysterical disorders. Treatment typically involved hypnotizing the patient before encouraging them to identify the factors precipitating the onset of their symptoms and to re-experience their emotions at this time, a process known as **catharsis**. Freud later rejected this method in favour of free association and the use of **psychoanalysis**.

The latter part of the twentieth century saw a revolution in the treatment of mental health problems and a strengthening of both the biological and psychological approaches. Humanistic therapies advocated by Carl Rogers added to those of Freud and the analysts, as did the behavioural and cognitive behavioural approaches led by theorists and clinicians such as Hans Eysenck and Stanley Rachman in the UK, and Aaron Beck and Donald Meichenbaum in the USA and Canada (see Chapter 2). Psychological therapies now provide effective treatment for conditions as diverse as schizophrenia, depression, and anxiety disorders.

Care in the community

Modern treatments have allowed thousands of individuals with chronic mental health conditions who would have required hospital care in the first half of the twentieth century to be treated in the community. The change from hospital to community care began in the UK in the 1950s, and reached its peak in the 1970s. Over this time, many people who had spent years, perhaps decades, in hospital were gradually moved back into the communities from which they came. This was not an easy process, as by the time these changes in care were enacted, many of these people had become totally institutionalized. Their behaviour was determined by the rules of the hospital, which were generally more accepting of deviance than the general population. They had limited self-care skills, as they had not been responsible for cooking, cleaning and other elements of self-care for many years. Often the impact of living in an institution was more disabling than the condition for which they had originally been hospitalized, which could have been as non-problematic as vagrancy or being an unmarried mother. As a result of these factors, people discharged into the community had to be taught how to survive outside the hospital environment. Without this, many struggled after discharge, ending up as 'rotating door' cases; that is, as quickly as they were discharged into the community, they were readmitted to the hospital.

To avoid these difficulties, modern treatment seeks to minimize the use of hospital facilities and to maintain people within the community in which they live. People with relatively minor mental health problems, including most people with anxiety or mild–moderate depression, are treated by their general practitioner (GP) in primary care. Even relatively serious mental health problems are usually treated through outpatient appointments or in the individual's own home by multidisciplinary teams of health care workers. Admission to hospital occurs only at times of crisis or exacerbation of problems, with discharge back to the community as quickly as is reasonably possible.

Multidisciplinary teams are typically led by a consultant psychiatrist who has medical responsibility for the care of their patients. They and the more junior doctors are medical graduates who have specialized in the care of the 'mentally ill'. At the time of writing they are the only members of the team who can prescribe medication, although many adopt other clinical interests and may be involved in the provision of other therapies. Nurses within the team have a specialized training in the care of people with mental health problems. They have a multifaceted role involving, among other things, monitoring an individual's progress, recommending changes in medication, providing basic psychological therapies and acting as advocate for the patient. More specialized professions may also be involved in the provision of care. Occupational therapists can help the individual develop or maintain life skills such as cooking or strategies for coping with stress. Clinical psychologists provide therapy for people with complex problems, and support others in their therapeutic work with **clients**, through **clinical supervision** and training in therapy skills. Finally, social workers help the individual deal with social problems such as lack of money or unemployment that may contribute to their problems.

Issues of diagnosis

The medical model

This book is generally organized around a set of diagnostic labels that can be ascribed to people with common mental experiences or who behave in similar ways – schizophrenia, depression and so on. The approach is rooted in the 'medical model', which assumes that mental health problems are the result of physiological abnormalities, generally involving brain systems. The disorder is considered as an illness, much as other medical problems are, and is therefore treated with physical treatments that modify the underlying biological disorder, the most common of which involves drug therapy. The type of treatment given is determined by a diagnosis, which is itself determined by the presence or absence of various signs or symptoms. This assumes that people with mental health problems are experiencing a state divorced from that of 'normal' individuals: a mental illness.

Classification systems

The historical roots of this approach lie in the work of Kraepelin in the late nineteenth century. He described a number of syndromes, each of which had a common set of symptoms which differed from those of other syndromes, in a classification system of mental health disorders which later formed the basis of the World Health Organization's (WHO) International Classification of Diseases (ICD: WHO 1992). Indicating how such systems have struggled to accurately identify and classify mental health conditions, this is currently in its tenth revision. The American Psychiatric Association (APA) devised its own classification system, known as the *Diagnostic and Statistical Manual* (DSM), which although having much in common with the ICD system, differs in a number of details. Like the ICD, it has changed over the years and, having first been published in 1952, is now in its fifth revision (**DSM-IV-TR**: APA 2000).

The DSM system is 'multi-axial'. That is, it allows an individual's mental state to be evaluated on five different axes:

- *Axis 1:* the presence or absence of most clinical syndromes, including schizophrenia, mood, anxiety, sexual and eating disorders
- *Axis 2:* the presence or absence of stable long-term conditions, including personality disorders and learning disabilities
- *Axis 3:* relevant information on the individual's physical health
- *Axis 4:* psychosocial and environmental problems
- *Axis 5:* rating of an individual's global level of functioning: from a score of 1 for persistent violence, suicidal behaviour or inability to maintain personal hygiene to 100, symptom free.

Classification systems provide a number of benefits, not the least of which is an apparent simplicity – many would say an oversimplification – of definitions of mental health problems. In addition, they provide those using the system with a dichotomous outcome that fits the medical model of treatment. Whether an individual has an 'illness' or not will determine whether or not they are treated, admitted to hospital and so on. Proponents of the medical model have argued that a reliable diagnosis that is consistent both within and between countries ensures that:

- any individual presenting with a set of problems will receive the same diagnosis across the world
- they will therefore receive the same treatment wherever they are in the world
- research that informs treatment focuses on the same condition wherever it is conducted.

Diagnoses are particularly important in relation to drug therapies where a diagnosis will determine which class of drugs is used to treat the presenting problem: antidepressants for depression, **major tranquillizers** for schizophrenia, and so on. An incorrect diagnosis will mean that incorrect medication is prescribed. In the case of research, incorrect diagnosis will result in unreliable results from any treatment trial and confuse rather than help the development of new treatments. Before considering how well the present diagnostic systems achieved these goals, it is important to indicate some fundamental scientific and philosophical drawbacks to this approach.

- The model implies a dichotomy between normal and abnormal mental states. An individual either is mentally ill or is not. This dichotomy is becoming increasingly difficult to sustain. Many 'abnormal' states ascribed to the 'mentally ill' have now been found to occur to large numbers of the 'normal' population; many people who live normal lives and who have never been considered in any way 'abnormal' report, for example, hearing voices in their head – almost a defining characteristic of schizophrenia.

- The model implies that when an individual is ill, they behave or experience mental events that are in some way abnormal and different from those of 'normal' people – an argument rejected by the findings of cognitive psychology. There is increasing evidence that while the thought content and behaviour of people with and without mental health problems may differ from the norm, the cognitive processes underlying them are essentially the same. This issue will be returned to on many occasions later in the book.
- The approach fails to recognize the experience of the individual; they are assigned a diagnosis and the diagnosis is treated, not the individual.
- The model implies that biological factors are primary in the development of mental health problems and that, therefore, biological treatments are also primary. This ignores findings that social and psychological factors appear to be critical in the development of mental health problems and that biological factors involved in mental health problems change as a result of changes in these factors (see Chapter 4). This also distracts from findings that pharmacological therapies may prove only partially effective in the treatment of a number of apparently biologically mediated conditions (such as schizophrenia, depression) and that psychological therapies have proved more effective than pharmacological in the treatment of many conditions.

Diagnostic consistency

Despite the development of clear criteria for each disorder, diagnosis is not a clear-cut process. Even within countries, levels of agreement on diagnosis may be low. In the 1960s, Beck et al. (1962) reported only a 54 per cent agreement between four psychiatrists on the diagnoses assigned to 154 patients based on their own interviews. By the mid-1980s, things had not changed. Lipton and Simon (1985), for example, compared the diagnoses made by hospital doctors with those made by an inspection team in one psychiatric hospital. While 89 patients were assigned a diagnosis of schizophrenia by the hospital doctors, the review team assigned only 16 such diagnoses. Originally 15 patients were assigned a diagnosis of depression; 50 received this on review. The goal of DSM is to minimize the possibility of such errors, and each new edition strives to make the criteria for each diagnosis more clear cut. Its latest version, DSM-IV-TR (APA 2000: the revised fourth edition), has been tested by a number of clinicians to ensure consistency of diagnosis, although its reliability still has to be formally assessed.

What even a clear diagnostic system may have difficulty in dealing with are the biases that clinicians bring to the diagnostic process. Clinicians may reach varying diagnostic decisions as a result of the different information they obtain either as a result of their consultative style or the biases they bring to the assessment. Diagnoses may also be influenced by clinicians' knowledge of the disorder or any previous diagnoses made by other doctors, the frequency with which the doctor has encountered the condition, and the costs and benefits of giving a diagnosis. Under conditions of uncertainty, for example, clinicians may diagnose a condition that they feel is likely to benefit the patient most and harm them least, even if it is wrong.

Diagnostic validity: schizophrenia

Validity of classification labels can also be difficult to achieve. Perhaps the most controversy lies with the diagnosis of schizophrenia. One of the important criteria for the diagnosis of schizophrenia when first identified by Kraepelin was that it was a progressive and deteriorating condition with no return to levels of functioning achieved before its onset. Bleuler (1908) later identified four fundamental symptoms of what he termed the group of schizophrenias: ambivalence, disturbance of association, disturbance of affect, and a preference of fantasy over reality.

Subsequent diagnostic systems have, until recently, adapted Kraepelin and Bleuler's diagnostic categories, and attempted to develop increasingly clear and unambivalent diagnostic criteria for various sub-types of the disorder. Until the mid-1990s, DSM-III (APA 1987) identified four types of schizophrenia:

- *simple:* progressive development of 'oddities of conduct', an inability to meet the demands of society, and withdrawal from everyday life
- *paranoid:* stable, paranoid **delusions**, frequently accompanied by auditory hallucinations that support these delusional beliefs
- *catatonic:* marked **psychomotor** disturbances, switching between extreme excitement, stupor and **waxy flexibility** in which the individual may be placed in a position and maintain it for several hours
- *hebephrenic:* changes in mood and irresponsible and unpredictable behaviour, accompanied by disorganized thought processes and speech that is frequently rambling and incoherent.

Unfortunately, this categorization disregarded any form of causal theory of linkages between the various symptom clusters, and may have actually inhibited our developing understanding of the nature and treatment of schizophrenia. A more useful classification system has now been derived from consideration of the causes of the symptoms of schizophrenia.

Factor analysis of the signs and symptoms of the various sub-types of schizophrenia has identified three clusters of symptoms, known as **disorganized symptoms, positive symptoms** and **negative symptoms** (Liddle et al. 1994) that tend to co-occur. The positive cluster includes hallucinations, delusions, disorganized speech or positive thought disorder. Negative symptoms denote an absence of activation, and include apathy, lack of motivation or poverty of speech. Disorganized symptoms include disorganized speech and behaviour, and flat or inappropriate mood. These may have differing biological and neuropsychological foundations, and prove a more useful way of categorizing the various schizophrenic-type disorders (see Chapter 6).

Even if diagnostic criteria have both high reliability and validity, they carry some negatives. Perhaps the most important is that the process of diagnosis implies the individual has an 'abnormal' medical condition. They 'medicalize' individuals and place them within the remit of the mental health profession, sometimes quite inappropriately. Until 1973, homosexuality was listed as a sexual disorder within DSM, legitimizing attempts at treatment and legislation against homosexuals. Now, the criteria for personality disorder include within them a number of characteristics that many would argue should be considered as personality styles, not mental disorders (Widiger and Costa 1994: see Chapter 11).

Cultural relativity

An important goal of DSM is to identify and diagnose mental health problems in a similar way across cultures. The approach assumes that medical illnesses will present in a universal way throughout the world. Whether this is actually the case is questionable. Work by the World Health Organization (1979), for example, suggested that people who develop schizophrenia presented in the same way in nine different countries. Their study was, however, compromised by their use of the same set of criteria to determine whether people had or had not schizophrenia in each country, and their exclusion from this diagnosis of those who presented with differing symptoms. Accordingly, while these data suggested that some people do present with similar problems across the world, they could not exclude the possibility that other people who may have had similar underlying problems may have presented in quite different ways.

One way in which people from different cultures have been found to present quite differently is through the reporting of negative emotions in terms of psychological or physical factors. Somatization involves the presentation or experience of physical problems rather than emotional ones: 'My heart is burning', for example, may imply depression or anxiety. This type of reporting is relatively rare in western cultures, and very common in Asians and countries such as Turkey, possibly because such cultures disapprove of the strong expression of emotions, particularly negative ones (Chen 1995). Seeking help for physical problems therefore becomes an acceptable route for help with psychological ones. This cultural relativism does indicate that it may be inappropriate to assume that a set of diagnostic symptoms may be appropriate for all cultures and at all times.

A social critique

In addition to the scientific critique, a number of social commentators have raised strong ethical objections to the medical model. Farber (1990), for example, argued that the medical model underestimates the individual's capacity for change, and consequently inhibits this capacity. At its most stark, the model assumes that unchangeable biological factors lead to psychological states that are distinct from the mental processes of 'normal' individuals. These may remit, either as a result of treatment or through natural recovery, but the individual is still prone to further episodes of the disorder.

Farber identified two types of medical models: one that assumes that mental disorders are the result of genetic and biological factors and the psychoanalytic model that assumes the adult disorders are the result of psychological, but biologically driven, mental structures that are set down in childhood and are unchangeable over the life course. He saw the ethical danger of the medical model in its legitimization of the health care professions', and therefore the state's, control of people considered as disordered. Perhaps the most extreme example of this has been various extreme left- and right-wing governments' use of psychiatry to control its dissenters. According to Farber, the medical treatment that people with mental health disorders receive prevents them from self-change and serves to reinforce assumptions that they are not capable of self-development and change. He also contended that such treatment is coercive, and that any attempt at self-change is viewed negatively and resisted: the patient who wishes to discontinue medical treatment, for example, is told that this is a sign that they are resisting treatment, and that they do not want to get 'well'. Only the experts know when people who are mentally ill are well enough to make authentic choices.

Having provided such a critique of the medical model, the astute reader may now be asking why the book is organized around a set of diagnoses which may be so seriously questioned. Their use here perhaps reflects a dilemma, and one of the reasons for their continued use by psychologists and others that reject the medical model. They provide a shorthand means of orienting the reader to the content of each chapter. Their use does not imply an acceptance of the medical model – even the 'reality' of the conditions described within them is occasionally questioned – and while biological explanations for each disorder are provided, this certainly does not indicate that these are considered the primary cause.

Alternatives to the medical model

Any alternative to the medical model needs necessarily to differ from it on some important dimensions. In particular, it needs to

- consider there to be no dichotomy between abnormal and normal mental states
- consider the social and psychological processes that lead to and accompany any mental health problems
- make the affected individual (and not their diagnosis) the focus of any assessment and treatment
- at least consider non-pharmacologically based interventions as primary.

Two alternative approaches that address these issues, at least to some degree, are the dimensional approach and psychological formulation.

Dimensional approaches

While accepting the benefits of some form of diagnostic system, a number of commentators (e.g. Widiger and Costa 1994) have challenged the categorical approach adopted by the DSM. In DSM, diagnoses are based on the presence of a number of symptoms, such as poor sleep, feeling depressed, and so on. It provides a categorical classification: the individual either has a disorder or does not. A dimensional approach rejects this all-or-nothing approach and the assumption that the mental states of people with a mental health problem are distinctly different from those of the 'normal' population. Proponents of the dimensional approach (e.g. Clark et al. 1995) argue that categorical models of psychopathology are challenged by a number of problems, including that of co-morbidity, in which a single person might satisfy criteria for more than one diagnosis, such as schizophrenia and affective disorder; heterogeneity, in which two people with the same diagnosis can present with entirely different patterns of symptoms; and the provision in DSM of a subcategory of 'not otherwise specified', which Clark and colleagues suggested seems to be a mechanism for assigning diagnoses that do not really 'fit'.

The dimensional approach suggests that people who are now diagnosed as having a mental disorder may better be considered to be at the extreme end of a distribution of normality, not categorically different from others. Many of us have been anxious or depressed at one time or another, felt like not engaging with the world, or slept poorly. These experiences are not unique to people with a depressive disorder. Whether or not we consider them to be problematic is dependent on the degree and intensity to which they are experienced. Dimensional approaches adopt this approach, and suggest it is the degree to which problems are experienced, not merely their presence or absence, that determines whether or not an individual has a mental health problem. This approach fits well with increasing findings that some 'symptoms' of mental health disorders, such as hearing voices, are relatively common within the general population, and may never lead an individual to seek help or impair their everyday living (see Chapter 6). As a compromise with the diagnostic approach, they suggest that if an individual scores above a threshold score, based on the severity and frequency of their experiences, they may be given some form of diagnosis.

The dimensional approach has a number of strengths. In particular it highlights which aspects of a person's life are problematic and for which they may require some form of help, and avoids 'forcing' the presenting problems into a diagnostic category into which they do not easily fit. What it does not address is the processes through which an individual developed their problems or an understanding of the factors that maintain them. This level of assessment is provided by the psychological formulation.

Psychological formulation

Diagnostic criteria are helpful in determining the pharmacological treatment that may benefit an individual. They are of less benefit to therapists using other treatment approaches. Here, any diagnostic label simplifies and reduces the information it carries to a degree beyond that which is useful. At its most basic, a clinician adopting a biological model of mental health disorders would aim to give a diagnostic label to a cluster of symptoms, and then provide the drug treatment related to that condition. The exact nature of the problems an individual faces or how they are expressed will be of only secondary interest. A person with schizophrenia who is hallucinating will be treated with drugs that stop hallucinations; the nature of the hallucinations will not influence the drug treatment given. A depressed individual will receive antidepressants regardless of the nature and causes of their condition.

A quite different view is taken by **psychotherapists**. From their perspective, the nature of the hallucinations or conditions that led to a period of depression are of paramount importance, and are the focus of any intervention. The diagnostic label assigned has little impact on the type of treatment given. A psychotherapist working with someone who is experiencing hallucinations, for example, would want to know their exact nature and content so they can apply specific techniques tailored to the specific needs of the individual to help them cope or respond to them more appropriately (see p. 146).

Psychological formulations attempt to identify the processes that led to and maintain the problems an individual is facing. These may be external: negative life-events, rape, bereavement, and so on. They may be internal: distorted interpretations of the world, **hyperventilation** leading

to panic disorder, and so on. They may be short-term or longer-term
sequelae to childhood events such as sexual abuse or poor parental relationships. The goal of the therapist is to identify the specific factors that
are leading to and maintaining the problem for the particular individual
they are working with at the time. These factors then become the target
for future interventions.

A formulation is an explanatory hypothesis about the nature of the
clinical problem. This usually reflects the theoretical orientation of the
therapist. For a cognitive therapist, it will address the nature of faulty
cognitions or maladaptive behaviours, how they were established, what
maintains them, and so on. A Freudian analyst would be concerned with
how an individual's behaviour is linked to unconscious processes and
their developmental history. It includes a number of 'best guesses' and
the causes of the problem, what is maintaining it, and how it may be
resolved. The formulation has two main functions: first, to guide the
therapist in what to do, and second, to help establish criteria for evaluating the intervention: to determine what are the goals of therapy and how
success or failure in achieving these goals is measured. Formulations are
not static. They may well change in the light of new evidence gained over
time, as will the focus and form of any intervention.

Formulations are guided by theory. These guide the questions asked
by a therapist and the formulation of the problem they establish. This, of
course, is both a strength and a weakness. A strength because they allow
the therapist to select, in a relatively parsimonious way, from the myriad
of potential contributors to a problem those most likely to be relevant. A
weakness because they may focus the therapist too exclusively on what
they deem to be important aspects of a client's experience and too little
on what may actually be important, but seem irrelevant to the therapist
as a result of their theoretical 'blinkers'. On this basis, some have argued
that good therapists are aware of several aetiological models and can
either integrate them into a meaningful synthesis or identify which are
relevant to particular clients. The validity of this approach is considered
more in Chapter 5, pp. 105–6.

The aetiology of mental health problems

There are a number of diverse literatures focusing on risk factors for
mental health problems. These do not act independently, but combine in
some way to influence the risk an individual has for developing a disorder. The rest of this chapter provides an introduction to each type of
explanation. The following chapters examine the issues in more detail.

- *Genetic models* consider how genetic factors influence an individual's risk of developing a mental health disorder. Genetic factors

have been implicated in conditions as varied as schizophrenia, **Alzheimer's disease** and depression.

- *Biological models* focus on biochemical processes, usually involving chemicals known as **neurotransmitters**, which mediate mood and behaviour. They also consider how damage to the brain can result in a number of mental health disorders.
- *Psychological models* focus on the internal mental processes that influence mood and behaviour. Unlike the genetic or biochemical models, there is no single explanatory paradigm. Instead, there are a number of psychological explanations of mental health disorders, the best known being psychoanalytic, humanistic, behavioural and cognitive behavioural.
- *The socio-cultural approach* focuses on the role of social and cultural factors in mental health disorders.
- *Systemic models* focus on the role of smaller social systems, frequently the family, in which the individual is situated. Disorders are considered to be the consequence of stressful or disordered interactions with families.
- *The biopsychosocial approach* attempts to integrate these various factors into a holistic causal model. This approach suggests that genetic or other biological factors may increase an individual's risk of developing a mental health disorder. However, whether the disorder will actually develop depends on whether the 'at risk' individual encounters factors such as social or family stress and/or whether they have the coping resources to help them cope with such stresses.

Genetic models

With the exception of egg, sperm and red blood cells, each of the approximately 100 trillion cells of the body contains two complete sets of the human genome: one set from the individual's father, the other from their mother. Each genome comprises 23 pairs of **chromosomes**. Each set of chromosomes carry the 60,000–80,000 genes that contribute to both the physical and psychological characteristics of the individual.

Each set of matched genes affecting the same processes are known as alleles. The instructions in the sets of genes from each parent may be the same or quite different, for example, blue versus brown eyes. Where the alleles are the same, the individual is described as homozygotic. Where they differ, they are termed heterozygotic. The expression of these 'competing' genes is determined by whether the genes are dominant or recessive. Some genes, such as those determining the eye colour brown, are described as dominant. When linked to a gene with other instructions they are expressed. Recessive genes are expressed only when matched with other recessive genes with the same instructions. The development of most mental health disorders is associated with recessive genes. If they were the result of dominant genes, their expression in each generation would be virtually guaranteed, resulting in continuing disadvantage and limited chances of reproduction.

Genetic studies of the aetiology of mental health problems have done so using several methods. Family studies measure whether those with genotypes that are more or less similar to the affected individual are at different risk for the disorder. If there is a genetic linkage in a disorder, one would expect someone with an identical genetic make-up (a **monozygotic (MZ) twin**), to be more likely to develop the disorder than a non-identical or **dyzygotic (DZ) twin**, who has roughly 50 per cent of genes in common, who in turn would be more at risk than a cousin or aunt with even less genetic similarity. Many family studies focus on the degree to which both MZ and DZ twins develop the same disorder. Where more MZ than DZ twins are concordant for the disorder, this is taken to imply some level of genetic risk. This approach has a number of limitations. Critically, not only do closer family members share more genes, they also share a more common environment. MZ twins, for example, tend to be treated more similarly than DZ twins. Any concordance for a condition may therefore be attributable to a shared environment rather than shared genes.

In an attempt to more carefully separate out environment from genetic factors, a number of studies have examined concordance rates in twins brought up in differing environments, usually as a result of adoption. This method typically identifies MZ twins separated close to birth and examines whether they are or are not concordant for the condition under examination. It is assumed that because the separated twins have a common genetic make-up and different environments any concordance for the condition under examination is the result of genetic factors. However, there are a number of reasons why any **heritability coefficient** determined by this method may not prove totally accurate. First, even twins that are separated have factors other than their genes in common. If nothing else, they have shared the same prenatal experiences that may determine risk for various disorders.

Another factor that can result in overestimation of genetic risk involves any genetic influence on the behaviour of a child, particularly where they are 'difficult' or 'problematic', instigating similar reactions from those caring for them. As a result, separated children may experience both a common genetic heritage and a common family background, despite their separation. Where the family reaction is one that itself contributes to risk for emotional or behavioural problems, this may result in high levels of concordance between twins being attributed solely to genetic factors using traditional analytical methods.

This kind of interpretive problem has resulted in new methodologies in this type of study. Rather than assume the nature of the environment in which the person lives, they have now begun to measure genetic, environmental, social and other life stresses. These data are then subject to complex statistical modelling techniques that allow the investigators to determine the degree to which both genetic and environmental factors contribute to the development of the disorder under investigation.

This type of research is able to identify the strength of any genetic linkage, but not isolate the nature or location of the gene or genes involved. Work on the human genome now permits this more fundamental research. Most disorders are likely to result from a number of genes (that is, they are **polygenic**), and in some cases problems may arise from the absence of a gene, rather than its presence. There is evidence, for example, of a gene locus on chromosome 4 that may be 'protective' against alcohol problems. Whatever the genetic linkages found, there is a general consensus that genes, at most, influence risk for a particular mental health disorder. It is also important to note that while risk for a particular disorder may be increased as a result of genetic factors, many if not most people with the disorder will not carry the relevant gene. Eighty-nine per cent of individuals diagnosed with schizophrenia, for example, have no known relative with the disorder. Not carrying the gene that increases risk for a disorder does not mean that you are immune from that disorder.

Despite this lack of absolute determinism, genetic technologies carry a number of social consequences. At its most extreme, social and political groups such as the Eugenics movement in the late nineteenth and early twentieth centuries advocated the use of selective birth control and sterilization to rid the nation of 'national and racial degeneracy' that was thought to result in mental illness, feeble-mindedness, criminality, alcoholism and sexual promiscuity. Ideas such as this gained widespread political support in the mid-twentieth century, and were used by Hitler to justify the mass extermination of people with mental health problems or learning difficulties.

The potential for testing for genes that confer risk of both physical and mental health problems also carries a number of challenges to modern society. At present, screening programmes for genetic risk of disorders such as cystic fibrosis, Huntington's disease, and breast, ovarian or colo-rectal cancer are now being widely instituted. These testing programmes bring with them a whole series of ethical dilemmas. The UK testing programme for genetic risk of breast cancer, for example, rates people as being at low (population), moderate or high risk of developing breast cancer. We are now learning how a generation of men and women cope with knowledge of their risk of this disease. So far, it seems that it is not easy, and testing seems to evoke high levels of health anxiety both in the short- and long-term (Brain et al. 2002). At a societal level, the likelihood of genetic screening for medical insurance and even job selection is increasing. Will genetic testing result in an underclass that will find it difficult or impossible to get insurance or even a job? Time will tell.

Biological models

Biochemical explanations of mental health problems focus on the bio-logical processes underlying mood and behaviour. Both are regulated by brain systems, whose actions are mediated by neurotransmitters. These systems allow us to perceive information, integrate that informa-tion with past memories and other salient factors, and then respond emotionally and behaviourally. Disruption of these systems as a result of inappropriate neurotransmitter actions results in inappropriate per-ception, mood and behaviour. The exact nature of the systems and the neurotransmitters involved in different mental health problems are considered in more detail in Chapter 3 and each of the chapters in Part II of the book.

Other biochemical processes have been implicated in some conditions. Hormones such as melatonin appear to be involved in the aetiology of seasonal affective disorder, a type of depression considered in Chapter 8. Other disorders may be the result of problems in the architecture of the brain. Schizophrenia, for example, may arise from degeneration or fail-ures of brain development that lead to fundamental errors in informa-tion processing, and disordered thoughts and behaviour. A second common condition, Alzheimer's disease, results from progressive neuronal damage evident through the deterioration of cognitive functioning in later life.

Biochemical models are often considered to be in opposition with psychological explanations: mental health problems are seen as either psychological in nature or to have a biological cause. A more appro-priate way of thinking about the two approaches is that they provide different *levels* of explanation, somewhat analogous to the levels of explanation provided by physics and chemistry. Biochemical processes underpin all our behaviour at all times. The act of writing this sentence is activating numerous sensory, motor and neuronal processes, all of which are mediated by chemical transmissions. But understanding these fundamental processes explains only part of the behaviour: it does not easily account for the motivation in writing it, the process of mental construction of the sentence, nor, indeed, my mood as it was written. To understand these, one needs to address the psychological processes driving the behaviour. In this way, both biochemical and psychological explanations of the behaviour are 'correct'.

Psychological models

In contrast to the biochemical and genetic models where most scientists and practitioners believe in a common process through which mental health disorders arise, there are many psychological models. There are many 'fringe' therapies, most of which have little or no theoretical rationale and whose practice may be somewhat dubious. There are also a number of 'mainstream' theories of mental health disorders and related treatments which largely reflect the development of more general psychological theories over the past century. The first psychological therapy to be practised was psychoanalysis in the beginning of the twentieth century, with Freud and his followers being the leaders of this movement. This was the dominant therapy for a number of years and is still practised, albeit with some modifications over 100 years after its inception.

Psychoanalytic principles were rejected by two therapies, both of which began in the 1950s and 1960s. **Behaviour therapy** (e.g. Wolpe 1982) rejected the notion of psychic processes influencing mood and behaviour and the unscientific nature of psychoanalysis. Its practitioners argued that behaviour is largely controlled by external events, and based its principles on the 'hard' science of operant and classical conditioning. At a similar time, humanistic therapies (Rogers 1961) rejected psychoanalysis, not because of its psychic nature, but because of the *nature* of its psychic phenomena. In contrast to psychoanalysis which assumes that behaviour and mood are influenced by past traumas, humanistic therapies are based on the assumption that behaviour is driven by aspirations towards the future, with the potential of **self-actualization** available to all. Therapy was designed to help the individual achieve their potential, not to resolve the traumas of the past.

The most widely practised therapy is a derivative of behaviour therapy, known as cognitive or cognitive behaviour therapy (Beck 1977). It considers our thought processes, or cognitions, as the prime determinant of behaviour and mood. It makes no assumptions of past trauma or future aspirations and is not based on a model of personality as are psychoanalysis and humanistic therapies. Instead, it focuses on how the thoughts we have at any one time influence mood and behaviour. It assumes that the cognitions that result in mental health problems are somehow 'faulty' and dysfunctional. Therapy focuses on changing them to more functional and less inappropriate ones through a number of educational and therapeutic strategies. It also retains a strong behavioural focus: distorted cognitions, for example, may be challenged by behavioural experiments designed to illustrate errors of thinking. Each of these models is described and discussed in more detail in Chapter 2 and the chapters in Part II.

Psychotherapy versus pharmacotherapy

It is possible to argue that, because biochemical processes underpin behaviour at a fundamental level, altering the levels of neurotransmitters that influence mood through pharmacological processes provides the most direct and effective form of treatment of mental health disorders. While there is some logic in this argument, it certainly does not hold for all cases and it implicitly assumes that psychological therapy does not influence the fundamental biological processes underpinning mental health disorders. This is not the case: there is a powerful reciprocity between the two forms of treatment. Psychological treatments do cause changes at the biochemical level: otherwise they would not alter mood. Similarly, **pharmacotherapy** alters cognitions and behaviour, the primary targets of most psychological interventions.

One argument favouring the use of psychological therapy is that many of the drugs prescribed are effective only while they are being taken. Once a course of drugs has finished, their action stops and the individual's biochemical status, and hence mood and behaviour, may revert to the state it was in before the treatment was commenced. To prevent this, many people are now being prescribed drugs such as antidepressants for much longer than was initially considered to be necessary. In contrast, some have argued that psychological therapy prepares the individual to cope with the stresses they face now and in the future, making them at significantly less risk of relapse once therapy is terminated.

Both arguments may be overstating the case. There is good evidence that many people maintain good mental health following cessation of pharmacological treatments, although the reasons for this may be more psychological than pharmacological. A depressed individual who has withdrawn from family and social life, for example, may benefit from a drug treatment that helps them re-engage with people and enjoy life more. The pleasure gained from this may, itself, increase levels of the neurotransmitters that prevent depression (serotonin and norepinephrine: see Chapter 3) and maintain them in a healthy state once drug therapy is stopped. If they had not re-engaged so positively, the risk of relapse may have been much greater.

It is also true that some individuals do not benefit from psychological therapies, or relapse following successful psychological treatments. They may forget, be unable to use the new skills they have learned, or feel so overwhelmed by circumstances that they once more experience a deterioration in their mental health. For this reason, some advocates of psychological therapy suggest the need for 'booster' sessions some months after the completion of therapy to help maintain a positive mental state.

Both pharmacological and psychological therapies are effective in treating most mental health conditions. Psychological therapies seem to be more effective than drug treatments in treating conditions such as anorexia, panic disorder and some sexual problems. In contrast, although psychological treatments are increasingly being used in the treatment of schizophrenia, the mainstay of treatment remains drug therapy. The relative effectiveness of the two forms of treatment for some conditions such as depression is still hotly debated (see Chapter 8). This debate is returned to in more detail in Chapter 3 and in each of the chapters in Part II of the book.

Socio-cultural models

All the models so far discussed assume that mental disorders arise as a result of problems within the individual, be they genetic, biochemical or psychological. By contrast, the socio-cultural approach assumes that external, social factors contribute to their development. Socio-cultural factors include a wide range of influences, from the family to wider socio-economic factors, some of which were identified in the British Psychiatric Morbidity Survey (Jenkins et al. 1998). This revealed increased rates of depression or anxiety among women, those living in urban settings, unemployed people, and those who are separated, divorced or widowed. Psychoses were more prevalent among urban than rural dwellers. Alcohol dependence was nearly twice as common among those who were unemployed than those who were employed: drug dependence was five times greater among those who were unemployed than those in jobs. People who are members of ethnic minorities or in the lower socio-economic groups are also more likely to experience depression, non-specific distress, schizophrenia or substance abuse problems than those in other sectors of society (Ulbrich et al. 1989). A number of, sometimes competing, theories to explain these differences have been proposed, each of which is discussed in more detail in Chapter 4:

Socio-economic status differences

- *Social drift:* this approach suggests that high levels of mental health problems among the lower socio-economic groups are the result of affected individuals developing a mental health problem, which renders them less economically viable. They may be unable to maintain a job or the levels of overtime required to maintain their standard of living, and drift down the socio-economic scale. That is, mental health problems precede a decline in socio-economic status.
- *Social stress:* this approach assumes that living in different socio-economic conditions results in differing levels of stress: the lower the socio-economic group, the higher the stress. That is, the stresses associated with social deprivation result in mental health problems.
- *Lack of resource model:* similar to the social stress model, this model assumes that those who are economically deprived have fewer resources to help them cope with any life demands they face. These resources may be economic, psychological, social or environmental. Poor mental health is thought to be a direct consequence of a lack of resources.

Gender differences

- *Willingness to express distress:* one theory is that gender differences in the **prevalence** of mental health problems are more apparent than real, and result from women's willingness to visit their doctor and complain of mental health problems. This theory has not been substantiated (Weich et al. 1998).
- *Role strain:* an alternative hypothesis suggests that women encounter more role strain and **spillover** between the demands of work and home than men. The resultant stress places them at increased risk for stress and mental health problems.

Minority status

- *Confound with social class:* this model suggests that the apparent relationship between minority status and mental health problems is spurious. It suggests that people in ethnic minorities largely occupy the lower socio-economic groups. That they also have higher levels of mental health problems is a result of this association, not of being a member of an ethnic minority per se.
- *The effects of prejudice:* this suggests a more direct link between ethnic minority status and mental health. Mental health problems may result from the additional stresses, including overt and covert prejudice, experienced by the members of minority ethnic groups.
- *Cultural transitions:* a further source of stress may be the tension experienced as individuals adopt or reject some of the norms of their own or other cultures. Both may result in feelings of alienation, rejection by members of differing cultures, and consequent mental health problems.

Systemic models

A more enclosed system that impacts on mental health is the family. Family system theorists consider the individuals within a family to form an interacting system. Each has a reciprocal influence on those around them. The behaviour of individuals within these systems, and the communication between them, can lead to individual members behaving in ways that seems 'abnormal'. Perhaps the most extreme form of family dysfunction occurs when a member of a family sexually abuses a child within it. Levels of sexual abuse are very high among women who seek psychological therapy for conditions as varied as depression, anxiety and anorexia (Jaffe et al. 2002).

One of the first models of family interactions in relation to mental health focused on people with schizophrenia. Brown and colleagues (e.g.

Brown et al. 1972) were the first to identify a family characteristic, now termed high negative expressed emotion (NEE), in which individuals who were prone to episodes of schizophrenia fared particularly badly. Individuals in families who were particularly critical, hostile or over-involved had a higher rate of relapse than those who did not experience this environment. Reducing levels of NEE resulted in a dramatic reduction in relapse rates. A second, more complex, family system is thought by family therapists to contribute to the development of anorexia in young women (Minuchin 1974). These and other family models of pathology are considered in more detail in Chapter 4 and other chapters in Part II of the book.

Biopsychosocial models

Evidence reviewed so far in this chapter has shown that living in a stressful environment, however defined, does not inevitably lead to mental health disorders, nor does carrying the gene for a particular disorder. Both sets of factors place an individual at increased *risk* for the disorder. Whether or not this potential is realized is the result of an interaction between these, and other, factors. An individual who has some genetic risk for depression, for example, is more likely to develop the disorder if they live in a stressful environment than if they never encounter such conditions. Someone without genetic risk for the disorder is less likely to become depressed, but they are not invulnerable. If they encounter certain environmental conditions they may still become depressed. The same factors may work by protecting an individual against risk of mental health problems. Some genes may protect against disorders. Similarly, some social environments may help an individual to develop resilience and be able to cope effectively with stress.

For most mental health problems, vulnerability to, or resilience against, mental health disorders are determined by a number of factors, some of which include

- *biological factors:* genetic make-up, viral infections, injuries
- *psychological factors:* childhood trauma, maladaptive cognitive responses to environmental events
- *social/environmental factors:* socio-economic stress, difficult personal relationships, lack of social support.

It is noteworthy that the boundaries between each of these dimensions of risk is somewhat fuzzy, and even this simple categorization fails to take account of the interaction between them. Those in the lower socio-economic groups, for example, may be more prone to viral infections or injury. People with more or less adaptive coping styles, as a result of previous family experiences, may respond to potentially stressful events in differing ways. Nevertheless, they indicate the key risk dimensions involved in the aetiology of mental health problems.

Diathesis-stress model

These factors have been placed into a simple biopsychosocial model known as the diathesis-stress model. In it, diathesis refers to the biological vulnerability an individual carries: stress involves any event or condition that interacts with this vulnerability to influence risk for the expression of the disorder. The lower the individual's biological vulnerability for a particular disorder, the greater the stress needed to trigger that disorder: the higher their biological vulnerability, the less stress is needed. The nature of both the biological vulnerability and the type of stress that triggers the problems is likely to differ across disorders. In the chapters in Part II of the book, each of the various factors that contribute separately to risk of mental health problems are identified and discussed. Note that in most cases, these risk factors can be combined into this diathesis-stress/biopsychosocial model, even when this is not explicitly stated in the chapter.

Some commentators (e.g. Johnstone 2000) have argued that while the diathesis-stress model acknowledges the role of stress in the aetiology of mental health problems, it still adopts an essentially medical model of mental disorders, as it suggests that stress acts as a trigger to provoke an underlying biologically determined disease process. In other words, the role of stress is relatively minor, and the role of biological factors remains primary. It does not accept that mental health problems can result from the experience of stress or negative events alone, without there being a biological propensity to respond to stress in a way that leads to mental health problems. As such, it maintains the medicalization of what is an essentially psychological phenomenon.

Chapter summary

1 Defining 'abnormality' in relation to mental health disorders usually involves: distorted cognitive processes, distress or dysfunction, and an unusual response to particular circumstances. It may also involve the individual being a danger to themselves, but this is relatively infrequent.

2 Diagnosis of mental health conditions, such as those within DSM and ICD classifications, largely follows the biological or disease/medical model of mental health established by Kraepelin in the late nineteenth century.

3 According to this model, accurate diagnosis is important to ensure consistent treatment and research in relation to mental health disorders.

4 Diagnosis is typically based on the presence of a number of symptoms including hallucinations, poor sleep, low mood and so on. This categorical approach leads to a dichotomous diagnosis process in which the individual either has or does not have a disorder.

5 Dimensional approaches state that the experiences of individuals with mental health disorders differ in degree from those of the 'normal' population but are not categorically different.

6 Psychotherapists generally find diagnostic labels to be unhelpful. Instead, they focus on the nature of the factors that contribute to and maintain the individual's problems. These become the focus of therapy.

7 A number of factors may contribute to the development of mental health disorders: genetic and biological factors, socio-cultural and family factors, and individual psychological factors. No one approach is able to explain the development of any one disorder, and most result from a combination of factors: the biopsychosocial approach.

For discussion

1 Should we limit the types of people with mental health disorders who are treated in the community? Should people such as psychopaths or so-called 'predatory' paedophiles thought to be at risk of reoffending be permitted to live or be treated outside hospital or prison?

2 What would you think of if told an individual is 'schizophrenic'? How may this alter your interpretation of their behaviour or your responses to them?

3 Some severe psychiatric conditions such as Huntington's disease in which the individual develops increasing muscular spasticity and mental deterioration leading to death in middle age can be predicted by genetic testing. It cannot be prevented, but those who have the gene for the condition may choose not to have children and pass the gene onto them. Would you want to know as a young person whether you carry the gene?

4 If offered the choice of medication or psychological therapy for a mental health problem, which would you choose – and why?

Further reading

Johnstone, L. (2000) *Users and Abusers of Psychiatry: A Critical Look at Psychiatric Practice*. London: Routledge.

Oken, D. (2000) Multiaxial diagnosis and the psychosomatic model of disease, *Psychosomatic Medicine*, 62: 171–5.

Sanua, V.D. (1996) The fallacy of the medical model and the dangers of psychotropic drugs: a mode of treatment for mental disorders, *Journal of Primary Prevention*, 17: 149–73.

2 The psychological perspective

There have been four major schools of psychological therapy since the late nineteenth century, each with a very different model of the causes of mental health problems:

- *Psychoanalytic:* views childhood trauma and the unconscious as the causes of problems in adulthood
- *Behavioural:* considers psychopathology to arise from conditioning processes
- *Cognitive or cognitive behavioural:* assume that the critical element of psychopathology is inappropriate, dysfunctional, cognitions
- *Humanistic:* considers psychopathology to be the consequence of deviation from the drive towards self-actualization.

To understand the rationale behind the therapies, it is necessary to understand the theories of aetiology upon which they are based. This chapter therefore provides both an overview of the theory that underpins each therapeutic approach and some of the strategies they use to achieve change. After reading it, you should have an understanding of the theory and some of the practice of each of the different approaches.

The psychoanalytic approach

Freud

Sigmund Freud (e.g. 1900) was one of the first therapists to explore the role of childhood factors and the unconscious in explaining problems of adulthood. His work, conducted in the late nineteenth and early twentieth centuries, was highly innovative, and based on his formulation of the unconscious, largely derived from cases he saw in his practice in Vienna.

Freud considered personality to have three basic components: the id, ego and superego. The **id** is driven by the basic instincts of sex and aggression, which Freud considered the basic motivating forces of human behaviour. It operates under the pleasure principle. That is, it seeks to maximize immediate gratification. It is greedy, demanding and has no natural self-control. The **ego** is the realistic component of personality. It operates under the reality principle and also works to maximize gratification, but within the constraints of the real world. The **superego** contains the individual's morals and societal values. It acts as the conscience, creating feelings of guilt if social norms are violated. These basic personality components are in a continuous struggle to control the individual. Sexual desire, for example, is rooted in the id. However, its immediate urge for sexual gratification is tempered by the superego's moralistic statements that such urges are a sin, and the ego's realistic consideration of the costs and benefits of various actions. The outcome of these competing processes is usually some form of socially acceptable sexual behaviour. However, should the id gain control, the likely outcome is rape or some other violent act.

Five stages of psychosexual development

According to Freud, the development of personality occurs through a five-stage sequence of psychosexual development. The first stage, known as the *oral stage*, is characterized by receiving gratification through oral means: sucking, crying or exploring objects with the mouth. The oral stage occurs between the ages of 18 and 24 months. At this time, children have only the id. Accordingly, the stage is characterized by an inability to delay gratification, and selfish and demanding behaviour. Immediately following this is the *anal stage*, which continues until the child is between 42 and 48 months old. At this time, children achieve gratification through anal means. Freud argued that the process of toilet training is the first time the child becomes aware of their actions on other people, and learns to modify their behaviour to gain gratification from them. If the child satisfies parental demands, it receives praise and approval. If not, it experiences disapproval. Realistic expectation of these outcomes is the beginning of the ego component.

The third stage of psychosexual development is the *phallic stage*. This continues through to the age of about 5 or 6 years. In this stage, the superego begins to develop as a result of the child's experiences of sexual conflicts and the means by which they are resolved. According to Freud, boys in the phallic stage develop incestuous wishes towards their mother, driven by the urges of the id. These desires are known as the oedipal complex. By this stage, the ego is able to judge the realistic consequences of these actions and recognizes that they would meet the disapproval of their rival, their father. The boy also recognizes that if he were to enter into open rivalry with his father, he would be defeated. He begins to fear that his father will castrate him to prevent him from becoming a future rival for his mother – a phenomenon known as castration anxiety. The boy resolves this dilemma by identifying with his father. This permits him, at least symbolically, to make love to his mother as does his father. As part of this identification process, he begins to adopt the father's beliefs and values. He begins to develop a superego.

The young girl develops her superego in a similar way. Freud suggested that when a girl enters the phallic stage she begins to recognize that she is different from boys. She experiences penis envy: she feels incomplete or inadequate as a result of her lack of a penis. She also believes that if she makes love with her father she will 'possess' her father's penis, at least temporarily. In addition, if she is made pregnant, she may bring a penis into the world by giving birth to a boy. In this way, the girl's basic sense of inferiority leads her to develop incestuous desires for her father. These feelings are resolved by the girl identifying with her mother, allowing her to symbolically make love to her father when her mother does so, and leading her to adopt her mother's moral values: her superego.

The fourth stage of development is the *latency stage*. It continues until puberty. During this stage, the individual channels their sexual and aggressive urges through age-appropriate interests and activities such as sports and hobbies. The final stage is the *genital stage*. This begins in puberty and continues throughout life. In it, the individual is driven by the two basic motivating forces: sex and aggression. Our bodies generate both sexual (libido) and aggressive energy. Healthy individuals discharge this energy through socially appropriate channels: sexual intercourse with age-appropriate adults, sports, career progression and so on. Where people fail to find such outlets, energy builds until it can no longer be contained and is released in an uncontrolled fashion, guided by unconscious influences. To prevent the inappropriate discharge of these forces, the individual diverts or blocks them through a variety of unconscious mechanisms.

Defence mechanisms

According to Freud, mental health problems are the result of either ego anxieties or the **defence mechanisms** it sets up to prevent these anxieties becoming conscious. Ego anxieties frequently relate to troubling experiences experienced in early childhood. These can lead the individual to become fixated at a particular developmental stage, and to behave in ways appropriate to that stage during adulthood. Such behaviour forms an unconscious defence against anxiety caused by the experience and its memories. Its function is to prevent recognition of the hurt that was experienced at the time. Individuals may also regress to previous levels

Table 2.1 Some adult personality characteristics associated with a failure to progress through Freud's development stages

Stage	Associated problems
Oral	Depression, narcissism, dependency
Anal	Obstinacy, obsessive-compulsive disorder, sadomasochism
Phallic	Gender identity problems, antisocial personality
Latent	Inadequate or excessive self-control
Genital	Identity diffusion

of psychosexual functioning through which they have successfully passed as a result of stresses in adulthood. The stage to which they regress is influenced by the severity of the stress, the similarity of the current stressor to problems experienced in previous stages, and the success with which each stage was passed through. Some of the repressed or fixated personality types in adulthood are summarized in Table 2.1.

A number of other defence mechanisms that do not involve regression may also be used to counter ego anxieties. The most basic Freudian defence mechanism is repression. In this, threatening material is unconsciously and actively blocked from awareness to prevent it from entering consciousness. Some other defence mechanisms are outlined in Table 2.2.

A classic case involving ego defence mechanisms was that of little Hans. This young boy had an extreme fear of horses, which Freud suggested indicated a fear of his father: that is, castration anxiety. Hans's defence mechanism was to displace the fear of his father to more acceptable objects, horses, which were large and strong like his father, and acted as symbolic representations of him. Another condition which Freud identified as a defence mechanism was bed wetting, which he considered a symbolic form of masturbation. Its perpetrators expressed their underlying sexual urges by converting them to a more acceptable physical symptom.

Criticisms of Freudian theory

Freud broke new ground to develop a complex model of human development. His contribution to the development of theories of personality and psychopathology is without question. However, his theories are beset with the problems of any theory, particularly one so encompassing, developed before our present rigour of science and its empirical process was established. Even though a number of researchers have developed experimental studies to assess Freud's theories (e.g. Dollard and Miller 1950), the theory is beset with such fundamental interpretive problems that whatever the results of such studies, they provide little

Table 2.2 Some Freudian defence mechanisms

Defence	Definition	Example
Repression	Blocking threatening material from consciousness	An adult who cannot recall being abused as a child
Denial	Preventing threatening material from entering consciousness	A parent who cannot accept the death of their child
Projection	Attributing one's unacceptable impulse or action to another	Someone who denies their homosexuality, and considers that homosexuals are constantly making sexual approaches
Displacement	Changing the target of an unacceptable impulse	'Kicking the cat' instead of whoever caused anger or upset
Reaction formation	Expressing the exact opposite of an unacceptable desire	A person who is considering ending a relationship, but continues to show strong affection for their partner
Sublimation	Expressing an unacceptable impulse in a symbolic manner	A child who, unable to satisfy a desire to handle faecal matter in the anal stage, becomes a gardener in adulthood
Conversion	Expressing painful psychic material through symbolic physiological symptoms	A soldier who finds it unacceptable to shoot others, develops paralysis in his hands
Undoing	A repetitive action that symbolically atones for an unacceptable impulse or behaviour	Repeated washing of hands following an extramarital affair

evidence to support or disprove Freud's theories. Because processes such as id drives, ego defences and fixation are abstract and supposedly operate at an unconscious level, there is no way of knowing for certain whether or not they are occurring. In addition, the theory provides few if any testable hypotheses. If an individual engages in a set of behaviours predicted by the theory, it may be considered supported. However, if they do not, the theory is not challenged or falsified, as it could be hypothesized that they did not do so as a consequence of the individual's defence mechanisms.

Some other criticisms of Freudian theory include the following:

- Freud's theories were based on interpretation of information gleaned from a relatively small and specific group of patients, in particular, middle-class Viennese women. The ability to generalize from these cases to the wider population is questionable.
- Freud's views on women were misogynistic and based on cultural attitudes of his time, rather than a true scientific perspective.

- Freud's theory changed over time, sometimes without clear rejection of previous versions. It is therefore difficult to know which theory should be tested.

Freud's contemporaries and descendants

Jung

Psychoanalysis now encompasses a diverse set of theories, all of which see childhood experiences or the unconscious as the driving forces of behaviour, but differ considerably from Freud's original theory. Carl Jung ([1912] 1956), for example, was seen by Freud as the 'Crown Prince' of psychoanalysis. However, his beliefs became less and less congruent with those of Freud, and he broke away to develop his own analytical psychology. Jung considered Freud's emphasis on sex as the major motivator of human behaviour to be simplistic and reductionist. By contrast, Jung emphasized the psychological and spiritual influences on behaviour. He also disagreed with Freud's notion that personality and adult neurosis are established in early childhood. He suggested that people are motivated by future goals rather than determined by past events. While Jung believed that our unconscious was developed through individual experiences, he also considered part of it to reflect universal themes and ideas. He considered this 'collective unconscious' to be biologically based and evident through symbols and myths common to all races and times – a sort of race memory that influences our reactions to the present world. Jung considered that the goal of personal development is to expand conscious awareness through the ego making contact with the unconscious. The ultimate end of this process is union between the conscious and the unconscious, although this is rarely completely achieved. In this, Jung was close to the humanistic school, considered later in the chapter.

Klein

A generation later, Melanie Klein (1927) focused on the psychological processes of young children, placing emphasis on the relationship between mother and child in the first few months of life. She considered psychic structures to evolve from human interactions rather than be biologically derived tensions. She also considered people to be driven by a need for human contact, and that conflicts and anxieties experienced by children arose from their relationships with adults rather than from sexual impulses. According to Klein, the mother is initially represented by the child as 'part-object' of the breast, and is experienced as either a 'good object' or a 'bad object'. She is good when the needs of the baby are met through feeding, bad when these needs are not met. The baby responds to the bad object with feelings of terror, insecurity and destructive rage.

Over time, the baby begins to see his or her mother as a more realistic 'whole object' rather than the part object of the breast, and to understand that good and bad can coexist in the same person. This revelation leads to a deep sense of disappointment and anger that a loved person can be bad as well as good. There is a primitive sense of loss and separation now the possibility of complete fusion with the 'good mother' is no longer possible. There may also be a sense of guilt that the child may be responsible for the end of this relationship. Klein did not suggest that this formed a coherent and conscious set of beliefs. Rather, she considered the awareness of the child to be fragmented and dreamlike. According to Klein, at times of stress or distress, adults may revert to this childhood understanding of the world or people as either good or bad – a process known as splitting. This is more likely to occur if the individual has been traumatized as a child, and may adversely influence adult relationships.

The practice of psychoanalysis

Despite the differences between the various psychoanalytical theories, they share a number of therapeutic goals, including gaining insight into the nature of the original trauma and bringing troubling material to consciousness so the individual can cope with it without the use of ego defence mechanisms. By removing the need for the ego to engage its defence mechanisms, the symptoms may be 'cured'.

Freudian psychoanalysis

Freud experimented with a number of therapeutic techniques, including hypnosis and a form of suggestion in which he sat behind the patient, held their head in his hands, exerted mild pressure, and suggested that the troubling material would be 'released' when he released the physical pressure. He stopped using these methods because he came to believe that the patient–therapist relationship was critical to good psychotherapy. Instead, he used the process of free association. This involved the client speaking aloud whatever came to mind, with the therapist making no conscious effort to monitor or censor their speech. To facilitate the process, the client lay down so they were unable to see the therapist's face and not be guided by any facial expressions resulting from their flow of thoughts.

Through free association, clients may remember actual childhood events. However, given the ego's use of defence mechanisms, such revelations are unlikely. Instead, the therapist is guided more by what the client does *not* say than what they do. Absences, where the client is unable to think of a word or finish a sentence, or abrupt changes in topic may indicate the proximity of sensitive issues. Errors, in which a client may mean to say one thing and actually say something different (the so-called 'Freudian slip') may also be indicative of sensitive issues that the therapist would then explore more deeply.

Another technique used by Freud involved the interpretation of dreams, which he considered 'the Royal Road to the unconscious'. An example can be found in Freud's (1900) interpretation of the dream of one woman which included images of flowers as table decorations for a party. When asked to freely associate to the elements in her dream, she associated *violet* with *violate*, a word carrying both sexual and aggressive connotations. Freud interpreted the flowers as symbols of fertility and the birthday as a symbol of an impending birth or pregnancy. Accordingly, her dreams symbolized her desire to become impregnated by her fiancé.

A third source of information about childhood experiences can be found through examination of the client's relationship with their therapist. Freud suggested that a client may develop strong positive or negative feelings towards their therapist, a process known as **transference**. Positive transference may result in the client becoming dependent on the therapist or even falling in love with them. Negative transference includes resentment and anger. According to Freud, these feelings reflect those held for significant others earlier in the client's life. If they fall in love with their therapist, for example, this may mean they have failed to resolve an earlier oedipal conflict. Freud used the transference process in two ways: First, as a diagnostic process, and second, for resolving earlier conflicts by 'working through' the transference process. Freud contended that once having achieved insight, the individual may still need to work through the issues raised by an understanding of the trauma. In a process known as catharsis, the individual is encouraged to expresses the emotions previously damped down by the defence mechanisms.

Contemporary psychoanalysis

Classical psychoanalysis was extremely lengthy. Freud preferred to see clients six times a week, and even 'mild' cases were seen for three sessions a week. In addition, because psychoanalysis used free association to bring insight into the clients' problems, and there may be weeks or even months between sessions in which significant insights were attained, analysis took many months or even years. More recent versions of psychoanalysis tend to be shorter, typically lasting fewer than 25 sessions. They have three distinct phases: beginning, an active phase, and termination. Beginning involves assessment, developing a therapeutic alliance and preparing the client for therapy. In the active phase, the therapist determines the direction of therapy and the issues addressed within therapy. Strategies may involve the use of interpretation of current feelings in terms of past experiences, and the elicitation of emotions experienced at the time of any trauma. Issues of transference are deliberately minimized, for example by discouraging client dependency. The end of therapy is a negotiated process, in which issues of loss and separation are considered and dealt with.

Most people who take part in psychoanalysis in Britain do so by seeking private therapy. Not surprisingly, most find it a useful experience.

> I found the process remarkably useful. No one to judge you, no one to comment – you don't even have to talk to anyone. It provides a space for me without pressure to explore issues that are important to me that I cannot speak – quite literally – to anyone else about. I feel my unhappiness stems from my poor relationship with my parents – and this has provided me with a means to explore this, and disentangle some of the issues that confuse me about this time.

Behavioural approaches

The roots of behaviour therapy lie in the theories of classical and **operant conditioning** developed in the early to mid-twentieth century by Pavlov ([1927] 1960) and Skinner (1953). Although differing considerably in their explanations of behaviour, both theories held that:

- Behaviour is determined by external events.
- Past learning experiences drive present behaviour.
- Behavioural change can be achieved through direct manipulation of external events. There is no need to explore or change the individual's 'psyche' or 'inner world'.
- The principles of learning are subject to scientific exploration and hold across all species: studies in rats and mice inform our understanding of human behaviour.

Classical conditioning

Classical conditioning was initially explored by Pavlov's work on the salivatory response of dogs. During his experiments he noticed that, on occasion, his dogs would salivate *before* being given food, a response he termed 'psychic salivation'. Exploration of the process through which this occurred led to the discovery of what is now termed classical conditioning. Pavlov considered salivation to be a basic reflex to the presence of food that required no learning: an unconditioned response to an unconditioned stimulus. The novel element of Pavlov's work was that he noted that other salient stimuli present at the time of the elicitation of the unconditioned response subsequently come to elicit the same behaviours: an initially neutral stimulus became a conditioned stimulus and elicited a conditioned response, identical to the unconditioned one. Learning the association between the neutral stimulus and unconditioned stimulus may take several pairings. Repeated presentation of the conditioned stimulus in the absence of the unconditioned stimulus will result in a gradual fading of response to it, a process known as extinction.

The link between these processes and emotional disorders was made when it became clear that conditioning experiences may influence emotional as well as behavioural responses to stimuli. Behavioural explanations of **phobias**, for example, assume that they result from a conditioning experience in which the inappropriately feared object or situation was associated with the experience of fear or anxiety at some time in the past. The conditioned stimulus subsequently evokes a conditioned fear response. The conditioning process can be so powerful when acute fear is experienced, that it may require only one conditioning experience to result in a long-term fear response that is difficult to extinguish. Being in a car crash, for example, may result in a phobic reaction to being in a car, and subsequent avoidance of being in a car or driving. This response has three components: a *behavioural element* involving avoidance or escape from the feared object, a high state of *physiological arousal* evident through a variety of symptoms including physical tension, increased startle response, tremor or sweating, and the *emotion* of anxiety and fear.

The most famous early example of the conditioning of a phobic response was Watson and Rayner's (1920) conditioning of 'Little Albert': 11-month-old Albert was a hospitalized child who had a fear of furry animals induced through the experimental association of loud noises at the same time as being given a rabbit to play with. Over time, he developed a conditioned fear (phobic reaction) to the presence of furry animals, a fear which generalized to similar looking stimuli including balls of cotton, white fur and a Santa Claus mask. Sadly, although Albert was subsequently allowed to play with the toys in the absence of the loud noises, he was discharged from hospital with his phobia intact – an outcome now deemed ethically unacceptable.

Operant conditioning

In contrast to the reflexive behaviour associated with classical conditioning, operant conditioning attempts to explain behaviours that are voluntary and purposive. Skinner's basic premise was that behaviour that is rewarded (reinforced) will increase in frequency or be repeated; that which is not rewarded or punished will decrease in frequency or not be repeated. His definition of a reinforcer was behavioural: that which is observed to increase the frequency or strength of a behaviour. He made no assumptions about internal mediating processes such as liking, pleasure or enjoyment.

Skinner distinguished between two types of reinforcer: *primary reinforcers*, such as food and water that have innate biological significance, and *conditioned reinforcers*, that have become associated with these primary reinforcers through a complex process of classical conditioning. In this way, reinforcers such as attention and social interaction, which are associated with the primary reinforcer of food and drink for young children, take on reinforcing properties in themselves.

Operant processes have been implicated in the development of a number of mental disorders. Lewinsohn et al. (1979), for example, considered depression to be the result of an individual being removed from a reward system they had previously occupied. Conversely, Seligman (1975) considered depression to arise from a failure to avoid negative stimuli within the environment. His theory stemmed from a series of studies in which animals received electric shocks they were either able or unable to avoid. Animals that could avoid the shocks seemed to experience no ill-effects. Those that could not exhibited what Seligman termed **learned helplessness**. They were apathetic and even when they were in conditions where they could avoid shocks made no attempt to do so. This was seen as analogous to some elements of depression.

Combining classical and operant conditioning

The classical conditioning model of phobias so far considered is adequate in its description of the process of acquisition of anxiety and phobias. However, it is less able to explain why they are maintained over long periods, as repeated exposure to the feared object or situation in the absence of any negative consequences should lead to a reduction of anxiety through the process of extinction. Mowrer's (1947) two-factor theory combined both classical and operant process to provide an explanation of this phenomenon. He noted that once a phobic response is established through classical conditioning processes, the affected individual tends to avoid the feared stimulus. This has two consequences. First, it prevents the classical conditioning process of extinction, as the individual does not experience the conditioned stimulus under conditions of safety. Second, because avoidance itself produces feelings of relief (it is reinforcing), the avoidance response is strengthened by operant conditioning processes. In this way, anxiety is potentially maintained over long periods.

Behaviour therapy

Behaviour therapy assumes behaviour to be governed by the laws of learning: disorders arise as a consequence of specific learning experiences and can be treated using the same principles. The type of therapy it engendered differed fundamentally from psychoanalytical therapies:

- It is directive: the therapist actively treats the client using methods based on learning principles.
- The goal of therapy is behavioural change, not personality reconstruction.
- Therapy is generally shorter than other forms of therapy.
- Interventions are condition-specific: there is no common therapeutic goal such as 'insight' or catharsis.

Classical conditioning-based interventions

Classical conditioning-based interventions have primarily been developed for the treatment of anxiety disorders including phobias. Techniques include systematic desensitization and flooding. The primary goal of both methods is to weaken and eliminate the conditioned fear response and to condition less aversive emotional associations to the previously feared object.

Systematic desensitization

Systematic desensitization involves the client being repeatedly exposed to a series of stimuli, initially somewhat distant from and then increasingly like the feared stimulus, while in a state of relaxation. At the beginning of the intervention, the individual is taught to relax using standardized relaxation procedures. At the same time, they construct a hierarchy of stimuli that progressively resemble the feared object or situation.

Therapy proceeds through a series of stages. In each stage, the client first relaxes and is then exposed to a stimulus within the hierarchy, starting with the most distant stimulus from the feared object or situation. On each occasion, they remain in the presence of the stimulus until they feel fully relaxed. This process is repeated several times until the stimulus no longer elicits an anxiety response. They then progress along the hierarchy, repeating the same procedures until they are able to cope in the presence of their feared stimulus or situation. These procedures are thought to have a number of conditioning effects. First, they extinguish the fear response to the stimulus. Second, by being relaxed in the presence of the feared stimulus, a process of counter-conditioning is established which conditions a state of relaxation to the previously feared stimulus (see Box 2.1).

Flooding

Systematic desensitization provides a gradual approach to the treatment of phobias and is user friendly, but relatively slow. Flooding involves a diametrically opposite approach. In it, clients are exposed directly to their most feared stimulus and encouraged to remain with it until they no longer experience any fear, a process that may take an hour or more. The therapy is based on the principles of *habituation*. We cannot sustain a fear response for prolonged periods of time – physical exhaustion

Box 2.1   Ruth's spider phobia: an example of a systematic desensitization programme

The image of an individual with a spider phobia is a person who when they see a spider becomes anxious and jittery, and usually asks for someone to remove it from their presence. But for Ruth, the problem was much greater. In the winter, she had no fear of spiders as she knew there were no spiders in her house. However, from spring to autumn her fear of spiders was so strong that she would not enter a room without someone first checking that there were no spiders in it. Similarly, she would not go into the hall or stairs of her house without a family member making checks. As a consequence, she remained restricted to one room in her house over the summer months, unless there was someone in the house who could check for her 'safety'. If she saw a spider, she hyperventilated and experienced the symptoms of panic, and would run as far away as possible from it.

Ruth entered a programme of systematic desensitization in the spring. She was taught to relax using a programme of deep muscle relaxation. At the same time, she developed a hierarchy of stimuli to be used in the desensitization programme. She also determined her desired end-point of the programme, which was to be able to enter a room where there may be a spider without undue anxiety and to be able to kill any spiders she noticed in the room. The initial hierarchy she and her therapist constructed included the following stimuli:

1 A pencil drawn line, resembling the leg of a spider.
2 A pencil oval, resembling the body of a spider.
3 A pencil drawn sketch of a spider.
4 A picture of an actual spider.
5 A dead spider in a jar.
6 A dead spider on a nearby table.
7 A live spider in a jar.
8 A live spider constrained by the therapist.
9 A live, unconstrained spider.

Ruth worked through this hierarchy over a period of weekly meetings. On each occasion, she used the relaxation techniques and was exposed to the relevant stimulus within the hierarchy on several occasions. Each time, she remained in the presence of the stimulus until she was fully relaxed and calm. The stimulus was removed and then re-presented, and the procedure repeated, until there was good evidence that she was fully relaxed at that stage in the hierarchy and she felt confident to move to the next stage.

Once she was able to be relaxed in the presence of a live spider, Ruth began a second hierarchy:

1 Walking into a room with a constrained spider in it.
2 Walking into a room with the possibility of an unconstrained spider in it, remaining by the door.
3 Walking into a room in which she knew there was a spider and killing it with a heavy object.
4 Walking into a room with the possibility of an unconstrained spider in it, and being able to sit down in the room for several minutes.

Not all people with a phobia of spiders would require such a gradual or extended treatment programme. Nevertheless, this programme provides an example of the use of systematic desensitization.

results in a diminution of a fear response even under circumstances that initially provoke high levels of fear. Accordingly, even though initial levels of anxiety or fear may be extremely high, if the client remains in the feared situation sufficiently long, they will experience a reduction in anxiety to normal levels. This low level of fear is then associated with the previously feared stimulus. Repeated flooding is usually necessary to fully extinguish some fear responses. Flooding can be an effective form of therapy (Wolpe 1982). However, many therapists prefer to use desensitization methods as they do not provoke the high levels of client distress associated with flooding. Nor do they run the risk of the recipient leaving before extinction of the fear is achieved, something that may actually add to their problems as avoidance of the feared stimulus is once more reinforced.

Emerging problems

While behavioural therapies achieved (and still do achieve) some notable successes, by the 1970s conditioning theories of the acquisition of fear and other emotional responses were finding it increasingly difficult to account for emerging experimental and clinical findings (Carr 1974):

- Many people with a phobia were unable to identify any traumatic conditioning incident.
- Many common phobias were to relatively benign stimuli (such as spiders).
- Many common phobias were to stimuli rarely if ever directly encountered by most individuals (for example snakes).
- By contrast, rates of phobias to many frequently encountered and potentially frightening stimuli (such as traffic) were relatively low.
- Phobias tend to 'run' in families.

Seligman (1970) provided one explanation of these findings. He suggested that some basic anxieties may be biologically 'hardwired'. This has survival advantages, in that avoidance of small, quick and possibly dangerous animals is likely to be of enormous benefit to individuals who live in a dangerous and wild environment. These instinctual reactions become problematic when we no longer live in these conditions, but because they are hardwired, we are unable to stop responding in this basic way.

While Seligman's theory gave some support to the behavioural model, other findings made it increasingly difficult to maintain purely behavioural models of fear acquisition. One of the most problematic findings stemmed from cases such as the individual whose initial fear of beetles generalized to a number of other stimuli including Volkswagen cars and the Beatles rock group (Carr 1974). While behavioural theory acknowledged the potential for the generalization of a fear response to stimuli that were similar to the phobic stimulus, this was based on the physical characteristics of the related stimuli. What was clear from cases such as this was that the associations between feared stimuli were of a semantic nature: the development of fear was based on cognitive processes.

Social learning theory

At the same time as these problems in explaining clinical phenomena became evident, other theorists were beginning to exploring the role of cognitive processes in directing behaviour. One influential theory to stem from this period was **social learning theory** (Bandura 1977). This suggested that we can learn fear responses without having direct experience of the feared object ourselves. Instead, fear is learned from observation of other people's responses, through a process known as **vicarious learning**. This provided a cognitive explanation of both the development of phobias to stimuli not encountered by the individual and of phobias running in families. Both result from observation of others' responses to feared stimuli. Bandura also provided a cognitive explanation of the therapeutic mechanisms of systematic desensitization and flooding: reductions in anxiety were the result of the individual's increasing confidence in their ability to cope with the presence of the feared object.

Cognitive approaches

Further pressure to integrate cognitive elements into behavioural interventions stemmed from the emerging cognitive therapies of Aaron Beck (1977) and Albert Ellis (1977). Both clinicians assumed that our cognitive response to events – not the events themselves – determines our mood, and that mental health problems are a consequence of 'faulty' or 'irrational' thinking. Emotional disorders result from *misinterpretations* of environmental events. These thoughts impact directly on our mood, our behaviour and our physiological state. Ellis referred to this process as the *A-B-C theory* of personality functioning. A refers to an activating event: something that triggers off an emotional response. C is the emotional or behavioural reaction to that event. B refers to the intervening cognitive processing, the individual's beliefs about the event that always occur between A and C.

Beck referred to the thoughts that drive negative emotions as automatic negative assumptions. They come to mind automatically as the individual's first response to a particular situation and without logic or grounding in reality. Despite this, their very automacity means they are unchallenged and taken as true. He identified two levels of cognitions. Surface cognitions are those that we are aware of. We can access them and report them relatively easily. Underlying these are a set of unconscious beliefs about ourselves and the world, known as cognitive schemata, that influence our surface cognitions (subsequent chapters provide a more detailed consideration of the nature of these schema in relation to depression, addictions and personality disorder). These, in turn, are thought to influence emotions, behaviour and levels of physiological arousal. In fact, there are powerful reciprocal relationships between each of these elements. How we behave affects our physiology, emotions and cognitions as much as our thoughts influence what we do and how we feel.

Beck hypothesized that our underlying beliefs about ourselves and the world develop in childhood. Some may affect an individual in their day-to-day life. Price (1982), for example, suggested that the schema underlying Type A behaviour, an aggressive time-urgent form of behaviour thought to increase risk for coronary heart disease, are low self-esteem and a belief that one can gain the esteem of others only by continually proving oneself as an 'achiever' and capable individual. These underlying beliefs underpin more conscious competitive, time-urgent or hostile thoughts. Other schemata, such as those underlying depression, may impact only at certain times in their life.

To explain why people with negative self-schemata are not in a permanent state of emotional distress or sadness, Beck suggested that vulnerable individuals are able to override negative schemata for much of the time. However, when they encounter stressful circumstances in adulthood, in particular those that echo previous childhood experiences (divorce or separation, for example, reflecting earlier experiences of parental rejection), underlying negative schemata are activated, influence their surface cognitions, and lead to depression or other emotional disorders. Evidence of the activation of underlying schemata at times of low mood can be found in experimental work reported, for example, by Miranda and Gross (1997). They studied the different reactions of people with and without a history of depression when asked to rate themselves on a series of self-descriptive adjectives either before or after listening to sad music designed to lower mood. The found no differences in self-ratings on measures taken before listening to the music. However, after listening to the sad music participants who had previously experienced a period of depression endorsed more negative attributes than those who had not been depressed, a finding they interpreted as indicating the presence of underlying negative cognitive schemata that were activated by the induction of low mood.

Alternative models of the emotions

In contrast to Beck's highly detailed and clinically rich models of depression and anxiety, other theorists have developed more general models of emotion (e.g. Smith and Lazarus 1993). In these models, the emotional response to a situation is considered to be a reflection of the individual's appraisal of the situation: different emotions are driven by different appraisals. Smith and Lazarus (1993) identified two types of situational appraisals: *primary and secondary appraisal*. Primary appraisal involves consideration of events in terms of their motivational relevance and motivational congruence. The first is an evaluation of the extent to which an event is personally relevant: the second refers to the extent to which it is consistent or inconsistent with an individual's desires or goals. Together, these appraisals drive the general valence of an emotional response: whether it is positive or negative. Events that are considered personally important and that are inconsistent with an individual's goals result in negative emotions: those which are personally important and consistent with their goals result in positive emotions.

The specific emotion experienced is contingent upon the secondary appraisal(s) linked to the primary ones. The four components of secondary appraisal are accountability (who is deemed responsible for the situation), problem-focused coping potential (whether or not any problem can be resolved), emotion-focused coping potential (how well the individual will be able to cope with the emotional consequences of the situation) and future expectancy (whether or not the situation is likely to resolve in a positive or negative way). Smith and Lazarus (1993) identified four groupings of secondary appraisals that link to 'negative' primary appraisals and lead to four *core emotions*. According to their model, anger is characterized by other-accountability (this bad situation is someone else's fault), guilt by self-accountability (this bad situation is my fault), anxiety by pessimistic or uncertain emotion-focused coping potential (I am not sure how well I can cope with this), sadness by pessimistic appraisals of both problem-focused coping potential and future expectancy (I am not sure I can resolve this problem and it is likely to end badly) and challenge is characterized by optimistic appraisals of both problem-focused coping potential and future expectancy (I think

I can resolve this problem successfully). While the model is perhaps too parsimonious in that it attempts to explain complex emotion reactions to events by a minimal number of cognitive processes, it has been relatively successful in predicting emotional responses to stressful events (e.g. Bennett et al. 2002).

Cognitive behavioural therapy

Acceptance of the role of cognitions in mental health disorders did not lead to the wholesale rejection of behavioural techniques. There has been a therapeutic evolution rather than revolution, and behavioural and cognitive techniques are now frequently used together under the rubric of cognitive or cognitive behaviour therapy. That said, the goal of cognitive behaviour therapy is now primarily one of cognitive change, albeit through the use of both behavioural and cognitive techniques.

Cognitive behaviour therapy has a number of common elements:

- Its primary goal is to change cognitive distortions.
- It is usually short-term.
- It maintains a large behavioural component.
- Therapy focuses on the here-and-now, although exploration of cognitive schemata may require some investigation of past events.
- It is directive: the therapist is active in identifying cognitive errors and helping the client change them.
- It focuses on skills (cognitive, behavioural) taught to the individual to help them cope better with their emotional problem. Meichenbaum (1985) referred to the therapist as 'educator'.

Beck, Ellis and other early cognitive therapists argued that cognitions did not follow the laws of learning – Ellis (1977) described faulty cognitions as 'magical', Beck (1977) described them as automatic assumptions. This meant that they required a different type of intervention than those targeted at behavioural change, which did follow the laws of conditioning. Beidel and Turner (1986) disputed this assumption and provided evidence of the operant conditioning of, at least, the reporting of cognitions and other 'internal experiences'. If cognitions could be changed by environmental contingencies, they argued, there is no need to use cognitive methods to change them.

These views gained some support from a British cognitive therapist. Teasdale (e.g. 1993) argued that changes in cognitions made within the therapy session were only short-term in nature. These led the individual to engage in behaviours that tested the old and new assumptions developed within the therapy session using the technique of behavioural hypothesis testing. Longer-term cognitive change occurred only *after* these new assumptions were behaviourally tested and confirmed.

This model suggests that the role of cognitive therapy is essentially one of encouraging the individual to engage in some form of behavioural intervention. An alternative, behavioural intervention in which the client is directly encouraged to test their assumptions without the cognitive preparation should prove equally effective in engendering emotional change. Because cognitive therapy has a significant behavioural component, tests of this hypothesis have been lacking, as any relevant comparisons have been between behaviour therapy and a combination of behavioural and cognitive therapy. However, since the early 1990s a number of studies have been conducted in which 'pure' cognitive therapies have been compared with 'pure' behavioural therapies. These have generally shown the cognitive interventions to be more effective than behavioural therapies and the combination of cognitive and behavioural interventions to be more effective than those that utilize just one intervention type.

Cognitive techniques

Perhaps the simplest method of changing cognitions is **self-instruction training** (Meichenbaum 1985). This involves interrupting the flow of stress or negative emotion provoking thoughts by replacing them with pre-prepared realistic or 'coping' ones. These typically fall into one of two categories: reminders to use any stress-coping techniques the person has practised, and reminders that they can cope effectively with the situation ('You can cope with this . . . you have before . . . remember to relax . . .').

A more complex approach, known as **cognitive challenge**, involves identifying and challenging the reality of the negative assumptions an individual is experiencing. In this, the person is taught to 'catch' their thoughts and identify the association between thoughts, emotions and behaviour. They then learn to treat their immediate negative cognitive response to particular situations as hypotheses or guesses, not reality; to challenge their veracity, and to replace them with more appropriate and less emotionally disturbing thoughts ('I'm feeling faint. I'm going to pass out and make a fool of myself' . . . 'Well, I've felt this way before and nothing bad happened – It won't happen this time . . .'). This skill can be practised within the therapy session, before being used in the 'real world'.

Ways of identifying and changing negative assumptions can be taught through the Socratic method or *guided discovery* (Beck 1977). This involves the therapist helping the client to identify distorted patterns of thinking that are contributing to their problems by directly challenging their assumptions. It encourages them to consider and evaluate different sources of information that provide evidence of the reality or unreality of the beliefs they hold. One technique that has been developed specifically to help identify and challenge core beliefs is known as the *downward arrow technique* (Beck et al. 1979). When clients express what seem to be inappropriate thoughts or reactions to events, the downward arrow technique can be used to identify distortions in core beliefs that are contributing to their problems. Key questions include:

- What is your concern about . . . ?
- What would the implications be . . . ?
- What would the consequences be . . . ?
- What would the ultimate consequences be . . . ?

An example of their use is provided by this extract from a session with a problem drinker adapted from Beck et al. (1993):

Therapist: You feel quite strongly that you need to be 'relaxed' by alcohol when you go to a party. What is your concern about being sober?
Client: I wouldn't enjoy myself and I wouldn't be much fun to be with.
T: What would be the implications of that?
C: Well, people wouldn't talk to me.
T: And what would be the consequence of that?
C: I need to have people like me. My job depends on it. If I can't entertain people at a party, them I'm no good at my job . . .
T: So, what happens if that is the case?
C: Well, I guess I lose my job!
T: So, you lose your job because you didn't get drunk at a party?
C: Well, put like that, I think I may have not had it in the right perspective.

Here, the downward arrow technique has been used both to identify some of the client's core beliefs and to get them to reconsider the accuracy of those beliefs.

Behavioural strategies

Behavioural interventions form an important element of many interventions. Two commonly used strategies in depression, for example, are behavioural activation and behavioural challenge. The first involves increasing levels of activity in a planned progressive manner. For those who are profoundly depressed this may involve planning times to get out of bed, go to the shops, and so on. For those who are less depressed, it may involve engaging in more social or 'pleasant' activities. Behavioural challenge involves setting up behavioural experiments within the therapy session or as homework that directly test the cognitive beliefs that clients may hold, in the expectation that negative beliefs are disconfirmed and more positive ones affirmed. In the above case, for example, the individual may be encouraged to go to a party and try not to drink, to see whether or not this has the disastrous consequences they originally hypothesized. Success in these tasks is thought to bring about long-term cognitive, behavioural and emotional changes.

Relaxation techniques

Some emotional disorders, such as anxiety and pathological anger, have a large physiological component varying from high levels of physical tension to hyperventilation (see Chapter 3). Chronic stress may also be associated with high levels of physical tension, which may not be so noticeable, but nevertheless may result in chronic tiredness, poor sleep, and increase an individual's vulnerability to a variety of health problems. Relaxation provides a mechanism for moderating this drive. Relaxation skills enable the individual to relax as much as is possible at times of both acute and chronic stress. This moderates the unpleasant symptoms experienced at such times as well as increasing actual or perceived control over the stress response – a valuable outcome in itself.

The relaxation process most commonly taught is a derivative of *Jacobson's deep muscle relaxation technique*. This involves alternately tensing and relaxing muscle groups throughout the body in an ordered sequence. As the individual becomes more skilled, the emphasis of practice shifts towards relaxation without prior tension, or relaxing specific muscle groups while using others, in order to mimic the circumstances in which relaxation will be used in 'real life'. The order in which the muscles are relaxed varies, but a typical exercise may involve the following stages (the tensing procedure is described in parentheses):

- hands and forearms (making a fist)
- upper arms (touching fingers to shoulder)
- shoulders and lower neck (pulling up shoulders)
- back of neck (touching chin to chest)
- lips (pushing them together)
- forehead (frowning)
- abdomen/chest (holding deep breath)
- abdomen (tensing stomach muscles)
- legs and feet (push heel away, pull toes to point at head: not lifting leg).

Monitoring physical tension

Where high levels of tension are clearly associated with specific stimuli, an individual may quickly learn to use relaxation techniques to help them relax at such times. Where people are more chronically stressed and perhaps less aware of any excess tension, learning to relax effectively may involve a more structured approach. This may begin by the individual learning to monitor their levels of physical tension throughout the day. Initially, this provides an educative effect, helping them identify how tense they are during the day and what triggers their tension. As they move through the practice stage, monitoring may help identify further triggers and provide clues as to when the use of relaxation procedures may be particularly useful. This phase may entail the use of a 'Tension diary' in which the individual typically records their level of tension on some form of numerical scale (0 = no tension, 10 = very high levels of tension) at regular intervals through the day.

In vivo relaxation

After a period of monitoring tension and learning relaxation techniques, individuals can begin to integrate them into their daily lives. At this stage, relaxation involves the individual in monitoring and reducing tension to appropriate levels while engaging in their everyday activities or at times of acute stress. Relaxation is best used initially at times of relatively low levels of excess tension. The consistent use of relaxation techniques at these times can prepare the person to cope with times of greater tension. An alternative strategy that many find useful involves relaxing at regular intervals (such as coffee breaks) throughout the day.

Stress inoculation training

The exact nature of any cognitive behavioural intervention will differ according to the nature of the presenting problem and resources of the individual in therapy. A number of these differing approaches are considered in the chapters in Section II of the book. However, one simple approach combining the various therapy components was developed by Meichenbaum (1985) in his approach to treating general stress. He suggested that the various strands of cognitive behavioural therapy could be combined into a simple iterative learning process. He combined these strands in two ways. First, he suggested that when an individual is facing a stressor, they need to keep three processes under review: check that their behaviour is appropriate to the circumstances, maintain relaxation, and give themselves appropriate self-talk. Second, he suggested that where a particular stressor can be anticipated, the opportunity should be taken to rehearse these actions before the event itself. Once in the situation, the planned strategies should be enacted. Finally, after the situation has occurred, time should be given to review what occurred and successes or failures learned from.

Experiencing cognitive behaviour therapy

Here are some views about the experience of cognitive behaviour therapy:

> I found it really helpful – but it was difficult. The therapist asked me to, like, question my thoughts. I found that really difficult. I

couldn't really work out what I was thinking . . . let alone try to question them! But I remember one appointment when we talked through how I felt when I went on holiday, and I felt really sad at the beginning of the session. By the end I felt really good about myself! And I began to see how thinking about things differently could help me feel better. In the end I found this part of therapy really useful.

I found the relaxation really good . . . I really enjoyed it. Yeah, it worked well – the rest wasn't easy. But I really valued the support of my therapist. I actually think that that was the most important thing I got out of therapy.

I found it good to take a gradual approach to dealing with my panics. The therapist was very good as they listened to my concerns, and gave me advice about what to do to stop me panicking. I don't think I would have liked just talking – and telling her about my childhood and so on – I can't see the point in that.

These comments reflect some of the problems that people face in cognitive behaviour therapy and the importance of the relationship between client and therapist, even in the relatively structured use of cognitive behavioural techniques. This issue is considered in more detail in Chapter 5.

Humanistic approaches

The humanistic school of psychology began in the 1950s in the USA. Its major figures include Carl Rogers (1961) and Abraham Maslow (1970). It developed largely as a reaction against both psychoanalysis and behaviourism, and formed a 'Third Force' countering both approaches. Humanists considered psychoanalysis to be too pessimistic as it emphasized the pathological, irrational, unconscious fragmentation of personality. Behaviourism was rejected because of its mechanistic approach to understanding the human condition. By contrast, humanistic psychologists wanted a psychology that focused on healthy, rational, higher motivations.

There are two common elements to the humanist approach:

- Behaviour is understood in terms of the subjective experience of the individual: the phenomenological perspective. This accepts the subjective experience of the individual as a valid source of information about their values, motives and the meaning of their behaviour.
- Behaviour is not constrained by either past experiences or current circumstances. The individual has 'free will' and makes

behavioural choices independent of past learning history or the unconscious influence of innate drives.

Models of the individual and neurosis

Rogers

Carl Rogers (1961) was one of the leading humanists. His theory of the individual has been termed a *self-theory*, in that it focuses on the individual's self-concept and their subjective experience of the world. His basic premise was that all individuals have an innate drive to grow, develop and enhance their abilities in ways they choose: a process he called self-actualization. This 'activating tendency' stimulates creativity, and leads us to seek new challenges and skills that motivate healthy growth. When the individual is in touch with their actualizing tendency, it directs behaviour in ways that foster positive growth and happiness. When they are not, the result is sadness, anxiety or depression.

He also noted that we live in subjective worlds of our own creation, formed by a process of perception: the *phenomenal field*. In many ways this maps on to reality, but it may also be distorted and inaccurate. Nevertheless, our reaction to events, be they emotional or behavioural, is based on our perception of the world, not 'objective' reality. Within this framework, the most significant element is the sense of self, our understanding of 'who we are'. Rogers considered the self to be constantly in a process of forming and reforming. We experience it as unchanging only as a result of biases and selectivity in attending those elements of our phenomenal field that are consistent with our prior experience. Our sense of self is influenced by past experiences, our present situation and expectations of the future. However, unlike the psychoanalysts, he argued that the past is only as important as the individual chooses to make it, through conscious choice. Free will allows us to break away from the past, and for our behaviour and emotions to be related more to the present, and perhaps the future.

Although the individual acknowledges their *actual self*, our actualizing tendency drives us towards another version of the self: the *ideal self*. This reflects who we would like to be: the goals and aspirations of our lives. Like the self, this is a changing and evolving concept. The degree to which the actual and ideal selves match each other has a profound effect on our emotions and behaviour. When the two are relatively similar (what Rogers termed congruent), we experience positive emotions. When the two are incongruent, we experience sadness and other negative emotions, and the actualizing process is inhibited.

For many, the beginnings of incongruence lie in childhood. Rogers argued that the way parental love and approval are given have a strong impact on the developing person. Subtle elements of parent–child interactions contribute to the development of pathology. One important process, known as *conditional positive regard*, occurs when parents simultaneously show both their disapproval of bad behaviour and of the child ('Your behaviour is bad, and I don't love you when you behave in this way'). Love and approval are granted only if the child behaves in a way that their parents want them to. As a result, children adopt their parents' 'conditions of worth'. That is, the child comes to associate their self-worth with their behaviour, and begins to adopt behaviours that are valued by their parents. The child begins to internalize the goals of his or her parents into its ideal self, and work towards achieving them rather than his or her own goals and aspirations. As a result, the child fails to progress towards self-actualization.

According to Rogers, three elements of the individual's interactions with others can facilitate their move towards self-actualization:

- *unconditional positive regard*: acceptance and love that is not contingent upon the individual behaving in required manner: 'I do not approve of your behaviour . . . but I love you nonetheless'
- *genuineness*: an environment in which the individual is able to freely express their own sense of self, rather than playing a role or hiding behind a façade
- *empathy*: an environment in which the individual is involved with people who can understand the world from their viewpoint – who share their phenomenal field.

Maslow

Rogers's work and beliefs about the development of the individual largely stemmed from his therapeutic work, which is considered later in the chapter. Others, such as Maslow, contributed to humanistic theory but not to the development of therapy. Like Rogers, he believed that the individual strives throughout their life to achieve their human potential: to achieve *self-actualization*.

Maslow (1970) believed that we are motivated to fulfil a variety of needs, which are hierarchically structured, starting with basic biological imperatives such as obtaining warmth and food. Self-actualization, he argued, can be achieved only by obtaining the needs of the highest tier of the hierarchy. In addition, the individual can progress up the hierarchy only if all the needs of each subordinate level are achieved. As a result, the individual is motivated to meet the needs within the different levels of the hierarchy and to progress upwards towards self-actualization. The hierarchy of needs described by Maslow had the following levels:

- *physiological*: including food, air, sleep, sex and so on
- *safety*: including both physical and psychological safety – stability, social order and so on

- *love and belongingness:* giving and receiving acceptance and affection
- *esteem:* feelings of self-respect, competency, and receiving the regard of others.

Once the basic needs of biological and physical security are met, the individual can engage in behaviours that allow them to express their potential for growth and to use their capacities to the fullest. Maslow referred to the needs at this level as *meta-needs*: those which are based on a desire to grow. The hierarchy is not rigid, and may differ across individuals or time, but holds for most people, most of the time.

Maslow considered a number of experiences to be related to self-actualization. He termed the most profound and vibrant level of being a *peak experience*, a period of intense emotion when we really feel what it is to be alive. Other, longer-term experiences of heightened awareness can also exist. In what Maslow termed a *plateau experience*, the individual may feel a sustained heightened appreciation of life over months or even years. These two factors are related to self-actualization but are not synonymous with it. According to Maslow, it is possible to have both these experiences without integrating them into the process of self-actualizing. Conversely, some individuals who live productive, self-actualized lives may never experience the shift of awareness associated with the peak or plateau experiences. Self-actualization results from a balance of needs being met and the individual achieving the 'full use' of their abilities, not just a transcendent episode.

Maslow considered self-actualizing to be something the individual actively works towards, but is achieved only by a small minority. It is not an inevitable outcome, and the individual may have to overcome obstacles or make choices that progress them towards actualization. A significant source of deviation from this process may be the culture the individual is situated within. Maslow contended that the western culture places great emphasis on material sources of gratification, which satisfy physiological and safety needs, but not the higher ones of love, affection and esteem.

Humanistic therapy

There are several schools of humanistic therapy, with the *client-centred therapy* of Rogers being pre-eminent. Rogers considered pathology to be the result of a deviation from the actualizing process, usually as a consequence of experiencing conditional positive regard. Therapy involves the individual realigning with their own actualizing tendency.

Early in the history of Rogers's therapy, he described his approach as non-directive. The role of the therapist was to help the individual explore issues relevant to them and their development, with an equal relationship between therapist and client giving the client control over the issues explored. However, careful analysis of therapy transcripts by Truax (1966) indicated that rather than act as a neutral facilitator, the therapist (in this case Rogers himself) unconsciously reinforced statements that indicated progress on the client's part, and ignored those that were less positive. Acknowledging the impossibility of total neutrality by the therapist, Rogers abandoned the term non-directive, but still emphasized that therapy should focus on the development of the individual, not the interpretations or actions of the therapist. The choice of the name 'client (later, person)-centred therapy' was deliberately chosen by Rogers to contrast with the medicalization and power structure implied by use of the term 'patient' by the psychoanalysts.

The goal of person-centred therapy is to provide an environment in which the individual can identify their own life goals and how they wish to determine them: to place them on the pathway to self-actualization. Rogers stated that therapy does not rely on techniques or doing things *to* the client. Rather, the quality of the interpersonal encounter is the most significant element in determining effectiveness. The goal of the therapist is to provide a setting in which the individual is not judged and can be free to explore new ways of being. That is, therapy provides the conditions necessary for growth identified earlier. To achieve this, the therapist must have three characteristics:

- they are integrated and genuine in their relationship with the client
- they gain an empathic understanding of the client's perspective and communicate this to them
- they provide unconditional positive regard.

Being genuine means that the therapist shares feeling or gives feedback about how they feel as a consequence of what the client is telling them. Such feedback may be positive or negative, and shows that the therapist is human with human feelings. It may involve expressions of sadness or even anger in response to individual's stories. Empathy involves the therapist gaining an understanding of the individual's situation, problems, feelings and concerns, from *their* perspective and showing the client that they have achieved this level of understanding. The most frequent method by which this is achieved is through a process of reflecting back the therapist's understanding of the client's perspective. The final component of the therapeutic relationship is that the therapist is not judgemental, and does not repeat the past experiences of conditional positive regard.

Rogers suggested that these three therapist characteristics can facilitate a shift from the externally imposed standards of others to the identification and shift to the pathway towards self-actualization. This is thought to be achieved through a series of seven stages (Rogers 1961) in which the client:

1 fails to acknowledge feelings, and considers personal relationships as dangerous
2 is able to describe their behaviour, but rarely their feelings, which are not 'owned'
3 can begin to describe their emotional reactions to past events, and recognize contradictions in their experience
4 develops an awareness of their current feelings, but finds it difficult to cope with them
5 begins to explore their inner life in a more meaningful and emotional way
6 is able to fully experience feelings while talking of past events
7 develops a basic trust in their own inner processes: feelings experienced with immediacy and intensity.

The therapist's actions facilitate each of these processes. Empathic feedback encourages and validates the exploration and expression of personal feelings and meanings of statements made in therapy. Acceptance and genuineness encourage the growth of trust in the self and increased risk-taking in the expression of previously withheld thoughts or emotions.

Experiencing person-centred therapy

Here are some reactions to this type of approach:

I found it really quite disconcerting. All my therapist seemed to do was to repeat back to me things that I'd said to him. I wanted someone to suggest things and advise me what to do to help me cope with my problems. But all he seemed to do was to avoid this and say it was up to me!

I really liked the space to sit and think – without someone on my back or things to deal with. Just thinking things through can help you change your perspective or think how do things different. Just unloading some of the shit I'd had during the week really helped.

I found it really useful – it gave me time to think and develop my plans for the future. Sometimes you need this sort of space, with someone you can trust and who does not sit in judgement on you – even if some of the things you say may not always put you in the best light.

These comments reflect some of the benefits that many people get from humanistic therapy. They also hint that different people may benefit from different types of therapeutic approach. The first person here, for example, may have benefited from a more structured form of therapy (see Chapter 5 for more discussion of this issue). Finally, they also hint at the non-specific benefits of therapy, which may just involve expressing negative emotions that cannot be expressed elsewhere.

How effective are the therapies?

The therapeutic approaches outlined in the chapter developed from different historical roots and at different times. Nevertheless, they are all still practised in one form or other, although the dominant method is now the cognitive behavioural approach. The reasons for adoption of cognitive behavioural methods can be attributed to a number of factors, including the dominance of cognitive psychology within the broader discipline of psychology and the accessibility of the approach to both practitioner and client. However, the strongest argument for its use is the evidence of its effectiveness relative to the other therapeutic approaches.

Meta-analyses

As the number of studies of interventions in specific conditions proliferate, comparisons between the various approaches have increasingly become condition specific. However, a number of **meta-analyses** have drawn together evidence of the relative effectiveness of each of the therapeutic approaches over a broad spectrum of disorders. These have consistently shown cognitive behavioural approaches to be superior to both psychoanalytic and humanistic approaches. One of the most stringent meta-analyses was reported by Shapiro and Shapiro (1983), who identified 143 studies that compared different therapies both to one another and to a control condition. They found the following **effect sizes**: psychoanalytic therapy, 0.40; behavioural therapy, 1.06; cognitive behavioural therapy, 1.42. These compared with an effect size for **placebo** interventions of 0.71. These data both emphasized the relative strength of cognitive behavioural interventions and showed the analytic therapies to be marginally less effective than placebo. M. Smith et al. (1980) had previously found a mean effect size of 0.63 for client-centred therapy, suggesting a modest benefit. However, they also found that this did not differ markedly from that achieved by placebo treatment and was significantly less than that achieved by cognitive or behavioural treatments.

While these data provide measures of the overall effectiveness of the therapies they do not necessarily indicate that cognitive behavioural strategies should be used in all cases. Schofield (1964), for example, suggested that humanistic therapies may be most effective with certain client groups sometimes known as *YAVIS* clients: young, attractive, verbally able, intelligent and successful. These individuals, who already bring significant resources and personal skills to the therapy session, may benefit most from a therapy that allows them to explore issues in a non-directive manner. Specific groups or subgroups of clients may therefore benefit best from differing interventions.

Therapist–client relationship

Of note also is that the qualities of the therapist may also contribute significantly to the outcome of therapy (see Chapter 5). Murphy et al. (1984), for example, asked clients to identify the most helpful component of a psychotherapeutic intervention. All reported that they found the *relationship* with the therapist more helpful than the therapeutic techniques they used. Not only do clients report benefiting from these relationship factors, but also they are predictive of treatment outcome in the treatment of conditions as varied as low social skills, family and marital problems, and depression (Keijsers et al. 2000). In a major review of the effectiveness of different components of therapy, Orlinsky and Howard (1986) noted that 47 per cent of studies that measured it reported that the genuineness of the therapist contributed, at least in part, to the outcome of therapy. The percentage of studies reporting an effect of empathy and warmth were 48 and 61 per cent respectively. Good therapy seems to require both the use of appropriate therapeutic methods and a good therapeutic style.

Chapter summary

1 Different psychoanalytic models of psychopathology place differing emphases on sexual and developmental issues. They are central to Freud's theory, but not those of Jung and Klein.

2 Despite these differences, psychoanalytical therapy is targeted at gaining insight into traumas that lay the foundations for future emotional problems. Insight may lead to catharsis, the expression of emotions previously withheld from consciousness by ego defence mechanisms. Therapy also focuses on within-therapy issues such as transference.

3 Behavioural therapies are based on classical and operant conditioning paradigms. These have been largely superseded by therapies that include a focus on dysfunctional cognitions.

4 Cognitive behavioural therapies place dysfunctional cognitions at the centre of psychopathology. Changing inappropriate cognitions necessarily results in changes of mood and behaviour.

5 Humanistic therapies aim to provide the individual with the emotional space to reorient them towards the path to self-actualization.

6 The key factor within humanistic therapy is the relationship between therapist and client, which removes conditions of worth imposed by parents and others, and allows the individual to move towards self-actualization.

7 Cognitive behaviour therapy has proven the most effective of the therapeutic approaches. However, many of the characteristics of the therapist–client relationship identified by Rogers have also proven important in the therapeutic process.

For discussion

1 Some clinical psychology training courses encourage their trainees to undertake a course of psychotherapy during their training. How might this be useful to their practice as clinicians? Should all clinicians receive some form of psychotherapy while practising?

2 One of the claims of the early behaviour therapists is that therapy could be delivered without the need of a therapist. Written and now computer-driven programmes could provide the skills and structure to treat mental health problems. Was this a realistic claim?

3 How accessible are the thoughts that influence mood, and how easy is it to change them?

4 What commonalities and differences are there between the various schools of therapy?

Further reading

Beck, A. (1977) *Cognitive Therapy of Depression*. New York: Guilford.
Berry, R. (2000) *Freud: A Beginner's Guide*. London: Headway.
Rogers, C.R. (1961) *On Becoming a Person*. Boston, MA: Houghton Mifflin.
Szasz, T. (1998) Discretion as power: in the situation called 'psychotherapy', *British Journal of Psychotherapy*, 15: 216–28.

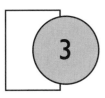

Biological explanations and treatments

3

The basis of biological explanations and treatments of mental disorders is that behaviour and mood are regulated by brain systems. These allow us to perceive information, integrate that information with past memories and other salient factors, and then respond emotionally and behaviourally. Their disruption results in inappropriate perception, mood and behaviour. This may occur as a result of structural damage, or disruption of chemicals, known as neurotransmitters, responsible for activating different areas of the brain. By the end of the chapter, you should have an understanding of:

◆ Basic neuro-anatomy as it relates to mental health disorders

◆ The neurotransmitter systems and the key neurotransmitters that influence mood and behaviour

◆ The drug treatments that are used to alter neurotransmitter levels and, hence, mood and behaviour

◆ Two physical interventions used to treat mental health problems: **electroconvulsive therapy (ECT)** and psychosurgery.

The behavioural anatomy of the brain

The brain is an intricately patterned complex of nerve cell bodies. It is divided into four anatomical areas: the hindbrain, midbrain, forebrain and cerebrum.

Hindbrain, midbrain and forebrain

The hindbrain contains the parts of the brain necessary for life: the *medulla oblongata*, which controls respiration, blood pressure and heart beat, the *reticular formation*, which controls wakefulness and alertness, and the *pons* and *cerebellum*, which correlate muscular and positional information.

Above these, lies the midbrain, which also contains part of the reticular system and both sensory and motor correlation centres which integrate reflex and automatic responses involving the visual and auditory systems and are involved in the integration of muscle movements.

Many of the key structures that influence mood and behaviour are situated in the forebrain. These include the following:

- *Thalamus:* links the basic functions of the hindbrain and midbrain with the higher centres of processing, the cerebral cortex. Regulates attention and contributes to memory functions. The portion that enters the limbic system is involved in the experience of emotions.
- *Hypothalamus:* regulates appetite, sexual arousal and thirst. Also appears to have some control over emotions.
- *Limbic system:* a series of structures including a linked group of brain areas known as the Circuit of Papez: hippocampus – fornix – mammillary bodies – thalamus – cingulated cortex – hippocampus. The hippocampus – fornix – mammillary bodies circuit is also involved in memory. The hippocampus is one site of interaction between the perceptual and memory systems. A further part of the system, known as the amygdala, links sensory information to emotionally relevant behaviours, particularly responses to fear and anger. It has been called the 'emotional computer' because of its role in coordinating the process that begins with the evaluation of sensory information for significance (such as threat) and then controls the resulting behavioural and autonomic responses.

Cerebrum

Above these three sets of structures lies the cerebrum. This is the part of the brain we are most familiar with, and is the most recently evolved part. It contains a number of structures:

- *Basal ganglia:* a dense mass of neurons at its core. It includes the corpus striatum responsible for complex motor coordination.
- *Cortex:* the convoluted outer layer of grey matter comprising nerve cell bodies and their synaptic connections. It is the most highly organized centre of the brain. Most cortical areas are involved to some degree in the mediation of any complex behaviour, although there are centres of functional control within it. It is divided into two functional hemispheres, linked by the *corpus callosum*, a series of interconnecting neural fibres, at its base. It is divided into four lobes: frontal, temporal, occipital and parietal (see Figures 3.1 and 3.2). As these are involved in the aetiology

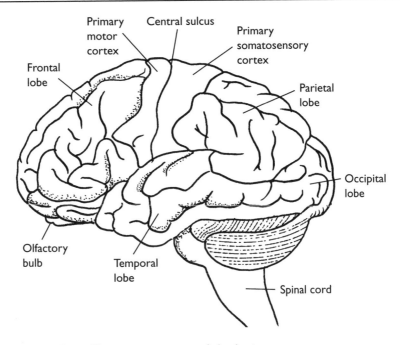

Figure 3.1 The gross anatomy of the brain

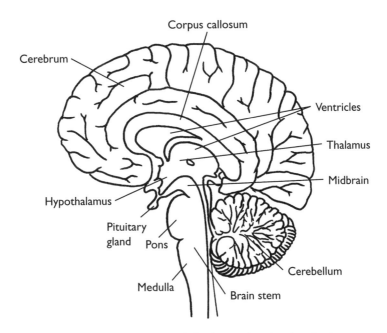

Figure 3.2 Cross-section of the brain showing key brain structures

of a number of mental health and neurological disorders, the function of each will now be considered in more detail.

Frontal lobes

The frontal lobes make up about one-third of the mass of the brain. The frontal cortex has an **executive function**, in that it coordinates a number of complex processes, including speech, motor coordination and behavioural planning. Loss of this executive function, as a consequence of damage, can result in a number of outcomes including diminished anxiety and concern for the future, impulsiveness, lack of initiative and spontaneity, impairments in recent memory, loss of capacity to think in abstract terms, and an inability to plan and follow through a course of action or to take account of the outcome of actions. Individuals with frontal damage become inflexible and rigid. They have difficulty in shifting from one concept or task to another and changing from one established habit or behaviour to another. This can result in **perseveration**, where a particular behaviour is continued even in the face of clear instructions to change. The frontal lobes also seem to influence motivation levels. Damage to them can lead to a condition known as adynamia, evident through a complete or relative lack of verbal or overt behaviour. The prefrontal lobes are connected to the limbic system via the thalamus and motor system within the cortex. Links between the prefrontal cortex and the limbic system are activated during rewarding behaviours.

Temporal lobes

Although their functions are distributed, there are clear functional centres within the temporal lobes. The location of these centres differs according to handedness. In those who are right-handed, the main language centre is located in the right hemisphere, and visuo-spatial processing is located in the left hemisphere. In left-handed individuals, there is less localization within hemispheres. The temporal lobes are also intimately involved in the sense systems of smell and hearing. They are responsible for the integration of visual experience with those of the other senses to make meaningful wholes. Disruption within the temporal lobes, for example as a consequence of temporal lobe epilepsy, can result in visual illusions or hallucinations. Olfactory (smell) hallucinations have also been reported, although less commonly. Reflecting the multifaceted functioning of the temporal lobes, these illusions or hallucinations may be accompanied by strong emotions, in particular fear (Hermann and Chabaria 1980). The temporal lobes have an important role in memory, and contain systems which preserve the record of conscious experience. Damage to one of the temporal lobes results in relatively minor memory difficulties, some of which may be evident on psychometric testing, but may not cause problems to the individual. Damage to both can result in profound memory deficits. Finally, they have an intimate connection with the limbic system and link emotions to events and memories.

Occipital and parietal lobes

These lobes are primarily involved in the integration of sensory information. Their functions are distributed and there are no clear functional centres. The occipital lobe is primarily involved in visual perception. Links to the cortex permit interpretation of visual stimuli.

The synapse

Each of the millions of interconnecting nerves within the brain is known as a neuron. Activation of systems within the brain is the result of small electrical currents progressing along many different neurons. Critical to the flow of this current are the small gaps between neurons, known as synapses. Here, chemicals known as neurotransmitters are responsible for activation of the system.

Each neuron has a number of fine branches known as axons at its terminal. At the end of these is an area known as the presynaptic terminal which, in turn, is in close proximity to the postsynaptic terminal within the axon of another neuron. Between them is an enclosed area known as the synaptic cleft (see Figure 3.3). Neurotransmitter chemicals

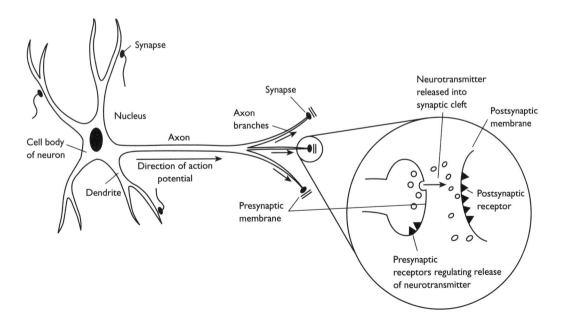

Figure 3.3   A neuron and close-up of the synaptic cleft

are stored within the axon in small pockets known as synaptic vesicles. Electrical stimulation of the nerve results in release of the vesicles' contents into the synaptic cleft. Once the transmitter has been released into the synaptic cleft, it moves across the gap between the two axons, where it is taken up by specialist cells within the postsynaptic membrane, known as receptor molecules. Once in the receiving neuron, chemicals known as second messengers are released and trigger the firing of the neuron, continuing the activity of the activated neurological system. If not all the transmitter is taken up by the postsynaptic receptor, further activation may be inhibited either by re-uptake of the unused molecules back into vesicles in the initiating neuron or degradation by other chemicals, such as monoamine oxidase released into the synaptic cleft.

Neuronal activity itself is mediated by small electrical impulses that travel down the nerve axon toward the nerve ending. When a neuron is at rest, the outside of the cell wall is lined with sodium ions, and the inside wall is lined with potassium ions. Nerve transmission is mediated by an electrical pulse moving through the nerve axon. When the neuron is stimulated by an incoming message at its receptor site, the sodium ions move from the outer side of the cell membrane to its inside. This starts a wave of electrochemical activity that continues down the length of the axon and results in it 'firing'. Immediately following this, the potassium ions shift from the inside to the outside of the neuron, returning it to its original resting state.

The neurotransmitters

A relatively small number of neurotransmitters have been implicated in the aetiology of the most common mental disorders. The effects of those considered in this chapter are summarized in Table 3.1, and are considered in more detail in the relevant chapters later in the book.

Serotonin

First identified in the 1950s, serotonin is an amino acid, and is synthesized from its precursor L-tryptophan. It is found in the striatum, mesolimbic, forebrain, cortex, hippocampus, thalamus and hypothalamus. It is thought to be involved in moderating mood, with low levels leading to conditions including depression and obsessive-compulsive disorder.

Norepinephrine

Norepinephrine is a second neurotransmitter involved in depression as well as a number of anxiety disorders. Among other areas, it is found in

Table 3.1 The key neurotransmitters, the drugs that affect them and their role in mental health disorders

Neurotransmitter	Primary disorder	Treatment*	Mode of action
Monoamine			
Serotonin	↓ in depression	Tricyclics	Prevent re-uptake
	↓ in obsessive-compulsive disorder	SSRIs	Prevent re-uptake
Catecholamines			
Dopamine	↑ in schizophrenia	Phenothiazines	Block receptor sites
		Reserpine	Block vesicular storage
Norepinephrine	↓ in depression	MAOIs	Prevent degradation
		Tricyclics	Prevent re-uptake
Amino acids			
GABA	↓ in anxiety	Benzodiazepines	Enhance GABA

* See pages 69–75

the hypothalamus, cerebellum and hippocampus. It belongs to a family of chemicals known as catecholamines.

Dopamine

Dopamine is one of the key neurotransmitters involved in schizophrenia. Neurons mediated by dopamine are found in the mesolimbic system, in a brain area known as A10, with links to the thalamus, hippocampus, frontal cortex and the substantia niagra. High levels of dopamine activity are associated with schizophrenia.

GABA

Benzodiazepines were found to be an effective treatment of anxiety before their mode of action was understood. It is now known that they enhance the action of a neurotransmitter known as gamma-aminobutyric acid (GABA). **GABA** carries inhibitory messages: when it is received at the postsynaptic receptor site it prevents the neuron from firing. Sites of GABA include the brain stem, cerebellum and limbic system.

The autonomic nervous system

Although most explanations of mental health problems focus on neuro-transmitters and neurological processes, another system, known as the autonomic nervous system, is also involved in some conditions, particularly those involving stress or anxiety. The autonomic nervous system links the brain to many of the body organs, including the heart, gut and smooth muscles. Its job is to control the activity of these organs in response to the various demands being placed on them, for example, by increasing heart rate, blood pressure and breathing rate during exercise. Overall control of the autonomic nervous system is provided by the hypothalamus. It receives blood-borne and nervous system inputs concerning the state of the body, such as oxygenation and acidity of the blood. In addition, it receives inputs from the cortex and limbic system regarding behavioural and emotional factors. Based on these various inputs, the hypothalamus either increases or decreases activity within the autonomic nervous system and the various organs it controls.

Autonomic processes

The autonomic nervous system comprises two subsystems, known as the sympathetic and parasympathetic nervous systems. These arise in the medulla oblongata in the brain stem and travel down the spinal cord. At various points along the spinal cord, they link with other nerves connected to target organs such as the heart, arteries, skeletal muscles and colon. The *sympathetic system* is involved in arousal, and its activity within the brain and spinal cord is controlled by norepinephrine. High levels of norepinephrine result in increased arousal and activation of the target organs. The *parasympathetic system* is involved in calming or reducing arousal, and its activity is controlled by levels of a neurotransmitter called acetylcholine. The two systems tend to work antagonistically and the level of physical activation of the individual at any one time is a function of the relative dominance of each system.

Endocrine responses

Neurotransmitters act quickly, but are unable to maintain activation for long. To enable a sustained response to stress, a second system is activated by the sympathetic nervous system. High levels of sympathetic nervous system activity cause part of the adrenal glands, known as the adrenal medulla which are situated above the kidneys to release hormonal counterparts of the neurotransmitters norepinephrine and epinephrine into the bloodstream. These travel to the target organs, are taken up by receptors, and sustain the action initiated by the neurotransmitters.

When the emotion of stress is experienced, the sympathetic nervous system gains dominance, activates the body and prepares it to deal with physical damage. At its most dramatic, this response is known as the *fight-flight response*. At such times, sympathetic activity is clearly dominant, the heart beats more quickly and more powerfully, blood is shunted to the muscles and away from the gut (hence the experience of 'butterflies'), skeletal muscles tense in preparation for action, and so on. The individual may shake, pace or want to engage in some form of physical activity. This ancient response is clearly advantageous at times when the causes of stress are acute and life threatening: chronic activation in response to long-term stress or short-term activation at inappropriate times, such as while in a supermarket or bus queue, is more problematic.

Drug therapies

Activation of brain systems is dependent on the activity of individual neurons, which are, in turn, mediated by the amount of neurotransmitter available at the postsynaptic receptor site. Too much and the system is overactive; too little, and it is underactive. The goal of drug therapies is to ensure appropriate levels of key neurotransmitters. They do this by one of two actions:

- *Increasing the availability* of the neurotransmitter by preventing re-uptake at the synapse, preventing degradation within the synaptic cleft, or replacing low levels of a particular neurotransmitter with its pharmacological equivalent. Drugs that increase the action of a neurotransmitter are known as **agonists**.
- *Decreasing availability* of the neurotransmitter by depleting levels of the available transmitter or replacing the active transmitters with an inert chemical. Drugs that inhibit the action of a neurotransmitter are known as **antagonists**.

Drugs are usually administered by mouth or injection into muscles, and then enter the bloodstream. They enter the brain by permeation from the small blood vessels that pass through it. Designing drugs to influence brain activity has not proven easy. The brain is protected from infection and other blood-borne insults by the blood-brain barrier. In the rest of the body, drugs pass from the blood vessels to target sites through pores in the walls of the blood vessels. The blood vessels in the brain lack these pores, and drugs have to pass directly through the cells of the blood vessel wall. This mechanism means that only drugs using relatively small molecules can pass this barrier, and even then their perfusion will be less than in the rest of the body.

Treating depression

Drugs that increase epinephrine: MAOIs

The first potent antidepressants to be developed were known as monoamine oxidase inhibitors (**MAOIs**). These prevent degradation of norepinephrine (and to a lesser extent, serotonin) by monoamine oxidase within the synaptic cleft and help sustain its action. As in the case of a number of early psychiatric treatments, the discovery of the anti-depressant qualities of MAOIs was accidental. Its first use was in the treatment of tuberculosis, where it was found to improve mood in those treated. MAOIs have since become a standard treatment for depression, with a success rate of about 50 per cent.

Despite this, MAOIs have to be used with some caution. As well as working in the brain, they prevent the production of monoamine oxidase in the liver and intestines, where it breaks down tyramine, a chemical that can result in potentially fatal and sudden increases in blood pressure if allowed to accumulate within the body. In order to prevent this, people who take MAOIs have to avoid foods such as cheeses, red wines, marmite, bananas and some fish that contain tyramine. Eating these foodstuffs may trigger a sudden and potentially fatal rise in blood pressure. Some newer MAOIs, known as reversible selective MAOIs, have been developed that avoid these problems. However, as more recent research has suggested that serotonin is more important in the aetiology of depression than norepinephrine, treatment has mostly changed to drugs that affect serotonin levels: the **tricyclics** and selective serotonin re-uptake inhibitors (**SSRIs**).

Drugs that increase serotonin: tricyclics and SSRIs

Two drug groups increase serotonin levels by inhibiting its re-uptake into the presynaptic terminal: the tricyclics (for example, imipramine, amitriptyline) and SSRIs (for instance, fluoxetine, sertraline). Tricyclics also increase levels of norepinephrine. The first tricyclic, imipramine, was used initially as a treatment for schizophrenia. It was unsuccessful in this, but did reduce levels of depression in many people. Between 60 and 65 per cent of those who take tricyclics experience some improvement of symptoms (Hirschfeld 1999). Its effect can take ten or more days to become evident, probably as a result of an initial reduction in the amount of serotonin produced at the presynaptic terminal in response to more being available within the synaptic cleft. Improvements in mood occur as the system adapts to the drug and begins to release normal amounts of serotonin again, with re-uptake prevention resulting finally in an increase in available serotonin. It is important to maintain a therapeutic regime for some months after changes in mood have been achieved: about 50 per cent of users will relapse within a year if tricyclic use is prematurely stopped (Montgomery et al. 1993).

Side-effects

SSRIs are a more recent pharmacological treatment. They increase serotonin levels without affecting norepinephrine levels. Although they may not be more effective than tricyclics, they have fewer side-effects such as constipation and dry mouth and are less dangerous in overdose. Rocca et al. (1997), for example, found that 56 per cent of people who took tricyclics reported an uncomfortably dry mouth, compared to 8 per cent treated with SSRIs. Tricyclics and SSRIs are now the pharmacological treatment of choice of depression; MAOIs may have therapeutic effects on some individuals who do not respond to these drugs, but the potential risks associated with their use generally make these a second-line treatment.

Side-effects such as a dry mouth may appear somewhat trivial, but they can have a significant effect on those taking these drugs, as one user pointed out:

> The worst thing about the drug was the dry mouth I got with it. And when I say 'dry mouth', I really mean it. My mouth and lips were dry all the time. I wanted to drink all the time, so I could refresh my mouth. But that didn't help much – so I ended up chewing gum all the time – and I hate gum! It may not sound much, but when you are already feeling down, it just adds to the bad feeling.

Another woman, who benefited from taking SSRIs, commented on a, perhaps, less obvious side-effect.

> Taking these drugs was great – I felt so much better on them. But one problem did arise. When I was depressed, the last thing I wanted to do was to have sex with my husband. Now, I can't wait . . . but the most frustrating thing is I can't climax! We have great fun, but it is so frustrating!

The Prozac story

Prozac (otherwise known as fluoxetine), an SSRI, has proven one of the more controversial psychiatric drugs yet prescribed. Eli Lilly, its makers, described it as the first of a new generation of side-effect-free antidepressants. In addition, it rapidly gained a reputation as the only antidepressant that could not only help people who were depressed, but also improve the quality of life of people who were not. It seemed to increase confidence, sociability and to reduce shyness and social anxiety. As a result, it became widely prescribed in the USA, among those who were depressed or who needed the emotional lift that it provided.

This initial success was soon mitigated by a series of claims alleging that Prozac had far more side-effects than were initially reported by its makers (see www.prozactruth.com), the most dramatic of which involved significant behavioural disinhibition that could result in either self-harm or violence towards others. Some of the links with violence were of a secondary nature. Lipinski et al. (1989), for example, reported significant levels of akathisia, a condition involving marked agitation and high levels of impulsiveness, in between 10 and 25 per cent of people prescribed Prozac. This may potentially be associated with suicide or aggression. A number of case histories have also indicated potential risks associated with taking Prozac. Rothschild and Locke (1991), for example, reported on three people who felt suicidal and attempted suicide while being prescribed Prozac. Perhaps the most notorious association between Prozac and violence was the case of Joseph Wesbecker, who shot 20 people in his former workplace, 8 of them fatally, before killing himself while he was taking Prozac (Geoffrey 1991). It is important to note that small case studies and sensationalist stories cannot be considered convincing evidence of a link between Prozac and dangerous behaviour, but they have increased the publicity surrounding prescription of the drug.

More empirical studies have indicated a smaller potential risk associated with Prozac than these initial studies may have indicated, and even these are open to alternative explanations. Jick et al. (1995), for example, identified over 170,000 people who had been prescribed one of ten antidepressants over a five-year period. They then compared suicide rates across the various types of antidepressant, reporting them as the 'rate of suicide per 10,000 person years'. The lowest rate of suicide, 4.7, was found among people taking Lofepramine; the mean rate was 10.8 suicides per 10,000 years. The highest rate of suicide was found among those taking Prozac: 19.0 suicides per 10,000 years. The authors noted that many people taking Prozac were at particularly high risk of suicide as a result of factors other than their medication, including a history of feeling suicidal and poor outcome on other antidepressants. After accounting for these factors, the increased risk of suicide in those taking Prozac was less apparent, although suicide rates remained a little higher than the average. Despite these cautions, this type of evidence has been sufficient to convince a number of judges in the USA that taking Prozac can result in a reduced mental capacity, and has led to acquittals following violent acts in people prescribed the drug.

Treating anxiety

Drugs that enhance the action of GABA: the benzodiazepines

Although their mode of action is not fully understood, a group of drugs known as benzodiazepines was found in the 1960s to be an effective treatment of anxiety. Benzodiazepines appear to enhance the action of GABA, but do not bind to the same postsynaptic receptor sites: the natural neurotransmitter that binds to these sites has not yet been identified. This class of drugs replaced the use of low doses of barbiturates, which made people drowsy, could prove fatal as they led to respiratory failure, and were highly addictive.

The first benzodiazepine was known as chlordiazepoxide (Librium). The best known, Valium, was marketed several years later. By the mid-1980s, benzodiazepines were the most widely prescribed **psychotropic medication**. However, their prescription has not been without cost. When their use is stopped, levels of anxiety frequently return to pre-morbid levels or above (Power et al. 1990). Sudden withdrawal of these drugs typically results in the rapid recurrence of previous symptoms combined with withdrawal symptoms, including sweating, shaking, nausea and vomiting. As a consequence of this, up to 80 per cent of people who stop taking benzodiazepines after a long period of use relapse and require further treatment. Many people have to be gradually withdrawn from the drugs over extended periods of time – often many months. Benzodiazepine use has also been associated with a number of undesirable side-effects, including drowsiness, memory loss, depression and aggressive behaviour including acute rage (Curran 1991). Long-term use may result in irreversible changes. Despite these concerns, benzodiazepines are still regularly prescribed, but now on a more short-term basis than previously. As well as impacting on sites within the brain such as the limbic system, they provide a relaxant effect as a result of their effect on GABA within the spinal cord.

Drugs that increase norepinephrine

There is some evidence that some anxiety conditions, and in particular panic disorder, are mediated, at least in part, by norepinephrine. For these conditions, treatment with antidepressants has proven more effective than with traditional anxiolytics (Bakker et al. 1999). Treatment is usually with tricyclics rather than MAOIs for safety reasons; although the primary effect of tricyclics is on serotonin, they also increase norepinephrine levels.

Drugs that increase serotonin

A further anxiety disorder, obsessive-compulsive disorder (OCD), appears to be mediated by the serotinergic system, making it treatable through the use of tricyclics and SSRIs.

Treating schizophrenia

Biological theorists have implicated dopamine in the aetiology of the positive symptoms of schizophrenia. Levels of dopamine are not raised in individuals with these symptoms. Instead, they appear to have an excessive number of dopamine receptor sites on the postsynaptic terminal, making them over-reactive to normal levels of dopamine. The goal of therapy is therefore typically to reduce the number of receptor sites accessible to the dopamine by filling them with inert drugs that mimic its chemical composition. A less frequent intervention involves reducing the amount of available dopamine.

Drugs that reduce dopamine levels

The phenothiazines
The origin of the present pharmacological treatment of schizophrenia lies in the observations made in the 1940s by a French surgeon, Henri Laborit, that one of the drugs he used as an antihistamine had a profound calming effect on his patients prior to surgery. The drug was Chlorpromazine. By the early 1950s, this was used experimentally with patients with psychotic symptoms, and rapidly became established as the primary treatment of schizophrenia.

Chlorpromazine belongs to a class of drugs variously known as **phenothiazines**, neuroleptics or major tranquillizers. They work by blocking the dopamine receptors in the postsynaptic receptor sites. Unfortunately, while successful in the short-term, their use results in a proliferation of dopamine receptor sites (Strange 1992), adding further to the sensitivity of the postsynaptic receptors and resulting in the need for long-term treatment. They also have a number of significant side-effects, and many clinicians maintain people with schizophrenia on the lowest effective dose or gradually reduce and stop medication after a period of time in which the individual is functioning normally.

The side-effects occur as a result of the drugs' impact on the extrapyramidal areas of the brain, including the substantia nigra, that are involved in the control of motor activity and coordination. The most common **extrapyramidal symptoms** are Parkinsonian symptoms. The main symptoms of this disorder include stiffness in the arms and legs, facial expressions that are flat and dull, and tremors, particularly in the hands. These symptoms can usually be relieved by drugs that reverse the effects of phenothiazines or a reduction in the amount of drug prescribed. About 20 per cent of those who take phenothiazines for an extended time develop a second condition, known as tardive dyskinesia (APA 2000). Its primary symptoms include involuntary writhing or tic-like movements of the face or whole body. Facial movements include involuntary chewing, sucking and writhing of the tongue in and out of the mouth. Body movements include jerky, purposeless movements of the arms, legs and torso. Its severity varies between a single symptom and a severe whole body problem. These symptoms are difficult to treat and can be irreversible. If detected early, and treatment is stopped immediately, most symptoms will remit. However, many symptoms are similar to those found in schizophrenia and may not be observed – or even result in increased phenothiazine being prescribed. The longer an individual has taken phenothiazines, the less likely their symptoms are to remit, even after the cessation of therapy.

Reserpine

A second approach to the treatment of schizophrenia involves reducing the amount of dopamine available to be released into the synaptic cleft. The action of a drug known as reserpine is to inhibit the synthesis of dopamine. Once existing stores have been utilized it can take up to two weeks for them to return to normal levels during treatment with reserpine.

Drugs that reduce NMDA levels

One additional form of drug has proven effective in the treatment of schizophrenia. Atypical neuroleptics do not work on the dopamine system. Instead they work on NMDA receptors. Activity in these is thought to be involved in the development of schizophrenia. Drugs such as phencyclidine (PCP 'angel-dust') and ketamine are thought to increase activity in these receptors and cause symptoms similar to those of schizophrenia. Their activity seems to be blocked by drugs such as clozapine and risperidone. These atypical neuroleptics are likely to prove a first-line treatment of schizophrenia in the future, as they may not only be more effective than phenothiazines, they also cause significantly less extrapyramidal symptoms (APA 2000). Success rates with phenothiazines of about 65 per cent are typical: for the new drugs the success rate is about 85 per cent (Awad and Vorungati 1999). Unfortunately, the medication also carries some costs. Between 1 and 2 per cent of those who take the drug will develop agranulocytosis, a potentially fatal reduction in white blood cells, resulting in a need for all those prescribed these drugs to have regular blood tests so they can be withdrawn before this disorder becomes problematic.

Adherence to drug treatments

Any drug can achieve its potential only if it is taken regularly and at therapeutic levels. This is not always the case: up to 50 per cent of those prescribed psychotropic medication either do not take the recommended dose or do not take the drug at all (a figure, incidentally, that reflects a more general failure to adhere to recommended medication of all types within the general population). This may be as a result of forgetting to take the medication. About 15 per cent of people forget at some time to take their medication when one tablet is prescribed, 25 per cent forget when two or three are prescribed, while 35 per cent of people forget if five or more tablets are prescribed (Ley 1997). One way of preventing poor adherence as a result of forgetting is to provide slow-release (depot) medication by injection, which requires those receiving it to have injections at regular intervals, rather than remember to take tablets several times a day. Phenothiazines are often given using this route.

More conscious decisions whether or not to take tablets are often based on a form of cost–benefit analysis, in which the benefits of taking medication, usually in terms of relief from symptoms, are weighed against the costs of taking it, usually the side-effects that accompany use of the drug. The more side-effects a drug has, the less likely those prescribed it are to adhere to its use, particularly where there are no immediate changes in symptoms when doses of a drug are taken or missed, as is the case for many psychiatric drugs. Demyttenaere et al. (1998) for example found that 36 per cent of people prescribed the tricyclic amitriptyline failed to take their medication, compared to 6 per cent of those prescribed the SSRI fluoxetine. Level of depression was not predictive of dropout. However, younger men who experienced severe side-effects were least likely to take the medication.

Not surprisingly, some side-effects are more problematic than others. Lingjaerde et al. (1987), for example, listed a hierarchy of side-effects that people receiving phenothiazines considered most troublesome. In ascending order, these were sleepiness, increased fatigability, weight gain, tension or inner unrest, and concentration difficulties. Extrapyramidal effects, which were the main concern of the prescribing psychiatrist, were rated as relatively unimportant. When asked whether they preferred depot or tablet medication, up to 80 per cent preferred depot (Desai 1999).

Other factors may also be involved. Joint therapeutic decisions between clinician and client improve adherence. Myers and Branthwaite (1992), for example, found that adherence was greatest when clients and not the doctor chose the times when they took their drugs. Finally, Sirey et al. (2001) found high adherence to medication to be associated with lower perceived stigma of taking drugs, higher self-rated severity of illness, age over 60 years, and absence of 'personality pathology'.

Electroconvulsive therapy

Electroconvulsive therapy (ECT) is the brief discharge of an electric current through the brain with the aim of inducing a controlled epileptic convulsion to achieve an improvement in an abnormal mental state. Its origins lie in observations made in the 1930s that stunned pigs appeared particularly sedated and quiet in abattoirs, and justified by the suggestion that people who had epilepsy rarely evidenced any form of **psychosis** and that mood following epileptic seizures often improved. (It is perhaps worth stressing that there is no evidence of any relationship between epilepsy and schizophrenia.) Extrapolating from these observations, physicians attempted to induce epileptic fits in an attempt to treat mood disorders, initially using injections of camphor to provoke seizures. Unfortunately, many people died receiving the therapy. An alternative approach was pioneered by two Italian psychiatrists, Ugo Cerletti and Lucio Bini, who found that they could induce seizures by applying electrical currents to patients' heads, and began their treatment of schizo-phrenia. Cerletti later abandoned ECT and sought alternative treatments, as a result of his concerns over the physical damage, including jaw dislo-cation and broken bones, and neurological effects such as memory loss that resulted from the seizures provoked by his treatment.

Until the 1950s, ECT involved placing electrodes on each temple and passing an electric current of between 65 and 140 volts through the 'paddles' for half a second or less. This provoked an epileptic fit lasting from half to several minutes. Initially, this was given 'straight', that is, with the patient fully conscious. Vigorous convulsive muscle activity frequently led to bone fractures until the introduction of the muscle relaxants given prior to ECT. As awareness of this paralysis led to high levels of anxiety on the part of the recipient, this was soon accompanied by administration of an intravenous barbiturate to render them uncon-scious during the procedure, a process known as modified ECT. More recently, the electrodes have been placed over the non-dominant hemi-sphere only, a process known as unilateral ECT. This is thought to result in fewer side-effects. Although schedules of treatment vary, ECT is typi-cally administered either two or three times a week in courses ranging from four to twelve treatments. Less commonly, it is given fortnightly or monthly for six months or longer to prevent relapse, as continuation or maintenance ECT.

Use of ECT

The use of ECT peaked and then began to decline substantially in the 1950s with the introduction of a range of psychotropic drug treatments. Nevertheless, its use is still recommended by psychiatric authorities for treatment of depression that is resistant to pharmacological intervention or where there is a strong likelihood of suicide (Freeman 1995). An American National Institutes of Health (NIH 1985) Consensus State-ment also suggested that ECT may form a primary treatment for 'certain schizophrenic syndromes'.

Just how ECT achieves any benefits remains unclear, although work by Ishihara and Sasa (1999) suggests that it may increase the sensitivity of postsynaptic neurons to serotonin in the hippocampus, increases levels of GABA and reduces levels of dopamine. These data explain the impact of this one procedure on both depression and schizophrenia.

The ECT controversy

The use of ECT has not been without controversy, and the literature seems to be divided largely into those who enthuse over its use and those who vehemently oppose it. Measured debate is less frequent. Those against its use oppose it on moral grounds as well as question its effectiveness. Thomas Szasz (1971), for example, argued that electricity as a form of treatment 'requires the sacrifice of the patient as a person, [and] of the psychiatrist as a clinical thinker and moral agent.' This negative view is endorsed by a number of psychological organizations, including the British Psychological Society, which considers that statute law should prohibit ECT in Britain. Even the psychiatric authorities that endorse its use have acknowledged the controversy. The NIH (1985) Consensus Statement observed that ECT had been used inappropriately to treat disorders where there was no evidence of effectiveness and that many of these efforts proved harmful. It also noted that the use of ECT as a means of managing unruly patients, exemplified in the film *One Flew over the Cuckoo's Nest*, contributed to the perception of ECT as an abusive instrument of behavioural control for patients in mental institutions. Issues of effectiveness are considered in the chapters on depression and schizophrenia, where ECT has been most widely used. The rest of this section considers some of the evidence of side-effects associated with ECT.

There are a number of short-term risks associated with ECT. First, those associated with being given an anaesthetic, and second, risk associated with fitting. Adverse events are rare, but do occur. The NIH Consensus Statement suggested a rate of up to 4.5 deaths per 100,000 treatments, a risk comparable to the use of short-acting barbiturate anaesthetics in other conditions. They also noted that the risk of physical injury was much less than in the past, with a complication rate of 1 per 1300 to 1400 treatments. Problems included tooth damage, vertebral compression fractures, uncontrollable fitting, peripheral nerve palsy and skin burns. Some people also perceive ECT as a terrifying experience, or regard it as an abusive invasion of personal autonomy. Some experience a sense of shame because of the social stigma they associate with it (NIH 1985).

Effect on memory

Perhaps the most problematic outcome of ECT is its effect on memory. People who have ECT typically experience an acute phase of confusion following treatment: it can take them five or ten minutes to remember who they are, where they are or what day it is (Friedberg 1977). It also impairs the ability to learn and retain new information for a period of time following administration and may impact adversely on memories of events that occurred months or even years before treatment. Squire and Slater (1983), for example, found that three years after receiving ECT, many people reported that their memory was not as good as it was six months before their treatment and thought that this decrement was related to having received ECT.

More objective studies of the impact of bilateral ECT have identified measurable long-term decrements in memory following its use. However, proponents of ECT note that the shift from bilateral to unilateral ECT has resulted in fewer memory problems. This defence was tested by Lisanby et al. (2000), who followed 55 people with major depression, randomly allocated to either unilateral or bilateral ECT. Prior to treatment, they obtained detailed autobiographical and impersonal memories and then tested recall of these memories immediately following the course of ECT and at two-month follow-up. A control group who did not have depression or ECT underwent the same testing procedures. All those who received ECT recalled less personal and impersonal memories, and in less detail, than controls on both testing occasions. By the second assessment, differences between the two groups who received ECT also emerged: those given bilateral ECT recalled less than those who had unilateral ECT.

Whether these findings are indicative of structural brain damage is unclear, although there appears to be little evidence of widespread significant damage. Devanand et al. (1994), for example, reviewed the literature examining cognitive side-effects, structural brain imaging, post-mortem studies and animal experiments. Their review acknowledged its cognitive effects, but could find little evidence of any structural changes following unilateral ECT.

Psychosurgery

The modern practice of psychosurgery began in the 1930s, when two Portuguese neurologists, Egas Moniz and Almeida Lima, began severing connections to and from the frontal lobes in people with 'psychoneuroses'. By 1936, the procedure had been developed into what was termed a prefrontal leucotomy (sometimes referred to as a lobotomy). This operation was initially fairly crude, as the surgeon had to estimate where to lesion the brain without any form of neuro-imaging and did so freehand. However, it has gradually become more precise in its anatomical location and procedures. Between 1936 and 1961, over 10,000 people received this type of treatment in the UK. Of these, an estimated 20 per cent of people with schizophrenia and about half those with depression gained some degree of benefit (Malizia 2000). However, 4 per cent died as a result of surgery, 4 per cent developed a severe loss of motivation and up to 60 per cent developed 'troublesome' personality changes, while 15 per cent developed epilepsy. Despite these problems, this approach had many advocates, probably because there were no viable alternatives to this treatment for much of this time.

Rates of psychosurgery have fallen dramatically since effective therapeutic alternatives have become available. Now, only about 20 operations are conducted in the UK each year, and only for conditions that have proven unresponsive to a variety of alternative treatments. New, more specific, surgical procedures have also been developed, including the stereotatic subcaudate tractotomy and stereotatic cingulotomy. Stereotatic interventions involve a device called a stereotatic frame which is placed over the brain during operations and, in combination with neuro-imaging, allows highly accurate lesions to be conducted. Neurosurgeons now use a 'conservative' approach, creating small initial lesions, which can be added to with later operations should this be required.

Most lesions are created with heated electrodes, with the exception of the subcaudate tractotomy which involves placing radioactive rods in the target area, which destroy parts of the subcaudate brain area through a brief burst of radioactivity before becoming inert. It is usually used for the treatment of severe, intractable depression. Stereotatic cingulotomy is the most commonly used procedure for the anxiety disorders, including OCD (see Chapter 7). The operation is conducted under general anaesthetic and involves placing electrodes into the cingulate bundle in each hemisphere. The tips of the electrodes are then heated to 85° centigrade for about 100 seconds.

Availability of psychosurgery

Psychosurgery is banned by law in countries such as Germany and some US states. To be given this form of treatment in the UK, an individual has to be resistant to all other attempts to treat the condition. In treating depression, for example, a candidate for surgery would typically have made more than 2 serious suicide attempts, have had an initial onset at least 18 years previously, and their present episode would have lasted 7 years without a period of remission of at least 6 months. They would have received over 30 ECT treatments, unusually large doses of anti-depressants, and be severely depressed on psychometric testing (Malizia and Bridges 1991). In England and Wales, a panel of 3 representatives appointed by the **Mental Health Act Commission** is required to assess that the person is providing full consent to the operation and that they are likely to benefit from it. In Scotland, this safeguard is evoked only if the person is detained for treatment against their wishes.

Post-operative effects

Since the advent of the newer operations, mortality has dropped to one in a thousand cases, and post-operative epilepsy to between 1 and 5 per cent (Jenike 1998). In addition, there is no evidence of reduced intellectual function following surgery. Indeed, many people perform better

Table 3.2 Summary of published outcome data for neurosurgery

Procedure	'Good' outcome (%)		
	Depression	OCD*	Anxiety
Stereotactic subcaudate tractotomy	53	44	43
Cingulotomy	34	56	50
Capsulotomy	60	93	
Stereotactic limbic leucotomy	55	67	27

* OCD: obsessive-compulsive disorder
Source: adapted from Jenike (1998)

on psychometric testing following surgery than before, perhaps because their depression is lifted and/or they are no longer taking antidepressant medication. Similarly, there is no evidence of significant 'personality changes' following neurosurgery, despite the potential for damage to the frontal lobe, which is considered by many to control functions considered fundamental to an individual's personality. The tests typically given in these studies do not test for subtle frontal lobe deficits, however, and Jenike (1998) acknowledged that the possibility of such damage cannot be excluded.

A number of people commit suicide following surgery. Whether this is a result of the surgical procedure or would have happened without this intervention is difficult to judge. It is possible that some people who view the operation as the treatment of last resort may commit suicide after disappointing results. Certainly, there is no evidence of this being a direct consequence of surgery. Jenike et al. (1991) found that 4 of a series of 33 individuals who underwent cingulotomy for the treatment of OCD committed suicide in the 13 years following the operation. All 4 experienced severe depression with prominent suicidal ruminations prior to surgery. The percentage of individuals to make a significant recovery following some form of psychosurgery is reported in Table 3.2.

How psychosurgery achieves these therapeutic gains is not fully understood. In OCD, it may sever the brain systems driving the behaviours (see Chapter 3). However, preliminary evidence suggests that people with OCD do not improve immediately following surgery. It may take several weeks or months before any benefits are observed. Jenike (1998) speculated that secondary nerve regeneration or metabolic alterations in brain areas other than those actually lesioned may be involved in any changes. What these may be, however, is unclear. This lack of understanding of what surgeons are actually doing provides critics of this approach with strong concerns about the nature and use of psychosurgery (www.antipsychiatry.org).

Chapter summary

1 The brain is divided into a number of anatomical areas, most of which are in some way related to functions that influence mood or behaviour.

2 Damage to most brain areas will result in deficits that may be evident as emotional or mental health problems.

3 Activity within the brain is mediated by neurotransmitters, which act at the neuronal synapse.

4 Neurotransmitters mediate the activity within brain systems that are responsible for mood and behaviour. The most important to mental health are serotonin, dopamine, GABA and norepinephrine.

5 Drug therapies affect the activity within brain systems by increasing or decreasing levels of neurotransmitters. Antidepressants increase the amount of serotonin (and to a lesser extent norepinephrine), anxiolytics increase levels of GABA, and neuroleptics decrease levels of dopamine.

6 ECT involves passing an electrical current through the temporal lobes of the brain to induce a seizure.

7 Treatment with ECT remains controversial; although it is now much safer than previously, it still evokes strong emotional arguments, among both those who support its use and those that oppose it.

8 ECT does appear to be linked to significant measurable memory problems, that last a significant period of time.

9 Psychosurgery is now used only in extreme cases of OCD or depression.

10 It achieves a moderate degree of clinical benefit in a population where previous, more conservative, treatments have failed, but carries with it a small but significant risk of subtle cognitive deficits.

11 How psychosurgery acts to relieve symptoms is not clear. It may interfere with activity within brain systems that mediate OCD or depression. However, the time frame in which changes occur following surgery indicates the possibility of other, as yet unknown mechanisms.

For discussion

1 Is ECT a degrading and dehumanizing form of treatment, or a useful alternative to drug or psychotherapy treatments?

2 Drug treatment for schizophrenia carries both risks and benefits. What considerations should a doctor have when prescribing phenothiazine medication?

3 Would you consider having ECT or psychosurgery if others thought you might benefit from either treatment?

4 If offered a choice, would you opt for a medical or psychological treatment for a mental health condition that could be treated with either approach?

Further reading

Gorman, J.M. (1998) *The Essential Guide to Psychiatric Drugs*. New York: St Martin's Press.

Jenike, M.A. (1998) Neurosurgical treatment of obsessive-compulsive disorder, *British Medical Journal*, 163 (suppl. 35): 75–90.

McCall, W.V. (2001) Electroconvulsive therapy in the era of modern psychopharmacology, *International Journal of Neuropsychopharmacology*, 4: 315–24.

Ratey, J. (2001) *A User's Guide to the Brain*. Boston, MA: Little, Brown.

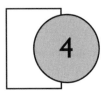

4 Moving beyond the individual

Very few of us live isolated lives that do not involve interacting with other people or wider society. These interactions impact on our mental well-being. Good relationships, for example, appear to be protective against mental health problems. Poor relationships or living in a stressful environment increase our risk for such problems. This chapter considers two important social factors that influence mental health: the family and the social environment in which we live. It then considers how some of these problems may be ameliorated through family therapy or the use of health promotion or other public health interventions. By the end of the chapter, you should have an understanding of:

♦ Theoretical models of the family and family problems

♦ Interventions that involve the whole family

♦ The impact of social and cultural factors such as socio-economic class, gender and ethnicity on mental health

♦ How health promotion and public health programmes may improve the mental well-being of individuals and populations.

Family models of mental health disorders

Family models of mental health disorders and their treatment are based on systems theory. This views the family or other social groups as an interrelated set of individuals. The behaviour of each person within the system does not occur in isolation. Instead, behaviour follows a principle of circularity in which no one behaviour is seen as starting or being the outcome of events. The behaviour of X affects Y, whose behaviour reciprocally affects X, whose response to this affects Y, and so on. Behaviours form a continuous causal loop, with no beginning or end-point. Change within this continuous set of behaviours can be achieved by intervening at any point in the system.

Systemic therapy

Systemic therapy involves the family, and sometimes extended family, with usually two or more therapists. The latter may not be obvious to the family, but they will know of their presence. Often a team of therapists sits behind a one-way mirror and tracks the progress of therapy. They may discuss issues raised within the session, identify the nature of the interactions among family members and develop intervention strategies. They provide support to the therapist in the room with the family, who may be too involved in managing the process of therapy to notice all the complex interrelationships that occur. These observers may take an active role. They may communicate with the therapist in the room, either by telephone or by the therapist stepping out of the room for consultations with them, and share developing formulations about the nature of the problem. They may even tell the therapist to take a particular action or ask a specific question. The experience of family therapy is therefore very different from that of individual therapy, as is reflected in these participants' negative and positive responses to an initial therapy session:

> I found it unpleasant and uncomfortable. We didn't all want to be there, and when we did get there, it was not at all clear what was going on. I didn't feel it right that we were watched by people through a mirror. You can't see their reaction to what's going on . . . that is really uncomfortable. I didn't like it at all. I don't think we'll come back.

> It was weird, and not what I expected. The therapist was moving about talking to us all. He even got some of us to move around! Not what you expect. I thought he or she would be quiet and make us take it in turns to talk to them. Not move around and interrupt and things . . . It was unnerving to know that people were watching through the mirror. But you couldn't see them, and I began to forget about them, especially when we were dealing with difficult things in the therapy session.

This chapter considers two systemic therapies that have emerged from very different theoretical perspectives. Other forms of family therapy are described in the following chapters as appropriate.

Structural family therapy

The structural school of family therapy was initially developed by Salvador Minuchin (1974). The basic premise underlying this approach is that families develop structures in order to carry out roles. Structures include the family rules that govern the way in which people relate to each other within the family. The father, for example, will relate to different people in different ways at different times: partner, father, disciplinarian, friend and so on. The rules that regulate these various relationships differ. However, each is governed by overt and covert rules.

Minuchin also identified a series of elements that combine to determine each family's organization and style of interaction. Subsystems are small units within the family that share a common element: generation, gender, interest and so on. One individual may be a member of several subsystems. Boundaries exist between subsystems and between the family and the outside world. According to Minuchin, clear boundaries are required to allow subsystems to carry out their specific functions and to develop autonomy and a sense of belonging. Problems arise when these boundaries are incorrectly established within families. Diffuse boundaries are highly permeable and information flows readily between subsystems. In such cases, family members are extremely close. Indeed, they may become too close, leading to a state of enmeshment in which individual members do not experience a state of autonomy or independence. Conversely, boundaries that are too rigid and which prevent information flow between subsystems result in a process of disengagement and emotional detachment between family members.

Subsystems are organized hierarchically. The parental subsystem is generally considered to be superordinate to others, such as sibling subsystems, and to have an executive function. It makes key family decisions. There may also be disruptions or temporary subsystems established, in the form of alliances. Here, members of different subsystems cooperate, typically on a short-term basis. Father and son may combine forces to influence the mother, and so on. These alliances, particularly if they are long-term, are thought to disturb the family hierarchy and to be an indication of dysfunction.

Minuchin identified the characteristics of functional families as having clear boundaries, appropriate hierarchies and sufficiently flexible alignments to adjust, change and foster individuals within them. Dysfunctional families have the opposite constellation of characteristics. According to Minuchin, when an individual presents with problems seen as requiring therapy, these 'symptoms' actually represent systemic problems. Minuchin's group associated particular diagnoses with specific types of family dynamics. Minuchin et al. (1978), for example, identified the characteristic of 'anorexic families', as being enmeshed, over-protective, rigid and conflict-avoidant, with unexpressed parental conflict. According to Minuchin, the stresses associated with an adolescent's push for independence within such a family increases the risk of the parental conflict becoming overt. To avoid this, the adolescent develops anorexic behaviours to prevent total dissension within the family. These behaviours may hold the family together as it unites around the 'identified patient' and deflect attention away from parental conflict.

The goal of therapy is to identify where these dysfunctions lie and to change them: to establish a 'normal' family structure in which the parental subsystem has executive powers, the boundaries between and around generations are clear, and long-term alliances do not exist. Each family member should have age-appropriate independence while still feeling part of the family.

Structural family therapy is behavioural, directive and dynamic. The therapist is active within therapy sessions. They may move about, change the positions of family members to develop or disrupt alliances, interrupt particular allegiance patterns and align with different members of the family. Treatment of the family involves three elements:

• challenging the family's perception of reality
• providing alternative possibilities that make sense to them
• once they have tried out new patterns of transactions, developing new relationships and structures that are self-sustaining.

The therapeutic process involves a series of stages:

1 *Joining with the family:* in this, the therapist enters the system, joining or establishing rapport by accommodating to the family's culture, mood, style and language. They may physically sit within the family and engage with them.

2 *Evaluating the family structure:* here, the therapist examines boundaries, hierarchies and alliances. This may be a very dynamic process. Individuals or subsystems are observed interacting using role play. The therapist may even set up conditions for these to be real interactions. Minuchin et al. (1978), for example, frequently held therapy sessions with the families of children with anorexia at lunchtime, when the family would be invited to have a meal together. These sessions could demonstrate, for example, the inability of parents to work together to encourage their child to eat, or a shifting pattern of coalitions between each parent and the child. This may then lead on to discussion among family members about the reasons for these various behaviours.

3 *Unbalancing the system:* during this phase, the therapist deliberately unbalances existing, dysfunctional, behavioural patterns in order to put the family into a state of disequilibrium. This process is highly directive and may involve the therapist aligning themselves with different subsystems or alliances. An example of this process can be found in the case of a depressed woman who

was pessimistic and hopeless at the start of a therapy session, but whose mood improved as she vented her feelings of frustration with her husband and her husband's family, who were critical and demanding of her. Rather than remain neutral, as would be the case in most one-to-one therapies, the therapist began to take sides with her husband, sympathizing with the problems he was having trying to keep everyone in the family happy, but also suggested that the two of them sat down and attempted to establish limits on the intrusiveness of his family on their relationship.

4 *Restructuring operations:* once the system has been unbalanced, attempts follow to establish a normative family structure. This may involve a series of strategies, including:

- *actualizing family transactional patterns:* this involves developing more appropriate transactional patterns through strategies including role play, guided practice, and physical manipulation of individuals into appropriate subsystems (that is, mother and father sitting together and combining to interact with members of other systems)
- *escalating stress:* this involves blocking recurrent inappropriate transactional patterns, and developing conflict in order to encourage new alliances within more appropriate subsystems.

It is assumed that any changes are mutually reinforcing and that the family will continue to develop without the need for further intervention. Therapy may nevertheless continue at weekly intervals for several months. One advantage of this approach is that it presents a clear model of therapy. Targets and goals are clearly stated. The process of change and the strategies through which they can be achieved are well delineated. However, its simplicity may also be a disadvantage, and many new therapists attempt to restructure the family before they have sufficient grasp of family rules. The application of too rigid a blue print of family functioning can have the effect of imposing the therapist's solution on the family, which may, of course, be incorrect.

Strategic family therapy

The strategic model of family therapy, led by (among others) Watzlawick et al. (1974), also focused on the interactions between family members. It assumed that families tend to organize themselves according to a particular sequence of repetitive interactions. Problems generally occur following a poor or unsuccessful adjustment at critical points in the family life cycle.

They noted that when a family faces a problem, its members typically interact in repetitive ways and use previously used strategies to deal with the problem. If this is successful, the problem is resolved. Where these strategies are unsuccessful, some families will adopt novel approaches in their attempts to resolve the problem. Others may continue to apply the same unsuccessful strategy to try to achieve change. Where this occurs, the attempts at problem resolution may themselves become the problem: perhaps more so than the original problem. An example of this process can be found in the man who responds to his wife's lack of engagement with him with upset and anger. In his anger, he attempts to persuade his wife to be more forthcoming in their relationship. However, in response to his anger, she becomes more withdrawn and avoidant, which results in him becoming more angry, her becoming more avoidant, and so forth. Here, his anger used in an attempt to change the original problem has become part of the problem, not the solution – as has the woman's withdrawal. It is important to note that *both* repetitive responses actually exacerbate the problem – not just his anger, which is what traditional individual therapy may focus on.

The goal of therapy is to identify and change these repetitive and, ultimately, destructive, attempts at problem resolution. The family's tendency to look for a cause of the problems and to attribute them to one individual is minimized, as this is seen as contributing to, rather than helping, the problem. The strategic school placed significant emphasis on both verbal and non-verbal communication between family members. All behaviour was thought to act as a form of communication. One cannot fail to communicate: inaction provides a message just as much as action.

The goal of strategic therapy is to disrupt behavioural cycles that maintain the problem, and to introduce the conditions for more appropriate transactional patterns. Therapy follows a number of discrete stages:

1 Detailed exploration and definition of the difficulties to be resolved.
2 Developing a strategic plan of action to break up the sequences of interactions that are maintaining the problem.
3 Delivery of the strategic interventions – often involving homework between therapy sessions, the goal of which is to disrupt the problematic sequences.
4 Feedback on the outcome of these interventions.
5 Reappraisal of the therapeutic plan, including revision of homework or other interventions employed.

The style of the therapist is one of emotional distance from the family. To avoid confrontation, they may adopt a one-down approach rather than expert position. They also do not insist that the whole family attends therapy sessions: they will work with whoever attends. Therapy focuses on two key strategies of change: positive reframing and paradoxical interventions.

- *Positive reframing* involves placing a positive interpretation on the behaviours that are contributing to the problem. That is not as difficult as it may sound because, according to the strategic therapists, these behaviours are erroneous but genuine attempts at resolving a problem. In this way, a couple who are constantly antagonistic towards each other may be told that the good thing about their arguing is that it shows they both have sufficient commitment to the relationship to continue fighting in an attempt to make it work. The goal of reframing is to challenge the family's perception of the presenting problem and to encourage them to redefine and give a new meaning to it. Having redefined the problem, the family can no longer apply the same solutions, and new solutions and patterns of interaction become possible.
- *Paradoxical interventions* involve those involved in the therapy being asked to engage in tasks that are paradoxical or contrary to common sense. The arguing couple, for example, may be asked to *continue* arguing – perhaps linked to the positive reframe of 'because this shows your continuing attachment to each other'. By the use of paradox, the therapist creates a therapeutic bind by suggesting that there are good reasons why it is advisable for change *not* to occur: while hoping to have the opposite effect. The paradox is intended to give the problem a new meaning and that those involved will be forced to decide on change or no change – itself a change within the system.

A number of paradoxical strategies have been identified. The above example is known as *symptom prescription*. A similar technique, known as *pretending*, involves a family member deliberately and consciously pretending to have a particular problem, with the family enacting their usual pattern around the presenting 'symptom'. Again, this is meant to disrupt the normal family interactions and facilitate behavioural change. The approach has a number of strengths, and the strategic group have reported some impressive therapeutic gains (Watzlawick et al. 1974). However, the ethics of the approach have been strongly questioned, as the power lies with the therapist and the method of treatment is not clear to its recipient. Box 4.1 illustrates both structural and strategic approaches.

How effective is systemic therapy?

This chapter has described two very different approaches to working with families; there are many other approaches, some of which will be described in subsequent chapters. Evaluation of the effectiveness of systemic interventions is therefore not a simple question. Different chapters in this book will show that systemic therapy has proven successful in the

Box 4.1 Jane's anorexia: an example of structural versus strategic therapy

Strategic and structural approaches view the problems that people have quite differently. Here are two formulations of the problems associated with anorexia.

A structural approach

Jane is an adolescent girl diagnosed as having anorexia in a family: the 'identified patient' indicative of structural problems. The therapist has heard how the mother and father try to encourage her to eat, but have so far failed to do so. The therapist diagnosed the issue as one in which the family has failed to accommodate her transitional stage from adolescence. The parents are observed as powerless to persuade her to eat, and seem to put their differences aside and unite in their concern to get her to eat.

A structural view of this situation would be that the family is enmeshed: they are overly concerned at their daughter's behaviour and so close to her that they deprive her of her independence and decision-making autonomy. The power invested in the girl to control the family has inverted the power hierarchy within the family, and the parental system is weak: they cannot get her to eat.

The goal of therapy is to remedy these deficiencies: in particular, to strengthen the parental subsystem and restore the appropriate power hierarchy. One way in which this may be achieved is for the therapist to actively change the structure and support the parents in their attempts to control the behaviour of their daughter.

A strategic approach

A different formulation of the problem may be gained by a strategic approach. One possible formulation is that as Jane entered adolescence she tried to gain more autonomy and independence. However, her parents were overprotective and controlling and did not accommodate to these changes. She therefore started to diet as an expression of control and autonomy. However, her dieting and loss of weight simply increased her parents' concern over her health and increased their desire to control her and ensure she ate 'properly'. Accordingly, they increased their attempts at controlling her eating. As a direct consequence, she rebelled and escalated her diet, which, in turn, increased her parents' concern and protective behaviour, which . . . The cycle continues. The pattern of interaction that is established is the main concern of the strategic therapist – not the initiating problem.

treatment of conditions as varied as schizophrenia, alcohol- and drug-related problems and anorexia: on occasion, it is more effective than individual therapy. A more statistical overview of the effectiveness of this approach can be found in the results of a meta-analysis reported by Shadish et al. (1993). They synthesized the results of 163 randomized trials, and found systemic (family or marital) therapy to be effective in the treatment of a wide range of problems including conduct disorder, phobias, schizophrenia, sexual problems and depression. The strategic model described above was one of the most effective interventions, with a success rate of about 65 per cent. The structural approach of Minuchin was generally less effective, although it has been used with some difficult to treat groups, including people with anorexia. Cognitive behavioural approaches, which are described in subsequent chapters in relation to specific problems, proved the most effective systemic intervention.

Psychosocial explanations of mental health problems

Risk for mental health problems has been linked to a number of social and economic factors. The results of the British Psychiatric Morbidity Survey (Jenkins et al. 1998) provided evidence typical of the wider findings. They conducted diagnostic interviews on 10,000 people who were either living in their own home or homeless and roofless. Among the former, they found relatively high rates of neurotic disorders (various types of depression or anxiety) among women, those living in urban settings, unemployed people, and separated, divorced or widowed individuals. Men were three times as likely as women to be dependent on alcohol, and twice as likely to be dependent on drugs. Unemployed people were twice as likely to abuse alcohol than employed people and five times more likely to be dependent on other types of drugs. Psychoses were more prevalent among urban than rural dwellers. The prevalence of neurotic disorders among hotel residents was 38 per cent; among night shelter residents, the prevalence was 60 per cent; among those sleeping rough, rates were 57 per cent. Rates of psychoses and alcohol and drug dependence were similarly high. The next sections consider possible explanations for consistent findings of higher levels of mental health problems among socially disadvantaged people and women.

Socio-economic status

Social causation versus social drift

Two hypotheses have been proposed to explain findings of higher rates of mental health disorders among people in the lower socio-economic groups. *Social causation models* suggest they result from high levels of stress experienced by the relatively less well off: that is, low socio-economic status 'causes' mental health problems. The *social drift model* opposes this view. It suggests that mental health problems lead to a decline in socio-economic status. According to this model, when an individual develops a mental health disorder, they become less economically viable. They may be unable to maintain a job or the levels of overtime required to maintain their standard of living. They therefore drift down the socio-economic scale: that is, mental health problems 'cause' low socio-economic status.

The evidence generally favours the causation hypothesis. Indeed, where there is social drift, this has been found to precede rather than follow episodes of depression (Moos et al. 1998). These effects may even be intergenerational. Ritsher et al. (2001) followed a cohort of people whose parents either had experienced an episode of major depression or were depression free. They hypothesized that if the social causation model held, the children of blue-collar parents were at increased risk of developing depression. If the social selection model held, having depressed parents placed participants at risk of a low socio-economic status. Their data supported the social causation hypotheses. The children of blue-collar workers were more than three times as likely to develop a major depressive disorder than those of white-collar workers. Parental depression did not predict the socio-economic status of their offspring. Neither was there any evidence of drift following the onset of depression.

These findings should not be surprising. The lower the individual is within the social structure, the greater the reported exposure to stressful life-events, hassles and problems, and the greater the emotional impact they have (House et al. 1991). Not having a job also appears to have negative effects on mental health. Ferrie et al. (2001), for example, found that insecure re-employment and unemployment following redundancy were associated with significant increases in minor psychiatric problems and high use of family doctors.

Differential vulnerability

Not only do people in the lower socio-economic groups experience more stresses than the better off, but also they often have fewer resources to help them cope with them. Hobfoll's (1989) *conservation of resources model* proposed that mental and physical health are determined by the amount of resources available to the individual. These may be economic, social (for example, family support), structural (such as housing), or psychological (for instance, coping skills, perceived control). A high level of resources is health protective. Low levels of resources place an individual at risk for mental health problems.

As well as more economic resources, people in higher socio-economic groups also appear to have more social and psychological resources known to be protective against mental health problems than the less well-off. Turner et al. (1999), for example, found that people in higher socio-economic groups reported higher levels of self-esteem and personal control over events than those in lower socio-economic groups. Both are known to be protective against depression. Social support, which is highly protective against a number of mental health problems (Kawachi and Berkman 2001), is also generally less available to those in the lower socio-economic groups. Ruberman et al. (1984), for example, found that measures of life stress, depression and social isolation were greatest among those with relatively few years in education. Similarly, Marmot et al. (1991) found that fewer male blue-collar workers than white-collar workers reported having a confidante who they could trust with their problems, or from whom they received practical social support.

Relativity issues

While social stress and lack of resources appear to be direct causes of many mental health problems, some theorists have argued that it is not an absolute lack of resources that results in stress or mental health problems. Rather, it is the knowledge that one is under-resourced in comparison to other groups within society. If everyone 'is in the same boat', a lack of resources is not problematic. This type of hypothesis has been derived from studies which have examined the physical health of whole populations. These have found that the highest levels of pre-mature mortality among western countries are not found among the poorest countries. Rather, they are found among the countries where there are the greatest disparities between rich and poor. Japan and Cuba, which perhaps represent the extremes of wealth across the western countries, both have low levels of premature mortality (see Wilkinson 1992). Both have relatively flat income distributions. Countries where the distribution of income is greater, such as the USA and the UK, have less healthy populations. These and other similar data led Wilkinson (1992) to suggest that we engage in some form of comparison of our living conditions with others in society, and that knowledge of a relative deprivation in some way increases risk of disease. Such a relationship is likely to be mediated through adverse mood states and stress, although studies of these processes are in their infancy, and the hypothesis has yet to be fully tested.

Gender differences

A number of theories have attempted to explain consistent findings of higher levels of mental health problems among women than men. One theory suggested that these differences were more apparent than real, and stem from women's willingness to report psychological distress and men's relative unwillingness to do so. This theory has not been substantiated, however, and a number of well-conducted prevalence studies have consistently found gender differences in rates of mental health problems when random populations have been closely interviewed about the presence of psychiatric symptoms (Weich et al. 1998). Other theories have suggested similar mechanisms to those used to explain socio-economic differences in health: differential exposure and vulnerability to stressors.

Differential exposure

The differential stress hypothesis suggests that women encounter more stress in their lives than men, and as a result are more prone to mental health problems. What evidence there is suggests that women experience more hardship in their work and family roles than men (Rieker and Bird 2000). In addition, women encounter more role strain and spillover between the demands of work and home. Even when working full-time, women tend to do more work in the home than their partners. The resultant stress may place them at increased risk for stress and mental health problems. These issues were clearly demonstrated in the findings of Lundberg et al. (1981), who found that female managers' stress hormone levels remain raised following work, while those of male managers typically fell. This effect was particularly marked where the female managers had children. It seems that men compensated for a hard working day by relaxing when they came home, while women continued to cope with the demands of family and home. These differences in exposure to stress may be exacerbated by women's lack of support or control within the family or at work.

Women are also more subject to physical assault within the family, rape and other traumatizing events than men. Although these events may be relatively uncommon, they may profoundly affect those involved and contribute to higher overall rates of anxiety or depression among women (Wetzel 1994). Cloutier et al. (2002), for example, found that 19 per cent of their representative sample of women in North Carolina had been the subject of sexual assault at some time in their life. These women were two and a half times more likely to report 'poor mental health' than women who had not experienced this. A final source of stress among women may be poverty. Strickland (1992) suggested that 75 per cent of those living in poverty were mothers and children. Vulnerability to mental health problems as a result of low socio-economic status may therefore particularly impact on women.

Differential vulnerability

An alternative approach to this issue suggests that women may be more vulnerable to some types of stress than men. Elliott (2000), for example, suggested that women have a higher dependence on the support provided by social networks than men, and may be differentially affected by events that disrupt them. Related to this may be problems associated with the loss of attachment to the extended family as children are more mobile and increasingly move from the family home as they mature. Finally, Simon (1995) suggested that women may react more strongly to work and family strains than men because of the importance that these roles have to their sense of worth.

Minority status

Minority status can be conferred by a number of factors: ethnicity, sexual choices, appearance and so on. However, it is usually taken to mean obvious differences as a result of ethnicity. Considering issues of ethnicity is not without its dangers. Nazroo (1998), for example, warned that ethnicity encompasses a variety of issues: language, religion, experience of races and migration, culture, ancestry and forms of identity. Each of these may individually or together contribute to differences between the mental and physical health of different ethnic groups. It is dangerous to reify 'ethnicity' as a single factor which alone impacts on mental health. Indeed, reported rates of mental health may differ not as a result of actual between-group differences, but as a result of the differing presentations of mental health problems in people from differing ethnic groups or cultures: people with psychological problems from some cultures, for example, rarely present with 'mental problems', but describe their problems in physical terms ('my heart is bad . . .' and so on). Any brief review of the relevant literature can only scratch the surface of a complex literature and suggest some issues that may explain some differences in some mental health problems across some minority groups.

Differential exposure

One explanation for higher levels of mental health problems among social minorities is that they are exposed to more stress than the majority groups as a consequence of their minority status. One general stress to which many people in ethnic minorities are exposed is that associated with low socio-economic status. Indeed, some commentators have suggested that any distress resulting from being within an ethnic minority is the result of occupying lower socio-economic groups, not being part of an ethnic minority per se. Ulbrich et al. (1989), for example, used data from a survey of 2115 adults to explore the role of race and socio-economic status on mental health in the USA. The minority group of interest here was black people. Overall, they found that occupational status, but not race, was related to distress. Other studies have found a more direct link between race, ethnicity and stress, not mediated by economic status (Williams 1999).

There are a number of social stressors to which minority social groups are uniquely exposed. One obvious stressor is that of racial prejudice. In an interesting examination of the effects of this type of stress, Clarke (2000) found that among a sample of young African American women, the more they reported experiencing racism, the greater their rises in blood pressure during a task in which they talked about their views and feelings about animal rights. They took this to suggest that they had developed a stronger emotional and physiological reaction to general stress as a result of their long-term responses to racism. A third source of stress experienced by ethnic minorities may be that resulting from tensions as individuals adopt or consciously reject some of the norms or mores of other cultures, including those of the host culture. Both may result in feelings of alienation, rejection by other members of the larger or one's own culture, and consequent mental health problems.

Minority status is not just conferred by visible differences. Sexual minorities also experience prejudice that may impact on their mental health. Cole et al. (1996), for example, found that healthy gay men who concealed their sexual identity were more likely to experience poor mental and physical health than those who were able to express their sexuality. The same research group found social rejection influenced mental health and even disease progression in HIV-infected men. Those who experienced social rejection evidenced greater immune system dysfunction and less time to a diagnosis of AIDS.

Differential vulnerability

As well as experiencing more stresses than the white majority, data from Ulbrich et al. (1989) suggested that differing ethnic groups may respond differentially to the stresses they face. They reported that economically deprived black people were actually exposed to fewer 'undesirable' events than their white counterparts, but that they reported more mental and physical health problems as a result of them. Conversely, white people were more vulnerable to economic problems than were their black equivalents. That is, there was something about how each group dealt with these stresses that placed them at differential risk of mental health problems, not the events per se. What these differences were and how they were generated is not clear. These differences held only among those in the lower socio-economic groups. Among the better off, there were no racial differences in the problems faced or the impact of those problems. Whether these findings would be replicated in other groups is not clear, and these data should be viewed only as preliminary.

Preventing mental health problems

Health promotion

According to the World Health Organization (1996), health promotion involves a variety of complex interventions at differing levels, targeted not just at preventing ill-health, but also at promoting positive health. This perspective involves:

- having a holistic approach to health
- respecting diverse cultures and beliefs
- promoting positive health as well as preventing ill-health
- working at a structural not just individual level
- using participatory methods.

Removing the jargon, this means that health promotion does not just work with individuals, but should work at a societal level to bring about improvements in health. It works with communities to meet their particular health needs, and attempts to improve health and quality of life, not just prevent disease. It can work at a legislative level, with communities, and groups and individuals within them. It can be conducted by a variety of people, some who would label themselves as workers in health promotion, many of whom would not. Some examples of the range of health promotion activities that can be conducted, in this case to minimize levels of alcohol-related problems, are outlined in Table 4.1. Here, interventions are targeted at the whole population of drinkers as well as those who drink to excess.

The link between poor mental health and socio-economic inequalities has led some commentators to suggest that the most compelling intervention strategies to reduce health inequalities are likely to be social, economic and political. From an economic perspective, strategies should include measures to reduce unemployment to the lowest possible level. The Swedish economic model identified a series of strategies that have proven effective in maintaining high levels of employment, including proactive employment exchange, high quality training aimed at providing skills required by the employment market, recruitment incentives for employers, and the right to temporary public employment in the last resort. Davey Smith et al. (1999) called for a series of differing economic measures. They argued for the implementation of 'affordable' basic income schemes as a means of ending poverty. These could take the form of a payment received by every person or household to provide a minimal income, with the amount paid based on age and family status. In addition, they suggested that all benefits to families with children which receive income support should be increased to avoid the next generation being disadvantaged from birth. They noted that a quarter of all children

Table 4.1 Examples of differing levels of health promotion targeted at minimizing alcohol-related harm

Level of approach	Examples of practice
Whole population	
Central government	Establishing drink-drive laws: reduces harmful effects of alcohol consumption Taxation: high taxation reduces consumption Government guidelines on consumption limits
Local government	Local police policies on policing public houses and drink-driving Licensing of new pubs and drinking time limits
Media	Drink-drive campaigns Television programmes on the harmful effects of alcohol and promoting sensible drinking
Supermarkets/shops	Giving priority to low-alcohol drinks on the shelves
Population of drinkers	
Individual pubs/brewers	Establishing local minibus services to prevent drink-driving Provision of low alcohol beers Discouraging the obviously intoxicated from drinking alcohol (in the USA, a bartender can be sued for an incident – e.g. car accident – involving a drunk individual if they served them alcohol while visibly drunk)
Supermarkets/shops	Policing of drinking-age requirements for purchase of alcohol
Problem drinkers	
Health care/social services	Provision of detoxification services Therapy to prevent excess alcohol consumption Therapy to prevent relapse in people who have successfully stopped or reduced their excess drinking

are born to mothers under the age of 25 years, and that the government should ensure that those under this age receive no fewer benefits than older individuals – as they did at the time of their paper. It is beyond the scope of the present volume to comment on the strengths and weaknesses of various economic systems. However, they have significant implications for mental health and should, therefore, form a legitimate area of influence for those involved in health promotion and public health.

Therapeutic interventions

Most interventions to promote or improve mental health have used much more limited approaches than these more radical ones. Interventions usually still focus on the provision of therapeutic interventions, albeit away from the traditional outpatient department or among new populations. Innovative developments include working with those at risk of developing mental health problems, the early detection and treatment of such problems, and the provision of counselling and therapy services within the community, GP's surgery or work settings. Other interventions have been aimed at preventing relapse in people already identified as having a mental health problem and who have received treatment from the health care services (Secker 1998). In other words, prevention attempts have generally focused on the health care/social services, individually targeted, end of the intervention spectrum.

Using the media

An important exception to this individual focus has been programmes that use the media to educate and influence people who may have, or are vulnerable to, mental health problems. One in four people are likely to experience mental health problems in their lifetime, of whom only a minority will access professional help (Jenkins et al. 1998). The mass media provides a means of accessing such individuals. One example of this approach was reported by Barker et al. (1993). They reported the outcome of a series of seven 10-minute programmes, covering a variety of mental health topics. An audience survey indicated that viewing the series led to attitudinal, but not behavioural changes: probably as much as could be expected given the brevity with which each subject was dealt with. The effects of a more substantial television series, 'Pssst . . . the really useful guide to alcohol', targeted at sensible drinking, were reported by Bennett et al. (1991). The programmes were designed to attract younger drinkers, and involved both media personalities and experts in educating viewers about what was meant by sensible drinking and providing models of sensible drinking: Rowan Atkinson, for example, provided humorous reminders of weekly sensible drinking limits. One of the presenters gradually cut his consumption over the course of the programme. Surveys conducted before and after the programme suggested that it improved knowledge of what was meant by sensible drinking among the general population, and resulted in a modest shift of attitudes among moderate–high drinkers towards drinking less.

Public education

Another health promotion approach involves providing relatively simple psychological interventions that are open to all: usually in the form of **stress management** classes. Brown et al. (2000) assessed one such programme. They ran eight free full- or half-day stress management workshops in a leisure centre following a publicity drive as part of the 'Healthy Birmingham 2000' programme. These taught attenders relaxation and other strategies for controlling their stress. Their comparison groups comprised people who took part in a day-long programme focusing on sessions on healthy eating, alcohol awareness and physical exercise and a group of people on a waiting list for future workshops. The event proved very popular and attracted both people who had seen a health professional, usually their GP, about stress-related problems and those who had not. The intervention also proved successful. Compared to baseline levels, participants in the full-day workshops showed significantly greater reductions in stress and anxiety three months following the workshop than those in the comparison groups: an impressive result given the relative brevity of the intervention and the wide range of people attending.

The working organization can also provide a setting in which people can learn stress management skills. One survey (Fielding and Piserchia 1989) found that about a quarter of large companies in the USA provide some form of stress management classes for their workers. In general, these have proven effective, although Oldenburg and Harris (1996) noted that they attract only between 10 and 40 per cent of the workforce, and that many of those that attend have little to gain, while many anxious individuals do not attend them.

Setting up and running these types of workshops while of benefit to those who attend is relatively time consuming and costly, so some groups have begun to explore alternative, more cost-effective approaches. One exciting approach is to provide stress management training or other psychological therapies online. A quick search through the Internet will show the hundreds if not thousands of private therapists that provide such a service. These tend to focus on treatment rather than prevention. However, larger scale prevention projects are also being set up. At the time of writing, an interactive web-based stress management programme is being set up by Unilever, which will be accessed through health clinics or online to interested individuals throughout Europe. This provides a structured approach to reducing stress as well as targeting behaviours that increase risk for heart disease, including an exercise programme and dietary advice. A more targeted approach was reported by Matano et al. (2000), who set up a web-site to provide advice on how to cut down alcohol consumption for a single large worksite. As with the Unilever project, levels of usage and its effectiveness have yet to be evaluated, but the potential for such interventions is impressive.

Organizational interventions

So far, the preventive approaches discussed have focused on helping people cope more effectively with the stress in their lives. A higher level intervention may involve reducing the causes of those stresses. While large-scale societal changes to improve mental health have proven difficult to implement and are constrained by political and economic factors, one area that can be more easily manipulated is the workplace.

One of the few worksite stress management projects to adopt a systemic approach to reducing stress was reported by Maes et al. (1998). Their intervention focused on modifying key aspects of the working environment in order to enhance mental well-being throughout the workforce of a major industrial producer. Their intervention drew upon studies that identified working conditions that can enhance both the well-being of workers and work production levels, including individuals working within their capabilities, avoiding short and repetitive performance tasks, having some control over the organization of work, and adequate social contact in the work situation. With these factors in mind, they attempted, within the constraints of production, to change the nature of each worker's job to bring it closer to the ideal. In addition, they trained managers in communication and leadership skills and identified methods through which they could recognize, and then prevent or reduce individual stress within the workforce. Although measures of 'stress' were not taken as part of the research programme, these changes resulted in an increase in the quality of work and lower absenteeism rates: both indicative of an increase in well-being at work.

Chapter summary

1 Both small and large social groups and other social influences impact on levels of mental health conditions.

2 Family models of mental health note the reciprocity between family members, and that mental health problems arise as a consequence of interactions between family members.

3 Structural family therapy adopts a model of a well-functioning family, based on the boundaries between units within the family. It uses behavioural strategies to shift dysfunctional families towards this model.

4 Strategic family therapy has no model of appropriate functioning. It uses two strategies of change: positive reframing and paradoxical manipulations.

5 Three major social variables impact on levels of mental health within the population: socio-economic position, gender and minority status.

6 Explanations for these differences include differences in levels of stress and coping resources and, perhaps, processes of social comparison.

7 Proponents of radical health promotion suggest that health inequalities can best be addressed through economic and political changes.

8 Those involved in promoting mental health have typically done so using more circumscribed interventions including using the media and open access classes to teach stress coping skills. Some projects have also addressed working environments to make them less stressful.

For discussion

1 All conditions treated with family therapy can also be treated by one-to-one therapy. What are the advantages and disadvantages of each approach?

2 Consider how you could promote mental health within the population or specific groups, such as working mothers or students, within the wider population.

3 If mental health disorders result at least in part from social conditions, should psychologists be actively involved in attempts to influence public health policy and relevant government decisions?

Further reading

Dallos, R. and Draper, R. (2000) *An Introduction to Family Therapy*. Buckingham: Open University Press.

Elliott, M. (2000) Gender differences in the causes of depression, *Women and Health*, 33: 163–77.

Secker, J. (1998) Current conceptualisations of mental health and mental health promotion, *Health Education Research Theory and Practice*, 13: 57–66.

Turner, R.J., Lloyd, D.A. and Roszell, P. (1999) Personal resources and the social distribution of depression, *American Journal of Community Psychology*, 27: 643–72.

Watzlawick, P., Weakland, J.H. and Fisch, R. (1974) *Change: Principles of Problem Formulation and Problem Resolution*. New York: W.W. Norton.

Wilkinson, M. (1992) Income distribution and life expectancy, *British Medical Journal*, 304: 165–8.

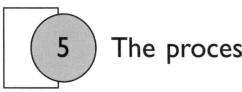

5 The process of therapy

Much of the focus of the following chapters is on the relative effectiveness of differing therapeutic techniques. This focus ignores the fact that therapy is, at its heart, a human enterprise, involving a relationship between client(s) and therapist(s). Therapy does not simply involve the systematic application of a set of techniques regardless of the therapeutic formulation, the client's needs and their response to therapy. This chapter therefore focuses on the process of therapy and how therapist and client factors affect the outcome of therapy. By the end of the chapter, you should have an understanding of:

- The process of assessment and intervention in clinical sessions
- Client factors that influence the outcome of therapy
- The characteristics of the therapist
- Their actions within the therapy session.

Therapy is often described as being conducted in the '50-minute hour'. That is, a client is often seen for a period of about 50 minutes, following which the therapist writes up their notes, considers the issues raised in therapy and perhaps plans how therapy will progress in the following session or sessions. The first one or two sessions are typically spent by the therapist gaining an in-depth understanding of some of the issues facing the client, why they chose to come for therapy at that time, what issues they would like to address in therapy, and what changes they wish to make. These introductory sessions are followed by a period in which the 'work' of therapy is conducted. The final sessions are spent considering how the individual will cope in the future and the process of disengagement from the therapist.

Assessment issues

Although it may be augmented by a variety of other methods, the clinical interview remains the main tool for gaining an understanding of clients' problems. Shea (1998) identified six goals of this introductory assessment:

- establishing a therapeutic relationship between client and therapist
- obtaining basic information about the client
- gaining an understanding of the problems they face
- arriving at a tentative formulation of the problems: what they are, what triggered them, and so on
- developing an intervention plan: work on relaxation, identify and change cognitive errors, increase activity, and so on
- decreasing the client's anxieties about therapy.

No one assessment interview is the same as others. Nevertheless, there may be considered a core 'set' of information that the therapist would wish to gain, including:

- *the presenting problem*: including the nature of the problem that led the person to seek help, the emotion and other problems they are experiencing, how long these have been present and whether they have occurred before, their impact on the day-to-day life of the individual, and how they are presently coping with their problems
- *the context in which the problem has arisen*: including the family and social context in which the person lives, the support or lack of it available to them, their work and any other relevant social issues such as legal problems
- *client characteristics*: including the client's strengths and weakness, what they want to achieve by coming to a therapist.

It is critical that the therapist not only listens to the client, but also observes them. They may check whether their appearance is suggestive of problems – are they neglecting themselves; does their appearance suggest they are depressed, manic and so on? The therapist may look for evidence of abnormal thinking. This may be so bizarre that it is self-evident. However, this is often not the case. Clients, understandably, present stories from their own perspective. This results in them presenting cognitive distortions as 'facts', the absolute belief in which may actually be their primary problem. Accordingly, issues have to be explored in some depth to allow the therapist to identify whether and where they think the individual's interpretation of events may be distorted. Further factors to consider are the client's mood. Are they severely depressed? Is their mood congruent with the story they are telling? Each may indicate the nature of the problem and the client's response to it.

This process is a critical phase in the process of therapy, as it will determine the formulation of the problem (see Chapter 1) and the way in which therapy will initially proceed. Surprisingly, perhaps, there is relatively little research assessing the reliability and validity of this process (Powell and Lindsay 1994). Certainly, the process is open to much the same biases as were raised in relation to the diagnostic process (see Chapter 1). Therapist factors that may lead to failures here include biases in the questions asked, misinterpretation of information given, and failing to identify relevant but subtle cues in what is said. Clients may also contribute to this process. Many find it difficult to tell a stranger their intimate and revealing secrets, and may deliberately withhold or play down important information, waiting till they have more trust in their therapist and confidence in telling them. In defence against these problems, it has been argued that the process of therapy involves the therapist in developing an understanding of the client's problems, and then testing and reassessing that understanding over the course of therapy. Accordingly, while an initial assessment may not match exactly with a client's problems, this process of checking and rethinking will result in an increasing understanding of their problem as therapy progresses.

Standardized interview schedules

Many therapists' initial assessment interview is relatively unstructured. However, a number of standardized interview schedules have been developed. These ask standard questions in a preordained sequence and are usually designed to identify whether or not an individual achieves the diagnostic criteria for a particular disorder. They are often used in clinical studies where it is important to identify the population being studied and ensure it is comparable with other populations with the same diagnosis. They are less often used in clinical practice.

Perhaps the most widely used is the Structured Clinical Interview (APA 2000) which is designed to elicit sufficient information to provide a DSM diagnosis. There are, however, a number of others, including the Diagnostic Interview Schedule (Robins et al. 1981) and the Diagnostic Interview Schedule for Children (Costello et al. 1985). Despite the use of such standardized instruments, agreement between observers on the diagnosis assigned remains less than perfect (see Chapter 1).

Other assessment approaches involve the use of self-rating questionnaires. These may measure both specific and more general issues. Some simply provide a measure of the severity of a problem. Others, such as the Beck Depression Inventory (Beck et al. 1961) provide cut-off scores, above which scores indicate the likelihood of someone being assigned some form of diagnosis were they to be given a formal diagnostic interview.

These types of assessments provide simple and relatively effective screening instruments for the presence of mental health problems, but do not provide sufficient detail to permit a full clinical picture to be developed. These measures have been used widely in clinical settings and have high levels of test-retest reliability and therefore provide a relatively consistent rating of client's functioning. Examples of this type of measure will now be described briefly.

Symptom-specific measures

• Beck Depression Inventory	Measure of depression with a cut-off score for a diagnosis of depression. Perhaps the most widely used measure of depression.
• General Health Questionnaire	Screening instrument for the recent onset of non-specific emotional problems. Often used to identify 'at risk' individuals in general populations.
• State-Trait Anger Scale	Measure of trait and situation specific-anger. As anger is not a 'diagnostic category' does not provide clinical cut-off scores.
• Michigan Alcoholism Screening Test	Measures the degree of alcohol dependence. Provides cut-off score to indicate need for clinical intervention.

General measure

• Symptom Checklist-90	Provides a general measure of psycho-pathology on nine scales: somatization, obsessive-compulsive disorder, interpersonal sensitivity, depression, anxiety, hostility, phobic anxiety, paranoid ideation, psychoticism.

Other measures

Many other assessment tools are also available. Observation of key behaviours is common. A therapist may visit the home of someone with obsessive-compulsive disorder, for example, and observe how they cope with issues related to their fears. Observation may also be conducted through role play. Assessment of cognitions, for example, may involve talking aloud while imagining oneself in a certain situation or during role play. A more grounded approach may involve a process known as thought sampling in which at pre-designated times, perhaps indicated by the beep of a timer or watch, an individual may speak aloud into a tape recorder the things they are thinking at that time. A final approach to assessment involves the use of diaries, which can be kept by clients and used to measure key factors within therapy including the frequency of panic attacks or episodes of anger, the nature of cognitive responses to certain events, and the frequency and effectiveness of the use of new coping behaviours such as relaxation or cognitive restructuring.

Working through the problem

By the end of the assessment phase, the therapist will have developed a preliminary understanding of the problems faced by their client: a formulation of the problem. This then guides the focus of the intervention. The content of the intervention phase sessions differs across therapies. In cognitive behavioural therapy, for example, the issues addressed in therapy may involve exploration of inappropriate cognitions or behaviour through Socratic dialogue, learning relaxation, and so on. Therapy sessions are typically divided into three phases:

- reviewing the homework conducted since the previous therapy session
- identifying and working on new issues either as part of a predetermined plan of therapy or as a result of issues that have arisen since the previous therapy session
- therapist and client considering how any new skills or insights may be applied in the 'real world', in the form of homework, which involves clients practising new skills in a formal pre-planned manner.

Some interventions, such as those teaching anxiety management skills (relaxation, self-instruction training), may follow a relatively structured form of intervention. They may even have manuals detailing the content of each week's therapy session. Other interventions, such as those involving people with anorexia or who are depressed, may be less structured and more led by client needs. The duration of therapy differs across therapies. Clients engaged in cognitive therapy may typically attend between eight and twelve weekly sessions, although this may vary markedly across conditions. Psychoanalytical therapy typically involves many more therapy sessions (see Chapter 3).

Some of the specific interventions that are carried out in this central phase of therapy have been considered in previous chapters and will be described in those chapters concerning specific disorders. Instead of reiterating these here, it is worth considering some of the more general elements of therapy that may be of benefit to individuals. Powell and Lindsay (1994) identified a number of key elements and processes common to many cognitive behavioural interventions in this phase, including the following:

- *Establishing realistic expectations:* the client is implicitly or explicitly given the understanding that they can achieve change, but is cautioned against expecting 'overnight cures' and to expect any changes to gradual rather than immediate.
- *Reinforcing progress:* clients are reinforced for successes they achieve, a process that increases their sense of mastery over their problems, and maintains or increases motivation to continue to deal with them.
- *Giving feedback on progress:* confidence in the client's ability to change is enhanced by feedback on progress. Critical to this process is the framing of problems encountered or 'failures' in a positive way. Rather than catastrophizing and considering a lack of success as evidence of a lack of ability or progress, they can be reframed in terms of an experience that can be learned from and which can help foster subsequent positive change.
- *Ensuring a graded approach to change:* progress is gradual, at a speed with which the client can cope. Cognitive behavioural programmes are often thought of as providing skills: the skill to identify and change maladaptive cognitions, to relax, to engage socially, to cope with intrusive 'voices', and so on. Like all skills, progress occurs through teaching simple skills under relatively easy circumstances, before increasing their complexity and using them in increasingly difficult situations. It is important that steps in progress are sufficiently large so the client has a feeling of progress, but not so difficult that they end in failure and the client becomes demoralized. Collaboration with the client in setting goals is essential.
- *Modelling:* again following the skills learning model, skills can be acquired through modelling by the therapist or other relevant individuals. Some interventions specifically targeted at teaching specific skills, such as social skills, may involve significant amounts of explicit modelling of new behaviours. Modelling may also be more implicit. Calm interactions or questioning of assumptions by the therapist may provide appropriate models of behaviour. The Socratic dialogue through which a therapist may identify and challenge maladaptive cognitions also provides a model that the client can then follow outside the therapy situation (see Chapter 2).
- *Rehearsing:* the more a new skill is practised, the easier it becomes to use, particularly at times of emotional stress. Accordingly,

clients in cognitive behaviour therapy are often asked to rehearse new skills, perhaps first in the therapy session and then at home. This combines with a graded approach to building up skills to optimize effective learning and behavioural change.

Moving to a more general set of principles, Frank (1961), in his seminal text, *Persuasion and Healing*, considered that people who enter therapy can be characterized as being demoralized, so much so that they have turned to others for help. He suggested that what we term therapy provides four common factors of benefit to such individuals:

- a relationship between client and therapist
- a setting that is socially sanctioned as a place of healing
- a theory to explain the development of the problem
- an intervention based on that theory.

Within therapy, sessions provide opportunities for learning, enhance the individual's hope for relief, and provide success experiences that increase their sense of mastery, overcome their feeling of alienation from others, and arouse them emotionally. Frank (1961) contended that these outcomes occur both within formal therapy sessions, and also in those we might consider less conventional such as with psychic healers and witch doctors.

Ending therapy

The ending of therapy has to be conducted with care, particularly when a client has been engaged in therapy for a significant period of time. Preparation for the ending of therapy tends to be more elaborate when therapy has been conducted over a long period of time and has dealt with intense or intimate issues than following brief and unemotional therapy, such as a stress management training group. Such preparation typically involves three elements:

- *a review of progress over the course of therapy:* including consideration of the client's initial level of functioning, the initial treatment goals, and how far they have progressed to meet them
- *an analysis of the progress of therapy:* analysis and feedback of how the client made progress, which may indicate and reinforce potential future actions to deal with similar problems
- *consideration of the future:* may involve consideration of what problems the individual may face in the future and how they

may work to prevent them occurring or deal with them should they do so.

The exact content of these issues will differ according to the therapeutic approach with which the client has been involved. The time they take to work through will also vary according to the duration of therapy – where this has been prolonged these issues may be dealt with over several sessions. The frequency of sessions may themselves be decreased towards the end of therapy as the client becomes more independent and as a preparation for coping without recourse to a therapist for some form of support. Finally, it is important to consider the possibility of a return to therapy should the client not be able to cope with future problems. Where feasible, it may be useful to consider how an individual may return to therapy should the need arise. An alternative approach, which is being increasingly used, is to plan a session some time into the future in which issues which have arisen since the end of therapy can be discussed and thought through, even if the individual is coping relatively well. These *booster sessions* have been shown to be effective in preventing at least some relapses.

Who benefits most from therapy?

Although this is a relatively under-researched area (Keijsers et al. 2000), what evidence there is suggests that the characteristics of those who take part in therapy have a significant effect on its outcome. Important factors include levels of motivation to change, hope, confidence in the ability to achieve a positive outcome, and the quality of the person's interpersonal and coping skills (see Roth et al. 1998).

Client characteristics

One of the first explorations of client characteristics that influenced the outcome of therapy was summarized by Schofield (1964), who suggested that humanistic therapies may be most effective with YAVIS clients. Young, attractive, verbally able, intelligent and successful individuals bringing significant resources and personal skills to the therapy session may benefit most from a therapy that allows them to explore issues in a non-directive manner. By contrast, people with severe personality disorders have poorer outcomes than more integrated individuals. In particular, they benefit little, or may even be made worse, by therapies that evoke high levels of emotion (see Chapter 11). Horowitz et al. (1984), for example, found that such people fared badly in bereavement therapy. Others who coped badly with this type of intervention were people who had lost their mother, had high levels of self-blame, or who were judged to have high levels of guilt or hostility. Psychopathic individuals seem to gain little from traditional therapies and may even become more 'effective' in their manipulative behaviour as a result of engaging in therapy (see Chapter 11).

Other research has shown that a high level of interpersonal functioning at the beginning of therapy is predictive of a good outcome at the end. People with good personal resources and who are responding to relatively short-term problems in their lives fare better than those with lower levels of personal resources and with longer-term problems. That is, therapy seems to be better at helping people whose problems are specific and circumscribed than those who have chronic, highly generalized problems and poor coping skills. Sadly, those with most to gain from therapy find it harder to achieve its benefits. Piper et al. (1991), for example, found that up to 83 per cent of individuals with a history of stable and satisfying relationships achieved significant gains following short-term psychoanalytic therapy compared to only 32 per cent of those without this history.

In a series of subsequent studies the same research team (Piper et al. 1999a, 2001) evaluated the joint impact of the ability to develop strong personal relationships and what they termed *psychological mindedness* on the outcome of therapy. Psychological mindedness is commonly regarded as a desirable attribute of clients being considered for dynamically oriented psychotherapy and is defined as the ability to identify dynamic (intrapsychic) processes and to relate them to their difficulties. Their studies generally supported this belief. They found that higher levels of both characteristics were associated with better short-term outcomes following both individual and group short-term dynamic therapy. However, only the ability to develop strong personal relationships was predictive of long-term outcome following individual therapy.

Perhaps not unexpectedly, the level of motivation to achieve change at the beginning of therapy is also associated with therapy outcome. Horowitz et al. (1984), for example, reported that people with high levels of motivation for psychoanalytic therapy and a strong concept of 'self' responded best to psychoanalytic techniques. Low motivation is associated with high dropout rates as well as unsuccessful therapy (Keijsers et al. 2000).

One research group (Beutler et al. 2000) summarized the relevant data, and identified six key client types that are predictive of therapy outcome, and the type of therapeutic intervention required:

- *high functional impairment*: need to consider hospitalization, use of medication, long and (at least initially) frequent treatment, with an urgency to achieve short-term therapeutic goals
- *high subjective distress*: most likely to benefit from interventions that reduce distress, including support, hypnosis and meditation

- *low subjective distress:* associated with low motivation and may benefit from strategies that increase arousal, including confrontation, peer evaluation and increased expressiveness
- *high social support:* require relatively brief interventions and are less likely to relapse
- *low social support:* need longer treatment and have poorer prognosis
- *high resistant:* benefit most from supportive, non-directive approaches or paradoxical interventions (see Chapter 4).

Client responses

The behaviour of the person in therapy has a significant effect on therapy outcome. Perhaps the most obvious marker of a poor therapeutic outcome is dropout from therapy. This is most likely among clients who find it difficult to engage in or who resist therapy, and where there is a relatively poor relationship between client and therapist (e.g. Piper et al. 1999b). As noted below, client behaviour can influence therapist behaviour. Hardy et al. (1998), for example, found that even in highly structured therapy sessions, therapists responded consistently to clients' interpersonal style. They tended to use more mood- and relationship-oriented interventions with over-involved clients, and more cognitive treatment methods with those who were under-involved. These responses may in turn influence clients' experience of therapy and how much they engage with emotional issues raised in therapy or try out strategies of change. Tang and DeRubeis (1999) also noted the importance of client factors in their three-stage model of sudden therapeutic gains within cognitive therapy. This suggested that gains are predicted, first, by the client responding favourably to education about the cognitive model of mood disorder. When this is followed by the experience of change in a critical belief or schema that leads to a sudden decrease in depression, this leads to an improved alliance between therapist and client and receptivity to cognitive interventions.

What makes a good therapist?

Therapists differ in their levels of skills and the personal attributes they bring to the therapy session. This has important implications for the outcome of therapy, even when relatively standardized therapeutic techniques are used. Not only do different therapists achieve differing levels of success using the same techniques, but also some studies have shown therapist characteristics to be more important predictors of outcome than the type of therapy used. That is, the variance in outcomes between therapists using the same treatment approach can be larger than that between differing treatments (see Roth et al. 1998). Huppert et al. (2001), for example, reported on the outcomes of 14 highly trained therapists involved in a large trial of the effectiveness of cognitive behaviour therapy for panic disorder. The intervention was highly standardized. Therapists were of proven high competence and were trained by experts in the therapeutic approach used in the study. They received extensive supervision during the trial. Despite this, there were marked differences in their effectiveness, with different therapists' success rates varying between less than 45 per cent to over 66 per cent. In general, good therapists achieve more consistent gains than poor therapists: even those who are least effective generally achieve some successes.

Therapists may vary across a number of factors, including:

- the therapeutic approach they adopt
- the extent of their training and years of experience as a therapist
- their skilfulness as a therapist, including persuasiveness, capacity for neutrality, the ability to make insightful links within therapy and to work with the client
- their personal qualities and interpersonal manner, including warmth, empathy, and genuineness (see Chapter 2).

Therapist experience

Many studies of factors that impact on therapy outcome have focused on the effects of relatively broad factors such as the length of therapist experience or how much training they have received. While these may have some merit, even where differences are found, any findings do not explain *why* these differences occur. It is also quite difficult to make strong predictions about the effect of experience on outcome. Do all therapists learn from their interactions with clients and gradually hone their skills and therapeutic effectiveness? Do some continue to make the same mistakes over time and not change in their effectiveness? Does the young, inexperienced therapist have an enthusiasm and closeness to their training that counters the experience but gradual distancing from closely supervised training of the more experienced therapist? Do good, intuitive therapists work effectively regardless of length of training? The many questions hidden in examination of associations between therapist experience and therapy outcome perhaps explain the inconsistent findings in the research literature.

In one of the first reviews of the relevant literature, Bergin (1971) examined 48 studies of the influence of therapist experience on therapy outcome: 53 per cent reported positive associations between length of therapist experience and positive outcomes. Only 18 per cent of trials using inexperienced therapists achieved significant clinical improvements. By contrast, Smith and Glass's (1977) meta-analysis of over 4500 studies revealed no effect of therapist experience, although most trials involved relatively inexperienced therapists and the lack of variance in therapist experience across the trials made it difficult to explore these issues.

Stein and Lambert (1995) restricted their review to the treatment of clinically significant problems. Assessing the experience of therapists proved difficult, with research reports typically reporting the training they received rather than their years of experience. Nevertheless, they identified a modest, but significant, association between length of therapist experience and outcome: longer experience was associated with a better outcome. Support for this conclusion can also be found in the study of Huppert et al. (2001) reported above. They found the most successful cognitive behavioural interventions were conducted by the most experienced therapists, regardless of their initial therapeutic orientation.

Therapist training

Evidence of the effect of therapist training is equally mixed. A number of studies have failed to find any effect of therapists' type or length of training on therapy outcomes. Orlinsky and Howard (1986), for example, reported significant variations across therapist effectiveness, but that this was not related to whether they were professionally trained. By contrast, Burns and Noen-Heoksema (1992) found that therapists with training in cognitive behavioural interventions were more effective in the treatment of depression than therapists with no training. These, and similar data, led Roth et al. (1998) to suggest that professional therapist training may be most important in relatively unstructured therapies in which the therapist has to develop their therapy in response to client disclosure and responses to treatment, and less important where therapy is standardized and based on a predetermined structure. Relatively untrained therapists may be effective, for example, in running stress management groups which follow a set sequence of teaching standardized skills including relaxation and self-instruction training, but less effective in therapy with depressed individuals, where there is no standard treatment protocol.

Gender and ethnicity

A number of studies have explored the impact of therapist and client gender and ethnicity on the outcome of therapy. Zlotnick et al. (1998), for example, found no impact of either variable on the outcomes of the NIMH depression trial (Elkin et al. 1994: see Chapter 9). A similar lack of association between the gender and/or the ethnicity of the therapist and outcome in a study involving treating cocaine-dependent individuals was reported by Sterling et al. (2001). Despite such findings, it is possible that in some cases, particularly where there are marked cultural differences between client and therapist, where language and understandings of mental health may differ markedly, both client's and therapist's ethnicity may have implications for the effectiveness of therapy.

Within-therapy factors

Regardless of training or experience, the real issue in therapy is whether the behaviour of the therapist within the therapy session makes a difference to its outcome. The answer here is unequivocal: it does. Several within-therapy factors have been shown to impact on outcome, including the acceptability of the treatment, the competence of the therapist, and the relationship that builds between client and therapist.

Treatment acceptability

Treatment acceptability refers to the degree to which clients accept and agree with a particular treatment model or technique. Clients will not benefit from entering into a therapeutic process if it is in some way unacceptable to them. Acceptability is influenced by the client's perception of the proposed treatment's sensibility, practicality, and potential for success: does it involve substantial 'homework', will it lead to high levels of distress, and so on? Interventions rated by clients as more acceptable are taken up more often than those rated as less acceptable (Reimer et al. 1992). It is therefore essential that the therapist checks out the acceptability of any proposed intervention with the client, and adjusts it accordingly.

Therapist competence

Therapist competence is clearly an important issue, even in standardized therapies. Several measures of therapist competence, for example, were taken by O'Malley et al. (1988) in the NIMH depression trial (Elkin et al. 1994: see Chapter 9). These included ratings of tape recordings of one therapy session, therapist reports and ratings from therapy supervisors. Therapist performance on these combined measures contributed to 23 per cent of the variance in therapy outcome, in contrast to 34 per cent of the variance which was accounted for by client characteristics (clients who were less well socially adjusted at baseline gained most). The NIMH trial used highly skilled therapists, possibly reducing the variance in outcome explained by this variable. A wider spread of skills may have resulted in therapist competence accounting for even more of the variance in outcome.

The therapeutic alliance

A further important factor within therapy is the strength of *therapeutic alliance* (Horvath and Luborsky 1993) between client and therapist. This is determined by the degree to which they agree over the relevance of the interventions offered, their short- and mid-term expectations of the outcome of therapy, and the personal 'bond' between client and therapist, based on the client's perception of the therapist as a caring, sensitive and sympathetic helping figure. Relevant data were subjected to meta-analysis by Horvath and Symonds (1991), who found that measures of therapeutic alliance explained 26 per cent of the variance in therapy outcome. The strength of alliance early in therapy may be particularly important: it appears less important later on. This may be a consequence of clients' increasing independence from the therapist as they improve, or perhaps because initial levels of alliance foster therapeutic change that becomes self-maintaining regardless of the later relationship between client and therapist. One encouraging finding of Horvarth and Luborsky (1993) is that a good therapeutic outcome can occur even where a therapeutic alliance has broken down, as long as it is subsequently redeveloped.

How these alliances are forged is a complex, and not yet fully understood, process. Crits-Cristoph et al. (1988) found that the accuracy or frequency of interpretations made by therapists during psychotherapy was unrelated to measures of the strength of therapeutic alliance. By contrast, Piper et al. (1993) found an inverse relationship between the number of interpretations made within therapy sessions and client ratings of alliance. Too many interpretations were seen as puzzling and annoying. People with poor relationship skills tended to have worse outcomes with high levels of accurate interpretations; those capable of maintaining relationships fared better. The strongest therapeutic alliances among clients with high personal relationship skills resulted from relatively low levels of accurate interpretations.

In a similar examination of therapist–client interactions, Beutler and Consoli (1993) found that directiveness was unhelpful with depressed clients who were resistant to problem exploration, but not with others. Studies of more subtle client–therapist interactions suggest that therapeutic gains are likely to be maximized where the therapist is appropriately responsive to the interpersonal style and psychological needs of the client on a moment-by-moment basis. Hardy et al. (1999), for example, found that the most effective therapists were those who were able to provide clients with a sense of security by responding to their changing attachment needs and allowing them to work in their *zone of proximal development* in which they could explore perceived threats and dangers but not be overwhelmed by them. This involved the therapist making decisions as to whether the client would benefit most from interventions they termed *containment*, in which the client was made to feel safe, or those that challenged them in some way.

A number of studies have focused specifically on therapeutic failures, where clients drop out from therapy. Hill et al. (1996) found that in all the cases they studied, dropout resulted from disagreement over strategies, therapist mistakes and negative feelings towards the therapist, that is: a breakdown of the therapeutic alliance. Importantly, these rarely resulted from one incident within therapy, and disagreements could often be resolved within the therapy session. Where the therapist was able to detect and respond effectively to disruptions in the therapeutic relationship, problems could be resolved and could even strengthen the therapeutic process. To do so, the therapist needed not only to identify when there was a therapeutic rupture, perhaps evident only through a subtle withdrawal by the client, but also to respond appropriately to it, generally by addressing and resolving issues arising from the precipitating issue.

Self-disclosure

Self-disclosure occurs when the therapist tells the client something about themselves relevant to the client's situation, including similar experiences, personal thoughts, feeling or reactions. Such a process is thought to increase the strength of relationship between therapist and client. Until recently the effects of this had not been evaluated in a structured manner. However, Barrett and Berman (2001) have now evaluated the effect of differing levels of therapist disclosure by systematically determining the degree of self-disclosure by the therapists. In conditions of high therapist self-exposure, clients reported both liking their therapist more and lower levels of symptom distress.

Specific techniques

So far, the discussion has ignored the use of therapeutic techniques and focused on the general characteristics of the therapist or therapeutic styles. The use of more specific strategies may also determine outcome. Teasdale and Fennell (1982), for example, measured outcomes in clients whose therapists systematically varied whether they used cognitive behavioural or a less focused and more general exploration of issues. Periods of 'pure' cognitive behaviour therapy resulted in greater changes in depressive thought content than similar periods of general exploration. Similarly, Oie and Shuttlewood (1995) found that therapy-specific factors such as the attention paid to dysfunctional attitudes and automatic thoughts were more associated with reductions in depression than more general factors such as clients' evaluations of the therapist or satisfaction with therapy in a study of group cognitive therapy for depression.

Bryant et al. (1999) considered both therapist and client characteristics associated with completion of homework assignments in a cognitive behavioural programme for depression. Therapist characteristics associated with high levels of completion were the review of homework assignments within therapy sessions and a composite measure of therapist competence, including items on collaboration, interpersonal effectiveness and development of appropriate cognitive interventions. That is, where clients developed a good rapport with the therapist and saw the value of the homework assignments, they actually did them.

Finally, Wiser and Goldfried (1998) found that the nature of therapists' control over the session strongly influenced clients' emotional experience during therapy. When therapists used reflection and acknowledgements, and did not direct the problem areas to be explored, clients reported high levels of both positive and negative emotions within therapy. At times when the therapist interrupted the client or increased their control over issues explored within the session, they reported a shift to low emotional experience, perhaps because they felt less emotionally engaged and less able to explore salient emotional issues when they were interrupted and controlled by the therapist.

Factors beyond the therapy situation

The typical therapy session lasts for one hour every one or two weeks. It is self-evident that the client spends more time in the 'real world' than they do in the therapy situation. Factors beyond the therapy situation can therefore have a significant impact on the outcome of therapy. One model of therapeutic change that took these factors into account was proposed by Teasdale (1993). According to Teasdale, cognitive change during therapy helps the client develop new, revised, beliefs about the world and themselves. However, these new beliefs are initially rather fragile, and how long they last, and their ability to influence mood and behaviour, is largely determined by events beyond the therapy situation. If events are in accord with the new schemata (that is, any hypothesis testing supports the new beliefs), they will be strengthened; if not, events may simply strengthen pre-existing schemata and make them more difficult to change in the future.

Chapter summary

1 Therapy can be divided into three phases: assessment, active intervention phase and ending. Different issues are dealt with in each phase.

2 Assessment ends in a psychological formulation, which is based on the therapist's theoretical understanding of the processes involved in developing particular problems and their therapeutic orientation.

3 The clinical interview remains the most used way of obtaining clinically relevant information, although this is often augmented by the use of psychometric instruments, diaries and perhaps observation of relevant behaviours.

4 The treatment phase includes a number of factors common to most, if not all, therapies and some specific to individual therapeutic approaches.

5 The ending of therapy involves a synthesis of what has happened within therapy and planning for how the individual will cope in the absence of therapy.

6 Therapy works best for people who have good coping skills, social support and who have short-term and specific problems. It is least effective for those without these advantages.

7 Therapist factors contribute significantly to the outcome of therapy: on occasion, more than their therapeutic approach.

8 Most therapists achieve some benefits with some clients; good therapists do so more consistently.

9 A number of therapist characteristics have been associated with therapy outcome, including their length of experience and the extent of their training. Gender and ethnicity appear to have little impact on therapy outcome.

10 Within-therapy processes are also important predictors of outcome. Of particular importance are the competence of the therapist (variations in outcome occur even among highly skilled therapists), the quality of the relationship between therapist and client, and the degree to which client and therapist share the same goals and can work together.

11 Some degree of self-disclosure may also facilitate the therapeutic process.

12 Specific therapeutic interventions may impact on specific outcomes: cognitive interventions impact on cognitive process, the degree of

therapist control within therapy will determine the experience of emotions within the therapy session.

13 Premature cessation of therapy is typically preceded by therapist mistakes, disagreement over strategies and negative feelings towards the therapist.

14 Events beyond the therapy situation also impact on outcome in a variety of ways.

For discussion

1 What may new or trainee psychotherapists gain from themselves being a client in psychotherapy?

2 What characteristics would you look for in a therapist if you were seeking therapy?

3 Would you be a good candidate for psychotherapy?

4 Should people seeking help for mental health problems be screened for their ability to benefit from psychotherapy, with those least likely to benefit being offered pharmacotherapy at an early stage?

Further reading

Beutler, L.E., Clarkin, J.F. and Bongar, B. (2000) *Guidelines for the Systematic Treatment of the Depressed Patient*. New York: Oxford University Press.

Keijsers, G.P.J., Schaap, C.P.D.R. and Hoogduin, C.A.L. (2000) The impact of interpersonal patient and therapist behavior on outcome in cognitive-behavioral therapy: a review of empirical studies, *Behavior Modification*, 24: 264–97.

Llewelyn, S. and Hardy, G. (2001) Process research in understanding and applying psychological therapies, *British Journal of Clinical Psychology*, 40: 1–21.

Roth, A., Fonagy, P., Kazdin, A.E. et al. (1998) *What Works for Whom?* New York: Guilford.

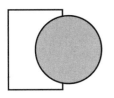

Part II
Specific issues

6 Schizophrenia

Schizophrenia is one of the most controversial psychiatric diagnoses. Over time, debates have addressed whether a distinct state of schizophrenia actually exists, whether it results from genetic or environmental causes, and whether it should be treated using drug therapy, ECT, or more social or psychological approaches. This chapter will address each of these issues. By the end of the chapter, you should have an understanding of:

- The nature of schizophrenia

- Alternative understandings of the 'symptoms' of schizophrenia

- The possible causal role of genetic factors, the family and psychosocial factors

- Neuronal and neurotransmitter models of the disorder

- Psychological models of the experiences of people diagnosed as having schizophrenia

- Differing approaches to the treatment of schizophrenia and their effectiveness.

The condition now labelled schizophrenia was first described by Kraepelin ([1883] 1981) using the term *dementia praecox*. This label was chosen to indicate that it was a progressive and deteriorating illness with no return to pre-morbid levels of functioning. Some years later, Bleuler (1908) identified four fundamental symptoms of what he termed the group of schizophrenias (literally, 'split mind'): ambivalence, disturbance of association, disturbance of mood and a preference of fantasy over reality. In retrospect, many of these people may actually have been suffering from a number of neurological disorders including a form of encephalitis known as *encephalitis lethargica* (Boyle 1990).

The nature of schizophrenia

The exact nature of schizophrenia remains hotly disputed. However, the consensus view is that it comprises a number of related disorders characterized by fundamental distortions of thinking and perception. Disturbances in thought processes are usually the most obvious symptom of schizophrenia. Conversations may lack coherence, jumping from topic to topic and idea to idea in an apparently incoherent manner. People with schizophrenia may use **neologisms** or make bizarre associations between words. They may feel that someone is putting thoughts into their mind and lose track of their conversation or thoughts, perhaps not completing sentences. They may have deluded and sometimes bizarre beliefs about themselves or others. These may include *delusions of control* (both being able to control others or being controlled by others), *grandeur* (believing they are rich, famous, talented) and *reference* (believing the behaviour of others is directly related to them: glances, looks, laughter are all seen as being directed at the individual). People with schizophrenia may also experience hallucinations, the most frequent of which are auditory. Their content may vary from the benign to the persecutory. The emotions that such people experience are often described as *flattened*. That is, they experience a general lack of emotional responsiveness, although they may be prone to apparently inappropriate mood states such as anger or depression as a consequence of internal thoughts or hallucinations.

Personal experiences

The experiences of people with schizophrenia vary markedly, as do the degree to which any experiences interfere with their life. Many people experience delusions over long periods without any significant impact on their life; for others the experience may be much more problematic. Two examples of this may be found in the experiences of Michael and David. Michael was a middle-aged man diagnosed with schizophrenia some years ago who was living a relatively normal life in a small flat in Cardiff. One of his delusional beliefs was that he is being attacked by lasers from an unknown, probably extraterrestrial, source:

> The lasers attack me. They aim for my head. I know when they are firing because I have pains when they hit me. They don't fire at me all the time. They come and go. I don't know what I have done to have them do this to me. But it's been going on for years. They usually hit me in the head, so I wear protection against it when they fire. I wrap metal foil over my head so it reflects the

lasers away . . . that way they can't get to me . . . I think they are
aliens that do this . . . The last time they fired at me was Sunday
morning. They woke me up – the lasers – with my head really
hurting. I couldn't get out of bed because of the pain. I had to
wear protection and take my time to get going because of the
pain . . . That was bad. Usually I can stop the lasers with the
metal, but it can get through sometimes.

(It is perhaps not coincidental that Michael had spent much of
Saturday night drinking beer in a local pub.)

A more acute and devastating set of delusional beliefs resulted in
David being admitted to hospital as he was running naked down the
middle of a city road proclaiming that he was the son of God come to
save us from our sins. At the time he was brought into casualty he was
proclaiming:

I am the messiah! I am David, savid, the saviour . . . I will save
you from the sins you have committed that commit you to the
heat of the hell not heaven of the Lord my God. You cannot hold
me . . . God is angry with you, the world, the whole round . . . the
devil will take you for your sins of holding me here. . . . the nine
that follow will kill you for holding the son of God in your
hall . . . I have come to save the world . . . you cannot hold
me . . . By the writings of Methuselah and the prophets and God
and Jesus I am here. God speaks to me! Not you! And he is angry
at the wickedness of the world and the work of the people and
the things they have done . . . the sins, things . . . wings of angels
will come for me to take me away from this hall.

About 1 per cent of adults are diagnosed as having some form of schizophrenia (APA 2000). Prevalence rates appear stable across countries,
cultures, and over time (but see the discussion of cultural relativity in
Chapter 1), with the onset of problems typically beginning between
the ages of 20 and 35 years. On average, women develop the condition
three to four years later than men and show a second peak of onset
around the menopause. It is an *episodic* disorder, with periods of acute
problems frequently separated by periods of remission. Wiersma et al.
(1998), for example, followed a cohort of individuals with schizophrenia
for a period of 15 years following their initial episode. Two-thirds of
those followed had at least one relapse and after each relapse one in six
did not recover: one in ten committed suicide over the course of the
study. Factors associated with a good prognosis included an acute onset,
the presence of an identifiable stress trigger, a predominance of positive
symptoms (see p. 129), good social support and no family history of
schizophrenia.

DSM diagnostic criteria for schizophrenia

For a diagnosis of schizophrenia to be made, DSM-IV-TR (APA 2000) states that two or more of the following symptoms should be present for a significant portion of time during a one-month period:

- delusions
- hallucinations
- disorganized speech: frequent derailment or incoherence
- grossly disorganized or **catatonic behaviour**
- negative symptoms: **flattened mood, alogia** or **avolition**

Only one of these symptoms is required if the delusions are bizarre or the hallucinations comprise a voice keeping up a running commentary on the person's behaviour or thoughts, or involve two or more voices conversing with each other. A second criterion is that the symptoms result in significant impairment. Four sub-types of schizophrenia, in which differing symptoms predominate, have been identified:

- *Disorganized:* in this, disorganized speech and behaviour, and flat or inappropriate mood are the dominant features.
- *Paranoid:* the commonest type of schizophrenia, characterized by stable, paranoid delusions. Auditory hallucinations may support these delusional beliefs. Disturbances of mood and speech, and catatonic symptoms, are not prominent.
- *Catatonic:* characterized by marked psychomotor disturbances. The condition varies between extreme excitement, stupor and waxy flexibility in which the individual may be placed in a position and maintain it for several hours. They may also evidence automatic obedience. These individuals may experience a dream-like state accompanied by vivid hallucinations. It is now rarely seen in industrial countries, though it remains common elsewhere.
- *Residual:* characterized by an absence of prominent delusions, hallucinations, disorganized speech, or grossly disorganized or catatonic behaviour. There is, however, continuing evidence of a disturbance, indicated by the presence of negative symptoms or two or more of the key symptoms in an attenuated form (see Table 6.1).

Alternative view of the symptoms

A different way to consider diagnostic criteria is to examine which symptoms cluster together, and to examine any underlying mechanisms that contribute to these symptom clusters. Factor analysis of the signs and symptoms of the various sub-types of schizophrenia has identified three

Table 6.1 Some of the most frequent symptoms
of acute schizophrenia

Symptom	% of cases
Lack of insight	97
Auditory hallucinations	74
Ideas of reference	70
Flattened affect	66
Suspiciousness	66
Delusions of persecution	64
Thought alienation	52

clusters of symptoms, known as disorganized, positive and negative symptoms (Liddle et al. 1994). The disorganized cluster is characterized by disorganized speech, behaviour and flat or inappropriate mood (or 'thought disorder'). The positive cluster includes hallucinations and delusions. Finally, negative symptoms denote an absence of activation, and include apathy, lack of motivation, or poverty of speech. Each of these may have different psychological and biological causes.

Deconstructing schizophrenia

The DSM-IV-TR criteria for a diagnosis of schizophrenia differ markedly from those of DSM-III (see Chapter 1), which differ from the alternative definitions of schizophrenia suggested by Liddle et al. (1994). This difficulty in establishing exactly what schizophrenia is presents clinicians and researchers with a fundamental problem when developing aetiological models or treatment approaches. So great is this difficulty, that many scientists and clinicians have begun to question whether schizophrenia exists in any form let alone how it is defined by DSM.

A fundamental problem with the DSM concept of schizophrenia is that different people given the diagnosis can present with very different experiences and problems: only two, potentially quite different, symptoms need be present to achieve a diagnosis of schizophrenia. This contradicts the notion of a disorder that has one underlying mechanism: if this were the case, all people should present with the same cluster of symptoms. A related point is that different people with schizophrenia respond to different medications, including **neuroleptics**, lithium and benzodiazepines. Others fail to respond to any of these medications. Accordingly, the course and treatment of the condition varies considerably across individuals. As Bentall (1993: 227) noted, 'we are inevitably drawn to an important conclusion: "schizophrenia" appears to be a disease which has no particular symptoms, which has no particular course, and which responds to no particular treatment'. On these grounds, he suggested that the diagnosis has no validity and that the concept of schizophrenia should be abandoned. Rather than attempting to explain multiple syndromes, future efforts should focus on explanations of particular behaviours or experiences: each of the various symptoms of 'schizophrenia' should be considered as a disorder in its own right, with differing underlying causes and treatments.

A further issue of relevance here is that the experiences of people diagnosed with schizophrenia are not exclusive to them. Many people who do not come to the attention of the psychiatric services also hear voices. What appears to distinguish between those who do or do not seek help for their 'problem' appears to be differences in individuals' responses to them and their ability to cope with them. Positive coping strategies include setting limits to the time spent listening to voices, talking back to them, and listening selectively to more positive voices (Romme and Escher 1989).

Having argued that attempts to link widely differing experiences under the rubric of 'schizophrenia' present significant problems, the following sections of the chapter generally reflect a more traditional perspective, and reviews research based on DSM or similar definitions of schizophrenia. Some may argue that this type of research is doomed to failure as it is seeking to identify causal factors for a condition that does not exist. More positively, it may still indicate some of the factors that increase risk or provide effective treatment for some or all of the experiences now considered under the rubric of schizophrenia. It also indicates some of the problems faced by theorists trying to explain common factors that contribute to the diverse experiences of people diagnosed as schizophrenic. As the research almost exclusively focuses on people with a diagnosis of schizophrenia, this term will be used throughout the sections, despite concerns about the validity of the concept.

Aetiology of schizophrenia

Genetic factors

Schizophrenia has been at the centre of a scientific debate concerning the role of nature and nurture in the development of mental health problems. Perhaps the dominant model of the aetiology of schizophrenia has considered it to have a biological cause, driven by genetic factors, although this has been hotly debated by those who favour environmental explanations. Evidence relating to genetic factors has therefore been closely scrutinized and has not been without controversy.

Table 6.2 Risk for schizophrenia (definite and probable) of relatives of people diagnosed with schizophrenia

Relationship	Percentage shared genes	Risk (%)
General population	N.A.	1
Spouses of patients	N.A.	2
Third-degree relatives	12.5	
First-degree cousins		2
Second-degree relatives	25	
Uncles/aunts		2
Nieces/nephews		4
Grandchildren		5
Half-siblings		6
First-degree siblings	50	
Parents		6
Siblings		9
Children		13
Siblings with one schizophrenic parent		17
Dizygotic twin		17
Monozygotic twin	100	48
Children with two schizophrenic parents	100	46

Source: adapted from Tsuang (2000)

Early genetic studies indicated that the risk for schizophrenia among relatives of an identified 'case' correlated with the degree of shared genes. Table 6.2 summarizes the findings of some early family studies, although weak study designs may have resulted in an overestimation of the strength of the family linkages. More recent and methodologically sound studies (e.g. Kringlen 1993) have reported concordance rates for schizophrenia in MZ twins of between 30 and 40 per cent and between DZ twins of 10–15 per cent, suggesting a part-genetically mediated risk for schizophrenia. While this evidence shows that schizophrenia runs in families, it does not necessarily mean that it has a genetic causation (see Chapter 1). Those closest to the affected individual may share a similar environment to them, or be affected by their behaviour. Attempts to disentangle environmental from biological issues have led to a number of studies comparing the risk for schizophrenia among relatives or twins of adopted-away children.

Close examination of these studies reveals a far from clear set of evidence. The Danish Adoption Studies (Kety et al. 1975), for example, traced the biological relatives of 34 adopted children who later developed schizophrenia and those of 34 control cases with 'clean pedigrees', and compared the prevalence of schizophrenia among them. Interestingly, they found only one person diagnosed as having chronic schizophrenia among the relatives of either cases or controls. Only when they extended the diagnoses assigned to one of *schizophrenic spectrum of disorders* comprising numerous diagnoses including borderline state, inadequate personality and uncertain schizophrenia did differences between the groups arise. Using these diagnoses, they found nine affected relatives in the families of the cases and two among the controls. This, some critics (e.g. Roberts 2000) have argued, provided no evidence that schizophrenia per se is inherited. Roberts also noted that at least some of the diagnoses assigned were taken from hospital notes and not confirmed by the research team, and that at least one person's reported diagnosis changed from inadequate personality to borderline schizophrenia over the course of two reports by the same research team. Worse was to come: subsequent reading of this individual's notes showed an initial diagnosis of bipolar disorder (Rose et al. 1984).

A more recent study of genetics reported by Tienari et al. (2000) compared rates of schizophrenia in the adopted-away offspring of both mothers diagnosed with schizophrenia and those without the diagnosis. Risk for schizophrenia was four times greater among the children of the women diagnosed as having schizophrenia than among the children of the comparison mothers: a total **incidence** of 8.1 per cent versus 2.3 per cent. However, this was not entirely due to genetic factors. Using data from the same study, Wahlberg et al. (2000b) reported an interaction between genetic and environmental factors. Children of women with schizophrenia who lived with adoptive parents with no communication disorder were not at increased risk for thought disorder. By contrast, the children of women diagnosed as having schizophrenia who were placed in families with evidence of communication deviance were at greater risk of developing schizophrenia than those with 'normal' mothers who were placed in such households. That is, the development of schizophrenia seemed to depend on both genetic risk *and* communication deviance within the adoptive family. Importantly, any communication deviance seemed to predate the adoption, and was not a consequence of the child's behaviour.

Together, these and other data have generally been seen by biological theorists as supporting a model in which genetic factors influence risk for schizophrenia, but do not form the single causal agent. They form a vulnerability factor rather than a causal factor. The search for the location of genes that increase risk of schizophrenia has also failed to yield definitive results, although loci on a dozen chromosomes have been implicated as likely sites (Tsuang 2000). Even genetic advocates such as Corsico and McGuffin (2001) have admitted that identifying the genetic linkages of schizophrenia presents 'great difficulties'. When considering the role of genetics in schizophrenia, one final cautionary note should be borne in mind: 89 per cent of individuals diagnosed with schizophrenia have no known relative with the disorder. Other factors are clearly implicated in the development of the disorder.

Biological mechanisms

The dopamine hypothesis

Much of the neurological research attempting to identify the causes of schizophrenia has been conducted on people who already are known to have the condition. This makes sense in some ways. But it provides significant problems for interpretation of much of the data. Johnstone (2000), for example, contended that any findings of neurological differences between people with schizophrenia and those without it may not indicate that these differences cause the condition. Rather, they may be explained by the effects of medication and/or the stress of experiencing vivid hallucinations or holding strong delusional beliefs.

Despite these provisos, a number of biological models of schizophrenia have been proposed. The first plausible theory involved the dopamine systems of the brain. Neurons mediated by dopamine are found in the limbic system, in a brain area known as A10, with links to the thalamus, hippocampus and frontal cortex, and the substantia nigra. The key feature of the dopamine hypothesis is that the experiences of people diagnosed with schizophrenia result from either an excess of dopamine, or the receptors at neuronal synapses being supersensitive to normal amounts of dopamine. Evidence generally supports the latter, but either way this theory suggests that at least some of the experiences of schizophrenia may result from excess activity in those parts of the brain controlled by dopamine.

Evidence of increased dopamine activity comes from a number of converging types of study (Lieberman et al. 1990):

- Amphetamine use increases dopamine levels and can produce experiences that mimic the positive symptoms of schizophrenia. Small controlled doses of amphetamines can produce schizophrenic-like symptoms in at least some naive subjects. These experiences may continue long after cessation of taking the drug. They do, however, mirror only one particular type of schizophrenia: paranoid schizophrenia.
- Some of the most effective drugs for treating both amphetamine psychosis and schizophrenia are the neuroleptic drugs known as phenothiazines (see Chapter 3), which block transmission of dopamine by preventing its uptake at the postsynaptic receptor site.
- Post-mortem evidence has shown a marked increase in dopamine receptor sites in people with schizophrenia in comparison to 'normal' controls, suggesting a supersensitivity to dopamine. How much of this is a consequence of medication and how much the disease process is in dispute.

Other evidence is less supportive of the dopamine hypothesis (Duncan et al. 1999):

- No direct evidence of pathologic dopamine neuronal activity has been consistently demonstrated, such as increased levels of dopamine, its metabolites or its receptors, that are not the potential results of antipsychotic drug treatment.
- One of the most effective antipsychotic drugs, clozapine, appears to work by its impact on the serotonin and not dopamine systems. This suggests that other neurotransmitters may be involved in schizophrenia.
- A substantial proportion of people with schizophrenia are resistant to treatment with neuroleptics, suggesting that dopamine systems may not always be involved in its aetiology.
- Schizophrenic-like experiences are rarely induced in 'normal' individuals when they are administered drugs that increase dopaminergic activity.
- Neuroleptics are only partially effective in alleviating the negative symptoms of people diagnosed with schizophrenia.

These conflicting findings may reflect problems in trying to collapse a number of differing biological processes under the rubric of one condition which may present quite differently in different people. However, instead of trying to identify specific biological substrates to specific psychological experiences, biological theorists continue to attempt to provide a model which explains all the experiences of schizophrenia. One way they have done this is to extend the number of neurotransmitters implicated in its aetiology. Duncan et al. (1999), for example, suggested that NMDA and serotonin dysregulation may also contribute to the disorder.

Neurological substrates

As well as errors in neurotransmitter levels, some studies suggest that negative, disorganized and some positive symptoms may result from damage to the neural systems themselves (Basso et al. 1998). The most common findings of brain scans include enlarged cerebral ventricles and decreased cortical volume especially in the temporal and frontal lobes. Post-mortem examinations have revealed reductions in neuron density and size in the limbic, temporal and frontal regions and that the connections between neurons are relatively disorganized. The various affected brain areas include systems that influence attention, memory and mood (limbic system), planning and coordination (frontal and prefrontal lobe), and acoustic and verbal memory (temporal lobes).

The length of time a person experiences any problems before receiving drug treatment is a significant predictor of long-term outcome. Lieberman et al. (1990) took this to indicate the neuronal degeneration is a progressive deterioration, resulting in a diminished ability of the individual to respond to antipsychotic medication. Provide treatment too late, and the degree of neuronal damage is too great to allow full recovery. Biological theorists have proposed a number of potential causes for any neural damage, as described next.

Excess dopamine

In an extension of the dopamine hypothesis, Lieberman et al. (1990) suggested that the initial trigger to a first episode of schizophrenia may involve increased dopaminergic activity, which results in positive symptoms. However, continued excessive dopamine activity leads to degeneration of the neurons in the dopamine systems, leading to exceptionally low levels of dopamine activity and, hence, negative symptoms.

Viral infection

There is consistent evidence that children born in the winter months are more at risk of developing schizophrenia than those born in the summer (Torrey et al. 1997). Why this should be the case is not clear. However, the best guess is that neural damage as a result of viral diseases, which are more prevalent during the winter, may be a causal factor. Supportive evidence was reported by Jones and Cannon (1998), who found that young children who had viral infections were five times more likely to develop schizophrenia than those who did not. Similarly, Takei et al. (1995) found that female (but not male) foetuses exposed to an influenza virus five months before birth were at increased risk of developing schizophrenia in adulthood than those that were not exposed. Larger studies in whole populations have not always supported these findings, however. While some studies have found the incidence of schizophrenia to be higher among cohorts of adults born close to times of childhood viral epidemics, this is not always the case (Battle et al. 1999).

Pregnancy and delivery complications

Pregnancy and delivery complications may also cause subtle brain damage that increases risk for schizophrenia. In a meta-analysis of eleven studies reporting relevant data, Geddes et al. (1999) compared data on 700 children who went on to develop schizophrenia and 835 controls. A number of delivery complications were implicated by their data, including low birthweight, prematurity, requiring resuscitation or being placed in an incubator, lack of oxygen, and premature rupture of the membranes.

Maternal stress

A number of studies have also implicated maternal stress in the development of schizophrenia. Van Os and Selten (1998), for example, found that the children of Dutch women who experienced bombing during the

Second World War during pregnancy were at increased risk for schizo-phrenia in comparison to control populations who did not. Interpreting these data is somewhat complicated as not all women may have experi-enced stress as a consequence of these factors. In addition, the cause of any relationship between maternal stress and subsequent disorders is far from clear. It could be mediated through hormonal changes at times of stress, changes in health behaviour such as smoking or alcohol use, delivery complications or some other mechanism.

Substance abuse

So far, the chapter has identified a number of factors that either increase risk of developing schizophrenia or explain the chronic degenerative changes associated with the condition. They have not considered what may actually trigger particular episodes. Such triggers may be psy-chological (see below). However, one biochemical trigger may also be implicated.

Stimulants can cause transient psychotic experiences and precipitate relapse of an existing psychotic condition (Satel and Edell 1991). Evid-ence that cannabis consumption can also increase risk of schizophrenia may be found in a longitudinal study of nearly 45,000 Swedish people reported by Andreasson et al. (1987). Those who used cannabis at the age of 18 were more likely to be admitted to hospital with schizophrenia over a 15-year follow-up period than those who did not. In addition, there was a dose–response relationship between the frequency of smok-ing cannabis and the risk of developing schizophrenia: the more canna-bis smoked, the greater the risk of developing schizophrenia. A potential biochemical route through which cannabis exerts this influence has also been determined. The active metabolite of cannabis (delta-9 tetrahydro-cannabinol) raises levels of cerebral dopamine and might precipitate psychosis. An alternative hypothesis is that people with the early experi-ences of schizophrenia may take cannabis as a form of self-treatment to alleviate either negative experiences or depression (Peralta and Cuesta 1992), reversing the causal link.

Psychosocial factors

The highest population rates of schizophrenia are among those in the lower socio-economic groups. Eaton et al. (1989), for example, calcu-lated that individuals in the lowest socio-economic group were three times more likely to be assigned a diagnosis of schizophrenia than those in the highest. This type of finding could have (at least) two implications. Either socio-economic status is a risk factor for schizophrenia, or schizo-phrenia is a risk factor for low socio-economic status: social causation versus social drift (see Chapter 1). Fox (1990) analysed both his own long-term data and that of other published work and found no evidence to support the social drift hypothesis. It seems that low socio-economic status is generally a cause rather than a consequence of schizophrenia.

One explanation for this finding is that the relatively high levels of stress associated with low socio-economic status may trigger the onset of schizophrenia in vulnerable individuals. This speculation is supported by findings that up to 24 per cent of episodes of schizophrenia seem to be precipitated by some acute life stress (Tsuang et al. 1986).

Long-term stresses also increase risk of initial onset of the condition. One long-term stressor may be the family in which the individual lives. One of the first theories to consider this issue identified the relationship between the child and their mother as a critical factor in schizophrenia. This psychoanalytic theory, developed by Fromm-Reichman (1948), suggested that schizophrenia is the outcome of being raised by a mother who appears warm and self-sacrificing, but is in reality self-centred, cold and domineering – the so-called *schizophrenogenic mother*. Fromm-Reichman suggested that the mixed signals that such a mother gives out confuses the child and makes their world difficult to interpret, a process that eventually leads to chaotic behaviour and cognitions. A similar theory was subsequently proposed by Bateson et al. (1956). Their 'double-bind' theory suggested that some parents frequently deal with their children in contradictory and confusing ways. They may, for example, tell their children they love them in a tone of voice that portrays the opposite, or ask them to do incompatible things: 'I think you should go out more often with your friends: please stay with me . . .'. Frequent exposure to these contradictory demands may confuse the person, and eventually prove so stressful that it results in the some or all of experiences of schizophrenia. Both models have some logic, but they have little evidence in their support.

One family theory has proven more robust. A critical element in the family process seems to be the degree of family criticism that the individual experiences. According to this model, the expression of high levels of negative emotional expression, hostility, or criticism may trigger a relapse in someone who has already had at least one episode of schizophrenia. The classic study of this phenomenon, now known as high negative expressed emotion (NEE), was conducted by Vaughn and Leff (1976) in a study of readmission rates of people with schizophrenia discharged from the Maudsley Hospital during the 1970s. Their findings were dramatic: those who were discharged to low NEE households were much less likely to relapse than those whose home was rated high in NEE. The effect of this type of environment is related to the amount of time it is experienced. Those who spent fewer than 35 hours a week in the home environment, because they went to work or a day centre, were significantly less likely to relapse than those who were exposed to these conditions for more than 35 hours a week. Evidence that family processes may also trigger the initial onset of schizophrenia in vulnerable individuals can be found in the Wahlberg et al. (2000b) study described earlier in the chapter.

A psychobiological model

So far, the evidence has implicated dopamine, subtle brain damage, and stress in the aetiology of the wider set of experiences of people diagnosed with schizophrenia. What it has not done is explain the episodic nature of the disorder or how psychosocial factors influence its course. The dopamine hypothesis can be extended to account for the stress–schizophrenia link, as there is evidence from animal studies that levels of dopamine increase at times of stress (Walker and Diforio 1997). In addition, rats sensitized by chronic amphetamine administration show increased behavioural responses and rises in dopamine levels in response to stress than control animals (Duncan et al. 1999). Together, these data suggest a possible stress-vulnerability model of schizophrenia involving three broad stages:

- The first stage is one of disordered neuronal development resulting from genetic, natal or perinatal factors. These problems underlie subtle early cognitive, motor and social impairments. They provide a *vulnerability* for schizophrenia.
- These deficiencies may lead to the second stage, which occurs in adolescence and early adulthood. At this time, stressful but normal human experiences, result in increases in dopamine activity. As a consequence of this neuronal disorganization, dopaminergic neuronal systems become sensitized to existing levels of dopamine and become more reactive to them, resulting in the positive symptoms of schizophrenia. The greater the stress experienced, the greater the risk of dysregulation and onset of schizophrenia.
- If prolonged or recurrent, high levels of dopamine can lead to the degeneration of neurons, leading to structural damage, and the onset of negative symptoms.

Accordingly, the dysregulation that underpins schizophrenia may be a consequence of both biological factors that increase vulnerability and may contribute to its chronicity, and stress factors that trigger or exacerbate the condition. Even this biopsychosocial model is too 'biological' for some critics (e.g. Johnstone 2000) who have argued that there are no compelling grounds to assume any biological underpinnings to either schizophrenia or its 'component' elements. They still do not feel the necessity to combine biological and psychological elements, arguing for a psychosocial rather than biopsychosocial model.

Psychological models

Psychological models offer an alternative understanding of schizophrenia. Rather than attempt to identify factors that trigger 'episodes' of 'schizophrenia', they attempt to explain the process that underlie each of the different types of experience reported by people assigned the diagnosis. They adopt a dimensional view to the understanding of these experiences (see Chapter 1), as they consider the experiences of people diagnosed as having schizophrenia to lie at the extreme of normal functioning rather than to be categorically different to 'normal'. These underlying cognitive processes are considered to be the same as those within the general population; only their content differs.

One way that schizophrenia can be considered from a psychological perspective is to consider the basic cognitive processes underlying some of the behaviours associated with schizophrenia:

- memory deficits are associated with an inability to link the separate elements of events into a cohesive, memorable and distinctive whole
- verbal 'hallucinations' may arise from abnormalities in speech perception and as a defence mechanism against the reality of traumatic memories
- thought disorder reflects a specific deficit in processing meaning, arising from unusual associative links within a semantic network
- negative symptoms are associated with deficits involving intelligence, executive function, memory and sustained attention.

A cognitive model of delusions

A further example of a psychological approach to explaining the experiences of people diagnosed with schizophrenia is afforded by the cognitive model of delusions developed by Bentall and colleagues. Perhaps the most common understanding of the delusional beliefs held by people with schizophrenia is that they are qualitatively different from the beliefs held by 'ordinary people'. Berrios (1991), for example, argued that delusions are 'empty speech acts' that refer neither to the world or the self: they are not symbolic of anything. By contrast, clinicians such as Bentall (e.g. Bentall et al. 2001) have argued that delusions are at the extreme end of a continuum of types of thought that runs from 'ordinary thoughts' to those that are bizarre and impossible, but all of which are the end-product of similar cognitive processes. Cognitions, including delusions, are seen as an interpretation of events; maybe even rational attempts to make sense of anomalous circumstances. While the thought content may be out of the ordinary, the psychological processes underpinning it are not.

Bentall and colleagues have focused particularly on explanations of one form of delusion involving persecutory beliefs. Their research has indicated that people with these types of belief have cognitive distortions common to many other disorders. Bentall et al. (2001), for example, found that people who experienced persecutory beliefs were more likely than depressed people or participants with no mental health problems to recall threatening themes in stories they were given to read as part of a memory test. They took this to indicate a general bias in their interpretation of events: not just those events that referred or happened to them directly.

The model of persecutory beliefs model developed by this group (Bentall et al. 2001) drew on the humanistic concepts of the actual and ideal self. They suggested that many people with schizophrenia have a poor self-image, and experience significant discrepancies between their actual- and ideal-self, that is, how they see themselves and how they would like to be. These discrepancies may be maintained by attentional and attributional biases, in particular, by considering negative events or outcomes of their behaviour to be the result of personal deficiencies. An awareness of the discrepancy between ideal- and actual-self may result in depression. Persecutory beliefs may occur as the result of a struggle to minimize the discrepancy. According to Bentall and colleagues, when discrepancies between actual- and ideal-self are activated by negative life-events or other triggers, the individual tries to minimize this discrepancy by shifting this attribution onto others, as a form of psychological defence: 'I think I am OK, even though others don't'. It may be less distressing for the individual to think others think poorly of him or her than to accept their own feelings of inadequacy. Bentall and colleagues further suggest that the natural history of schizophrenia within the family can be explained by this model, as attributional styles may be learned from other family members, and parental criticism may precipitate relapse by triggering actual–ideal self-discrepancies.

A trauma model of hallucinations

Romme and Escher's (1989) model of hallucinations considered them to be a normal response to traumatic events, particularly bereavement and sexual or physical assault. They considered that their function is to draw attention to emotional traumas that need resolving and to provide a defence against the emotional upset associated with the memories by placing them into the third person. This may be considered a form of dissociation similar to that involved in the processing of traumatic memories discussed in Chapter 9. The goal of therapy should therefore be to help people develop strategies to understand the meaning of the voices they are hearing, not to rid the person of their voices.

A coping model

A final, and related, approach to considering the experiences of people diagnosed with schizophrenia is that they are the end-point of a sequence of poor coping strategies in the face of life stresses. Analysis of the 'early signs' that indicate the future onset of what DSM would term an episode of schizophrenia often presents a pattern of behaviours involving withdrawal from friends and family, spending increasing amounts of time socially isolated perhaps in one room, poor sleep leading to tiredness to the point of exhaustion, losing the structure of the day and perhaps starting to take drugs to relieve distress and low mood (see Box 6.1). These conditions are not so far removed from conditions of sensory deprivation which are known to result in delusional thinking and hallucinations in most people. This model suggests that the experiences of

---

Box 6.1   Early signs of relapse

Birchwood and colleagues (2000) ask clients to tick off a checklist of 'early signs' which they experience at different times within a process of relapse. Others ask them to identify them through discussion. Here are some of the early signs identified by a number of people using this approach, roughly in the order in which they occur at times up to several months before any obvious 'relapse':

Sean

- sleeping later in the morning
- reduced contact with people – staying in
- loss of interest in music
- anxiety
- smoking and drinking more
- paranoia – think I'm being poisoned
- depression
- erratic eating
- stop shaving
- litter around the house – don't clean up, live in a mess
- fear
- mental exhaustion – peripheral hallucinations, flashes of light and dark.

Tony

- abusing drugs and alcohol
- distrusting people
- hostile towards people
- sleep deprivation
- erratic mood swings
- comfort eating
- tired and lethargic
- alienation from friends and family
- crying

- racing thoughts
- anger and violent behaviour towards parents
- smoking cannabis during work hours
- find it difficult to separate thoughts from reality
- washed out on jobs – verbally abusive
- lack of concentration.

Emerging pattern

The pattern that emerges from these, and other, descriptions is that these people when faced with a particular life stress withdraw from the world, spend increasing amounts of time on their own, become extremely tired to the point of exhaustion, lose the structure of the day and perhaps start taking drugs to relieve their discomfort. These conditions are not so far removed from conditions of sensory deprivation which are known to result in delusional thinking and hallucinations. This suggests that the experiences of people diagnosed with schizophrenia are perhaps not so far removed from those of other people. It may be that their eventual 'relapse' is more the inevitable end of a sequence of poor coping behaviours that places them at risk of unusual experiences rather than the onset of a 'disorder' that is removed from the experience of the rest of the population.

people diagnosed with schizophrenia are perhaps not so far removed from those of other people. It may be that their eventual 'relapse' is more the inevitable end of a sequence of poor coping behaviours that places them at risk of unusual experiences rather than the onset of a 'disorder' that is removed from the experience of the rest of the population.

Treatment of schizophrenia

Antipsychotic medication

Most people diagnosed with schizophrenia receive some form of medication, although dosages may be reduced or even discontinued during periods of remission. Chlorpromazine, haloperidol and clozapine are three of the most commonly used drugs (see Chapter 3). Their most striking effect is one of sedation. They also have a direct effect on hallucinations and delusions, although their effectiveness varies markedly between individuals. Chlorpromazine and haloperidol seem to affect only the positive symptoms of schizophrenia: clozapine, a relatively new drug, is more successful at treating the negative symptoms as well, and is often effective when other treatments fail. Antipsychotic medication has been so successful in treating people with schizophrenia that the average hospital stay has declined to less than 13 days, when formerly it was months, years, even a lifetime. Although antipsychotic drugs may be an important protective factor against relapse, relapse rates of 40 per cent in the first year following treatment initiation and 15 per cent in successive years are typical (Sarti and Cournos 1990). Overall, they appear to delay relapse rather than prevent it.

The use of antipsychotic drugs is also not without problems. They have a variety of side-effects that frequently lead those receiving them to minimize or stop their use. Side-effects of chlorpromazine, for example, include a dryness of mouth and throat, drowsiness, visual disturbances, weight gain or loss, skin sensitivity to sunlight, constipation, and depression. More problematic, however, are what are known as extrapyramidal symptoms. These include the symptoms of Parkinsonism and tardive dyskinesia (see Chapter 3), which have been estimated to affect over a quarter of individuals who receive medium to long-term neuroleptic treatment. Treatment by clozapine does not carry this risk, but those who receive it may be at risk of a condition known as agranulocytosis, which results in significant impairment of the immune system.

Adherence with antipsychotic drug regimes can be as low as 25 per cent among people living in the community (Donohue et al. 2001). This does not seem to be associated with socio-demographic variables, severity of the disorder, or even the extent to which people experienced extrapyramidal symptoms. Instead, low adherence seems to be related to attitudes towards medication, expectations of drug effectiveness, available social support, and the quality of the therapeutic alliance (Donohue et al. 2001). Poor memory may contribute to accidental adherence.

Strategies to maximize adherence include education, developing a high quality therapeutic alliance, and the use of memory aids for those with a poor memory. Depot injections may also be of benefit. One relatively new strategy to educate and motivate people to take medication is known as motivational interviewing (Miller and Rollnick 2002). This neutral approach does not involve attempts at persuasion to take medication. Instead, it encourages the client to choose whether or not to take their medication as a result of a careful exploration of the costs and benefits of medication use. This process provides some degree of control to the client, improves the therapeutic alliance as the therapist is not seen as coercive, allows any misunderstandings about medication to be identified and corrected, and seems to be more effective in encouraging drug use than direct attempts at persuasion (Coffey 1999).

Minimizing drug usage: early signs

The psychological and physical consequences of long-term drug treatment of schizophrenia have led clinicians to seek innovative methods by which medication usage can be minimized. One approach, involving 'early signs', is based on findings that many people with schizophrenia and their families can detect subtle changes in behaviour and mood that precede a relapse (see Box 6.1). Herz and Melville (1980), for example, found that 70 per cent of people with schizophrenia and 93 per cent of their families were aware of such changes. These experiences frequently followed a regular and predictable order, the progression of which typically occurred in a period of less than one month, but in some cases may appear up to one year before the onset of significant problems. The 'early signs' approach assumes that while a person is well, they may be placed on a reduced level of drug treatment or even withdrawn from them completely. When they experience changes that indicate risk of relapse, these should trigger the individual to seek help (often following a prearranged care plan) and receive intensive drug and/or psychological therapy to prevent relapse and maintain their recovery (Birchwood et al. 2000).

This approach can be effective. Gaebel et al. (2002), for example, compared outcomes in 363 people with schizophrenia who received either intermittent (early signs intervention) or continuous medication following either a first episode or multiple episodes of schizophrenia. Those people treated using the early signs approach used less medication over a two-year period than those in the continuous medication condition. Despite this, there were no differences in effectiveness between the treatments on measures of psychopathology, social adjustment and subjective well-being.

ECT

ECT (see Chapter 3) has been a front-line treatment of schizophrenia in the past, and has achieved some success. A meta-analysis by Tharyan (2002) concluded that about half those treated with ECT showed short-term improvements in general functioning when compared to those given placebo. This effect, however, did not last. Moreover, ECT is less effective than antipsychotic drug treatment. Combining antipsychotic drugs and ECT is of benefit only in the short-term, and only one out of every five to six people will benefit. For these reasons, ECT in the treatment of schizophrenia has largely been curtailed, with an increased emphasis on medication and psychosocial treatments.

Psychological approaches

Psychoanalytical approaches

One of the first psychosocial treatments of schizophrenia was developed by Harry Stack Sullivan in the early part of the twentieth century. Sullivan (1953) considered schizophrenia to involve difficulties in living arising from problems in personal and social relationships, and that 'personality warps' were the lasting residue of earlier unsatisfactory personal experiences. His treatment approach involved examination of the individual's life history and the historical roots and current ramifications of their maladaptive interpersonal patterns, evident in their relationship with their doctor and in daily life. Characteristic difficulties were thought to include a basic mistrust of others, and a marked ambivalence in relationships, with swings between a longing for, and a terror of, close relationships. Resolution of this conflict through the psychotherapeutic process was thought to result in improvements in psychosis, and maturation of the patient and their non-psychotic personality. While Sullivan's interventions were important, as they encouraged the psychological treatment of people with schizophrenia, the approach has been found to be less effective than supportive therapy, and is no longer carried out.

Family interventions

The recognition that high NEE was contributing to relapse in schizophrenia resulted in a number of studies of family interventions targeted at its reduction. In one of the earliest of these, Leff and Vaughn (1985) randomly assigned people with schizophrenia who had at least 35 hours per week face-to-face contact with family members in a high NEE household to a family intervention or usual care condition. The intervention included a **psycho-educational programme** that focused on methods of reducing NEE within the household, family support and the opportunity for family therapy. The programme was highly successful. Nine months after the end of therapy, 8 per cent of the people in the treatment group had relapsed, in contrast to 50 per cent of those in the comparison group. By two-year follow-up, 40 per cent of the treatment group and 78 per cent of the control group had relapsed.

A similar therapeutic approach was adopted by Falloon et al. (1982). Their intervention included education about the role of family stress in triggering episodes of schizophrenia and working with the family to develop family problem-solving skills. Their results were equally impressive. At nine-month follow-up, 5 per cent of the people in families receiving treatment had relapsed, in contrast to 44 per cent of those receiving standard medical treatment. By two-year follow-up, relapse rates were 16 per cent and 83 per cent respectively. On the basis of this and other related evidence, Pharoah et al. (2000) concluded that family interventions reduce risk of relapse by about half in comparison to standard medical care. They also noted that family interventions decreased the frequency of admissions to hospital, time spent in hospital, and improved compliance with medication regimens.

Cognitive behaviour therapy

Two forms of cognitive behaviour therapy are increasingly being used with people who have schizophrenia. The first, stress management, involves working with individuals to help them cope with the stress associated with psychotic experiences. The second, known as belief modification, involves attempts to change the nature of delusional beliefs the individual may hold.

Stress management

Stress management approaches involve a detailed evaluation of the problems and experiences an individual is having, their triggers and consequences, and any strategies they may use to cope with them. Problems are identified and the therapist and client work together to develop specific coping strategies to help the client cope more effectively with them. Potential strategies include cognitive techniques such as distraction from intrusive thoughts or challenging their meaning, increasing or decreasing social activity again as a means of distraction from intrusive thoughts or low mood, and using breathing or other relaxation techniques to help them relax (see Chapter 2).

In one long-term study of this approach, Tarrier et al. (2000) randomly assigned people diagnosed with schizophrenia to either drug therapy alone, or in combination with stress management or supportive counselling. The stress management intervention involved twenty sessions in ten weeks, followed by four booster sessions over the following year. By the end of the first phase of treatment, those who received this intervention evidenced a greater improvement than those in the supportive counselling group, while people who received only drug therapy showed a slight deterioration. One-third of the people who received stress management achieved a 50 per cent reduction in psychotic experiences; only 15 per cent of the supportive counselling group achieved this level of benefit; 15 per cent of the stress management group and 7 per cent of the supportive counselling condition were free of all positive symptoms. None of those in the drug therapy group achieved this criterion. One year later, there remained significant differences between the three groups, favouring those in the stress management condition. By two-year follow-up, however, although people who only received drug therapy had significantly more problems than those in the active treatment groups, there were no significant differences between the stress management and supportive counselling groups.

Belief modification

Belief modification involves the use of two cognitive interventions, verbal challenge and behavioural hypothesis testing, to counter delusional beliefs and/or hallucinations. Verbal challenge encourages the individual to view a delusional belief as just one of several possibilities. The person is not told that the belief is wrong, but is asked to consider an alternative view provided by the therapist. New possibilities may then be tested in the 'real world' as appropriate. A similar process is used to challenge hallucinations, focusing on the patient's beliefs about their power, identity and purpose. Behavioural hypothesis testing involves challenging any thoughts in a more direct, behavioural, way.

Reflecting the novelty of this approach, the number of studies to evaluate this type of intervention is relatively small. Nevertheless, Jones et al. (2000) conducted a meta-analysis on the results of four randomized controlled trials of belief modification, and found that it reduced both the frequency and impact of hallucinations. In addition, while it had only a minimal impact on measures of conviction in delusional beliefs, it did reduce the amount of distress associated with them. Overall, people who were taught ways of challenging their delusional beliefs or hallucinations were half as likely to relapse as those who were not.

Three of the studies analysed by Jones et al. (2000) involved specific interventions. One of them, reported by Haddock et al. (1998), compared a cognitive approach involving challenging the content of auditory hallucinations with one based on distracting from them. Both treatments were equally effective in the short-term, reducing the frequency of hallucinations and minimizing their impact on daily life. However, those who were taught to challenge the content and nature of the hallucinations reported stronger beliefs that the voices were their own thoughts than those in the distraction condition.

A more multifaceted intervention was reported by Drury et al. (2000). Their intervention involved both individual and group cognitive therapy in which participants learned to cope with delusions and hallucinations. In addition, they took part in a six-month long family psycho-education programme and an activity programme including life-skills groups. The effects of this intervention were compared to those of an activity programme involving participants in sports, leisure and social groups. The short- and mid-term impacts of the intervention were impressive. Those in the active therapeutic programme recovered more quickly following the relapse that brought them into therapy. By nine-month follow-up, 56 per cent of the control group still had moderate or severe problems, in comparison to 5 per cent of the intervention group. By five-year follow-up, however, there was no evidence of any long-term differences between the two groups on measures of relapse rates or levels of positive symptoms. To achieve longer-term benefits, it may be necessary to introduce a second, perhaps less extensive, 'booster' intervention.

Chapter summary

1 Schizophrenia is one of the most disabling mental health disorders.

2 DSM identifies four types of schizophrenia: disorganized, paranoid, catatonic and residual.

3 An alternative classification system identifies two clusters of symptoms. Positive symptoms include hallucinations, delusions and thought disorder, and negative symptoms are those related to a general lack of motivation.

4 Concerns over the nature of schizophrenia have led some to argue that the concept can no longer be considered valid. Instead, they have argued that the various experiences of people diagnosed as having schizophrenia would be better considered as separate and unrelated factors.

5 There is no exclusive 'cause' of schizophrenia, although a number of factors have been implicated including genetics and social and family stress.

6 The biological bases for schizophrenia include disruption of the dopamine system and neuronal degeneration, partly as a consequence of perinatal factors, partly due to excess dopamine.

7 Psychological models adopt a dimensional view of the disorder and attempt to understand the psychological processes that contribute to the experiences of people diagnosed with schizophrenia rather than to identify triggers to a 'condition' in which the individual differs categorically from the norm.

8 Treatment is largely with phenothiazines such as chlorpromazine and newer drugs including clozapine. These seem to delay rather than prevent the onset of further problems.

9 The high level of side-effects associated with these drugs has led to a number of innovative strategies to minimize their use, including the relapse prevention strategy known as 'early signs'.

10 Drug therapy may be significantly augmented by family therapy, particularly for those who live in a high NEE environment, which has been shown to profoundly alter the course of schizophrenia.

11 Newer cognitive techniques may also be of benefit, although their long-term benefits are yet to be evaluated.

For discussion

1 Is the diagnosis of schizophrenia a valid one?

2 Should people with schizophrenia receive genetic or family counselling when planning a family?

3 Should family or cognitive therapy form the first-line treatment for schizophrenia, with drug therapy used only if this is unsuccessful?

Further reading

Bentall, R.P., Corcoran, R., Howard, R. et al. (2001) Persecutory delusions: a review and theoretical integration, *Clinical Psychology Review*, 21: 1143–92.

Birchwood, M. and Spencer, E. (2001) Early intervention in psychotic relapse, *Clinical Psychology Review*, 21: 1211–26.

Birchwood, M., Fowler, D. and Jackson, C. (eds) (2000) *Early Intervention in Psychosis*. London: Wiley.

Boyle, M. (2002) *Schizophrenia*. London: Routledge.

British Psychological Society (BPS) (2000) *Recent Advances in Understanding Mental Illness and Psychotic Experiences*. Leicester: BPS.

Liddle, P., Carpenter, W.T. and Crow, T. (1994) Syndromes of schizophrenia: classic literature, *British Journal of Psychiatry*, 165: 721–7.

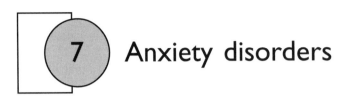

7 Anxiety disorders

Anxiety is a useful emotion. Without it, we are likely to be reckless and engage in dangerous activities that could lead to harm or even death. It therefore has strong survival benefits for both the individual and the species. However, when levels of anxiety become inappropriately high, they stop being a proportionate response to the threats within the environment and become problematic to the individual experiencing them. The anxiety disorders lie at the extreme end of the distribution of anxiety within the population. They fall under the DSM category of neurotic and stress-related disorders. This chapter will focus on three diagnoses within this group: generalized anxiety disorder, panic disorder and obsessive-compulsive disorders. Each represents a differing response to either specific or diffuse causes of anxiety. By the end of the chapter, you should have an understanding of:

- The nature and aetiology of each condition from a number of theoretical perspectives
- The types of interventions used to treat each disorder
- The relative effectiveness of each of these interventions.

Generalized anxiety disorder

DSM-IV-TR (APA 2000) defines generalized anxiety disorder (GAD) as excessive or ongoing anxiety and worry, occurring on more days than not, over a period of at least six months. In addition:

1 The person finds it difficult to control the worry.
2 The anxiety and worry are regularly associated with three or more of the following:

- restlessness or feeling keyed up or on edge
- being easily fatigued
- difficulty concentrating or mind going blank
- irritability
- muscle tension
- sleep disturbance.

3 The anxiety, worry or physical symptoms cause significant distress or impairment.

The worries reported by people with GAD usually relate to minor or everyday matters, which they may acknowledge as such, but nevertheless find difficult to control. At any one time, between 3 and 4 per cent of the population will be experiencing levels of anxiety diagnosable as GAD, with the prevalence in women being about twice that in men (Jenkins et al. 1997). GAD usually begins in childhood or adolescence. Once established, it tends to be a chronic disorder: up to 80 per cent of people diagnosed with GAD report having been worried or anxious all their lives (Butler et al. 1991).

Aetiology of generalized anxiety disorder

Genetic factors

The influence of genetic factors on the risk of developing GAD appears to be modest. Hettema et al. (2001b), for example, obtained a lifetime history of GAD through interviews with 3100 twin pairs. Concordance rates between the pairs were relatively low, leading them to estimate the heritability of GAD to be about 15–20 per cent across both sexes. Other studies have found no differences in concordance rates between MZ and DZ twins. Nevertheless, a meta-analysis by Hettema et al. (2001a) indicated a heritability coefficient of 0.32, suggesting that genetic factors influence the risk of whether some people will develop GAD.

Biological mechanisms

Chronic anxiety appears to be associated with overactivation of a brain system involving the septohippocampal system and the Papez circuit (see Chapter 3). Gray (1983) called this the behavioural inhibition system (BIS), because activation of these brain circuits is thought to interrupt ongoing behaviour, and redirect attention to signs of danger. According to Gray, the BIS receives information about the environment from the sensory cortex. It then checks this against predictions it makes about future changes. When a mismatch occurs, the system is activated and the individual experiences the emotion of anxiety.

In GAD, the criteria for such discrepancies may be 'set' too low, resulting in the individual constantly responding to perceived mismatches and the system being chronically activated. This system appears to be mediated by norepinephrine and serotonin, and is linked to the sympathetic nervous system via the amygdala and hypothalamus (see Chapter 3). Accordingly, it can initiate and maintain high levels of arousal when activated. A final brain and neurotransmitter system involved in anxiety uses the GABA receptors which control activity within the hypothalamus and sympathetic nervous system. Low levels of GABA result in high levels of activation of these neuronal pathways, resulting in the fight-flight response at times of high stress (see Chapter 3). However, in contrast to panic disorder, measures of sympathetic nervous system reactivity suggest this system is actually less reactive to stress in people with GAD than in 'normal' people, perhaps as a consequence of chronic activation.

The role of norepinephrine in GAD is not clear. Baseline levels appear not to differ from normal. However, people with GAD show a subnormal response to drugs that influence norepinephrine levels, which may indicate that the receptivity of norepinephrine at the postsynaptic site has become less sensitive to the norepinephrine as a result of initially high levels (Spiegel and Barlow 2000).

Psychoanalytical explanations

Freud distinguished two routes to adult anxiety, both of which have their roots in childhood: too rigorous punishment and over-protection. He suggested that both 'neurotic' and 'moral' anxiety begin when the child is repeatedly punished for, or prevented from, expressing their id impulses. This leads them to believe that such impulses are dangerous and have to be controlled. In adulthood, when parental control is no longer available, they are associated with high levels of anxiety. By contrast, if a child is protected from threats and frustrations it will not develop defence mechanisms adequate to dealing with the demands of adult life. As a consequence, relatively small threats result in feelings of high levels of anxiety.

Evidence in support of these explanations are generally circumstantial. Chorpita and Barlow (1998), for example, found over-protectiveness, excessive punishment and critical comments as a child to be associated with high levels of anxiety in adulthood. Conversely, Raskin et al. (1982) found no relationship between excessive discipline or parental protection and the development of GAD. However, even if these factors do contribute to GAD, they do not require a psychoanalytic explanation. A more cognitive explanation may be that they result in the child believing they have little control over their environment or come to consider it as particularly punishing or threatening, both of which may predispose them to GAD.

Humanistic explanations

A further explanation of any link between parental control and the development of GAD is provided by the humanists. Humanists consider GAD to occur when individuals fail to accept themselves for who they are. As a consequence, they experience extreme anxiety and are unable to fulfil their potential as a human being. According to Rogers (1967), this negation of self arises from the childhood experience of excessive discipline. If the individual is subject to criticism and harsh standards as a child, they adopt the standards of those around them, and receive conditional positive regard for doing so. They subjugate their own beliefs and desires and try to meet these externally imposed standards by repeatedly denying or distorting their true thoughts and experiences. Despite such efforts, threatening self-judgements can break through and cause intense anxiety. While theoretically elegant, this theory has not been subject to empirical testing, and the importance of these processes is largely unknown.

Socio-cultural factors

Social stress influences the prevalence of GAD. It is more prevalent among people in lower socio-economic groups than the more economically advantaged (Blazer et al. 1991). Ethnic minority groups, who tend to occupy the lower socio-economic groups and who may experience additional pressure because of their ethnicity, also experience relatively high levels of GAD.

Levels of GAD are higher in urban than rural countries and rise and fall in parallel with major societal changes, including war and political oppression (Compton et al. 1991). As coping with the demands of everyday living becomes more complex, so too does the proportion of the population experiencing GAD. Prevalence levels in the USA, for example, rose from 2.5 per cent in 1975 to 4 per cent by the early 1990s (Regier et al. 1998). Finally, GAD can be triggered by adverse or traumatic life events. Blazer et al. (1987) found that men who reported four or more stressful events in the preceding year were eight times as likely to develop GAD than those who reported three or less.

Cognitive behavioural explanations

The best behavioural model of the acquisition and maintenance of anxiety is that of Mowrer (1947). His *two-factor model* stated that fear of specific stimuli is acquired through classical conditioning, and maintained by operant conditioning (see Chapter 2). That is, a classically conditioned fear response is maintained by avoidance of the distress associated with a conditioned aversive stimulus. The feelings of relief when this occurs form an operant conditioning process that reinforces avoidance of the feared object. Avoidance also inhibits the extinction process by preventing the individual experiencing the feared situation in the absence of negative consequences.

While an effective model of the acquisition and maintenance of specific fears, the model cannot easily explain the diffuse anxiety associated with GAD, and more cognitive models have been developed to account for this phenomenon. According to Beck (1997), people who experience high levels of generalized anxiety initially interpret a relatively small number of situations as dangerous and threatening. Over time, they apply these assumptions to more and more situations and develop an increasingly generalized anxiety. Beck identified a number of common *unrealistic assumptions*, including 'a situation or a person is unsafe until proven safe', and 'it is always best to assume the worst'. Both social and childhood factors may influence cognitive processes experienced as an adult (see Chapter 2).

An alternative cognitive model of GAD was developed by Wells (1995), who proposed that the core feature of GAD was excess worry. He identified two types of worry experienced by people with GAD. *Type 1 worries* are the typical worries that most of us experience, albeit at an amplified level: worries related to work, social, health and other issues. Type 2 worry, or 'meta-worry', involves the negative appraisal of one's own worries: 'worrying will drive me mad . . .', 'I worry about my worries taking me over . . .'. Type 1 worries are relatively common in population samples. *Type 2 worries* are common in samples of people with GAD. Wells (1995) therefore suggested that individuals with GAD are defined by high levels of Type 2 worries.

The clinical picture is more complex than this, however, as despite these negative beliefs about their worries, people with GAD also hold some positive ones: 'Worrying helps me cope with my problems . . .'. As a result, they may be motivated to continue worrying, despite the discomfort experienced while doing so. In this way, worrying acts both as the cause of their stress and as a means of coping with it. In the light of this, people with GAD frequently try to avoid the need for worry in the first instance, although this can be difficult because of the wide range of stimuli that may trigger their worries. Other coping strategies commonly used to reduce worries, once initiated, include reassurance seeking, distraction, and attempts at controlling thoughts. The latter may, ironically, actually increase the accessibility of worries.

Claire provides an example of the worries and meta-worries that people with GAD experience:

> It's a family joke, but it's true . . . one day we set off from home
> to shop in Nottingham – a journey of about an hour and a
> half . . . and from the minute we got in the car I was worried
> about where we were going to park, what the traffic would be like

when we got there, and so on. I just worried the whole trip and drove my family mad. It sounds funny, but it's true!

I worry about everything and nothing. I worry if the kids are late back at night. They know I worry, so they really try to be back on time. I've given them a mobile phone so they can ring me if there are any problems or if they are going to be late . . . and they do because they know I'll be in a right state when they get home if they don't. I worry about the food – I won't eat it if it's over the recommended date even though my husband assures me that that's OK and we're not going to get any disease. You name it, I'm sure I've worried about it.

It does get me down . . . I can see me worrying myself into an early grave . . . But I can't stop worrying. My husband says 'Just get on with things, try not to worry'. But I can't. I sit and knit or watch the television in the evening trying not to worry about things, but once something's on my mind it's really difficult to stop – however hard I tell myself to. I worry about my health – the slightest thing, and I'm off to the doctor. I know I'm going to worry about things when we have stopped talking. Sometimes it really feels as if I'm going mad. It does get me down, because every day I cannot relax and just get on with things like most people. Mind you, I think many people worry too little . . . just cruise through life without a care in the world . . . that can't be right either . . .

What sounds even more mad is that I worry about NOT worrying. What if the worrying I do does stop bad things happening. I know it doesn't really, but I could never forgive myself if something happened to the children and I had just been getting on with things and didn't have their safety in mind. I could never forgive myself. What sort of a person would that make me – not caring for them when they were in danger?

Treatment of generalized anxiety disorder

Cognitive behavioural treatment

Behavioural treatments of GAD initially involved exposure to feared situations combined with a procedure known as response prevention. In this, the individual was exposed to their feared situations, frequently in a graded manner starting with the least feared. On each occasion, they remained in the presence of the feared object until they were no longer anxious: that is, they were prevented from their escape response. This was thought to extinguish the fear response as the individual learned the lack of association between the stimulus and its expected negative consequences.

Unfortunately, while effective in the treatment of some other anxiety disorders, these methods proved of little value in the treatment of GAD as the situations that threatened people with GAD were so diffuse. Cognitive behavioural interventions did not prove effective in the treatment of GAD until they incorporated three key strategies:

- cognitive restructuring of anxiety-provoking thoughts
- relaxation training
- worry exposure assignments.

Cognitive restructuring involves identifying the cognitions leading to anxiety and challenging any inappropriate assumptions. Strategies may be rehearsed in the therapy session before being used in the situation in which the client feels anxious. *Relaxation training* involves a structured programme of learning to physically relax and to slow and control breathing at times of anxiety. *Worry exposure* follows an exposure and response prevention approach. Many people with GAD attempt to mentally block or distract from negative or catastrophic thoughts. As a result, they fail to extinguish the associated anxiety, and continue to be worried by them in the long-term. Worry exposure is the mental equivalent of exposure programmes used in the treatment of phobias (see Chapter 2) or triggers to panic (see p. 163). It involves the individual focusing on their frightening or catastrophic thoughts or images for increasing periods of time, eventually up to between 25 and 50 minutes. Anxiety typically rises then falls, as the images are held and the individual habituates to them.

This approach has proven relatively effective. Butler et al. (1991), for example, reported that 42 per cent of participants in a cognitive behavioural programme achieved clinically significant changes in behaviour, cognitions and anxiety, compared to only 5 per cent of those who received only behaviour therapy involving exposure and response prevention methods. Similarly, Borkovec and Costello (1993) found this approach to be more effective than relaxation alone or non-directive counselling. At twelve-month follow-up, they found 58 per cent of people who received the combined intervention were relatively symptom-free compared to 33 per cent of those in the relaxation only group, and 22 per cent of those receiving non-directive counselling.

Psychoanalytic therapy

One study has examined the effectiveness of psychoanalytical therapy in the treatment of GAD, comparing it with a cognitive intervention (Durham et al. 1994). Psychoanalytical therapy involved the exploration and understanding of the individual's problems within the context of their current relationship, their developmental context and in terms of the transference and resistance within the therapeutic relationship (see Chapter 2). The cognitive behavioural approach followed that described above. Levels of contact were similar across both interventions. Cognitive behaviour therapy proved significantly more effective than psychotherapy, both immediately following therapy and at six-month follow-up. By this time, 76 per cent of those receiving cognitive therapy were 'better' or 'very considerably' improved; 42 per cent of those in psychoanalytic therapy achieved the same levels of success. Using a more conservative criterion of 'return to normal functioning', the results were less supportive of analytical therapy: 20 per cent of those receiving psychoanalytical therapy achieved this criterion in comparison to 66 per cent of those in the cognitive therapy condition. Dropout from therapy was much lower in the cognitive therapy group than in the analytic therapy condition: 10 versus 24 per cent respectively.

Pharmacological therapy

Benzodiazepines have frequently been used in the treatment of GAD, achieving an overall success rate of about 35 per cent (Davidson 2001). A further 40 per cent of people show moderate improvement but still have some symptoms of GAD. However, benzodiazepines bring with them a number of drawbacks, particularly when used in the long-term, including impaired cognitive performance, lethargy, drug tolerance and dependence, depression and relapse upon withdrawal and are no longer considered the drug treatment of choice (Davidson 2001). Not only are tricyclics and SSRIs safer, but also they are more effective than benzodiazepines. Both types of antidepressant appear equally effective, although the superior side-effect profile of SSRIs is generally considered to make them the treatment of choice. Rocca et al. (1997), for example, compared the effectiveness of the tricyclic imipramine, the SSRI paroxetine and a benzodiazepine in the treatment of GAD. From the fourth week of treatment, both antidepressants proved more effective than the anxiolytic. However, the levels of side-effects were greater among those prescribed the tricyclic, as were the dropout rates (31 versus 17 per cent) making paroxetine the more effective treatment.

Studies comparing the efficacy of benzodiazepines (valium and lorazepam) and cognitive approaches have shown similar or greater initial gains in the pharmacologically treated groups, but that the cognitive approach is more effective in the medium and long-term. Power et al. (1990), for example, evaluated a number of treatments including cognitive therapy alone, diazepam alone and drug placebo alone. Significant treatment gains were found in 85 per cent of those treated with cognitive therapy, 68 per cent of those treated with diazepam and 37 per cent in the placebo condition. Six months after the end of treatment, most of those in the cognitive therapy group had maintained their therapeutic gains, while many of those receiving medication had relapsed, presumably because they had not learned to control the symptoms of anxiety masked by the use of benzodiazepines until their withdrawal. The percentage of people to achieve complete recovery at this point were 70, 40 and 21 per cent respectively.

Panic disorder

A panic attack is a period of intense fear or discomfort that reaches a peak within ten minutes, and is associated with at least four symptoms that include breathlessness, palpitations, dizziness or trembling, feelings of choking, nausea and tingling sensations in the arms and fingers.

A common feature of a panic attack is known as hyperventilation, which involves rapid short inhalations and exhalations. As a result, carbon dioxide is rapidly exhaled and not absorbed through the lungs into the bloodstream, and oxygen is over-absorbed, leading to the symptoms described above. As the breathing response is triggered by high levels of carbon dioxide within the circulation, the physiological trigger to breath does not occur, resulting in feelings of shortness of breath, which encourage further over-breathing. It is at times such as this that the eponymous 'brown bag' can come in useful. Placing one over the mouth and nose ensures that the person rebreathes the carbon dioxide they are exhaling, increases its absorption from the lungs into the blood, stabilizes the breathing pattern and stops the symptoms.

Frequent unexpected panic attacks form part of the criteria for a diagnosis of panic disorder (APA 2000). Also required are a persistent concern about having additional attacks, worry about the implications of the attack or its consequences, and attempts to avoid situations in which panic attacks have previously occurred.

Charles Darwin provided one of the first descriptions of a panic attack, when he described one of his own. He was not unusual: about one-quarter of the general population will experience an occasional and unexpected panic attack at some time. However, the number of people achieving the diagnostic criteria for panic disorder is much less. Wittchen and Essau (1993), for example, estimated that about 2 per cent of the general population will develop repeated panic attacks, diagnosable as panic disorder.

Aetiology of panic disorder

Genetic factors

Evidence that risk for panic disorder has a genetic component can be found in studies such as that of Torgersen (1983), who found concordance rates of 31 per cent between MZ twins, and zero concordance between DZ twins. Similarly, Kendler et al. (1993) found concordance rates among female MZ twins of 24 per cent and 11 per cent between DZ twins. These and other data placed within a meta-analysis by Hettema et al. (2001a) indicated that panic disorder has a heritability coefficient of 0.40, suggesting that genetic factors will have some influence on whether an individual will develop panic attacks.

Biological mechanisms

A central element of the panic response is a high level of physiological arousal, triggered by hypothalamic activity and mediated by the sympathetic nervous system. This response is driven by the neurotransmitter and hormone norepinephrine, and to a lesser extent, epinephrine. When the emotion of anxiety is experienced, these both activate the body and prepare it to deal with physical damage (see Chapter 3). At its most dramatic, this response is known as the fight-flight response. At such times, the heart beats more quickly and more powerfully, blood is shunted to the muscles and away from the gut (hence the experience of 'butterflies'), skeletal muscles tense and blood pressure rises. These and other processes prepare the body for rapid and dramatic action. In the case of panic disorder, this may be apparent through running away from a feared situation, or shaking, breathlessness and dizziness as the person hyperventilates. The feeling of palpitations can be so extreme that they can lead to fear of having a heart attack.

Two further biochemical systems also seem implicated in the development of panic disorder. The effectiveness of tricylics and SSRIs in treatment studies has implicated the role of serotonin in the disorder, although the exact nature of the relationship between panic and serotonin levels is far from clear. The success of modern benzodiazepines in treating the condition has also implicated a role of GABA. The amygdala is involved in the generation of fear, and its activity is controlled by GABA: low levels of GABA lead to high levels of fear (Goddard et al. 2001). GABA receptors also control activity within the hypothalamus, and hence the sympathetic nervous system.

Socio-cultural factors

As with GAD, high levels of social stress increase risk for panic disorder. The highest rates of panic disorder are among widowed, divorced or separated individuals who live in cities. Limited education, early parental loss, or physical or sexual abuse also increase risk for the disorder (Ballanger 2000), as do many of the factors that increase risk for GAD (see above).

Psychological explanations

Psychoanalytic and humanistic theories do not discriminate between panic disorder and GAD, and the models outlined above hold for both disorders. Both explanations also receive limited empirical support, as people with panic disorder frequently recall their parents being overly concerned and protective of them as a child (Parker 1981). Mowrer's (1947) model of fear acquisition and maintenance can provide only a partial explanation of panic disorder, as it assumes high levels of conditioned anxiety to be triggered by the presence of a feared stimulus. It has difficulties in explaining high levels of anxiety in the absence of an obvious stimulus: a defining characteristic of panic disorder.

More recent aetiological models have considered how cognitions can lead to episodes of panic in the absence of any obvious trigger. The most influential of these cognitive models is that of Clark (1986), which identified three triggers to panic attacks:

- fear-related cognitions related to a particular stimulus or situation
- high levels of physiological arousal associated with different emotional states
- other events that may result in a physical disturbances.

According to Clark, each of these factors trigger the central cognitive element of panic disorder, which is the interpretation of bodily sensations in a catastrophic fashion. The sensations that are misinterpreted are mainly those involved in the normal anxiety response. Other triggers include tension associated with other strong emotions such as anger, raised heart rate as a result of caffeine ingestion, and so on.

Catastrophic misinterpretation involves perceiving these sensations as more dangerous than they really are, in particular, believing they are signs of serious physical or mental health problems, such as a heart attack. These thoughts lead to activation of the flight-fight response involving an increase in levels of physiological arousal, which is again interpreted in a catastrophic fashion ('Yes, my heart really is pounding: I really am heading for a heart attack'). These anxiety-laden cognitions, in turn, lead to a further increase in bodily sensations, which lead to further levels of anxiety: a vicious circle which culminates in a panic attack (see Figure 7.1).

Once an individual has developed a tendency to interpret bodily sensations catastrophically, two further processes contribute to the maintenance of panic disorder. First, because they are frightened of certain sensations, they become hypervigilant and repeatedly scan their body checking for them. This internal focus of attention results in them noticing sensations that most people would not be aware of. Once noticed, these are taken as further evidence of the presence of a serious physical or mental disorder. Second, safety behaviours, usually involving not

Situation

Figure 7.1   The panic cycle

entering, or leaving a feared situation at the onset of symptoms, tend to maintain the individual's negative interpretations. Such avoidance, the second stage of Mowrer's model, prevents the individual from learning that the symptoms they have experienced are not as dangerous as they consider, and prevents the extinction process. The case of Sue provides an example of these processes:

> When did it begin? I remember my first panic – who wouldn't?
> It was in the car park in Tesco's. I remember feeling a bit faint.
> I thought I was going to pass out. I thought I would look such a
> fool if I did. Stupid to pass out in a car park. And everyone would
> look at me . . . Now I know it was a panic attack. But when it
> happened I didn't have a clue what was going on. I felt bad for no
> reason . . . I didn't think I was going to die or anything like that,
> but I was frightened I would collapse and end up in hospital.
> I think I could have got over it OK, but the next time I went
> shopping, I began to think about things again. I wondered

whether there was anything about Tesco's or shopping that might bring it on again. Perhaps I had pushed myself too hard . . . I was in a bit of a rush when it happened – I don't know. They weren't very sensible thoughts, really. But I suppose they began to wind me up. Anyway, the next time I went shopping . . . yes, I had another attack. That was it really, I just thought, 'I'm not going there again.' So I started to shop in other places, but I began to worry that the same thing would happen, and then I had another panic while I was out, and that just confirmed my worries. In the end, it got easier to stay at home out of the way than to go out.

I quite like it at home. I feel safe, and I watch TV without any hassle. My friends come and see me, so it's not as if I don't have a life. I was never one for going out much. If I go out, then I worry before I set off, and while I am out. I often have a panic, so it's just not worth going out. I can get to the local shop if I go with my husband. And I can go in the car with him – as long as I don't have to get out. But I don't like to go far . . .

The example of Sue fits Clark's (1986) model of the development of panic disorder. She also hinted at a further factor that can contribute to the development of the disorder or its associated problems: a process known as secondary gain. Being restricted to the house was quite pleasant for Sue. She gained sympathy from her husband, and quite enjoyed being at home. These secondary rewards contributed to the maintenance of her avoidant behaviour once it had been initiated.

Clark's model has been experimentally tested in a number of ways. One set of studies examined the impact of cognitions on emotions and panic. Clark et al. (1988), for example, asked a group of individuals with panic disorder and 'normal' controls to read out loud a series of pairs of words. Some of these pairings included combinations of body sensations and catastrophes typically made by individuals while panicking: 'breathless – suffocate', and so on. Each group was asked to rate their anxiety before and after reading the cards and to rate any changes in any panic symptoms. The manipulation proved unexpectedly powerful. Ten out of the twelve people with panic disorder, but no controls, had a panic attack while reading the cards.

The impact of differing attributions about the cause of panic-like symptoms on emotions has also been measured. These have been manipulated by providing different types of information to people in whom panic-like symptoms are induced by a number of chemical means. The general hypothesis of such studies is that individuals who can attribute their symptoms to the procedure are less likely to become anxious than those who cannot do so. In one such study, Rapee et al. (1986) gave different information about the sensations likely to be experienced as a result of a single inhalation of 50 per cent carbon dioxide and 50 per cent oxygen to people with panic disorder. Half their participants were given a detailed explanation of all the possible sensations they could experience, and told they resulted from inhalation of the gas. The others were given no explanation of what to expect. As expected, participants in the detailed explanation group reported less catastrophic cognitions and less anxiety than those in the naive condition.

Treatment of panic disorder

Cognitive behavioural interventions

Some of the most successful treatment programmes for panic disorder have been based on Clark's aetiological model. Clark et al. (1994), for example, developed a two-phase treatment approach. The first phase involved teaching clients the cognitive model of panic. The second phase involved three elements:

- relaxation to reduce physiological arousal at the time of stress
- cognitive procedures to change panicogenic cognitions
- behavioural procedures in order to control panic symptoms.

Relaxation involves learning to physically relax and to slow and control breathing. These techniques can be applied before potential panic attacks, for example when approaching a situation where a panic attack has occurred previously, and during them. Cognitive procedures include self-instruction and cognitive challenge. Self-instruction training involves developing a series of 'calm-down' statements the client can use at times when they are feeling panicky. These pre-rehearsed statements may include reminders that their symptoms will not actually result in their feared outcome and to use coping strategies such as relaxation. Cognitive challenge involves identifying the cognitions contributing to panic, and trying to challenge any inappropriate assumptions.

The goal of the behavioural procedures is to teach the individual, through direct experience, that the outcome they fear at times of panic will not actually happen. Increasingly, therapists instigate the symptoms of panic within the therapy session and practice its control through the use of cognitive and relaxation techniques. Symptoms may be generated by a variety of procedures including reading lists of words linking bodily sensations and catastrophic outcomes or hyperventilating. These behavioural experiments can be used to show how thoughts and behaviours influence symptoms previously considered the result of unknown factors and rehearse the use of cognitive and relaxation panic control strategies. Once control over symptoms has been achieved within the therapy session, these skills can be used in real-life situations. This may be done in a graduated process, starting with relatively easy circumstances and moving on to more difficult ones.

Over 80 per cent of individuals are typically panic-free at the end of therapy using this approach, in contrast to about 12 per cent of those in no treatment control groups. Clark et al. (1994), for example, reported outcomes following cognitive behaviour therapy, applied relaxation, the tricylic imipramine and a **waiting list control** period. Participants in the cognitive therapy group took part in twelve sessions over a period of three months, followed by up to three booster sessions over the following three months. Imipramine was withdrawn after six months. At one-year follow-up, all three treatments proved more effective than no treatment. However, cognitive therapy was the most successful at this time, with 85 per cent of individuals being panic free, in contrast to 60 per cent of those who received imipramine or who were taught relaxation. Of note, is that 40 per cent of those receiving imipramine and 26 per cent of those receiving relaxation sought an alternative therapy in the year following the intervention. Only 5 per cent of the cognitive therapy group did so.

Pharmacological interventions

Both benzodiazepines and SSRIs have proven effective in the treatment of panic disorder: at least in the short-term (Ballenger 2000). So much so, that at least one study has shown drug therapy to be more effective than cognitive therapy within this time-frame. Bakker et al. (1999) reported a study comparing the relative efficacy of an SSRI (paroxetine), a tricyclic (clomipramine) and cognitive therapy in the treatment of panic disorder. Paroxetine proved more effective than cognitive therapy over the twelve-week intervention period. While this outcome is notable, it is important to note that the therapeutic gains reported are those achieved while on the drug. The problem with drug treatments is often one of relapse once they are stopped. Relapse rates as high as 50 and 60 per cent have been reported following withdrawal of benzodiazepines and of between 20 and 50 per cent following withdrawal of tricyclics and SSRIs (Spiegel et al. 1994). In addition, long-term use of benzodiazepines may result in problematic withdrawal symptoms and exacerbation of anxiety to beyond pre-medication levels (see Chapter 3). Antidepressants also have a number of side-effects that result in dropout rates of between 25 and 50 per cent (Gould et al. 1995): reported dropout rates from cognitive therapy vary between 15 and 25 per cent. The hypervigilance associated with panic and anxiety disorders may mean that those treated are highly sensitized to any side-effects, and that *any* medication is likely to result in high levels of reported side-effects.

Combining interventions

Given the potential short-term gains of benzodiazepines and the long-term benefits of cognitive behaviour therapy, a number of clinicians have considered the effectiveness of combining the two approaches. The results of such studies have generally been disappointing. Combined interventions appear less effective than cognitive therapy alone. Barlow et al. (2000), for example, found significant gains six months following the end of all therapy in 32 per cent of participants who received cognitive therapy, 20 per cent of those prescribed imipramine and 26 per cent who received a combination of drug and psychological therapy.

The reason for these disappointing results may lie at the heart of the mechanisms of change in cognitive therapy and pharmacotherapy. Central to change in the cognitive model is a reduction in catastrophic beliefs and increased control over symptoms at times when anxiety or panic were previously experienced. These are achieved by learning to cope with the symptoms of panic through challenging catastrophic beliefs and the use of relaxation at times of potential panic. The use of anxiolytics may prevent either of these from occurring, as use of the drug inhibits the arousal and catastrophic cognitions central to panic. Once off the medication, recipients may once more experience the arousal in response to environmental or physical cues, which triggers catastrophic thoughts they have not learned to cope with, and the problem may reappear. Worse, when their symptoms reappear they may feel more out of control and less confident in their ability to cope with them than previously (Westra and Stewart 1998).

Obsessive-compulsive disorder

Obsessive-compulsive disorder (OCD) is a chronic and disabling condition. It typically involves intrusive thoughts that some form of harm will occur if the individual does not perform certain acts of rituals, the performance of which results in a reduction of the anxiety. Fear of contamination, that one's thoughts can harm others, and eternal damnation are relatively common. Behaviours or thoughts to counter these fears can include ritual and repeated washing, to the point of developing skin problems, checking up to twenty or more times that an action has been actually done, and engaging in ritual behaviour or thoughts. DSM-IV-TR defines obsessions and compulsions in the following way.

Obsessions

- Recurrent and persistent thoughts, impulses or images that are experienced as intrusive and inappropriate and that cause marked anxiety or distress. In addition:

- these are not simply excessive worries about real-life problems
- the person attempts to ignore or suppress them with some other thought or action
- the person recognizes that they are a product of his or her own mind.

Compulsions

- Repetitive behaviours (for example, hand washing, checking) or mental acts (such as praying, repeating words silently) that the person feels driven to perform in response to an obsession, or according to rules that must be applied rigidly
- The behaviours or mental acts are intended to prevent or reduce distress, or preventing some dreaded event or situation; they are not connected in a realistic way with what they are designed to neutralize or prevent or are clearly excessive.

To be assigned a diagnosis of obsessive-compulsive disorder, these compulsions cause marked distress, last at least one hour a day, or significantly interfere with the person's normal routine functioning. Although clinical levels of obsessional behaviour are relatively infrequent, estimated at about 3 per cent of the population (Karno et al. 1988), Rachman and de Silva (1978) found that some level of intrusive thought was reported by almost 90 per cent of a non-clinical sample. The disorder typically has an early age of onset and prolonged duration. Of those adults diagnosed with the disorder in Karno's study, 20 per cent developed the disorder in childhood and 29 per cent developed it during adolescence.

An example of the nature of OCD and the problems associated with it is afforded by Stephen, who was a factory worker frightened of catching venereal disease from 'contaminated' parts of his work area that he believed someone with this problem had touched. To avoid this, he engaged in a number of protective behaviours, including turning on taps using his elbows, waiting by doors so that someone else would open them and using disposable towels to avoid the possibility of contamination. Because the man had been in his work area on one occasion, he washed his hands frequently through the day to make sure no stray contamination affected him. On each occasion he washed his hands until his skin was raw and bleeding. If he touched an area he 'knew' to be contaminated, he became extremely anxious and had to wash his hands repeatedly until he could reassure himself that he was not contaminated and reduce his anxiety. He described his situation as follows:

> I am frightened to touch anything M has been in contact with – well I won't touch it. I know he had venereal disease and he could have AIDS, and you know how it can spread . . . and you cannot,

like, avoid it. It's invisible – and I can't take the risk of coming into contact with it. I was really angry when he came into where I work. It's one thing avoiding things when I could kick doors open, but when I knew he had touched my workbench, I was horrified ... because I didn't want me and my family to get the disease, and I didn't know how to avoid it. I washed and scrubbed it down with disinfectant and rubbed my hands raw – but you can never guarantee that things are entirely clean. So, I start each day by cleaning my work area, hands, and arms for security ... to protect me and my family from the dirt that this man has spread ... Once that's done, I can relax ... I've got eczema on my hands because of the washing and they get really sore but it's worth it. It stops me worrying about things – and that's a lot worse. If I worry I think about getting AIDS and dying and my family dying. I just can't stop until I've got things sorted.

From the minute I come into work, I get really anxious. I get anxious on the way to work, because I have to face the risk of catching venereal disease ... it feels such a relief when I have finished washing, even though my hands are sore. I wash before I go home, and I take my clothes off before going into the house when I get back from work. I put them in the washer and wash them straight away – my wife can't touch them ... I have a shower before I do anything else and wash myself thoroughly. I would never forgive myself if I brought the disease into the house ... I leave my shoes outside.

I don't care if other people use my work bench – unless they work with M. I don't worry for them – that's for them to look out for. But if they don't get a disease it doesn't reassure me, because I know that these things are hidden ... just because they don't seem to have the disease doesn't mean they don't have it. If they know M, then I have to redo the washing, because I worry that they may be contaminated.

Aetiology of obsessive-compulsive disorder

Genetic factors

Evidence of a genetic risk for OCD is mixed. Carey and Gottesman (1981), for example, reported an 87 per cent concordance between MZ twins and a 47 per cent concordance for DZ twins, supporting a part genetic explanation for risk of the disorder. By contrast, Andrews et al. (1990) found no evidence of higher concordance in MZ versus DZ twins. Family studies have also produced mixed results. While a number of these have reported higher than population levels of OCD among the relatives of people identified as having the disorder, Black et al. (1992) found that 2.5 per cent of their large sample of relatives of people with OCD had the disorder: a figure similar to the 2.3 per cent prevalence among their control group and population norms.

Biological mechanisms

Biological theorists have identified two interconnected brain systems that are implicated in OCD. The first is a loop connecting the orbito-frontal area, where sexual, violent and other primitive impulses normally arise, to the thalamic region, where the individual engages in more cognitive and perhaps behavioural responses as a result of this activation. A second loop again connects the orbito-frontal region to the thalamic region, but via the corpus striatus. The striatal region is thought to control the degree of activity within the systems. It tends to filter out high levels of activity within the orbito-frontal area so that the thalamus does not over-respond to these initial impulses. In OCD, it may fail to correct overactivity in the orbito-frontal-thalamic loop, and as a result the individual over-responds to environmental stimuli, and is unable to prevent their cognitive and behavioural responses to them. The first system appears to be mediated by the excitatory neurotransmitter glutamic acid. The second system appears be mediated by a number of neurotransmitters including serotonin, dopamine and GABA.

Psychoanalytical explanations

Freud's (1922) model stated that OCD is the result of the individual's fear of their id impulses and their reactive use of ego defence mechanisms to reduce the subsequent anxiety. This 'battle' between the two opposing forces is not played out in the unconscious. Instead, it involves explicit and dramatic thoughts and actions. The id impulses are typically evident through obsessive thoughts, while the compulsions are the result of ego defences. Two ego defence mechanisms are particularly common in OCD: undoing and reaction formation. *Undoing* involves overt behaviours designed to counter the feared outcome: washing to avoid contamination, and so on. *Reaction formation* involves the adoption of behaviours diametrically opposed to the unacceptable impulses. The compulsively clean individual, for example, may harbour strong 'inappropriate' sexual compulsions that are countered by their cleanliness and orderliness.

Freud considered OCD to originate in difficulties associated with the anal phase of development. He suggested that children in this stage gain gratification through their bowel movements. If their parents prohibit or curb this pleasure through, for example, over-zealous potty training, this may result in a state of anger and aggressive id impulses expressed through soiling or other destructive behaviour. If the parents respond to this with further pressure, and if they embarrass the child in attempts to encourage toilet training, the child may feel shame and guilt as a consequence of their behaviour. So, the pleasure of the id begins to compete with the control of the ego. If this continues, the child may become fixated in this stage and develop a obsessive personality. Traumas experienced in adulthood may result in a regression to this stage if the passage through it is incomplete.

Not all **psychodynamic** theories are in agreement with Freud, although all agree that the disorder represents competition between aggressive impulses and attempts at controlling them. Kleinian analysts suggest that as a consequence of stress some individuals may lose the ability to see both good and bad in the same object. Rather, they consider them to be either good *or* bad: there is a *splitting* of good and bad with no shades of feelings in between. Obsessive-compulsive disorders arise where the individual protects themselves against these 'bad' thoughts that would make them a 'bad' person through the use of obsessional behaviours.

Behavioural explanations

The behavioural model of OCD is based on the two-process model of Mowrer (1947): fear of specific stimuli is acquired through classical conditioning and maintained by operant processes. What differentiates OCD from a phobic or panic disorder is that anxiety arises in conditions from which the individual cannot easily escape. As a result, reductions of distress are achieved by engaging in covert or overt ritual or obsessive behaviours, including repeated checking or hand washing, or repetition of cognitive or behavioural sequences designed to reduce the anxiety associated with the particular stimulus. These form escape or avoidant behaviours, and reduce anxiety in the short-term. However, they maintain longer-term anxiety and avoidant behaviour, as the affected individual fails to learn that no harm will occur in their absence. The individual also attempts to prevent initial contact with a feared stimulus.

Cognitive explanations

Two distinct types of cognitive theories have tried to explain the phenomena associated with OCD. Cognitive deficit theories (Reed 1985) suggest that obsessional behaviour results from a general failure in cognitive control, and inadequate memory and decision-making abilities. Critiquing this approach, Salkovskis and Kirk (1997) argued that these theories fail to adequately address a number of features of OCD. In particular they noted:

- People with OCD do not appear to have general memory and decision-making problems: their problems are situation specific. Although they may, for example, check many times that the

door of their house is locked, they may have no problems lock-
ing a kitchen cupboard door.
- Similarly, people with OCD may be frightened of a specific type
  of contamination or contamination from a particular source. They
  do not have a general problem in deciding what is clean and
  what is dirty.
- Obsessional individuals show no evidence of memory problems
  outside areas directly linked to their obsessional problems. They
  may check because of *concerns* about their memory, not because
  of any actual inabilities.

Salkovskis's own model (Salkovskis and Kirk 1997) is a development
of the behavioural models of OCD. He suggested that obsessions are
intrusive cognitions which the individual interprets as indicating they
may be responsible for harm to themselves or others unless they take
some form of action to prevent this. This belief leads to a state of fear or
distress which the individual tries to reduce by trying to suppress these
thoughts, and by taking actions intended to reduce their responsibility
for any negative outcomes. The latter may include compulsive behaviour,
avoidance of situations related to the obsessional thoughts, and seeking
reassurance to dilute or share responsibility.

Unfortunately, attempts at suppression of thoughts paradoxically make
them more frequent and salient (stop reading, and try not to think of a
white bear in the next minute, and see for yourself!). In a rather more
empirical test of this phenomenon, Salkovskis and Kirk (1997) reported
a series of single-case studies in which people with OCD used a diary to
record the frequency of intrusive thoughts during alternate days in which
they either attempted to suppress their thoughts or not. They found a
clear difference in the number of intrusive thoughts during each phase of
the study: during 'suppression' days, levels of intrusive thoughts were
about double the rate reported on non-suppression days. Avoidance
or escape from the feared situation prevents extinction of the anxiety
response. Accordingly, both types of coping efforts may lead to a worsen-
ing spiral of intrusive thoughts, negative emotional reactions and compulsive behaviours.

Treatment of obsessive-compulsive disorder

Behavioural and cognitive behavioural approaches

Behavioural treatment of OCD typically involves exposure and response
prevention. In this, the individual is exposed to their feared stimulus,
frequently in a graded manner, and then helped to prevent avoidance
through their use of escape rituals, that is: 'contaminating' hands and
then not washing them. This is thought to extinguish the fear response

as the individual learns the lack of association between the occurrence of harm-related thoughts and any expected negative consequences. Relaxation may also be taught to help people cope with the high levels of physiological arousal associated with the fear response.

Many clinical studies using this approach achieved moderate success, although complete remission was achieved by less than half of those who engaged in such programmes (Salkovskis and Kirk 1997). Behavioural treatments were also difficult to apply to people who ruminated or who had no ritualistic behaviour, and treatment refusals and dropouts were relatively common. Accordingly, as models of the disorder have evolved, so have the treatment programmes, which now focus increasingly on the cognitive factors that maintain the disorder.

Cognitive interventions focus on reducing the frequency of both overt (such as checking) and covert (for example, cognitive rituals) obsessional behaviours by:

- teaching the client that obsessional thoughts are irrelevant to further action
- altering the interpretation of obsessional thoughts – in particular challenging misinterpretations of responsibility
- challenging the belief that the consequences of not engaging in safety behaviours will be catastrophic.

The cognitive approach still involves exposure to a feared stimulus and response prevention. However, these procedures are augmented by a number of cognitive strategies, including challenging inappropriate thoughts, mind experiments, behavioural hypothesis testing and thought stopping. Mind experiments allow the individual to test the validity of their expectations, particularly focusing on the threat associated with their thoughts. Someone who is frightened that their thoughts may kill someone, for example, may be encouraged to test the reality of this assumption by a mind experiment in which the therapist and then client test out a similar assumption – let us hope with no negative effects!

Thought stopping is the converse of cognitive challenge. In it, the client is taught to distract from their thoughts rather than challenge their content. Learning thought stopping involves a progressive series of steps. Initially, the client relaxes in a comfortable chair and is asked to think about the thoughts they wish to distract from. Once this is established, the therapist interrupts this train of thoughts by, quite literally, startling the client from them (by saying 'Stop!' loudly and making a loud noise). At this juncture, the client is asked to concentrate on a pre-prepared image or thought totally different from their initial ones. This process is repeated, gradually reducing the strength of external stimulus and then making this an internal cue in which thinking the word 'Stop' is associated with a transition from threat-based thoughts to some other image or thought. The goal is to make distraction a classically conditioned response that the individual can trigger when they feel overwhelmed by their anxiety-provoking thoughts.

Comparisons between behavioural and cognitive approaches have failed to consistently identify which is the superior; indeed, one study found a cognitive intervention to be less effective than a behavioural one. McLean et al. (2001) compared the effectiveness of a purely behavioural intervention (exposure and response prevention) and a cognitive intervention involving challenging cognitions thought to underpin the disorder, with a particular focus on inflated responsibility, overestimation of threat, and intolerance of uncertainty. The researchers defined a measure of clinical recovery as evidence of a 'reliable' reduction in symptoms and being 'in the dysfunctional range'. Using these criteria, 16 and 38 per cent of participants in the cognitive and behavioural groups respectively had made significant recoveries by the end of treatment. At three-month follow-up, the figures were 13 and 45 per cent respectively.

Unfortunately, the method of cognitive therapy used in the study may not have been optimal. In the behavioural programme, participants were exposed to their feared stimuli on several occasions in the presence of the therapist, and remained with them without responding with safety behaviours until their anxiety had significantly diminished, facilitating the extinction of their anxiety response (and possibly resulting in cognitive change: see Chapter 2). In the cognitive intervention, participants were similarly exposed to the feared stimuli, but only to practise their cognitive skills. They did not remain with the feared stimulus until their fear had diminished. Participants may have left the presence of the feared stimulus while still highly anxious. This procedure may therefore have maintained or even exacerbated their initial levels of anxiety and obsessional behaviour. The relative failure of the cognitive approach may therefore be of no surprise.

No difference in effectiveness between cognitive and behavioural therapy was reported by Cottraux et al. (2001) when cognitive therapy involved challenging assumptions underlying the obsessional behaviour, but did not use exposure and response prevention methods. Finally, Van Oppen et al. (1995) found cognitive therapy combined with exposure and response prevention to be superior to behaviour therapy. It seems that 'pure' cognitive interventions without exposure/response prevention are less effective than exposure/response prevention alone. However, a combination of both approaches may be most effective. This outcome is in keeping with Teasdale's (1993) assertion that cognitive changes made in therapy sessions are relatively transient: only when they are behaviourally validated will any changes become fully integrated into the individual's **cognitive schema**.

Pharmacological interventions

Until the advent of SSRIs, the pharmacological treatment of choice for OCD was clomipramine, a tricyclic. This has been shown to be effective in the treatment of OCD independent of any affect on mood. The Clomipramine Collaborative Study Group (1991), for example, found an average 40 per cent reduction in OCD symptoms following treatment with clomipramine, in comparison to improvements of up to 5 per cent achieved by placebo. Where the effectiveness of clomipramine and SSRIs has been directly assessed, both treatments seem to be equally effective, and to have similar levels of side-effects (Freeman et al. 1994). Most people relapse after prematurely discontinuing treatment, and it may take many months before a maximum response is achieved. Pato et al. (1988), for example, reported that 16 out of 18 people treated with clomipramine relapsed within 7 weeks of stopping taking the drug, despite some of them having been on the drug for over a year.

Surgical approaches

Treatment of OCD by surgery is generally performed only in people with severe problems that have not responded to other treatment approaches. The most common surgical procedure for people is stereotatic subcaudate cingulotomy (see Chapter 3). This has proven of some value in this limited group of individuals. Jenike et al. (1991), for example, reported that 25–30 per cent of a series of cases improved significantly following surgery. However, 9 per cent developed epilepsy, while 10 per cent committed suicide. Whether this was as a result of changes in mood as a result of surgery, disappointment at the failure of the treatment of last resort, or pre-existing suicidal ideation was not clear. In one of the relatively few studies to use a control group in an evaluation of the surgical treatment of OCD, Tan et al. (1971) investigated the effects of a bimedial leucotomy, a procedure no longer used due to its high level of adverse effects. At five-year follow-up, 50 per cent of the patients who had surgery were rated as 'much improved' on measures of obsessive symptoms, compared to 23 per cent of those in their medical treatment group. For measures of anxiety, the corresponding figures were 89 and 63 per cent. This remains one of the few studies of the long-term outcomes of psychosurgery in OCD. How psychosurgery achieves its effects is unclear, although the best hypothesis is that it severs connections between the orbito-frontal and thalamic areas, damping down the activity within this circuit and hence the OCD symptoms.

Chapter summary

1 Generalized anxiety disorder (GAD) is an excessive, long-term, diffuse and inappropriate anxiety.

2 It is partly genetically mediated via the septohippocampal system and Papez circuit, in the behavioural inhibition system. Activity of

this system is dependent on levels of norepinephrine, serotonin and GABA.

3 Psychoanalytical explanations consider it to arise from excess punishment or protection during childhood. These lead to distorted id impulses or inadequate defence mechanisms.

4 Humanists consider GAD to be the result of deviation from the pathway to self-actualization as a result of conditions of worth imposed by others distorting the idealized self, and then the actual self.

5 Levels of GAD vary according to the social and economic stress across the population and time.

6 Cognitive models of GAD emphasize the role of worry and meta-worry in maintaining anxiety.

7 Pharmacological treatment may be equally or more effective than psychological therapies in the short-term. Cognitive therapies are most effective in the long-term.

8 Panic disorder occurs when an individual experiences repeated unexpected panic attacks.

9 It has a modest genetic heritability, and is mediated by high levels of norepinephrine and low levels of GABA.

10 Cognitive models provide an explanation of the triggering of panic in the absence of obvious triggers: people with the condition experience catastrophic cognitions in response to internal, usually physiological, stimuli.

11 Cognitive behavioural interventions appear to be the most effective treatment for the disorder.

12 Obsessive-compulsive behaviour is the result of anxiety triggers the individual is unable to avoid.

13 Psychoanalytic theories and cognitive theories agree that compulsions form part of a repertoire of safety behaviours the individual uses to reduce the threat associated with the anxiety. They disagree about their nature and causes.

14 The symptoms of OCD appear to result from lowered serotonin levels and raised dopamine levels, affecting the functioning of areas of the frontal cortex and basal ganglia.

15 Cognitive behavioural therapy combining exposure/response prevention and cognitive restructuring may prove the most effective treatment for OCD, although evidence is mixed, and many people do not benefit from this or pharmacological therapy.

16 Relapse following the cessation of pharmacological therapy is common.

17 Psychosurgery may be the treatment of last resort for OCD.

For discussion

1 What strategies may increase or decrease levels of worry in GAD?

2 What factors would indicate either psychological or pharmacological approaches being the treatment choice in people with an anxiety condition?

3 How important are cognitive processes in the development of anxiety disorders?

4 Each of the anxiety disorders described appears to be mediated by different biological substrates. With this in mind, consider whether the various conditions should be seen as differing presentations of similar, related disorders, or whether they are, in fact, unrelated disorders.

Further reading

Clark, D.M. and Fairburn, C.G. (eds) *Science and Practice of Cognitive Behaviour Therapy*. Oxford: Oxford University Press.

McNally, R.J. (2001) On the scientific status of cognitive appraisal models of anxiety disorder, *Behaviour Research and Therapy*, 39: 513–21.

Van Balkom, A.J., van Oppen, P. and Vermeulen, A.W. (1994) A meta-analysis on the treatment of obsessive compulsive disorder: a comparison of antidepressants, behavior and cognitive therapy, *Clinical Psychology Review*, 14: 359–81.

Western, D. and Morrison, K. (2001) A multi-dimensional meta-analysis of treatments for depression, panic, and generalized anxiety disorder: an empirical examination of the status of empirically supported therapies, *Journal of Consulting and Clinical Psychology*, 69: 875–99.

Zvolensky, M.J. and Eifert, G.H. (2001) A review of psychological factors/ processes affecting anxious responding during voluntary hyperventilation and inhalations of carbon dioxide-enriched air, *Clinical Psychology Review*, 21: 375–400.

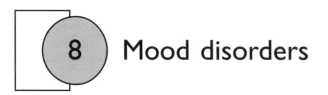

8 Mood disorders

Mood disorders are those in which depression is a significant symptom. What determines the differing diagnostic categories are the causes of depression and conditions with which it coexists. Here, we consider three types. Major depression is a condition in which the individual experiences a significant degree of impairment as a result of depression. Seasonal affective disorder is a condition also involving periods of depression. It differs from major depression in that, as its name implies, it is a seasonal condition, occurring only in winter. Finally, bipolar disorder is a condition in which the individual fluctuates between periods of profound depression and manic behaviour. The chapter also considers the causes of suicide (not all of which are associated with depression) and treatment of people who have unsuccessfully attempted suicide. By the end of the chapter, you should have an understanding of:

♦ The nature and aetiology of depression, seasonal affective disorder and bipolar disorder from a number of theoretical perspectives

♦ The causes of suicidal behaviour

♦ The types of interventions used to treat each disorder

♦ The relative effectiveness of each of these interventions.

Major depression

DSM-IV-TR (APA 2000) defines a major depressive episode as the presence of at least five of the following for at least two weeks:

- depressed mood
- markedly diminished interest or pleasure in almost all activities
- significant weight loss or gain, or increase in or loss of appetite
- physical agitation

- fatigue or loss of energy
- feelings of worthlessness or excessive guilt
- reduced ability to think, concentrate or indecisiveness
- significant distress or impairment.

Depressed people are characterized by emotional, motivational, physiological and cognitive problems. They feel low in themselves and gain no pleasure from their usual activities. They are frequently unmotivated to take voluntary action, often spending considerable time in bed or withdrawing quietly from the company of others. They may be markedly slow in their activities or speech. They generally hold negative views about themselves and marked pessimism about the present and future. They may feel out of control and helpless to change their situation. Some, but by no means all, will experience suicidal thoughts or actions. Depressed people often report confused or slow thoughts, and difficulties in retaining information or solving problems.

About 5 per cent of the population will be clinically depressed at any one time; 17 per cent will experience significant depression at some time in their life (Angst 1999). About a quarter of depressive episodes last less than one month; a further 50 per cent resolve in less than three months. Between 25 and 30 per cent of people remain depressed one year after onset, while nearly a quarter remain depressed for up to two years. The typical age of onset of a first episode of depression is between the ages of 24 and 29. Women are at least twice as likely as men to report depression, with lifetime prevalence rates among women being 26 per cent compared to 12 per cent for men (Keller et al. 1984).

Aetiology of major depression

Genetic factors

Although there have been some negative findings, there is an increasing consensus that genetic factors influence risk for major depression. McGuffin et al. (1996), for example, found that MZ twins had a 46 per cent chance of being concordant for depression, while DZ twins had a concordance rate of 20 per cent. Similarly, Wender et al. (1986) compared rates of depression in the relatives of adult adoptees who developed depression and a group of adoptees matched on measures of age, socio-economic status and time spent with biological mother, who did not. The relatives of adoptees who had experienced depression were 8 times more likely to have had a period of major depression and 15 times more likely to have attempted suicide than the biological relatives of index cases. Levels of mild depression did not differ across the groups.

Biological mechanisms

Both norepinephrine and serotonin have been implicated in the aetiology of depression. It was initially thought that low levels of either neurotransmitter impacted on mood. This simple model is now being challenged by recent data. It seems that mood is the result of an interaction between both serotonin and norepinephrine systems. It may even be the result of interactions between these and other brain systems. Rampello et al. (2000), for example, argued that mood is a consequence of an imbalance between several neurotransmitters, including serotonin, norepinephrine, dopamine and acetylcholine. It is possible that serotonin provides overall control of a variety of brain systems, and that low serotonin levels disrupt activity within these systems which results in depression. The major brain area involved in depression is the limbic system. According to the psychobiological model, these processes are triggered by both social and psychological factors, with genetic factors influencing the degree of stress required from each domain before an episode of depression is triggered.

Socio-cultural factors

A number of social stresses have been shown to increase risk for depression. Prevalence rates of depression are relatively high among the poor, ethnic minorities and those with poor social or marital support (Jenkins et al. 1998). Many people experience a combination of factors that make them particularly prone to depression. Brown and Harris (1978), for example, found that working-class women who had three or more young children, lacked a close confidante, had no outside employment, and whose father had died while they were young, were more prone to depression than those with the opposite constellation of circumstances. Economically deprived individuals tend to experience more negative life-events than those who are better off, and may have fewer social and financial resources with which to deal with them (House et al. 1991). Many people in minority ethnic groups may have to cope with adverse economic circumstances. In addition, they may have to contend with issues of prejudice and integration with the majority population that can cause significant stress (Clarke 2000). More acute life stresses, such as divorce or separation, may also trigger episodes of depression. Conversely, a good social support network can be protective (Paykel 1994).

Explanations of why women report more depression than men vary. Initially dismissed as a *reporting bias*, there is now mounting evidence that there are real gender differences in the prevalence of depression (Weich et al. 1998). Social explanations of these phenomena suggest that women now experience more responsibilities and lower quality of life than men. Women tend to have lower status jobs and have more spillover between work and home (Bird and Rieker 1999). That is, when they finish work they are more likely than men to take on the domestic role and continue working. Women may also be more subject to cultural pressures, including those to conform to western ideals of attractiveness, than men, adding further to their stress. A more psychological explanation suggests that women are more likely to attribute failure to personal characteristics than men, making them more prone to self-blame and low self-esteem. In addition, Holen-Hoeksema (1990) argued that when men experience circumstances that may lead to depression, they are more able to distract from any negative thoughts than women, who are more likely to focus on issues and their possible causes, increasing the salience of potentially depressing cognitions.

Psychodynamic explanations

Freud ([1917] 1957) considered depression to be a similar process to grieving. During grieving, the individual regresses to the oral stage of development as a defence mechanism against overwhelming distress. This involves complete dependency on the loved one, as a consequence of which they merge their identity with them and symbolically regain the lost relationship. In addition, through a process known as introjection, they direct their feelings for the loved one into themselves. These feelings may include anger as a result of unresolved conflicts. This reaction is generally short-lived, but can become pathological if the individual continues to introject their feelings in the long-term, leading to self-hatred and depression.

Freud suggested that 'normal' depression results from an imagined or symbolic loss. Events are seen as somehow removing the love or esteem of important individuals, and the depressed person introjects their negative feelings towards the individual who is seen as rejecting them. Those most prone to depression are people who fail to effectively progress though the oral stage of development (see Chapter 2), because they are either gratified too much or too little at the time. Such people remain dependent on others for love and approval through their lives, and are susceptible to events that trigger anxieties or experiences of loss.

Behavioural explanations

Behavioural theories of depression typically focus on operant conditioning processes. Lewinsohn et al. (1979), for example, suggested that depression is the result of a low rate of positive social reinforcement. This leads to low mood and reductions in behaviour intended to gain social rewards. The individual withdraws from social contacts, an action that may actually result in short-term increases in social contact as they gain sympathy or attention as a result of their behaviour. This may establish a further reinforcement schedule, known as *secondary gain*, in which the individual is rewarded for their depressive behaviours. This phase, however, is usually followed by a reduction in attention (further reducing the frequency of rewards available from the environment) and mood.

Learned helplessness

As noted in Chapter 1, there has been a shift from behavioural to cognitive behavioural explanations of the emotional disorders. This may be exemplified by the changes made to Seligman's (1975) learned helplessness theory over time. Seligman's theory suggested that depression results from learning that one's physical or social environment is beyond one's personal control. The term learned helplessness stemmed from animal experiments in which animals were typically placed in an area from which they could escape, for example by jumping over a low barrier. Following a mild electric shock, the animals quickly learned to jump over the barrier to avoid it. However, when they were prevented from doing so by being placed in a harness, they eventually stopped trying to avoid the shock even when the possibility of escape was open to them. They had learned that they could not avoid the shock, and expressed their helplessness by inertia and not trying to change the situation. A number of studies used differing procedures to induce learned helplessness both in animals and humans. Those that went through these procedures evidenced 'symptoms' similar to clinically depressed individuals, including lack of motivation, passivity, and disrupted learning.

This behavioural model of depression was revised in the late 1970s by Abramson et al. (1978), partly in response to the developing paradigm of cognitive psychology. The revised learned helplessness theory suggested that depression was the result of three key attributions for negative events. Internal ('It is my fault'), global ('Whatever I do, it never works') and stable ('It always happens to me') attributions are likely to lead to depression. The opposite constellation of attributions is protective against depression. More recently, Abela and Seligman (2000) stated that these attributions will result in depression only if they produce a sense of hopelessness: that is, a belief that the individual has no response available to them that will alter the situation and an expectation that desirable outcomes will not occur.

Cognitive explanations

Matching these changes in the learned helplessness model, behavioural explanations of depression have largely been superseded by cognitive ones, the best known of which is that of Beck (1997). Beck argued that depression results from inaccurate cognitive responses to events that affect us. In depression, the immediate response to such events is what Beck termed automatic negative thoughts. These seem immediate and valid, and are often accepted as true. However, they systematically misinterpret events in ways that lead to depression. Errors that typify such

Table 8.1 Some examples of Beck's depressogenic thinking errors

Absolutistic thinking	Thinking in 'all-or-none' terms: 'If I don't succeed in this task I am an absolute failure. I am either the best teacher, or I am nothing . . .'
Over-generalization	Drawing a general (negative) conclusion on the basis of a single incident: 'That's it – I always fail at this sort of thing . . . I can't do it!'
Personalization	Interpreting events as personal affronts or obstacles: 'Why do they always pick on ME . . . ? That's how it always feels, even when I'm not to blame.'
Arbitrary inference	Drawing a conclusion without sufficient evidence to support it: 'They don't like me . . . I could tell from the moment we met . . .'
Selective abstraction	Focusing on an insignificant detail taken out of context: 'I thought my lecture went well. But that student who left early may have been unhappy with it. Perhaps the others were as well but didn't show it . . .'.

thinking include over-generalization, selective abstraction and dichotomous thinking (see Table 8.1). They influence what Beck referred to as the *cognitive triad*: beliefs about our self, events or other people that affect us, and our future.

According to Beck, our conscious thoughts are distorted by underlying depressogenic schemata. These are unconscious underlying beliefs about ourselves and the world that influence conscious thought and are established during childhood. Negative events in childhood, such as parental rejection, for example, establish negative cognitive schema about the self and the world. For most of the time, these beliefs are not particularly salient, or else the individual would be chronically depressed. However, when we encounter stressful circumstances in adulthood, and particularly those that echo previous childhood experiences (divorce or separation, for example, reflecting earlier experiences of parental rejection), underlying negative schemata are activated, influence our surface cognitions, and lead to depression (see Chapter 2 for further discussion of this issue).

There is good evidence that some (negative) schemata are more accessible at times of low mood than at other times. By contrast, others may remain salient throughout the life course (see Chapter 11). Whether either type of schemata is irrevocably established in a critical period during childhood has been questioned by Meichenbaum (1985) who suggested that such schemata are more malleable than this, and change as a consequence of events over the life course. Determining which explanation is right has proven extremely difficult. Clinical practice has shown that some negative schemata beginning in childhood, endure over long periods, and can be difficult to change. However, this does not necessarily reflect a childhood critical period when such schemata are laid down. An alternative explanation may be that childhood beliefs are maintained by continuously distorted interpretations of events, perhaps because nothing happens to make the individual question their initial assumption. Indeed, an individual's own behaviour may result in these beliefs being reinforced. A girl who does not believe that her parents love her, for example, may react against them and cause them to treat her more severely or rigidly than would otherwise have been the case, providing some support for the initial belief. Over time, this belief and its associated behaviours may spill over to other relationships, resulting in relationship problems that continue for many years. Here, the schema laid down in childhood are maintained in adulthood not because of a critical period, but because the woman's behaviour as an adult continued to elicit responses that reinforced her childhood beliefs.

There is a strong reciprocity between mood and cognition: negative cognitions lower mood and low mood increases the salience of negative cognitions. Depressive thoughts, for example, can be triggered in non-depressed subjects following mood induction techniques in which people read aloud a series of adjectives describing negative mood states. Depressed people recall more negative experiences than non-depressed people do (Lloyd and Lishman 1975) (see also Chapter 2). However, there has been some debate as to whether cognitive distortions contribute to the initiation of clinically significant episodes of depression or follow its onset. The answer now seems that both are true. Lewinsohn (1988) found that negative thinking, self-dissatisfaction and high life stress preceded an episode of depression: poor social relationships and reductions in positive rewards accompanied it. Similarly, Rush et al. (1986) found that women who continued to hold negative cognitions at the end of a period of treatment for depression were more at risk of relapsing than those who were more positive by the end of therapy.

Depressive realism

One final commentary on cognitive models of depression suggests that depressed individuals may actually be 'right', and the rest of us 'wrong'. The depressive realism hypothesis (Haaga and Beck 1995) suggests that depressed people may actually be more accurate in their world evaluations than those who are not depressed. A number of experimental tests have supported this theory. Depressed individuals, for example, are more accurate than non-depressed people in their evaluations of how favourably or unfavourably others judge them and in their judgements of how much control they have in an experimental situation (Alloy and Abramson 1979). Those going through therapy for depression may actually benefit as a result of their cognitions becoming *less* realistic, albeit more positive.

Treatment of major depression

Biological interventions

Antidepressants

There are now three types of antidepressants in general use: MAOIs, tricyclics and SSRIs. Historically, MAOIs proved reasonably effective, achieving clinically significant changes in about 50 per cent of the people prescribed them. However, the dangers associated with their use (see Chapter 3) have meant they are used less as other drugs have become available. Now, the two key drug therapies for depression are the tricyclics and SSRIs. The two drugs seem equally effective, with between 60 and 65 per cent of individuals who take them reporting significant improvements in mood (Hirschfeld 1999). Where SSRIs gain their advantage is in their side-effect profile. Rocca et al. (1997), for example, reported 56 per cent of users complaining of a dry mouth following treatment with tricyclics compared to 8 per cent treated with SSRIs. The percentages to report constipation were 39 and 8 per cent respectively. Anderson (1998) reported that 14 per cent of people on tricyclics discontinued their use due to adverse side-effects in comparison to only 9 per cent of those receiving SSRIs. Whatever type of drug is given, it is important to maintain a therapeutic regime for some months after therapeutic gains have been achieved, as about 50 per cent of users will relapse within a year if their use is prematurely stopped (Montgomery et al. 1993).

St John's wort

A radical shift from traditional pharmacology is found in treatments using extracts of the plant Hypericum perforatum, more popularly known as St John's wort. Its mode of action is little understood, but it does seem to benefit those receiving it. A meta-analysis conducted by Linde and Mulrow (2002), for example, identified 14 trials that compared preparations of hypericum against placebo or antidepressant medication. The percentage of people to clinically improve following treatment with hypericum preparations and placebo were 56 per cent and 25 per cent respectively. Comparisons with antidepressants revealed few differences in benefit, with clinical gains in 50 per cent of those treated with hypericum compared to 52 per cent with standard antidepressant treatment. Of those treated with a combination of hypericum and antidepressant 68 per cent evidenced clinically significant improvements. St John's wort seemed to be more acceptable to those prescribed it than standard pharmacological medication, with dropout rates due to side-effects averaging 2 per cent among those prescribed hypericum in contrast to 7 per cent of those receiving standard antidepressants.

St John's wort does have some side-effects, including gastrointestinal discomfort, fatigue, dry mouth, dizziness, skin rash and hypersensitivity

to sunlight. Of more concern is that it may also interfere with the effectiveness of Indinavir, a protease inhibitor used in the treatment of AIDS;
Cyclosporin, an immunosuppressive drug used to protect patients from
organ rejection after heart transplantation; and Warfarin, an anticoagu-
lant. As a result, its use has to be limited in some cases.

Electroconvulsive therapy

Evaluations of the effectiveness of ECT have, in the past, compared
its effectiveness with that of pharmacotherapy in a general population of
depressed people. More recently, the success of antidepressants in treating depression, and a concern over the acceptability of ECT as a first-line
treatment (see Chapter 3), have resulted in it being used increasingly as a
second-line treatment for those individuals who do not respond to pharmacological, and perhaps psychological, treatments: so-called treatment-
resistant cases. At this point, ECT does appear to have some benefit, and
given the lack of response to other treatments, any gains at this point
may be considered a success (McCall 2001).

Perhaps more controversial has been the question whether ECT should
be continued over an extended period of time to maintain initial improvements in mood, or whether drug therapy is sufficient. Gagné et al.
(2000) explored this issue by comparing outcomes over a period averaging about three years in a group of people initially treated with ECT and
then maintained on either antidepressants or antidepressants plus ECT.
ECT was initially delivered once-weekly, and then gradually increased
to once-monthly. Their findings appeared to support the use of maintenance ECT: 7 per cent of those receiving continuation ECT plus antidepressant compared to 48 per cent of those only receiving antidepressants
relapsed over this time. However, they also noted that participants in
the ECT condition received more time with their doctor than those who
received medication as a result of their clinic visits. In addition, those
who did not attend their ECT clinic were vigorously followed up and
encouraged to attend, potentially resulting in more immediate remedial
action should the individual have started to become depressed than among
those treated only with antidepressants. Both may have contributed to
the better outcome in this group.

Psychological interventions

Cognitive therapy

The seminal cognitive treatment of depression was developed by Beck
(1977). Despite its name, cognitive therapy has its historical roots in
the behavioural treatment of depression, and still maintains a strong
behavioural element. It typically involves a number of strategies,
including:

- *an education phase* in which the individual learns the relationship between cognitions, emotions and behaviour
- *behavioural activation* and *pleasant event scheduling* to increase physiological activity, and engagement in social or other rewarding activities
- *cognitive rehearsal* in which the individual develops and practises cognitive or behavioural strategies to help them cope with behavioural hypothesis testing or other situations that have previously been problematic
- *behavioural hypothesis testing* in which the individual deliberately tests the validity of their negative assumptions, in the hope of disproving them.

Despite the emphasis on cognitive causes of depression, treatment may first involve a behavioural technique, involving increased engagement in physical activities. For those who are profoundly depressed, this may simply involve planning times to get out of bed, go to the shops, and so on. For those who are less depressed, it may involve engaging in social or 'pleasant' activities. Cognitive factors are usually addressed only after the client has experienced some improvement in energy or mood. At this time, they are taught to identify 'faulty thinking' that leads to low mood and to use cognitive challenges to counter it. In addition, the client is typically given homework to do between sessions, usually involving some form of behavioural hypothesis testing or practice in the use of new coping skills. Hypothesis testing involves direct, behavioural challenges of negative cognitions. Someone who is not sure they will be able to cope with a particular situation, for example, may be encouraged to enter the situation and try to cope with it. Such tasks should be selected with care. The therapist, at least, should be confident the client will be able to cope with the situation, as failure will reinforce negative expectations: the very thing the task was set up to disprove. Because there can be a significant risk of relapse in the year following cessation of therapy, one or two 'booster' sessions during this period can be a useful means of preventing relapse.

By the mid-1980s, there was a general consensus that cognitive therapy was at least as effective as antidepressant therapy in the treatment of both moderate and severe depression. This consensus was broken following publication of the results of the most influential treatment trial so far conducted. The National Institute of Mental Health (NIMH) Depression Collaborative Program (Elkin et al. 1989) was a particularly important trial as it was the first to compare two psychological treatments, cognitive therapy and **interpersonal therapy** (based on humanistic principles), with both pharmacotherapy (imipramine) and a placebo drug intervention.

By the end of the 16-week treatment phase, all the interventions appeared to be equally effective. The only between-group differences to reach statistical significance indicated that the pharmacological intervention was significantly more effective than the placebo intervention. Of those in the interpersonal psychotherapy condition 55 per cent were clinically 'improved', in comparison to 57 per cent in the active drug intervention, 51 per cent in the cognitive therapy group and 29 per cent in the placebo group. For those who were severely depressed, cognitive therapy proved significantly less effective than pharmacotherapy.

This secondary finding caused a significant amount of debate and discussion, not least because its results led both the American Psychiatric Association and the US Agency of Health Care Policy and Research to recommend against the use of cognitive therapy for more severe cases of depression. However, the results have been questioned from a number of perspectives. Psychiatrists were puzzled by findings that the effectiveness of the placebo was much greater than is typically found. Psychologists were surprised that the cognitive intervention proved less effective than in earlier studies. So much so, that Jacobson and Hollon (1996) suggested that it had been implemented by insufficiently skilled therapists at some sites. Subsequent data have also challenged this short-term finding. DeRubeis et al. (1999), for example, compared the short-term outcomes of antidepressant medication and cognitive behaviour therapy in people with severe depression in subgroups of four major randomized trials. In contrast to the NIMH study, both cognitive therapy and pharmacotherapy fared equally well in the short-term treatment of people with severe depression.

The long-term results of the NIMH study were more favourable to the psychological interventions (Shea et al. 1992). At one-year follow-up, those who had received cognitive therapy fared best, with success rates of 30 per cent for those in the cognitive behaviour therapy group, 26 per cent for those in the interpersonal therapy group, 19 per cent for those in the imipramine group, and 20 per cent for those in the placebo group. By this time, 14 per cent of the successfully treated individuals in the cognitive therapy group had relapsed compared to 50 per cent of those in the antidepressant group. Here may lie the advantage of cognitive over pharmacological therapy. Relapse rates following discontinuation of drug therapy are often much higher than those following cognitive therapy, even when the initial treatment is successful. Even when medication is given for one year to maximize its effectiveness, the same pattern of results has been found – albeit with a smaller difference between the conditions (Evans et al. 1992).

Suicide

Suicide is not an affective disorder. Nor is it uniquely associated with depression. Nevertheless, it is an important topic and is more strongly associated with depression than any other mental health disorder considered in this text. So, it is discussed in this chapter.

Suicide rates vary across countries. For example, Russia has an annual rate as high as 40 per 100,000 people, while Greece has as few as 4 per 100,000 (World Health Organization: www.who.int). Suicide rates also vary over time. Among British women, for example, suicide rates have fallen since the early 1970s; among men, a decline in suicide rates between 1960 and 1975 has been followed by a steady increase over the subsequent ten years (McClure 2000). In 2000, the UK rates were 11.7 per 100,000 men and 3.3. per 100,000 women – a substantial difference. Attempted suicide is particularly common in young people: two-thirds of all cases are below the age of 35 years of age (Hawton 1997).

Only about half of those who commit suicide have an identified mental health problem, the most common being depression, substance-related disorders and schizophrenia. About 15 per cent of those with each disorder kill themselves (Meltzer 1998). Suicide is less strongly associated with severe than with moderate levels of depression, as those who are severely depressed may lack the volition to act on their feelings. Indeed, people who are depressed may kill themselves as their depression begins to lift because they are still hopeless but have some increased impulsivity and motivation.

Bronisch and Wittchen (1994) reported that 56 per cent of their sample of people with a diagnosis of depression reported thinking about death, 37 per cent reported a wish to die, and 69 per cent had suicidal ideas. However, these thoughts were not exclusive to depressed individuals: 8 per cent of a comparison group who had never been assigned a psychiatric diagnosis reported having suicidal ideas, and 2 per cent had made a suicide attempt. Suicide in people with schizophrenia is more often a result of demoralization than the result of hallucinations or delusions. Other risk factors include being male, single, living alone, poor sleep, impaired memory and self-neglect (Bronisch 1996).

Wolfersdorf (1995) summarized the psychological characteristics of individuals who attempted suicide as involving thoughts of worthlessness, guilt, despair, depressive delusional symptoms, inner restlessness and agitation. Those who commit suicide are also more likely to have pre-morbid characteristics that include high levels of impulsivity, irritability, hostility and a tendency to aggression (Bronisch 1996).

Aetiology of suicide

Socio-cultural factors

Suicide is lowest among those who are married or co-habiting, and highest among divorcees. Three times as many women attempt suicide as men: conversely, three times as many men actually succeed in their attempt.

About 60 per cent of attempted suicides occur after the individual has been drinking alcohol (Royal College of Psychiatrists 1986).

The types of problems that trigger attempted suicide vary according to age. Hawton's (1997) summary of the data suggested that 72 per cent of adults who committed or attempted suicide had difficulties in interpersonal relationships, 26 per cent had employment problems, 26 per cent had difficulties with children, while 19 per cent had financial problems. The high levels of emotional lability associated with adolescence may make adolescents particularly prone to suicide. Sexual problems may also be a particular risk factor among adolescents. Remafedi et al. (1998), for example, found that 28 per cent of homosexual or bisexual males but only 4 per cent of heterosexual male adolescents had ever considered or attempted suicide. For females the corresponding figures were 21 and 15 per cent. Among older people, suicide may occur as a consequence of increasing disability: 44 per cent of one sample of elderly people apparently committed suicide to prevent being placed in a nursing home (Loebel et al. 1991). Suicide among those who have recently been bereaved is also frequent.

A more theoretical social model of suicide was developed by Durkheim ([1897] 1951) who identified three types of suicide: anomic, altruistic and egoistic. According to Durkheim, *anomic suicide* occurs when the social structure in which an individual lives fails to provide sufficient support for them, and they lose a sense of belonging – a state known as anomie. High levels of anomie occur at times of both societal and personal change, including economic stress, immigration and social unrest. *Altruistic suicide* occurs when an individual deliberately sacrifices themself for the well-being of others or the community. Finally, *egoistic suicide* occurs among those not governed by the norms of society, who are outsiders or loners in a more permanent state of alienation than those who commit anomic suicide.

Psychoanalytic explanations

According to Freud ([1920] 1990), suicide represents a repressed wish to kill a lost love object, and is an act of revenge. Hendin (1992) identified a number of other psychoanalytic processes that may lead to suicide, including ideas of effecting a rebirth or reunion with a lost object as well as self-punishment and atonement.

Cognitive explanations

Many people who attempt suicide have deficits in memory and problem-solving skills, even in comparison to non-suicidal depressed individuals (Schotte and Clum 1987). These deficits make it difficult for such individuals to cope successfully with stressful circumstances effectively and likely to use ineffective coping strategies, including suicide.

A more elaborate cognitive model of suicide was developed by Rudd (2000), based on Beck's model of emotional disorders and his own clinical experience. According to Rudd, the components of the underlying cognitive triad are the self as worthless, unloved, incompetent and helpless, others as rejecting, abusing, judgemental and the future as hopeless. Key assumptions are those of perfectionism ('If I am perfect, people will accept me'), with the resultant behaviour including subjugation in relationships and perfectionism. In contrast to depression, where sadness predominates, the suicidal individual may experience a range of emotions including sadness, guilt and anger. Thoughts may focus on revenge, but this will not lead directly to suicidal behaviour. Thoughts and emotions associated with suicide occur at the same time as high levels of physiological arousal and agitation: the profoundly depressed non-aroused individual will not have the motivation to attempt suicide. Risk of suicide varies over time, with periods of acute risk interspersed with lower levels of risk. High levels of risk occur when multiple risk factors converge. These may include situational stress, activation of negative schema, emotional confusion and deficient coping skills.

Here are the desperate words of a married woman close to suicide, for whom the events of many years previously held a continuing and damaging influence:

> I just can't go on . . . I'm bad . . . dirty . . . The things I did before were bad. I did things with men that I shouldn't even at the age of 6 . . . that makes me a whore . . . That's why I was raped at 11. I'm dirty . . . bad . . . a tart . . . and I can't keep trying to change, to be good. Whoever I love I make feel bad because I am me . . . because I am dirty. I can't do anything to change things . . . because I am bad, dirty . . .

> I can't think of a way out of things. I've tried for 30 years not to be bad. But I can't stop it. There's so many things I have done that make me bad . . . I just can't make myself good.

> There's nothing to live for. My husband and my daughters. . . . They'll get along without me. They don't need me. I make them unhappy and when I am gone they will be happy again. They don't deserve to have me pulling them down, making them unhappy. That's why the best thing to do is to kill myself . . . end my misery and theirs.

Treatment of attempted suicide

Problem-solving therapy

People who attempt suicide and have a mental health problem may benefit from treatment of this disorder regardless of its influence on their mood or behaviour. They may also benefit more directly from addressing the factors that contributed to their suicide attempt. One way through which this can be achieved is through the development of strategies to cope more effectively with the problems they face. The key elements of this approach include:

- both client and therapist gaining a good understanding of the nature of the problems
- identifying in what ways the situation could be improved: the desired goals (such as better relationship with partner)
- identifying strategies by which these goals can be attained (for example, talking more, going out together, and so on).

This approach can be used with individuals as well as couples and even families. Therapy sessions may be frequent in the early stages of therapy, and then more widely spaced as the individual begins to cope better with their problems. Therapy may also involve relatively few sessions: partly because this may be the only form of therapy acceptable to those who attempt suicide, partly to facilitate early client independence (Hawton 1997).

Evaluations of the effectiveness of this approach have generally supported its use. Indeed, in a meta-analysis of psychosocial interventions following suicide attempts, van der Sande et al. (1997) found problem-focused and cognitive behavioural interventions to be the only interventions to prove effective in this group. Salkovskis et al. (1990), for example, compared a brief, five-session cognitive-behavioural and problem-solving approach with routine outpatient care. In the six months following the intervention 25 per cent of those in the active intervention group engaged in at least one further suicide attempt, in comparison to 50 per cent of those who did not receive the intervention.

Seasonal affective disorder

Seasonal affective disorder (SAD) was only recognized as a distinct disorder by Rosenthal and colleagues in the mid-1980s (Rosenthal et al. 1984). DSM-IV-TR (APA 2000) described it as having the following characteristics:

- a regular temporal relationship between the onset of an episode of depression and a particular time of year
- full remissions occur at regular times of the year
- two major depressive episodes that fit these criteria have occurred in the previous two years
- any seasonal depressive episodes outnumber the number of non-seasonal episodes of depression.

The characteristics of SAD appear to be quite different from major depression, and include increased appetite and carbohydrate craving, an associated increase in weight, and increased duration of sleep, as well as other depressive symptoms. Winter episodes typically begin in November and last about five months. People with SAD benefit from living in lower latitudes with shorter winter periods. Their symptoms get worse if they move in the opposite direction (Rosenthal et al. 1984).

Those whose symptoms are so severe that they receive a diagnosis of SAD may be a subgroup of individuals who experience particularly problematic symptoms over the winter. Less dramatic seasonal changes in activity and weight levels occur within the general population. Terman (1988), for example, reported that 50 per cent of the general population reported lowered energy levels, 47 per cent reported increased weight, while 31 per cent reported decreased social activity in the winter months; 25 per cent reported that these changes were sufficiently marked to signify a personal problem. Wicki et al. (1992) found that 3 per cent of their German cohort developed either SAD or 'subsyndromal' SAD twice in two consecutive years. Rates of SAD in Scotland are in the order of 3.5 per cent (Eagles et al. 1999).

Aetiology of seasonal affective disorder

Explanations of SAD are almost uniquely biological.

Genetic factors

Reflecting the relatively recent interest in SAD, there are few studies examining the role of genetic factors in its aetiology. However, Madden et al. (1996) examined concordance for SAD in a large sample of MZ and DZ twins. They also measured a number of environmental variables and were able to determine the relative importance of genetic and environmental variables. They concluded that about 29 per cent of the variance in the risk for developing SAD was attributable to genetic factors.

The melatonin hypothesis

Melatonin has been implicated in SAD. It is a hormone whose release is triggered from the pineal gland in the base of the brain by darkness, and is found mainly in the midbrain and hypothalamus. It controls sleep and eating. In mammals that are living wild, the release of melatonin as the nights get longer reduces their activity, slows them down, and prepares them for winter rest or hibernation. According to the melatonin theory of depression, it has the same effect in humans, although most of us are able to override its effects and carry on without problems. However, some individuals appear particularly vulnerable to increased levels of melatonin in the winter months and experience a significant slow-down, evident in the symptoms of SAD (Blehar and Rosenthal 1989). In the reverse of SAD, some individuals seem to be affected by low levels of melatonin in the summer and experience periods of high mood and elation. Evidence of the role of melatonin is somewhat conflicting. While some studies have found an association between levels of melatonin and the onset and severity of SAD, this is not always the case, and its role in the aetiology of SAD is not yet fully understood.

Circadian hypothesis

In a twist to the melatonin hypothesis, Lewy et al. (1998) suggested that rather than the level of melatonin being the determinant of mood, it is the times at which it is secreted that are important in the onset and maintenance of SAD. In their circadian hypothesis, they suggested that 'normal' depression can result from poor sleep resulting from disruption of the circadian wake–sleep cycle. In the case of SAD, they suggested that changes in the times of dawn and dusk in the transition from summer to winter changes the time that melatonin is released, shifting the circadian rhythm of sleep, and taking it out of alignment with other biological rhythms. The goal of therapy is to rephase the wake–sleep cycle to that of the summer. According to Lewy and colleagues, this may be achieved through exposure to light early in the morning, which helps maintain the summer wake–sleep cycle and delays the secretion of melatonin until later in the day. This, combined with earlier times of sleep in the evening, should prove an effective treatment for SAD. Their own work supported this hypothesis, with findings that light therapy in the morning was more effective than if it was provided in the evening: an effect that seems to hold as long as the individual maintains their summertime waking and sleeping times (Lewy et al. 1998).

Serotonin hypothesis

The final hypothesis suggests that at least some of the mechanisms underlying SAD may not be peculiar to this particular syndrome, and may be those that underpin other forms of depression. A number of factors tie serotonin to the aetiology of SAD. Serotonin is involved in the control of appetite and sleep, and is a precursor to melatonin. Serotonin levels vary seasonally, and reducing serotonin levels by removal of a precursor to serotonin known as tryptophan from the diet results in depressive symptoms during the summer in people who typically develop winter SAD (Neumeister et al. 1997). Further evidence of a role for serotonin has come from treatment trials involving SSRIs. Both sertraline and fluoxetine have proven moderately effective in the treatment of SAD. However, these are generally not as effective as light therapy (Partonen and Lonnqvist 1998), suggesting that while serotonin levels may be implicated in SAD, they do not provide the entire picture.

Treatment of seasonal affective disorder

The recognized treatment of SAD is known as 'bright light' treatment which serves to lower levels of melatonin. In this, the individual is typically exposed to high levels of artificial light, varying from 2500 lux for a period of 2 hours to 10,000 lux for half an hour each day over a period of between one and three weeks. For comparison, light in the house typically measures 100 lux or less. Outside lux levels may vary between 2000 lux or less on a rainy winter day and 10,000 lux in direct sunshine.

These interventions are effective. In a meta-analysis of the relevant studies Terman et al. (1989) reported significant improvements in 67 per cent of people with mild SAD, and 40 per cent of those with moderate to severe levels, treated with light therapy: results that were significantly better than those of placebo treatments. A more recent trial was reported by Sumaya et al. (2001). In it, people with depression were subject to three conditions in a random order: a therapeutic dose of 10,000 lux for 30 minutes daily for one week, a non-therapeutic dose of 300 lux over the same time period (placebo), and a no-treatment period. After light treatment, 50 per cent of those receiving the active treatment no longer met the criteria for depression. Levels of depression did not change following either the placebo or no-treatment phases. Nevertheless, there can be a considerable placebo response to light therapy, sometimes equalling that of active therapy. Wileman et al. (2001), for example, randomly allocated people with SAD to either an active (four weeks of 10,000 lux exposure) or placebo (four weeks of 300 lux) condition. Immediately following treatment, 30 per cent of those in the active treatment and 33 per cent of those in the placebo treatment were no longer depressed; 63 per cent of those in the active group and 57 per cent of the placebo group showed 'significant' improvements. Despite findings such as this, light therapy remains the pre-eminent treatment for SAD.

Bipolar disorder

People with bipolar disorders experience both depression and periods of mania. According to DSM-IV-TR, mania involves at least three of the following:

- inflated self-esteem or grandiosity
- decreased need for sleep
- more talkativeness than usual or pressure to keep talking
- flight of ideas or the experience that thoughts are racing
- distractibility

- increased activity or psychomotor agitation
- excessive engagement in high-risk activities.

Manic individuals move rapidly, talk rapidly and loudly, and their conversation is often filled with jokes and attempts at cleverness. Flamboyance is common. Judgement is often poor, and individuals may engage in risky and other behaviours that they regret when less manic. They may also become extremely frustrated by the actions of others, who they see as preventing them achieving their great plans. Of interest is that while many people appear extremely happy while in a manic episode, this may not always be the case.

DSM-IV-TR described two types of bipolar disorder:

- *Bipolar disorder I:* individuals typically experience alternating episodes of depression and mania, each lasting weeks or months. Some individuals may experience several episodes of either mania or depression, separated by periods of 'normality', in sequence. Some people may swing between depression and mania in one day.
- *Bipolar disorder II:* depressive episodes predominate. The individual may swing between episodes of hypomania (an increase in activity over the normal, but not as excessive as mania) and severe depression. In addition, they will not have experienced an episode of mania.

Between 1 and 1.5 per cent of the adult population will experience bipolar disorder at any one time, with disorder I being the most prevalent (Bebbington and Ramana 1995). While the overall prevalence among men and women does not differ, women seem to have more depressive and fewer manic episodes than men and to cycle between these episodes more frequently (APA 2000). Prevalence levels do not differ across socio-economic or ethnic groups. The first episode of bipolar disorder usually occurs between the ages of 20 and 30. Over half of those who have an initial episode of major depression and at least 80 per cent of those who have an initial episode of mania will have one or more recurrences (APA 1994). Each episode may last days, weeks or, in some cases, years. The seriousness of the disorder tends to increase over time, although after about ten years there may be a marked diminution in severity.

Aetiology of bipolar disorder

Genetic factors

An early review of the genetics of bipolar disorder by Allen (1976) reported overall concordance rates for MZ twins of 72 per cent, while concordance rates for DZ twins averaged 14 per cent. More recently, these estimates have been reduced to 40 per cent and between 5 and 10 per cent respectively (Craddock and Jones 1999). Attempts to identify the locus of the genes that contribute to risk for the disorder have suggested that it may lie on chromosomes 4, 6, 12, 13, 15, 18 and 22 (Berretini 2000), suggesting a multi-gene contribution to risk.

Biological mechanisms

Given the role of serotonin and norepinephrine in depression, it would seem logical to assume that they also play a role in mania. However, the biological model that has emerged is not as simple as may have been expected. Data on norepinephrine are consistent with a simple model of mood disorders. High levels of norepinephrine are associated with elevated mood and mania; low levels result in depressed mood. No such relationship has been found for serotonin levels. Indeed, mania has been associated with low levels of serotonin (Mahmood and Silverstone 2001) – just as in depression. This finding is perhaps relevant to psychological studies that suggest manic behaviour may be somehow 'masking' depressed mood. Data such as these have led some researchers to suggest a *permissive theory of bipolar disorder*, in which low serotonin levels somehow permits the activity of norepinephrine to determine mood. Low serotonin combined with low norepinephrine results in depression; combined with high norepinephrine, it results in mania.

A second model of bipolar disorders moves from consideration of neurotransmitters to the electrical conduction of whole neurons. Two processes involved in nerve transmission may be implicated: disturbances in activity of second messengers known as *phosphoinositides*, that instigate the firing of nerves including those involved in moderating mood, and altered sodium and potassium activity in the same neurons (see Chapter 3). In mania, second messenger activity or sodium and potassium transport across the cell membrane may be excessive and result in overactivity of the neuron system; in depression, there may be low activity in the neurons (Lenox et al. 1998).

Psychoanalytic explanations

Psychoanalysts view mania as an extreme defence mechanism to counter unpleasant emotional states or unacceptable impulses. Katan (1953), for example, suggested that as periods of mania frequently follow states of depression, the conflict in mania may be of a similar nature to that in depression. People who pass from depression into mania maintain their preoccupation with a real or fantasized loss. In the manic state, this anxiety is externalized. Aggressive drive is directed outwards, and the individual reacts to external objects in the same manner as introjection directs anger inwards in depression.

Cognitive models

As in psychoanalytic models, the cognitive model of Winters and Neale (1985) suggested mania is a defence reaction against depression, arguing that a combination of low self-esteem and unrealistic standards of success may drive both depressive and manic episodes. According to Winters and Neale, when individuals with this constellation of cognitive schemata experience an adverse event, they either experience the emotions of depression and cognitions related to low self-esteem, or a defensive reaction against them, in which they adopt the *manic disguise* through which they report normal self-esteem levels. Why such individuals adopt differing strategies at different times is unclear. However, it may be a result of the acceptability of each response to those around the affected individual. Where the expression of negative emotions is unacceptable, they may adopt a manic coping style, which may be rewarded by continued or even increased social contact with important others. Despite this social reinforcement, however, the individual may eventually be unable to continue with these behaviours, and their depression may 'break through'. They then swing into a depressive episode.

In one of the few experimental tests of the manic defence hypothesis Lyon et al. (1999) compared the attributions made by people with bipolar disorder who were either manic or depressed and 'normal' controls, in response to hypothetical positive and negative events. Both groups of people with bipolar disorder attributed personal responsibility for more negative events and for fewer positive events than those in the control group. By contrast, when asked to endorse a number of positive and negative attributes as descriptors or 'self', both controls and people with mania endorsed largely positive items. Those in the depressed group endorsed mostly negative items. On a subsequent memory test of these words, however, people who were both manic and depressed recalled more negative words than the normal controls. Lyon and colleagues took this pattern of results to indicate that while people with mania explicitly made positive attributions about themselves, underlying this was a set of negative beliefs about self: the manic defence.

These experimental data are in accord with the experience of Helen, who had experienced significant mood swings for many years. When she was in a manic phase, she typically wore livid coloured clothes, used bright and excessive make-up, and was generally hyperactive, gregarious and had difficulty in concentrating on one thing at a time. She looked like she was having fun. Talking to her about her experiences gave a different impression:

> I know it looks like I'm having fun, being happy and all that.
> But it's not how I feel. I feel driven by things, it's like there's
> something in me driving me, making me do things wild. Like the
> make-up, it's all over my face, and I don't like it but I do it. I feel

really down sometimes while I'm acting all manic. It's not like I choose to though, it's like it's happening despite how I feel – it's not happy. I really don't like it. And I don't like people around thinking I'm happy too . . . it's really weird.

Treatment of bipolar disorder

Lithium therapy

Standard antidepressants are typically not used in the treatment of bipolar disorder, as they may provoke rapid mood swings rather than stabilize mood. Instead, lithium bicarbonate tablets are used to moderate mood swings. Lithium typically achieves this within 5 to 14 days in about 60 per cent of cases, and has to be taken continually to minimize risk of the onset of depression or mania. Suppes et al. (1991) reported relapse rates 28 times higher among individuals who stopped taking lithium when not experiencing symptoms than those who continued its use. How it achieves these therapeutic gains is unclear. It may act on all three processes that appear to influence mood: increasing serotonin activity, regulating the activity of second messengers, and/or correcting sodium and potassium activity within the neuron.

Despite its therapeutic potential, the effectiveness of lithium in clinical practice has been less than was hoped for, possibly because of poor adherence to recommended treatment regimes. Between 18 and 53 per cent of those receiving treatment do not adhere to the recommended regime (Guscott and Taylor 1994). Reasons for this include side-effects of weight gain, problems with coordination and tremor, excessive thirst, memory disturbances and tremor. Psychological factors include a dislike of medication controlling mood, feeling well and seeing no need for medication, and missing the highs of hypomania. In addition, many users complain of a 'damping down' of all emotions all the time, which they find problematic. A further caution is that the window between ineffective and toxic doses of lithium is narrow. Too high a dose will result in lithium intoxication, the consequences of which include nausea, vomiting, tremors, kidney dysfunction and, potentially, death. Accordingly, levels of lithium have to be regularly monitored by blood testing, a further disincentive to adherence.

Cognitive behavioural approaches

The biological model of bipolar disorder has been dominant for some years, and it is only recently that attempts to change the course of the disorder using cognitive behavioural methods have been attempted. These have been remarkably successful, adding to the effectiveness of lithium therapy in all the reported trials (see Scott 2001). Scott et al. (2001), for example, randomly allocated people with bipolar disorder into treatment either with lithium alone or in combination with cognitive therapy. The cognitive therapy involved three elements:

- an educational phase to prepare people for the cognitive approach
- a focus on cognitive behavioural methods of symptom management including establishing regular activity patterns and time management, as well as challenging dysfunctional thoughts
- anti-relapse techniques.

The latter involved developing strategies for managing medication, individual coping strategies to deal with stress, or seeking help at times of the onset of signs of relapse. Each intervention lasted six months. By this time, those in the combined intervention showed more improvements on measures of general functioning and depression than those in the drug treatment group. The data on relapse were equally impressive. Those who received the combined intervention were 60 per cent less likely to relapse than those in the drug only condition.

Chapter summary

1 Major depression involves significant psychological impairment lasting at least two weeks. About one-third of the people who become depressed will remain depressed one year later.

2 Psychodynamic explanations consider depression to result from the symbolic loss of love or esteem. Negative feelings towards the responsible person are internalized and result in depression.

3 Socio-cultural explanations focus on differentials in stress and coping in different social groups.

4 Genetic factors contribute to the risk of depression.

5 Low levels of serotonin may result in depression as a result of a loss of control over a number of brain systems, including those mediated by norepinephrine and dopamine.

6 Behavioural theories suggest that depression is the result of a lack of social reinforcement.

7 Cognitive theories consider negative automatic thoughts and dysfunctional schemata to be causal.

8 Both pharmacological and cognitive interventions appear to be equally effective in the short-term treatment of depression. Cognitive interventions may be more effective in the long-term.

9 St John's wort may prove an effective natural therapy.

10 ECT may be effective for some 'treatment-resistant cases', but continued use of ECT to maintain any gains remains controversial.

11 While individuals with serious mental health problems may be at increased risk of suicide, so are individuals without such disorders.

12 In adults, the primary trigger to a suicide attempt is interpersonal problems.

13 Freud considered suicide to be an attempt at revenge on a hated individual.

14 Cognitive explanations suggest that poor problem-solving skills and feelings of being worthless and rejected combined with situational stress, emotional confusion, and high levels of physiological arousal place an individual at risk of committing suicide.

15 Interventions that increase problem-solving skills appear to reduce the risk of suicide.

16 SAD appears to result from disordered melatonin and circadian rhythms.

17 Bright light therapy appears to be the most effective treatment of SAD.

18 Bipolar disorder is the result of neural mechanisms involved in the transmission of information along the neuronal axis.

19 The primary treatment of the disorder involves lithium medication, although cognitive behavioural interventions also appear to be of benefit.

For discussion

1 Jacobson and Hollon (1996) argued that the short-term findings of the NIMH depression study were flawed as a result of the inexpert implementation of cognitive therapy. Given the spread, and possible dilution, of therapist skills away from centres of excellence, is this an argument for the use of pharmacological therapies in preference to the psychotherapies?

2 Consider why the relapse rate among people with depression treated with antidepressants is significantly higher than that among people treated with cognitive therapy.

3 Is SADness in winter a common phenomenon? If so, why?

Further reading

Beck, A.T. (1977) *Cognitive Therapy of Depression*. New York: Guilford.

Dalgleish, T., Rosen, K. and Marks, M. (1996) Rhythm and blues: the theory and treatment of seasonal affective disorder, *British Journal of Clinical Psychology*, 35: 163–82.

DeRubeis, R.J., Gelfand, L.A., Tang, T.Z. et al. (1999) Medications versus cognitive behavior therapy for severely depressed outpatients: mega-analysis of four randomized comparisons, *American Journal of Psychiatry*, 156: 1007–13.

Linde, K. and Mulrow, C.D. (2002) St John's wort for depression, *Cochrane Database of Systematic Reviews*, Issue 1.

Lyon, H.M., Startup, M. and Bentall, R.P. (1999) Social cognition and the manic defense: attributions, selective attention, and self-schema in bipolar affective disorder, *Journal of Abnormal Psychology*, 108: 273–82.

Partonen, T. and Lonnqvist, J. (1998) Seasonal affective disorder, *Lancet*, 352: 1369–74.

Van der Sande, R., Buskens, E., Allart, E. et al. (1997) Psychosocial intervention following suicide attempt: a systematic review of treatment interventions, *Acta Psychiatrica Scandinavica*, 96: 43–50.

Trauma-related conditions

This chapter focuses on three types of problems that may occur as a result of significant trauma experienced by the individual either as an adult or child. The first, post-traumatic stress disorder (PTSD), is widely acknowledged as a natural response to being involved in or seeing highly traumatic events. The other two conditions explored in the chapter are rather more controversial. Indeed, their very existence has been called into question. The chapter explores evidence relating to two apparent responses to childhood trauma: hidden and recovered memories, and dissociative identity disorder (DID), previously known as multiple personality. By the end of the chapter, you should have an understanding of:

♦ The nature and treatment of post-traumatic stress disorder

♦ The controversy surrounding 'recovered memories'

♦ The controversy surrounding dissociative identity disorder

♦ Treatment approaches used in DID.

Post-traumatic stress disorder

The DSM-IV-TR criteria for a diagnosis of PTSD are that the individual has experienced or witnessed an event that involved actual or threatened death or serious injury, or a threat to the physical integrity of self or others, and that their immediate response involved intense fear, helplessness or horror. In the longer term, the individual must have experienced three clusters of symptoms lasting one month or more:

 • *Intrusive memories:* the trauma is re-experienced through intrusive thoughts, flashbacks or nightmares. Such review may be deliberate as the individual ruminates about the traumatic event. Images may also spring unbidden to mind, in the form of flashbacks. These images often feel as real as the event, but may be fragmentary or partial. Emotions and sensations associated with the trauma may be relived with similar intensity to those felt at the time. Images are often described as if being in a film of the incident. Initially, the person may feel they are actually 'in' the film: as they recover, they feel they are watching the film as an outside observer. That is, they begin to, almost literally, feel more detached from the trauma.

- *Avoidance:* the adoption of activities or behaviours to avoid re-minders of the traumatic event. This may involve mental defence mechanisms including being unable to recall aspects of the trauma, emotional numbness, or detachment from others, as well as phys-ically avoiding reminders of the trauma.
- *Arousal:* persistent feelings of over-arousal that may be evidenced by irritability, being easily startled or hypervigilant, suffering insomnia, or having difficulty concentrating.

The triggers of PTSD vary widely, and include war experiences, child-hood sexual and physical abuse, adult rape, and natural and technolo-gical disasters. Perhaps the most frequent cause of PTSD is road traffic accidents: about 20 per cent of those involved develop some degree of PTSD (Ehlers et al. 1998). About 1 per cent of the general population will have PTSD at any one time (Kessler et al. 1995). Prevalence rates among groups that regularly encounter traumatic events are much higher. Bennett et al. (in submission), for example, found a prevalence rate of 22 per cent among emergency ambulance personnel, while rates among combat veterans from Vietnam are as high as 30 per cent for men and 27 per cent for women (Kulka et al. 1990). PTSD often begins within a few weeks of the precipitating event, but can re-occur after symptoms have faded as a result of further trauma or life-events as diverse as trauma anniversaries, interpersonal losses, and changes in health status. Here is the story of Ron, which shows how both the situation and the reaction of the people around him can contribute to the development of PTSD

At the time this happened, I was working in a small hut on an industrial estate. They had been building some more units and had a crane on a lorry to lift things around the site. This was right next to our office. You couldn't see it, because there were no windows on that side of the hut, but you knew it was there . . . I don't know why, but on the day of the accident they were using the crane without stabilizing it by putting the legs onto the ground. The upshot of this was that the crane toppled over and fell onto the building I was in. The first we were aware of things was a lot of shouting and mechanical noises we now know were it toppling. Then there was a great crash and the arm of the crane smashed through the building. I was in there with my mate. Amazingly, neither of us were actually hit by the thing. But we were both trapped by debris from the building. I think I was knocked out for a while because I cannot remember in detail what happened, but it could only be for a minute or two. I wasn't hurt too badly, but I was trapped. The worst part of it all, was just having to wait to get out. I was frightened that the gas pipes were fractured and the image of dying in a fire went through my mind. I hate being unable to move and all sorts of things went through my head about what would happen to me while I couldn't move. I felt really frightened until I could hear people coming to dig us out, and they lifted the heavy stuff off me and I could move . . .

Once I was out, I went to the sick bay and was sent home. I told them I was OK, just 'cos I wanted to get home and get out of it. I was driven home and spent the rest of the day like a zombie. I just phased out. I didn't want to talk about it. Kept myself to myself. I slept OK. I hate missing work so I went in the next day. My mates took me to look at the hut, and they were saying how lucky we were to get out alive. Everyone I met said the same thing! I know they were being friendly, but that made things worse, and I began to think about things more and more. I felt shaky and sick . . . In the end, I had to go home.

The nightmares began a couple of days later. I dreamt that I was in the building – this time I was watching the crane fall even though I didn't in real life and felt trapped as it hit. Each dream was terrifying and I woke up sweating and breathing hard. I could dream two or three times a night. I had to get up and watch TV, have a cup of tea and fag to help me calm down after them . . . I couldn't go back to sleep. I took about eight or nine weeks off work because of all this. I was just too knackered to work.

I was also pretty uptight during this time. I'm usually very easy going. But I ran into problems with the wife because I was so difficult to live with . . .

The dreams gradually got better and I forced myself to go back to work. I had a few panic attacks when I went back to start with because I was working in a temporary building which had no windows, so I panicked at the thought of things that were happening outside. The new office has large windows, and that's OK for me now.

Aetiology of post-traumatic stress disorder

Biological factors

The brain systems involved in PTSD are thought to be those involved in processing emotions and memory, in particular, the amygdala and hippocampus. The hippocampus is responsible for storing and retrieving the memories. It is linked to the amygdala, the area of the brain particularly associated with the formation of conditioned fear responses. Both the hippocampus and the amygdala are activated either in establishing memories of the event and its associated emotions, or in recalling them. Two stress hormones appear particularly implicated in establishing traumatic memories: norepinephrine and cortisol. Increases in these hormones generally enhance memory, although the levels that may occur at times of traumatic stress may actually be toxic to brain tissue and result in neuronal death, damaging the memory systems. Norepinephrine release has been found to produce high states of arousal and fear, and intense visual flashbacks in some, but by no means all, cases (Leskin et al. 1998). Brewin (2001) speculated that flashbacks may occur when information is transferred from the amygdala to the hippocampus. The sympathetic nervous system (see Chapter 3), controlled by the hypothalamus and levels of norepinephrine, is responsible for the high levels of physiological arousal associated with the condition.

Conditioning models

The conditioning model of PTSD (Foa et al. 1989) is based on Mowrer's (1947) two-factor theory. That is, it considers PTSD to be a classically conditioned emotional response. Re-exposure to similar contexts or stimuli re-evokes memories of the event and the conditioned fear response. Avoidance of reminders of the trauma not only prevents distress, but also prevents habituation of the fear response to stimuli associated with the event. As a result, occasional and accidental encounters with relevant stimuli result in flashbacks and other cued memories. A major limitation of this approach is that it cannot explain why many people experience flashbacks and memories in the absence of such cues: memories in the forms of dreams, for example, are frequently reported by those with PTSD. This phenomenon may be better explained by cognitive models of PTSD.

Cognitive models

There are two types of cognitive model of PTSD: social cognitive models that emphasize the massive readjustment often needed to integrate traumatic experiences into the individual's view of the world, and information-processing theories that focus on how trauma-related information is represented in the memory system.

The first social cognitive model of PTSD, developed by Horowitz (1986), was strongly influenced by psychoanalytic theory. He proposed that PTSD occurs when the individual is involved in events that are so horrific they cannot be reconciled with the individual's view of the world. The belief that one may die in an incident, for example, may shatter previous beliefs of invulnerability. To avoid this ego-damaging discrepancy, defence mechanisms of numbing or denial are evoked. However, these compete with a second innate drive, known as the *completion tendency*. This requires the individual to integrate memories of trauma into existing world models or schema: either to make sense of them according to presently held beliefs about the world or to change those beliefs.

The completion tendency maintains trauma-related information in active memory in an attempt to process it. Defence mechanisms try to stop these memories entering consciousness. The symptoms the individual experiences are the result of fluctuating strengths of these competing processes. When the completion tendency breaks through the defence mechanisms, memories intrude into consciousness in the form of flashbacks, nightmares and unwanted thoughts or emotional memories. When the defence mechanisms are effective, the individual experiences periods of numbness or denial. Once the trauma-related information is integrated into general belief systems, the symptoms cease.

Brewin (2001) added a second level of information processing to the conditioning model of PTSD. His model suggested that the individual can both deliberately choose to address their traumatic memories, and that memories may also come to consciousness without deliberate recall. Deliberate processing of traumatic memories involves accessing what Brewin labelled *verbally accessible memories* (VAMs), which can be intentionally retrieved and progressively edited. He termed memories that cannot be deliberately accessed *situationally accessible memories* (SAMs). These are conditioned memories, which often take the form of nightmares or flashbacks. They are triggered by deliberate conscious processing of VAMs or other external, conditioned triggers. Brewin suggested that the hippocampus is the neural centre involved in processing VAMs. The amygdala may be involved in processing the more emotionally laden SAMs. Brewin, like Horowitz, suggested that emotional processing results from a drive towards resolution of conflict between previously held schemas and new information. The activation of SAMs provides the detailed information needed to allow cognitive readjustment to the trauma. Once integration has been achieved, the symptoms of PTSD will resolve.

Psychosocial model

Rather than focus on the cognitive processes involved in PTSD, Joseph et al. (1995b) explored a wider set of factors that influence the development and course of the disorder. These included:

- *Event stimuli:* iconic representations of the event held in immediate memory.
- *Event cognitions:* memories that provide the basis for re-experiencing phenomena or intrusive memories – similar to Brewin's SAMs.
- *Appraisals and reappraisals:* the individual's thoughts about the incident – similar to Brewin's VAMs. These involve interpretation of information relevant to the incident, drawing on past representations and experiences. They may take the form of automatic schemata linked to strong emotional states triggered by stimuli associated with the trauma or more considered attempts to think through and perhaps reappraise the meaning of the event.
- *Coping attempts:* flashbacks and emotional memories of the event may result in coping attempts intended to minimize emotional distress. These usually take the form of avoidance of reminders, memories or similar emotions and activities to those associated with the event. Coping strategies may also involve attempts at inhibiting unwanted memories (although these may prove difficult: see p. 170).
- *Personality:* this will influence the cognitions and emotions experienced at the time of a traumatic incident, the appraisals made in response to it, and subsequent coping strategies. Accordingly, personality has a significant impact on whether or not the individual develops PTSD and its course.
- *Social support:* an important mediator of the response to trauma, perhaps because talking to other people helps the individual assign new meanings to the event and provides support for the expression of negative emotions.

Joseph et al. (1995b) provided evidence linking each domain of their model. Here we examine the linkages between factors associated with two emotions that are predictive of PTSD: shame and guilt. Both emotions are associated with attributions of internal control and a negative outcome ('I could have done something to stop it – and I didn't'). These, in turn, may be driven by the individual's attributional style, a trait (personality) variable. Whether the individual feels guilt or shame will also affect the coping strategies they adopt. Strong feelings of guilt may be associated with intrusive thoughts and images to which the individual responds by attempting some form of reparative action. Shame may evoke attempts at avoidance and denial. Finally, social or crisis support has been shown to reduce long-term trauma following events such as the *Herald of Free Enterprise* disaster in which 193 people died (Joseph et al. 1996).

Two personality constructs appear to be particularly associated with the development of PTSD. Negative affect, or neuroticism, has been found to be predictive of the development of PTSD symptoms in some studies (e.g. Bennett et al. 2001). It may be predictive of PTSD as it is indicative of a propensity to appraise events as negative and threatening, and to dwell on such events. Studies have also found an association between the avoidance and numbing symptoms of PTSD and **alexithymia** (e.g. Fukunishi et al. 1996), characterized as a paucity of emotional experience and awareness, with an associated poverty of imagination and a tendency to focus upon the tangible and mundane (especially perhaps the physical symptoms of emotional responses). This may inhibit the processing of emotional experiences into general schemata, and place the individual at risk for recurrent memories of the frightening event.

Treatment of post-traumatic stress disorder

Preventing PTSD by psychological debriefing

Psychological debriefing is a single-session interview conducted immediately following a traumatic event intended to help those involved cope with their emotional responses to the trauma, and prevent the development of PTSD. It involves encouraging the individual to talk through the event and their emotional reactions to it in detailed and systematic manner. It is thought to aid integration of incident memories into the general memory system. Debriefing is now regularly offered following traumatic incidents, despite increasing questions about its effectiveness. Rose et al. (2002), for example, concluded from their meta-analysis of four well-conducted randomized controlled trials of debriefing that it not only may be ineffective in preventing PTSD, but also may actually increase risk for the disorder. None of the studies using this method found a reduced risk for PTSD in the three to four months following the incident. The two studies that reported longer-term findings found that those who received debriefing had nearly twice the risk of developing PTSD than those who did not receive the intervention. That is, debriefing seems to inhibit long-term recovery from psychological trauma. A number of explanations have been proposed for these findings, although each remains speculative:

- 'secondary traumatization' may occur as a result of further imaginal exposure to a traumatic incident within a short time of the event
- debriefing may 'medicalize' normal distress, and increase the expectancy of developing psychological symptoms in those who would otherwise not have done so
- debriefing may prevent the potentially protective responses of denial and distancing that may occur in the immediate aftermath of a traumatic incident.

Although psychodynamic approaches have been used to some benefit for people with PTSD (Marmar 1991), the most frequently used interventions in the treatment of PTSD are based on cognitive behavioural principles.

Exposure techniques

The principles underpinning exposure methods in the treatment of PTSD are that the individual will ultimately benefit from re-exposure to memories of the event and their associated emotions. The conditioning model suggests that distress lessens as the individual's emotional response to these memories habituates over time. A more cognitive explanation is that exposure leads to reconciliation between memories and the meaning of the traumatic event and pre-existing world schema. Only by accessing and processing these memories will resolution occur.

Exposure therapy may lead to an initial exacerbation of distress as upsetting images, previously avoided where possible, are deliberately recollected. To minimize this distress and to prevent dropout from therapy, Leskin et al. (1998) recommended a graded exposure process in which the individual initially talks about particular elements of the traumatic event at a level of detail they choose over several occasions until they no longer respond with a stress response. Any new, and potentially more distressing, memories are avoided at this time, and become the focus of the next levels of intervention. Reactivation of memories by this procedure involves describing the experience in detail, focusing on what happened, the thoughts and emotions experienced at the time, and any memories that the incident triggered. This core approach may be augmented by a variety of cognitive behavioural techniques including relaxation training and cognitive restructuring. Relaxation may help the individual control their arousal at the time of recalling the event or at other times in the day when they are feeling tense or on edge. Cognitive restructuring may help the individual address any distorted cognitions they had in response to the event and make them less threatening ('I'm going to die! . . . It felt like I was going to die, but actually that was more my panic than reality . . .').

A number of studies have shown exposure-based therapy to be superior to no treatment and alternative active interventions including supportive counselling and relaxation therapy without exposure (Keane et al. 1989). Foa et al. (1991), for example, randomly allocated female rape victims to either a waiting list control condition, self-instruction training, supportive counselling or an exposure programme. Participants in each of the active interventions evidenced greater gains than those in the waiting list condition. Immediately following the intervention period, participants in the self-instruction training condition fared best. By three-month follow-up, however, those in the exposure programme reported significantly less intrusive memories and arousal than participants in the other conditions. Similar results were reported by Marks et al. (1996) in a comparison of relaxation, exposure alone, cognitive restructuring alone, and exposure plus cognitive restructuring. By the end of the intervention phase, all the other treatments proved superior to relaxation, with no differences in effectiveness between them. By three- and six-month follow-up, the exposure programme proved superior. It seems that self-instruction and other cognitive techniques may help participants cope with the anxiety and other emotions evoked in the early stages of exposure programmes, while exposure to traumatic memories is critical to long-term benefit. The optimal treatment seems to involve a combination of self-instruction training or other cognitive strategies in the early stages of therapy combined with gradual exposure to traumatic memories.

Treating people with PTSD may not require large amounts of specialist training. Gillespie et al. (2002) taught health care staff with minimal background in cognitive behavioural therapy how to provide an exposure-based intervention for PTSD in response to a large bomb which exploded in the small Northern Irish town of Omagh in 1998. Staff received a two-day workshop plus telephone contact with an expert in the treatment of PTSD and therapy supervision. The effectiveness of their intervention was similar to those reported in previous studies involving expert therapists.

Eye movement desensitization and reprocessing (EMDR)

The most recent, and controversial, treatment of PTSD, known as EMDR, was discovered by chance by Shapiro (1995). She noticed that while walking in the woods her disturbing thoughts began to disappear, and when recalled were less upsetting than previously. This change was associated with her eyes spontaneously moving rapidly backwards and forwards in an upward diagonal. Since then, the procedure has been developed into a standardized intervention and subject to a number of clinical trials in the treatment of PTSD.

Treatment typically involves recall of target memories by the client as visual images along with a negative cognition that goes with the image, framed in the present tense ('I am terrified'). The client next rates the strength of emotion evoked by this process. They are then asked to track the therapist's finger as it is moved increasingly quickly back and forth across their line of vision. After 24 such movements, the client is instructed to 'Blank it out' or 'Let it go', and asked to rate their level of emotion. This procedure is repeated until the client experiences minimal distress to the presence of the image and negative cognition. If no changes occur, the direction of eye movements is changed.

EMDR incorporates exposure to elements of the trauma stimulus. An important question is therefore whether the addition of the eye movements enhances the effect of exposure. This does not seem to be the case.

While EMDR is certainly more effective than no treatment, it appears no more effective than standard exposure programmes. Davidson and Parker (2001) used meta-analysis to examine the effectiveness of EMDR in the treatment of PTSD in comparison to no treatment, non-specific treatment and the exposure methods described above. While their analyses indicated a modest benefit for EMDR when compared to no treatment or non-specific treatments, its benefits were similar or less than those resulting from exposure approaches. In one such study, Devilly and Spence (1999) randomly allocated people with PTSD into either an exposure-based programme combined with cognitive challenge of irrational trauma-related cognitions or EMDR. Combining data from a number of measures of PTSD revealed a clear advantage for the exposure group in comparison to EMDR immediately after the intervention was finished, and at two-week and three-month follow-up. The differences between the two groups became larger over time.

Pharmacological interventions

A variety of drug types have been used in the treatment of PTSD to some effect, including antidepressant MAOIs, SSRIs and tricyclics (see Chapter 3). Stein et al. (2002), for example, conducted a meta-analysis on nine short-term studies of antidepressants in the treatment of PTSD. The overall effects of the interventions were significantly greater reductions than placebo on global measures of functioning and the core PTSD symptoms of intrusion and avoidance. SSRIs seemed the most pharmacological effective intervention.

Recovered memory

Since the late 1980s, a number of clinicians have argued that many adults who were traumatized as children had repressed all memories of these events, and that these memories could be recovered only in the course of psychological therapy. In a seminal text, Bass and Davis (1988) argued that such repression is not unusual, and advised therapists to accept their 'recovered memories' of sexual abuse, and to suspend disbelief even if they found some parts of their history doubtful. Memories have been recovered in considerable detail up to 40 years after the alleged trauma. Individuals may describe partial or complete memory loss for periods of months or years while they are growing up. Between 20 and 60 per cent of women either in therapy or who have completed therapy report periods of forgetting some or all of the abuse they have experienced (e.g. Loftus and Ketcham 1994).

The nature of the abuse reported varies considerably, although it is often repeated sexual abuse; 6 per cent of telephone calls received by the

British False Memory Society in the mid-1990s reported incidents of ritual satanic abuse, while 18 per cent of callers to its US equivalent reported similar allegations. No cases of this level of abuse have been substantiated in either country, including those subject to in-depth judicial review. Individuals identified as abusers, usually parents or other family members, frequently deny the episodes and claim that they have been wrongfully accused: that is, that the recovered memories of abuse are false memories. Recovered or false, the negative impact these accusations can have on families is often profound.

Explanations of recovered memory

The recovered memory phenomenon has engendered considerable controversy and debate. Three differing explanations for this phenomenon have been proposed.

Accurate accounts

Recovered memories are accurate accounts of previously forgotten events, and should be accepted as such even in the absence of corroborative evidence. Explanations of why these memories are apparently forgotten focus on both unconscious mechanisms that prevent the laying down of easily retrievable memories at the time of any traumatic incident and problems of recall. The first involves a process known as dissociation. This is an altered state of consciousness in which ordinary perceptual and cognitive functioning is impaired: events feel unreal and distant from the individual. Dissociation may occur during the traumatic experience and act as a defence that prevents the individual from experiencing the full emotional impact of what is happening. Retrieval of associated memories is poor, as little if any ordinary conscious processing took place at encoding. What memories there are may be fragmented, but vivid and intense. Hunter (1997) described three forms of dissociation that have been reported by child abuse victims: out-of-body experiences in which events were seen as happening to someone else who looked like the victim, conscious attempts to 'blank out' memories of the assaults during or after they had happened, and the creation of an imaginary world to which the respondent could escape and feel safe during or after the abuse. Failure to recall events is thought to be the result of denial and long-term dissociation that prevent the retrieval of information once in memory stores.

Illusions

Recovered memories are illusions: false memories resulting from the therapy process itself (Zola 1998). Such memories are 'implanted' by therapists who have decided that the patient is an abuse victim and who use therapeutic techniques to persuade the client to remember these forgotten episodes of abuse in order to 'recover'. The likelihood of suggestive influences leading to memory errors is increased by the perceived authority and trustworthiness of the therapist, and their repetition and plausibility.

Normal forgetting

Recovered memories are not 'special', but are the result of normal forgetting (e.g. Loftus and Ketcham 1994). This explanation may be particularly relevant to single traumatic episodes, but has more difficulty in accounting for the forgetting of repeated traumatic episodes.

Evidence of recovered memory

Protagonists on each side of the debate have interpreted research findings both to support their case and question those who disagree with them. The debate has drawn on research related to normal memory processes as well as more clinical issues.

Age at time of incident

Recovered memories are sometimes described from before the age of 2, and often in significant detail (Loftus and Ketcham 1994). Morton et al. (1995), for example, reported that 26 per cent of allegations involved abuse that began when the claimant was aged between 0 and 2 years old. This, argue opponents of recovered memory, makes such memories unlikely to be accurate. Most people are unable to recollect experiences from the first two to three years of their lives, as the cortical areas that eventually become the sites for permanent memory storage are undergoing a process of maturation at this time that makes them unable to process and store information needed for long-term recall.

Evidence of emotionally intense memory distortion

Some clinicians (e.g. Terr 1991) have argued that trauma-related memories are not subject to the normal processes of memory decay and distortion over time, and are therefore more accurate than 'normal' long-term memories. This claim can be challenged, partly by the mechanisms of avoidance and dissociation described above that are thought to interfere with the accurate perception of events. Empirical evidence also suggests this is not the case. Neisser and Harsch (1992), for example, asked students one day after the *Challenger* disaster, in which a space shuttle burst into flames on lift-off, to describe their personal memories of the event: where they were at the time of the incident, and so on. Two years later, when asked to redescribe their memories, the accounts of one-third of the students differed substantially from their initial memories. Of note was that there was little relationship between the accuracy of recalled 'facts' and students' confidence in their ability to recall them. The *Challenger* disaster may not have been sufficiently traumatic for those not directly involved to result in unchangeable memory traces. Whether more salient emotional events can evoke differing memory processes is unclear, although a number of case studies in which long-term emotional memories show discrepancies with actual events suggest not (Zola 1998). Of course, this argument may challenge the accuracy of recall of events, but not statements as to whether or not particular incidents actually happened.

Corroboration

Gaining corroborative evidence of child sexual abuse is clearly problematic. Nevertheless, Feldman-Summers and Pope (1994) found some degree of corroborative evidence in 47 per cent of the cases they examined, including the abuser acknowledging some or all of the remembered abuse or someone else reporting abuse by the same perpetrator. Similar levels of corroboration, 41 per cent, were reported in an unrelated survey of British clinical psychologists (see Brewin and Andrews 1998).

Conditions of recall

Clearly, if recovered memory is a therapy-generated phenomenon, the majority of memories should reappear during therapy. This does not always appear to be the case. Feldman-Summers and Pope (1994) found that although over half such memories were recovered in the context of therapy, 44 per cent of their respondents stated that recovery had been triggered exclusively in other contexts. By contrast, Goodyear-Smith et al. (1997) reported summary data from several papers indicating that in over 80 per cent of cases of sexual abuse, memories had emerged while complainants were undergoing psychotherapy.

Attempts to forget

A key factor in the repressed memory debate is the assumption that those who remember childhood trauma as an adult have used unconscious coping mechanisms that result in them 'forgetting' the trauma they have undergone. If this is the case, then one would assume that a significant percentage of people who undergo other traumas as a child would engage in similar coping strategies and have similar problems of recall. Evidence to suggest this may not be the case can be found in studies of children who have gone through traumatic events which are a matter of historical record, including kidnap, the Holocaust and witnessing parental murder, and can accurately recall them (see Zola 1998). In each case, there was no evidence of repressed memory; indeed, many people had very vivid and detailed recall of events they would like to have been able to forget.

Proponents of the repressed memory hypothesis counter these data by suggesting that sexual abuse is different from other trauma and that it has specific and unique consequences for coping. They argue that because abuse is usually carried out by parents or significant others rather than strangers and occurs in isolation rather than with companions, the effects are unique. It has also been suggested that memories of single one-off events of trauma are generally retained, whereas repeated and prolonged trauma is repressed (Terr 1991). The exact memory mechanisms that may result in these differences are unclear.

Evidence of the creation of false traumatic memories

Those who argue against the concept of recovered memory suggest that such memories result from therapists' questioning and planting suggestions of childhood abuse in people to whom this has not happened. There is a large body of evidence suggesting this is a possible explanation for at least some cases of recovered memory. In a naturalistic example of this, Piaget (1954) as an adult was able to recall in some detail memories of his being kidnapped as a child of 2 years of age. This despite the event never having occurred, and being a story told to him by a family nurse. More experimental evidence has been provided by Loftus and Coan (1998). In one study, adults were asked about childhood events, one of which had never occurred, in the presence of other family members, who 'reminded' them of the event during the interview. Subsequently 6 of the 24 participants in the study 'remembered' the false episode as real and provided additional details about it. Using a similar method, Hyman et al. (1995) asked college students about various childhood events that had never happened, including an overnight hospitalization for an ear infection. At the end of the first interview, in which no participants 'recalled' the false events, they were encouraged to try to remember more information about them before the next interview. During a second interview, a quarter of the participants remembered detailed information about the false event.

Retraction

Although the percentage of people to do so is unknown, many people who recall traumatic memories eventually retract these memories and claim that the events never actually occurred: that they are a consequence of within therapy processes. Here, for example, is the testimony of Clare, who retracted her claims of sexual abuse by a family member. Her story here focuses on the power that her therapist had over her, how he shaped her 'memories', and how she latterly recognized his negative influence over her:

> Looking back, it's difficult to see how things could have got this far, and been so destructive. How could a relationship with a therapist become the only – the total – focus of my life for three years? How could I have sold my soul, my very self, to another human being? How could I have fallen under the spell of a man who, it turns out, had problems in his own life; a man so inadequate himself that he needed me and others to be 'sick' in order for him to be powerful and strong. I trusted this man with my life – my soul. I shared everything with him – my dreams, the desires of my life. I confessed my sins to him. He was my partner, mother, father, sister, best friend, and teacher. My role model. He was everything to me. Whatever he said, I agreed with. How could he be wrong? My life became so linked with his life, my ability to think for myself disappeared. I thought what he wanted me to think. I believed what he wanted me to believe. I became what he wanted me to become.

Overview of the evidence

Brewin and Andrews (1998) considered the evidence relevant to each of these explanations. They suggested the present state of the evidence is

- the age at which the majority of events are said to have occurred extends beyond the period of the infant amnesia
- corroboration occurs with reasonable frequency given the nature of the alleged incidents
- the content of most recovered memories concern a variety of events known to occur with reasonable frequency, and is not limited to child sexual abuse
- well-trained therapists not using inappropriate techniques have reported clients recovering memories
- the context of recall is not limited to the therapist's office.

On this basis, Brewin and Andrews suggested that the evidence is not sufficient to rule out the possibility that recovered memory may genuinely occur, at least in some cases, and that each case should be taken on its own merit. Nevertheless, because there is serious doubt over the accuracy of at least some recovered memories, a number of professional bodies have developed guidelines about how clinicians should respond to reports of 'recovered memory'. Those of the Australian Psychological Society (www.psychosociety.com.au) are typical:

- 'memories' that are reported either spontaneously or following the use of special procedures in therapy may be accurate, inaccurate, fabricated or a mixture of these
- the level of belief in memories, all the emotion associated with the memory, does not necessarily relate to the accuracy of the memory
- the available scientific and clinical evidence does not allow accurate, inaccurate, or fabricated memories to be distinguished in the absence of independent corroboration.

Psychologists/therapists should:

- be alert to the ways they can shape the memories reported by clients through the expectations they convey, the comments they make, the questions they ask, and the responses they give to clients
- be aware that clients are susceptible to subtle suggestions and reinforcements, whether intended or unintended
- be empathic and supportive of the reports of clients, while ensuring they do not jump to conclusions about the truth or falsity of their recollections of the past
- inform any client who recovers a memory of abuse that it may be an accurate memory of an actual event, may be an altered or distorted memory of an actual event, or maybe a false memory of an event that did not happen.

Dissociative identity disorder

A defining characteristic of individuals with a diagnosis of dissociative identity disorder (DID) is that they behave as if they possess two or more distinct identities or personalities, known as *alters*. In contrast to the past, where people with DID (or multiple personality as it was previously known) reported relatively few alter personalities, the average number of alters is about 15, and some individuals exhibit more than 100. According to DSM-IV-TR, the diagnostic criteria for DID are:

- the presence of two or more distinct identities or personality states, each with its own relatively enduring pattern of perceiving, relating to and thinking about the environment and self
- at least two of these identities or personality states recurrently take control of the person's behaviour
- inability to recall important personal information that is too extensive to be explained by ordinary forgetfulness
- the disturbance is not due to the direct physiological effects, substance abuse or a general medical condition.

Aetiology of dissociative identity disorder

The nature and, indeed, existence of 'true' DID is just as hotly debated as the existence of recovered memories, and the arguments are very similar. Some contend that its existence is self-evident, and that there are too many people experiencing these symptoms to deny the reality of the problem. Others reject the concept, arguing that the symptoms are invented by the individuals reporting them, or even implanted in their consciousness by over-zealous therapists. The two dominant theories of DID are that it is either the result of childhood trauma or a socially constructed system created by the affected individual and shaped by the therapist.

Childhood trauma

Proponents of the childhood trauma model (e.g. Gleaves 1996) suggest that the experience of severe trauma during childhood produces a mental 'splitting' or dissociation as part of a defensive reaction. The abused child learns to dissociate, or enter a self-induced hypnotic state, placing the memory of the abuse in the subconscious as a means of coping with the trauma. These dissociated parts of the individual 'split' into alter personalities that, in adulthood, manifest themselves to help the individual cope with stressful situations and express resentments or other feelings that are unacceptable to the primary personality.

The number of alters depends on a number of factors, such as the severity and time period of the abuse. Each alter has a job within the system. Most alters protect the host personality from memories of the trauma. It is common for each alter to guard a particular memory. Some alters are aware of other alters; others do not know of their existence.

Most alters do not see themselves in the physical body they are in: children see themselves as four feet tall, girls see themselves as women, and so on. They may be of different nationalities and races. Some may speak different languages. Alters may have different facial expressions and different mannerisms. There are many different kinds of alters and all systems are different, but there are some of the more common types of alter, here described by someone living with a partner who experienced DID (www.mpdfriends.homestead.com):

- *Host:* this person can either be the original birth child, or can be an alter that is the main personality presented to the outside world.

- *Original Birth Child:* this person may be awake and functioning, or said to be asleep. This person is sometimes referred to as the core personality.

- *Child Alters:* child alters (or 'littles' as they are affectionately known) can range from the age of an infant upwards. These are the alters that took much of the abuse, and often carry a large number of memories. They display behaviour that is appropriate for their age. Often they carry much pain, both physical and emotional.

- *Teens:* most systems have teen alters. These alters were often the ones who went to school, and were out for those years.

- *Gatekeepers:* some systems have a gatekeeper, who directs and has control of the body. They may also control the length of time an alter is in body. They do not often come out themselves, but just seem happy to observe and direct the others.

- *Internal Self Helpers:* these internal self helpers keep the alters safe. They usually know all the alters and the details of the abuse the alters endured. They are very helpful in therapy, and help the therapist understand why a particular alter feels the way they do, or decide the action of a particular alter. They also decide what information is passed to other alters and to the host.

- *Protectors:* protectors protect(!) the system from outside threats. They can usually talk hard, or fight, or do whatever is necessary to keep the system safe. They often use anger as a defence. They are especially protective of the child alters.

Switches between alters often result from some sort of stress or upset, which causes another alter, usually a protector alter, to emerge. Stresses can include comments by others, seeing the abuser, an unexpected touch, arguments and aggression – even having sex. Sel (1997) suggested that the individual has an ecosystem of alters who compete with each other to gain control over the output channels. The alter that most successfully maintains an emotional equilibrium is most likely to be best adapted. When the individual moves to a different context, different cognitive schema may be more adaptive and the dominant alter will switch.

Socio-cognitive model

By contrast, socio-cognitive theorists (e.g. Merskey 1992; Spanos 1994) have argued that DID is a set of beliefs and behaviours constructed by the individual themselves in response to personal stress, therapist pressure and societal legitimization of the construct of 'multiple personality'. They suggest that DID has become a legitimate way for many people to understand and express their failures and frustrations, as well as a tactic for the manipulation of others. According to this account, individuals diagnosed as having DID learn to portray themselves as possessing multiple selves and to reorganize and elaborate on their personal biography to make it consistent with their understanding of what it means to be a 'multiple'. That is, they actively construct their various selves. They have further argued that psychotherapists have contributed to the development of this disorder by encouraging clients to construe them-selves in this way and by providing official legitimation for the different identities their patients enact.

The two poles of this argument are perhaps best considered in a large review by Spanos (1994) in which he gave the socio-cognitive critique of the disorder, and the defence of the psychiatric model provided by Gleaves (1996). This next section considers their arguments in some detail.

Problems of prevalence

The prevalence of DID has changed over time, increasing substantially since the 1980s. Spanos (1994) argued that if DID were a naturally occur-ring state, this degree of change would not occur, and that it represents an increase in the social construction of the condition by therapists and clients. Spanos further noted that among 'investigators who are sym-pathetic to DID', diagnostic rates are extremely high. Modestin's (1992) survey of Swiss psychiatrists, for example, suggested that about 1 per cent of cases seen within their psychiatric system were diagnosed as having DID. He also found that while 90 per cent of the psychiatrists he surveyed had not seen a case of DID, three reported seeing more than twenty people with the disorder: 66 per cent of the cases were reported by less than 0.1 per cent of the psychiatrists surveyed. He suggested that these clinicians may have either misidentified symptoms as evidence of DID or encouraged their clients to construct various manifestations of the disorder.

Gleaves responded to this argument by suggesting that it is not sur-prising there were differences in observation rates among differing clinicians. According to Gleaves, this may have been a result of different referral rates, an unwillingness among some clinicians to give a diagnosis of DID, and a reluctance among the same clinicians to ask the questions that would lead to this diagnosis being assigned. He also suggested that the increase in reported prevalence may be a function of previous misdiagnoses as a result of it being a relatively new diagnostic category, increased awareness of the prevalence and problems of child abuse, and increased interest in dissociative states. Finally, he suggested that a critical factor may simply be the trend toward a lessening of scepticism about the condition among therapists. He cited a number of studies involving large numbers of patients and clinicians (e.g. Ross et al. 1989) in which the diagnosis of DID was more evenly spread across psychi-atrists than the study of Modestin (1992). He also noted that there are now several methods of assessment of DID, all of which have been found to have high reliability and inter-rater agreement (Steinberg et al. 1993). This consistency of diagnosis using standardized measures should indicate a reliable diagnosis, unbiased by therapist beliefs.

Teaching multiplicity

Spanos's most critical attack on clinicians who diagnose DID is that they lead their patients either covertly or overtly to report the presence of alters. He noted that proponents of DID have described a large body of symptoms that indicate the possible presence of the disorder and justify probing to confirm a diagnosis, including depression, periods of missing time, headaches and impaired concentration. One clinician even argued that a smooth complexion may be indicative because the regular switching between personalities prevents the formation of wrinkles. Merskey (1992) suggested that highly leading and suggestive procedures are frequently used, to the point that some therapists insisted to doubting patients that they were multiples and supplied them with the names of their alters. Allison and Schwarz (1980) contended that clients are frequently reluctant to accept they are multiples and, under these circumstances, should be actively persuaded by their therapist.

The generation of alters often occurs in the privacy of the consultation following use of hypnotic techniques. Spanos (1994) argued that the use of persuasive techniques or suggestion while under hypnosis may itself result in some individuals reporting alters and subsequently behaving as if they were 'multiples'. The role of hypnosis in generating alters was challenged by Gleaves (1996), who noted that the percentage of patients diagnosed with DID following hypnosis varied between 4 and 27 per cent across studies. Ross and Norton (1989), for example, found no differences between the clinical presentation, symptomatology, or number of alters, of people who were, or were not, treated using hypnosis.

Finding evidence of suggestion in clinical sessions is difficult, as their content is rarely made public. However, Spanos was able to review the transcripts of the interview of a suspected murderer, Ken Bianchi, who was found to have DID by Schwarz (1981) and who confessed to a murder perpetrated by an alter named Steve. Spanos argued that the instructions given to Bianchi led him to report having an alter, as they repeatedly informed him that there was another individual within, who could be addressed. When Spanos et al. (1985) used this procedure with naive participants under hypnosis in an experimental study, most participants enacted the symptoms of DID by adopting a different name, referred to their primary personality in the third person, and displayed amnesia for their alter personalities after termination of the hypnotic interview. The participants maintained their role successfully in a second session by exhibiting marked and consistent differences between their primary and secondary personalities on a variety of psychological tests.

Gleaves (1996) responded to findings such as this by arguing that while they raise interesting questions about the capacities and workings of the human mind, they do not indicate that DID is necessarily created within the therapy session. According to Gleaves, these analogue studies produced phenomena that were only superficially similar to DID. Participants did not experience any of the established features of DID, such as episodes of time loss, depersonalization or derealization, or hearing voices, in any of these studies. According to Gleaves, just because some people can replicate some of the symptoms of DID does not invalidate the concept: a person may replicate depression, anxiety and so on, without challenging the reality of the condition.

Further evidence countering the role of the therapist in developing a diagnosis of DID can be found from studies showing significant evidence of DID pathology prior to any therapist contact. Coons et al. (1988), for example, reported that amnesia (a core symptom of DID) was present in all of 50 of their sample of people with DID at the time of their first presentation to the mental health system. Gleaves (1996) also reported evidence of symptoms including journals in differing handwriting or memories of dissociative experiences going back to childhood. Some of this evidence could be verified by family members and friends.

Motivation, legitimation and DID

Spanos (1994) argued that people may seek or collude with a diagnosis of DID as a means of gaining the support of their therapist and others. He suggested that the idea of being a multiple may provide some people with a viable and face-saving way to account for personal problems as well as a dramatic means of gaining concern and attention from significant others. Spanos suggested that people who seek help and are diagnosed with DID are often unhappy and insecure people with a strong investment in gaining the interest and approval of their therapist. By contrast, therapists are highly valued by their clients and their suggestions are treated seriously. This combination of therapists 'on the look out' for signs of DID and clients wanting to create a good impression with their, valued, therapist may result in a gradual shaping of responses to fit those of DID. Spanos (1994) did not claim that people with DID are necessarily faking their multiplicity. Rather, they have come to adopt a view of themselves that is congruent with the view conveyed to them by their therapist, to adopt and believe in their presentation as someone with multiple alters.

The wider social environment may also be supportive of their diagnosis. Spanos (1994) argued that support for DID has almost taken on the characteristics of a social movement. People with DID and therapists participate regularly in workshops and conferences, and both those affected and their therapists frequently have access to national newsletters that provide ongoing legitimization for the multiple-self enactments. All this may reinforce the presentation of self as someone with multiple alters. Gleaves (1996) contended that this is not always the case, and that therapy is not always easy for patients with DID. Many people with the symptoms of DID experience hostile reactions from professionals and public alike. Many are told they are lying or faking, or even that their therapist is crazy.

Gleaves (1996) noted that some protagonists have suggested that some people with DID are attention seeking. By contrast, he contended that many are actually secretive about their condition and conceal their disorder for fear of being labelled as crazy and typically have an avoidant style that inhibits disclosure of their abuse histories (Kluft 1994). This speculation was supported by Fink and Golinkoff (1990), who found that people with DID evidenced relatively low levels of histrionic behaviours and emotional lability, and were more intellectualized, obsessive and introvert than a comparison group of people without the disorder. However, while this may indicate a general unwillingness to portray themselves to the general public as DID sufferers, it does not counter the argument that expression of multiple personalities develops over time as a result of therapist–client interactions.

DID and child abuse

Findings that people with DID report extremely high rates of childhood sexual or physical abuse (e.g. Ross et al. 1991) has led some theorists to suggest that dissociation as a result of repeated sexual abuse is almost a defining characteristic of DID. In response to this, Spanos (1994) argued that the apparently high level of association between child sexual abuse and the phenomena of DID may both be spurious and the result of therapist and client beliefs about the nature of the phenomenon. He suggested that:

- Child sexual abuse is relatively common in the USA, and rates are particularly high among those who seek psychiatric help. High rates among people who develop DID may therefore be indicative of these high background rates rather than indicative of risk for DID.
- Because some clinicians consider a history of sexual abuse to be a possible sign of DID, they may be more likely to expose abused than non-abused patients to hypnotic interviews and other procedures that result in 'multiplicity'.
- Some patients with DID do not remember being abused until their multiplicity is discovered in the course of therapy. Any recovered memories should be treated with some caution (see above).
- Therapists may disbelieve DID patients who claim not to have been abused and may be probed repeatedly in an attempt to unearth such memories. When patients believe they may be fantasizing, their uncertainty may be presented to them as evidence that they are unwilling to face the fact of their abuse (Bliss 1986).
- Many patients with DID report not just sexual abuse, but also that this was ritualistic and long-term. These histories are usually identified following a series of leading questions under hypnotic suggestion, and none have been found to be substantiated.
- Some of the data related to abuse are not in accordance with data on memory recall and typical patterns of abuse. Ross et al. (1991) reported on the age of earliest sexual abuse reported by their patient group. Over a quarter reported being abused before

the age of 3 years, and 10 per cent reported being abused before the age of 1 year. These ages are much younger than is typical in cases of sexual abuse (see Chapter 10) and prior to the establishment of neural substrates that permit long-term recall (see p. 212).

In a more recent defence of the concept of DID, Gleaves et al. (2001) considered that it achieves the criteria for a valid and meaningful diagnosis, perhaps more than many other more accepted psychiatric diagnoses. The diagnostic process, including interview and psychometrically validated questionnaires, can both reliably detect the disorder and discriminate it from others. Most people with the condition experience all the core primary dissociative symptoms (identity confusion, identity alteration, amnesia, depersonalization and derealization), unlike those with, say, schizophrenia (see Chapter 6). Finally, the diagnostic label has predictive utility: it can predict the types of problems an individual will experience in the future. These factors they argued, in combination with their refutation of the socio-cognitive model provide evidence of the validity of the disorder as a true representation of the experiences of some individuals.

As with recovered memories, it is difficult to dismiss the phenomenon of DID. It is also possible to see how on some occasions, at least, the behaviours associated with DID could be generated within the therapy session. Perhaps, therefore, DID should be accorded the same cautionary acceptance as that given to recovered memory. Perhaps that last word should go to a sceptical and cautious clinician, who told me:

> I believe. Once you have seen someone like this, it is difficult to see how they could be constructing it. When they switch from alter to alter, the differences in speech, their manner, things they tell you, and so on, are so different and rapid – and so consistent over time. It is difficult to see how this could be constructed by the individual.

Treatment of dissociative identity disorder

Not surprisingly, both Spanos (1994) and Gleaves (1996) disagreed over the treatment of DID. Spanos contended that the goal of treatment is to help clients accept that their alter identities are real personalities rather than self-generated fantasies. Gleaves contended that the opposite is true. He argued that the central goal of treatment should be to help the individual understand that the alters are in fact self-generated, not to convince them that they are real people. He argued that therapists working with people with DID should emphasize the fundamental nature of the disorder as a difficulty in integrating various aspects of the personality rather than a profusion of personalities (Fraser 1992).

Even among therapists that accept the reality of the multiple selves, the goals of therapy differ. Some (e.g. Spiegel 1993) suggest the goal of therapy is to move the individual towards a sense of integrated functioning. This can be achieved by:

- recalling repressed memories
- detraumatizing these memories so that recall does not result in reversion to other alters
- integrating the alters and primary personality.

Techniques such as psychodynamic therapy and hypnosis have been used to help individuals recover memories from the past (e.g. Kluft 1999). These approaches have to be used with care because the individual may revert to another alter when exposed to traumatic memories. In addition, some alters may take on a 'protective' role and attempt to protect the primary personality from suffering the pain of recalling traumatic experiences by, for example, becoming self-destructive or aggressive (see Kelly 1993).

Once memories have been recovered or recalled, they can be detraumatized using exposure techniques similar to those used in the treatment of PTSD. Because the reaction of someone with DID is to avoid recall of memories, this type of exposure work is difficult, and the traumatic nature of the memories may usefully be minimized at any one time. Advocates of EMDR suggest that this may form a useful intervention when used in combination with relaxation techniques, as this technique is thought to assist the person recall memories without the full-blown emotional effects (but see the cautionary results in relation to PTSD).

For most therapists, the ultimate goal of therapy is to integrate the various alters into one cohesive personality, a process known as fusion. In this state, the person is aware of all their behaviours and thoughts and accepts them as their own. Oke and Kanigsberg (1991) used a combination of play, guided imagery, life skills teaching, projective techniques and group therapy to help bring awareness and understanding of other selves, and through this eventually achieve cohesion between all alters. Unfortunately, the effectiveness of this and similar types of intervention is limited to descriptions of interventions with no outcome data or case reports, which by their very nature tend to be positive (few therapists like to broadcast their failures widely, and most journals are biased against publishing 'negative results'). Their efficacy or otherwise has yet to be fully investigated.

A more fundamental cautionary note has come from people with DID themselves. Many sub-personalities reject integration as a therapeutic goal, as they see integration as a form of death (Spiegel 1999). In support of this stance, Rossel (1998) argued that in a disintegrating postmodern world, it is of little benefit to attempt to achieve integration. Instead, the individual should be open to the experience of shifting between alters, which should be construed as a positive and comfortable experience, not a negative, destructive one.

Chapter summary

1 PTSD has three central symptoms: intrusive memories, attempts at avoidance of these memories and high levels of arousal.

2 The neurological substrates of PTSD are the amygdala and hippocampus that together mediate fear and memory, and link the two together. High arousal is mediated by the sympathetic nervous system.

3 The conditioning model of PTSD provides a partial explanation of the phenomenon, but cognitive models such as that of Brewin provide a more in-depth understanding.

4 Clinical incident debriefing is often provided at traumatic incidents. Evidence is mounting that this may actually inhibit long-term recovery from psychological trauma.

5 Exposure methods may prove the best intervention for PTSD, particularly when combined with strategies to help clients cope with any emotional distress triggered by the therapeutic process.

6 EMDR appears to be of no more benefit than exposure methods.

7 Since the 1980s, an increasing number of people have begun to report recovered memories of trauma, usually sexual trauma, experienced in childhood.

8 Three explanations have been proposed to account for this phenomenon: the memories are real and have been hidden as a result of a number of unconscious self-protective mechanisms; they are the result of therapists' shaping clients apparent recall of past events that did not in reality occur; they are incidents forgotten as a result of normal forgetting processes.

9 Arguments about which of these explanations are correct have focused on a number of issues: the age at the time of the incident, distortions in memory over time, mixed levels of corroboration of events, and experimental evocation of false memories.

10 Brewin and others have suggested that while some memories may be false, others may be truly repressed and recovered. Each case should be considered on its own merits.

11 The clinical model suggests that DID is a response to repeated childhood sexual trauma involving severe dissociation at the time of the trauma, resulting in the development of 'alters' or alternative personalities.

12 The socio-cognitive model suggests this is a response to therapist and social pressure to behave in a way that suggests multiple personalities.

13 Debate about which of these models has focused on differing explanations of the prevalence of the disorder, whether therapists can 'teach multiplicity', social and therapist pressures to present with DID, and the relationship between childhood abuse and DID.

14 While some cases of DID may be created by the process of therapy, others may represent a 'real' clinical condition. Each case should be considered on its own merits.

For discussion

1 How should we treat people following a major trauma?

2 What factors may contribute to the development of PTSD?

3 Is there such a thing as 'recovered memory'?

4 What are the causes of DID?

Further reading

Brewin, C.R. and Andrews, B. (1998) Recovered memories of trauma: phenomenology and cognitive mechanisms, *Clinical Psychology Review*, 18: 949–70.

Buckley, T.C., Blanchard, E.B. and Neill, W.T. (2000) Information processing and PTSD: a review of the empirical literature, *Clinical Psychology Review*, 20: 1041–65.

Cason, D.R., Resick, P.A. and Weaver, T.L. (2002) Schematic integration of traumatic events, *Clinical Psychology Review*, 22: 131–53.

Gleaves, D.H. (1996) The sociocognitive model of dissociative identity disorder: a reexamination of the evidence, *Psychological Bulletin*, 120: 42–59.

Gleaves, D.H., May, M.C. and Cardena, E. (2001) An examination of the diagnostic validity of dissociative identity disorder, *Clinical Psychology Review*, 21: 577–608.

Joseph, S., Williams, R. and Yule, W. (1995) Psychosocial perspectives on post-traumatic stress, *Clinical Psychology Review*, 15: 515–44.

Loftus, E.F. (1996) The myth of repressed memory and the realities of science, *Clinical Psychology: Science and Practice*, 3: 356–62.

Spanos, N.P. (1994) Multiple identity enactments and multiple personality disorder: a sociocognitive perspective, *Psychological Bulletin*, 116: 143–65.

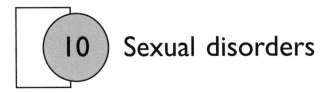

Sexual disorders

There are two categories of sexual disorders: *sexual dysfunctions*, which involve a problem in sexual response, and *paraphilias*, which involve repeated and intense sexual urges, behaviour or fantasies in response to objects or situations that society deems inappropriate. This chapter examines both types of problems. It considers problems that some people experience during the sexual act, focusing on the male problem of failing to achieve an erection and its female 'equivalent', known as vaginismus, and considers how these may be treated. It then describes the aetiology and treatment of paedophilia and transvestism. Finally, the chapter considers the problems faced when an individual questions their very sexual identity and wishes to change it: gender identity disorder. By the end of the chapter, you should have an understanding of:

- ◆ The nature and aetiology of erectile dysfunction, vaginismus, paedophilia, transvestism and gender identity disorder
- ◆ The types of interventions used to treat each disorder, and their relative effectiveness.

Sexual dysfunctions

The sexual dysfunctions are those that involve a problem with the sexual response. They include disorders of desire, such as an aversion to sexual activity and low sexual drive, problems of orgasm including premature ejaculation in men and a failure to achieve orgasm in both men and women. Here, we consider two conditions: erectile dysfunction in men, and a condition known as vaginismus in women. Both problems markedly interfere with, or may prevent, the sexual act. Both are treatable using relatively simple behavioural and pharmacological interventions.

Erectile dysfunction

A DSM-IV-TR diagnosis of erectile failure requires persistent or recurrent inability to gain or maintain an adequate erection until completion of sexual activity, which results in marked distress or interpersonal difficulties. It is a fairly common disorder, particularly among older men, although younger men are not immune. Laumann et al. (1999) reported a 7 per cent prevalence among men aged 18–29. The prevalence rate was 9 per cent for men aged 30–39, 11 per cent for those aged 40–49 and 18 per cent for those aged 50–59. Some of the causes of erectile dysfunction are physical, including high blood pressure, and the long-term effects of drugs such as alcohol, heroin, marijuana and cigarettes. However, Masters and Johnson (1970) found a relevant physical condition in only 7 out of 213 men they assessed; the most common causes of the problem are psychological. These may be immediate or remote:

- *immediate:* performance anxiety, lack of adequate stimulation, relationship conflicts, lack of partner intimacy, poor partner communication
- *remote:* childhood sexual trauma, unresolved partner or parental attachments, sexual identity or orientation issues.

Aetiology of erectile dysfunction

Psychodynamic explanations

According to Janssen (1985) erectile failure results from an oedipal conflict constellation involving fear of castration or incest, uncertainties in sexual identity, incestuous object choices, latent homosexual tendencies and fear of aggressive-phallic impulses. These may develop as a result of factors that inhibit appropriate passage through the oedipal stage of psychosexual development (see Chapter 2). In a case example, Janssen described one man who reported that as a child his mother had turned to him to discuss matters relating to her relationship with his father. When his father became aware of this, he became angry and abused his mother. The client feared that he too would become the focus of his father's wrath and experienced a conflict in wanting to defend his mother, but to avoid confrontation with his father. This prevented his successful resolution of the oedipal conflict. In adulthood, the fear of his aggressive father prevented him developing appropriate emotional and sexual relationships with women. Treatment involved dealing with his relationship with his father, not any explicit sexual function.

Cognitive explanations

In a more cognitive explanation, Bancroft (1999) argued that anxiety adversely affects sexual performance as a result of cognitive and perceptual factors. He suggested that men's sexual excitement depends on a delicate balance between excitatory and inhibitory mechanisms. Two key inhibitory processes are performance anxiety and fear of negative outcomes. Both may lead to a process coined by Masters and Johnson as *spectating* in which the individual becomes so concerned by the adequacy of their performance or the consequences of potential failure that they distract from sexually arousing cues, and lose their erection. Evidence in support for Bancroft's model can be found in a number of laboratory studies which have shown performance demand to increase sexual arousal in most men, but to have the opposite effect on those with erectile dysfunction. In addition, the presence of non-sexual stimuli is more disruptive to men with the disorder than those without (Cranston-Cuebas and Barlow 1990).

Many men set themselves inappropriately high levels of performance to which they aspire. Zilbergeld (1992), for example, noted that men frequently buy into the fantasy that their performance is the 'cornerstone' of every sexual experience and that a firm erection is the key element of every sexual encounter: views not necessarily subscribed to by their female partners. According to Zilbergeld, a failure to achieve this ideal results in fears of dysfunction, loss of masculinity, and declining interest in their partner.

Treatment of erectile dysfunction

Anxiety reduction and desensitization

The classic treatment programme for erectile failure, known as *sensate focusing*, was developed by Masters and Johnson (1970). It involves a structured approach, designed to take the stress out of the sexual act. It begins with the couple learning to touch each other in pleasurable ways, but with a mandate not to touch each other's genitals. Their goal is to enjoy the intimacy of touch, not to give or receive sexual pleasure. Once couples are comfortable with non-genital sensate focusing, they are directed to gradually make genital contact and to give and receive pleasure doing so. At this time, they are still mandated not to attempt intercourse, nor for the male to try to achieve or maintain an erection (although this typically occurs). Finally, when the couple are comfortable with this level of intimacy, they may progress to full intercourse. This is a frequently applied intervention; although there are relatively few studies of its effectiveness, it is generally considered to be highly effective (Hawton et al. 1986).

Cognitive techniques

There are relatively few formal assessments of cognitive interventions in the treatment of erectile failure, although Goldman and Carroll (1990) reported the outcomes of a number of workshops in which participants were given appropriate sexual information and inappropriate cognitive concerns were challenged. Participants showed significant changes in knowledge and attitudes towards sex, and reported increased sexual frequency and satisfaction in the short-term; no long-term data were reported.

Interpersonal interventions

Hawton et al. (1992) reported that the most important predictor of outcome following a programme of sensate focusing and graduated stimulation techniques was the couples' ratings of marital communication before treatment. Three domains are the main foci of interpersonal interventions (Rosen 2001):

- status and dominance issues
- intimacy and trust
- loss of sexual attraction.

Each of these may be more or less salient in the lifetime of a sexual relationship. Status and dominance issues may be salient when one partner loses a job or achieves promotion; intimacy or trust issues may be salient following an affair, while loss of sexual attraction may follow weight gain or some other physical or psychological changes. Following an intervention addressing these factors, Hawton and colleagues reported that 70 per cent of couples reported a positive outcome.

Medical approaches

Perhaps the best known pharmacological treatment for erectile failure is Sildenafil, more popularly known as Viagra. This works on the smooth muscle of the penis. It is an inhibitor of the enzyme phosphodiesterase type 5 (PDE5) which normally breaks down cyclic guanosine monophosphate (cGMP), a chemical that brings about smooth muscle relaxation, and maintains the erectile response. It is generally effective in treating erectile dysfunction, whatever the cause. Goldstein et al. (1998), for example, reported that 70 per cent of men treated with Viagra reported improvements in the quality and frequency of erections; 70 per cent of attempts at intercourse were successful, in comparison to 22 per cent of attempts by those treated with placebo. PDE5 is predominantly found in the penis. However, it is also found in other areas of the body. As a consequence, about 16 per cent of users experience headaches,

10 per cent experience facial flushing, with other effects such as gastro-intestinal upset and alterations in colour vision being somewhat rarer. One of the more dramatic side-effects was thought to be the onset of a heart attack, but this is now thought to be a result of exercise, not the drug (Holmes 2000). One of the benefits of Viagra is that it enhances the sexual response rather than initiates it. Erection therefore follows sexual stimulation, and does not immediately follow taking the drug, as is the case in some alternatives. Erection may also be achieved by vacuum pumps, direct injection of drugs into the penis and the use of prostheses. Each method has achieved some success, and many continue to be used, but less so in the light of the development of Viagra and similar drugs (Ralph and McNicholas 2000).

Vaginismus

Vaginismus is the recurrent or persistent involuntary spasm of the musculature of the outer third of the vagina that prevents sexual intercourse. It can cause considerable distress or interpersonal difficulties. It is thought to be one of the most common of the female psychosexual dysfunctions, although its exact prevalence rate among the general population is unknown. About 20 per cent of women experience occasional pain during intercourse, but less than 1 per cent are thought to have vaginismus (Heiman and LoPiccolo 1988).

Aetiology of vaginismus

Psychoanalytic explanations

Classic psychoanalytic theory considers vaginismus to result from unresolved psychosexual conflicts in early childhood. Women with the condition have been characterized as fixated or regressed to the pre-oedipal or oedipal stages. According to Abraham (1956), in less severe cases, women are not able to transfer their libidinal energy from their father to their husband/partner. In more severe cases, women remain fixated on their mothers, and have a poor prognosis.

Behavioural explanations

According to behavioural theory, vaginismus is a phobic reaction to actual or imagined negative experiences related to penetration. Fear or anxiety concerning penetration results in high levels of sympathetic nervous system activity, one of the results of which is involuntary vaginal muscle spasm. These fears may, in part, arise from ignorance of sexual issues. Three other factors may increase the fear reaction (Ward and Ogden 1994). First, a mother who is frightened of intercourse may pass a fear of pain to her daughter. Second, the experience of sex may be painful for the affected woman, and memories of pain trigger the symptoms: nearly three-quarters of women with vaginismus in Ward and Ogden's sample reported this type of fear. The third issue involves a fear of punishment related to sexual guilt. Ward and Ogden (1994) found that many women with vaginismus experienced sexual guilt, stemming from a belief that 'sex is wrong', which led to a fear of punishment for engaging sexual acts. Childhood sexual trauma and a background of religious orthodoxy may also contribute to the conditioning of fear or guilt in relation to intercourse.

Treatment of vaginismus

Psychological approaches

One way of reducing anxiety associated with the sexual act is through the use of sensate focus techniques, with a gradual progression to genital touching. However, the most common treatment of vaginismus involves systematic desensitization together with the use of graded dilators. This may be conducted in combination with education, homework assignments and cognitive or relaxation therapy. In this procedure, the woman, and in some cases a physician, inserts dilators of gradually increasing size into the vagina until the woman is relaxed and the involuntary spasm is not triggered by the entry of an object into the vagina. When she is able to accommodate a fairly large dilator, the woman may be encouraged to keep it in place for several hours every night. This type of approach has proven very effective. Masters and Johnson (1970), who pioneered this approach, reported complete success with no relapse in the treatment of 29 women with this condition.

The paraphilias

Defining which of the various forms of sexual activity is 'normal' and 'abnormal' is not unproblematic. However, a number of sexual behaviours are generally considered to be 'abnormal'. These are referred to as the paraphilias, which include behaviours that are legal, such as fetishism and transvestism, and some that are illegal, in particular, paedophilia (see Table 10.1).

Many people who engage in paraphilic behaviour do not experience distress as a result, nor do they seek help to change the nature of their

Table 10.1   Some of the more prevalent paraphilias

Fetishism	Recurrent intense sexual urges, sexual arousing fantasies or behaviours that involve the use of non-living objects, often to the exclusion of all other stimuli; common fetishes are to women's underwear, boots and shoes
Exhibitionism	Recurrent urges to expose the genitals to another person of the opposite sex – often while having sexually arousing fantasies
Voyeurism	Recurrent and intense urges to secretly observe unsuspecting people as they undress or have intercourse
Sadomasochism	Sexual stimulation through the act of being humiliated, beaten, bound or otherwise made to suffer, or being the one to inflict such acts
Frotteurism	Repeated and intense sexual urges to touch and rub against non-consenting others

sexual interest. As a consequence, people who engage in unusual sexual behaviour may be considered as at the edge of the distribution of sexual interests rather than disordered. With this in mind, DSM-III stated that any paraphilic behaviour had to result in distress on the part of the individual before a diagnosis of a 'disorder' be assigned. However, following strong criticism of this laissez-faire approach, DSM-IV stated that paedophilia was to be considered a disorder regardless of the perpetrator's emotional reaction to their behaviour. In its latest version, DSM-IV-TR now states that exhibitionism, frotteurism, sexual sadism and voyeurism are also now to be considered 'disorders' if the person acts on their desires, even though their behaviour may not cause them any distress or 'impaired functioning'. The medicalization of sexual behaviours is increasing. Relatively few people receive a diagnosis of paraphilia, but the number of specialist web-sites and other services suggests that these behaviours are more prevalent than this would suggest.

Aetiological explanations have tried to identify common pathways to all the paraphilias. Accordingly, while the next sections consider the aetiology and treatment of paedophilia and transvestism in some detail, the general process by which these conditions develop could be applied to all the paraphilias.

Paedophilia

DSM-IV-TR defined paedophilia as 'recurrent intense sexual urges and sexually arousing fantasies involving sexual activity with a prepubescent child or children' and that the person has acted on these urges, or the sexual urges or fantasies cause marked distress or interpersonal difficulty. In addition, the person has to be at least 16 years old and at least 5 years older than the other child or children involved. Note the emphasis on the victim's sexual maturity, not age. Legal definitions lay clear boundaries as to the age at which consenting couples may have intercourse. Violation of these limits will result in an individual being termed a sex offender, but not a paedophile unless the other child is pre-pubescent.

Paedophilic behaviours vary. Some paedophilic individuals may look at and not touch a child. Others may want to touch or undress them. When sexual activity occurs, it often involves oral sex or touching the genitals of the child. In most cases, except incest, there is no penetration. Where sex is penetrative, it is usually with older children and may involve threats or force. More typically, however, paedophilic individuals depend on persuasion, guile and 'friendship' (Murray 2000). Paedophilic individuals who are attracted to females usually prefer 8–10-year-olds, while those attracted to boys prefer slightly older children (APA 1994). Most are relatives, friends or neighbours of the child. Greenberg et al. (1993) reported that 33 per cent of people who engaged in paedophile behaviour abused only boys, 44 per cent only girls, and 23 per cent abused both boys and girls.

Prevalence levels of paedophilia are extremely difficult to determine. Most surveys report the prevalence of people who have been sexually abused rather than the prevalence of perpetrators. Barbaree and Seto (1997), for example, calculated that at least 7 per cent of US females and 3 per cent of males have experienced some form of childhood sexual abuse, although some surveys suggest even higher prevalence rates.

Aetiology of paedophilia

Theories of the aetiology of paedophilia are limited and focus more on social and psychological factors than biological ones. These separate into long-term background factors and proximal factors that form more immediate triggers to such behaviour.

Long-term risk factors

Many child sex offenders report that their early parent–child relationships were disruptive and/or that they have experienced childhood sexual abuse: up to 67 per cent of respondents in one survey (Hanson and Slater 1988). These data are extremely difficult to validate. Many people who engage in paedophilic behaviour have a vested interest in reporting such events as a way of minimizing their own responsibility for their actions or gaining the sympathy of others. Attempts at validation by asking the alleged perpetrators are equally likely to result in misreporting.

In an attempt to minimize these problems, Dhawan and Marshall (1996) used detailed interviews and questionnaire methods to try to corroborate or challenge any misreporting. They concluded that 50 per cent of imprisoned people who engaged in paedophile activities had been sexually abused as children. What this, of course, does not explain is why such episodes predict later sexual offences. If these incidents were particularly traumatic, one might expect a rejection of sexual relationships with children in order not to repeat the trauma.

Behavioural theories (e.g. Barbaree 1990) suggest that child offenders develop a strong sexual attraction to children following pairings of sexual arousal and images of children. These associations typically occur in early adolescence, and may initially be accidental. However, they may be strengthened by masturbation to images of children and the use of pornography. In a partial test of this model, Barbaree and Marshall (1989) measured the sexual response to pictures of female children and mature women among men who had either sexually abused children not in their family, committed incest, or claimed to have no sexual interest in children. Their findings were somewhat surprising. Less than half of the non-familial offenders and only 28 per cent of those who had committed incest were more sexually stimulated by pictures of young women than those of mature women. In addition, 15 per cent of men who reported no sexual interest in children were more sexually aroused by pictures of children than of mature women. While the conditioning model may hold for some individuals, it does not hold for all.

These data indicate that sexual interest is not the only factor that influences the sexual choices of paedophilic men. Another important factor may be a failure to develop satisfying psychological and sexual relationships with adults. Many people who engage in paedophile behaviour report high levels of loneliness, perhaps arising from inadequate attachment styles developed as children (Ward et al. 1996). As a result, some seek out intimacy with children, with whom they find it easier to instigate both a physical and non-physical relationship, and who are easier to control. However, this is certainly not the case for all those who engage in paedophile behaviour, emphasizing that the route to paraphilias differs widely between individuals.

Proximal factors

Pithers (1990) added to these background factors by examining the more immediate antecedents to any sexual offence. He suggested that the desire to engage in paedophile behaviour is frequently triggered by low mood as a result of stress or conflict. As a result, individuals seek some way of decreasing these negative feelings, and allow themselves to enter a high-risk situation. This may appear the result of seemingly irrelevant decisions that place them in increasing proximity to potential victims. Once in this situation, they are overwhelmed by the potentially powerfully rewarding feelings associated with paedophile acts. They focus on these rather than the long-term negative outcomes to the situation, and as a result engage in some form of paedophile behaviour. Once the immediate 'rush' has receded, they may once more experience remorse, but feel out of control of their behaviour, a negative mood state that may trigger the cycle again.

Up to two-thirds of those imprisoned for sexual offences either deny or minimize their own role in the offence. Barbaree (1991) identified three types of denial:

- complete denial that anything took place
- admission of sexual relations, but denial that it was an offence
- admission of physical contact but denial of any sexual elements.

He also noted three types of minimization, involving denial of harm to the victim, the extent of previous offences, and responsibility for offences. Common cognitive distortions are that children are as interested in sex as adults, that they seek out sex with adults, and that they enjoy and benefit from the experience. Some of these may be truly believed by the individual. Others may be deliberate falsification, to minimize negative reactions from others (see Box 10.1).

Treatment of paedophilia

As sexual activity with young persons is against the law, treatment is usually initiated in a prison or a secure forensic facility. Even here, engagement in treatment programmes is not compulsory, and only about 25 per cent of those offered treatment choose to engage in treatment programmes.

Physical treatments

Physical treatments suppress sexual urges and behaviour, but do not change the object of sexual desire. Two surgical procedures, castration and neurosurgery, are no longer considered ethically acceptable. However, chemical approaches involving administration of drugs that block the production or action of androgens, hormones that influence the male sexual response, remain in use. These have achieved modest results. Berlin and Meinecke (1981), for example, followed 20 men treated with androgen-blocking drugs; 3 repeated their offences while taking medication, and relapse rates were high following cessation of therapy. A major problem for anti-androgen treatments is that between 30 and 100 per cent of the people prescribed these drugs do not take them (Barbaree and Seto 1997). Many of those who stop taking them presumably do so because they want to reoffend, as they do not change any of the beliefs

Box 10.1   Differing paedophile behaviours

Not all people who engage in paedophile acts have the same motivation and act in the same way. Here are two contrasting cases, with very different outcomes.

John

John was a 30-year-old man, admitted to hospital as a result of a period of severe depression. Prior to his depression he had been a teacher in a school in the north of England. Although there was no evidence that he had engaged in paedophile acts with any children, his name was found on a distribution list for child pornography kept by a paedophile ring. His house was raided and paedophile materials were found in it. He was therefore charged by the police, and found guilty of using child pornography. The school at which he worked was notified of this outcome and he was immediately dismissed from his job.

He was married at the time that this occurred, but was immediately asked to leave the marital home and his wife began divorce proceedings. He moved to London, where he could be 'lost among the crowd' and had some family contacts. There he became profoundly depressed, and was admitted to hospital where he entered into therapy for his depression. After he began to trust his therapist, he started to tell his story.

He admitted to the use of child pornography for sexual pleasure, and that he was particularly turned on by pictures of young boys. His marriage had been functional and pleasant, but not sexually satisfying. He had had a number of age-appropriate homosexual relationships prior to his marriage, but these had generally ended disastrously. He was aware that his sexual interest was inappropriate and felt ashamed by it. He did not try to condone his behaviour, but thought that while he had no physical contact with young boys, even using photographs in this way was exploitative and morally unacceptable. His depression was a consequence of the loss of his job and his marriage, the probability that he would never find work again, and the shame he felt as his behaviour had been made public. He lived alone and avoided company other than his immediate family. He left his flat only rarely, and deliberately avoided places where children may congregate.

Because he found his sexual interests inappropriate and shaming, he was motivated to engage in therapy. He began a programme of masturbatory reorientation. In this, he began to masturbate to images of young children to achieve sexual excitement, before shifting the focus of his images to those of more mature boys or young-looking men. He found the image of one young-looking male Hollywood star (who will remain nameless!) particularly exciting. This programme worked very well, and he found that he could become sexually excited by the images of age-appropriate men.

Despite these gains and the claims he made about only using child pornography, his behaviour followed the pattern suggested by Pithers (1990) on at least one occasion. At this time he was feeling depressed, and decided to go for a walk, which drew him 'accidentally' to a shopping area frequented by local school children, and 'he happened to pass by a [public] toilet' when a young boy walked into it. At this point, he was excited by the thought of seeing the young child expose himself, and followed him into the toilet. There, he watched him use the urinal. The child was unaware of his presence, and there was no social or physical contact with him. Nevertheless, the incident highlighted the need to set up a relapse prevention programme, in which he drew up a list of alternative behaviours to do when he felt depressed or the need for sexual excitement. The alternative behaviours he engaged in were fairly limited, and included calling his family on the telephone or visiting them, and focusing on chores or tasks about the house. The one thing that he determined not to do was to leave the house, to walk randomly about, as this inevitably would lead to his 'accidentally' walking into high-risk areas. Both interventions progressed well after this point, and he was eventually discharged.

Stephen

By contrast, Stephen was more manipulative in his behaviour. He was a man in his late fifties, already living in London at the time of his offences. His history was one of befriending single mothers with adolescent daughters. After a (short) period of time, he had typically moved in with these women, and encouraged their daughter to join them in bed in the morning, so 'they could be a proper family'. When this was an established habit and the woman was not present, he had succeeded in having sexual intercourse with at least two of these girls. He came into therapy a few months before he was due in court. It quickly became clear that he considered his behaviour to be acceptable and justified. He told his therapist that he considered he was helping these girls in their sexual journey, 'because it was better that a sexually experienced man bring them into the sexual world rather than some spotty adolescent who would fumble around and not know what he was doing'. He stayed in therapy for a few sessions, all the time claiming that his behaviour was justified, and then stopped attending immediately before his attendance in court. He did not attend court, and could no longer be found at his flat.

or attitudes that drive deviant sexual behaviours. In addition, the drugs have a number of side-effects, including weight gain and reducing the size of testes, which may discourage their use. Finally, these treatments are effective only in individuals with abnormally high testosterone levels. Most people who engage in paedophile acts do not have these levels of testosterone, so would not benefit from the treatment even if they were fully compliant with the therapy.

Behaviour therapy

Both aversion therapy and masturbatory reconditioning methods have been used in the treatment of paedophilia. In aversion therapy, an inappropriate sexual stimulus is paired with an aversive event such as mild electric shock or strong aversive odour. This process is thought to condition a negative emotional state to the presence of the sexual stimulus. Most studies show some reduction of arousal to stimuli of young children. However, this may not result in reductions in offences. Rice et al. (1991), for example, followed 136 non-familial child molesters, 50 of whom received aversion therapy, following their discharge from a maximum security prison. Over a period of about six years, 31 per cent were convicted of a new offence. Recidivism rates were no lower among those who received aversion therapy than those who did not.

Masturbatory reconditioning involves the individual initiating a sexual response through the use of their favoured sexual images. Once they have achieved an erection, they switch to more appropriate images, such as a naked woman or man. They continue to masturbate to orgasm, when they concentrate deeply on this image. This approach may be combined with a graded series of 'normal' images, from less to more typical of the desired sexual focus. This approach has a number of advantages over aversion therapy. First, it is less ethically challenging and more acceptable to potential recipients. Second, it does not involve laboratory equipment and can be practiced between therapy sessions. Although there is little empirical evidence of its effects, it is considered to be moderately effective (Laws and Marshall 1991).

Relapse prevention

Relapse prevention involves teaching the individual to

- identify situations in which they are at high risk of offending behaviour
- get out of the risky situation
- consider lapses as something to be learned from
- identify factors that led to relapse and plan how these could be avoided in the future.

The relapse prevention programme described by Marques et al. (2000) is typical of its type. It involved an intensive inpatient programme conducted in a secure forensic hospital and a one-year support programme following discharge. Participants were given sexual education and taught general coping skills such as relaxation, stress and anger management, as well as social skills. More specific interventions included identifying the behaviours that preceded offending behaviour and addressing how these may be interrupted. It also dealt with issues of responsibility and minimization. Over a five-year follow-up, this intervention had a known re-offence rate of 10.8 per cent in contrast to the 13 per cent rate among those who did not receive the intervention – a modest, but significant difference. The programme was most successful with offenders who had male victims, and less successful with those who had female victims, although why is not clear.

The effectiveness of therapy

Measuring the outcome of offender programmes is difficult. Self-report change must be treated with caution, and data on relapse is usually obtained from official records, which can measure only reoffending of which society is aware. Convincing research on the outcome of treatment programmes is therefore lacking. Despite this, Hall (1995) reported a meta-analysis on the effectiveness of a variety of interventions. Of note is that many people were excluded from both types of interventions for a number of reasons including an extensive offence history, denial of offences and behavioural disturbances while in prison. Overall, the most effective interventions were relapse prevention programme and hormonal therapy, with neither proving more effective than the other. Average known reoffence rates following taking part in relapse prevention programmes were 15 per cent over a period of three years, in comparison to an average rate of 35.5 per cent among those not involved in such programmes. With hormonal therapy, known reoffence rates were 22 per cent over an average of ten years: rates of those who received no intervention averaged 36 per cent. Hall (1995) noted that up to two-thirds of participants refused hormonal therapy, and 50 per cent of those who started then discontinued treatment. By contrast, only one-third of those offered relapse programmes either refused or dropped out of them. He took this to indicate that relapse prevention programmes may prove the treatment of choice.

In an attempt to engage more people in therapy, Marshall (1994) used a group approach to shift people from a state of denial or minimization to one where they accepted responsibility for their actions. Their intervention comprised a series of group meetings, which participants entered as necessary and left when they had significantly improved. In it, they recounted their version of events that led to them being there, focusing on issues of blame and responsibility. Where there was evidence of denial or minimization, other group members were invited to challenge these interpretations, following which they retold their story taking account of these challenges and with less distortion. Marshall (1994) reported that those who went through this procedure showed significantly less denial and minimization than at baseline. While this appears a promising procedure, it is not clear how much the participants reported change simply to escape the group, and how many had made real and substantial changes.

Can we predict who will reoffend?

Identifying those who are at risk of reoffending is not an exact science. However, a number of clinicians have identified factors that may be predictive. Quinsey et al. (1995), for example, were able to correctly classify 72 per cent of reoffenders, as they had a previous criminal history, violent convictions, were unmarried, scored highly on a psychopathy checklist (see Chapter 11) and had a previous record of sexual offences. They suggested that these factors, combined with evidence of an individual's response to therapy, may inform decisions about length of sentence and release from prison. Once discharged from prison, sex offenders are now monitored by police and in some cases the public. In some states in the USA, for example, known paedophilic individuals who live in the community have to advertise this fact to those who live in the area. Some are calling for this approach to be adopted in Britain. Such knowledge, however, is not without its dangers. On the day of writing this section, the UK news reported that a person charged with paedophilia had been battered to death in his own house by vigilantes. The approach may also be counter-productive from a surveillance perspective. In the USA, the whereabouts of about 80 per cent of paedophilic individuals released into the community is known by the police and social services. The equivalent figure in Britain is over 90 per cent. Many sex offenders fear public retribution, and would hide rather than announce their behaviour to the general population.

Transvestic fetishism

Transvestism involves wearing the clothing of the opposite sex. DSM-IV-TR defined transvestic fetishism as

- recurrent, intense, sexually arousing fantasies, sexual urges or behaviours involving cross-dressing over a period of at least six months in a heterosexual male
- these fantasies, sexual urges or behaviours cause clinically significant distress or impairment in social, occupational or other important areas of functioning.

There is little evidence of an analogous form of the disorder in women. Boys who grow up to engage in transvestite behaviour do not engage in 'feminine' behaviours before puberty, nor do they cross-dress. Similarly, men who are transvestites are unremarkably masculine in their adult hobbies and career choices.

Transvestite boys usually begin cross-dressing at puberty, and rarely later than mid-adolescence. This typically results in sexual excitement, although many people report that they dress in this way because they like the feel of the clothes and that there is no sexual motivation to their behaviour. Some adolescents wear female clothes occasionally; others compulsively wear them under their masculine clothes. Attempts at passing off as a woman are rare in adolescence. However, cross-dressing is frequently accompanied by fantasies of being female, and these fantasies may form the nucleus of sexual fantasies.

In a survey of over 1000 adult transvestite men, Docter and Prince (1997) reported that 40 per cent of their sample experienced sexual excitement and orgasm 'always' or 'often' when they cross-dressed. Only 9 per cent of the sample said they never experienced this. Cross-dressing frequently elicits less and less sexual excitement as the individual grows older and may eventually have no discernible sexual association. However, the desire to cross-dress may remain the same or even grow stronger, and may be accompanied by feelings of comfort and well-being. Lack of opportunity to cross-dress can result in a lowering of mood and marked irritability. As a result, many transvestites continue to wear women's undergarments beneath the normal male clothes.

Among Docter and Prince's (1997) respondents, 87 per cent reported being exclusively heterosexual; 83 per cent were either married at the time of the survey or had been married; 32 per cent of their wives knew they cross-dressed before marriage; 28 per cent were completely accepting of the behaviour once they became aware of it, while 19 per cent were 'completely antagonistic'. It is common for transvestite men to stop cross-dressing in the early months or years of relationships with a new partner, although many revert to cross-dressing in time. Many enjoy 'normal' heterosexual intercourse. Others need props such as wearing feminine attire to achieve sexual pleasure.

As social reaction can be very negative to transvestic behaviour, it usually takes place in arenas where such behaviour is acceptable, including the home, or transvestite clubs or organizations. Nevertheless, Docter and Prince (1997) reported that 71 per cent of their sample had cross-dressed in public: 10 per cent had ridden on a bus or train while cross-dressed, 28 per cent had eaten in restaurants, 26 per cent used the ladies' toilet and 22 per cent had tried on feminine clothing in stores. When asked their preferred gender identity, 11 per cent preferred their masculine self, 28 per cent preferred their feminine self and 60 per cent preferred each equally.

Some people experience guilt and shame as a result of their feelings and behaviour. Such individuals may make repeated, frequently unsuccessful, efforts to overcome their perceived anomaly. They may destroy their wardrobe of feminine clothes, before acquiring new ones in the following weeks and months. This cycle may occur repeatedly in younger people who later become more accepting of their feelings. In Docter and Prince's sample, 70 per cent reported having purged their wardrobe on at least one occasion, and 45 per cent reported seeking counselling as a result of their feelings.

No formal epidemiological study of the prevalence of transvestism has been conducted, and its prevalence within the population is unknown.

Aetiology of transvestic fetishism

As with paedophilia, a number of social and psychological risk factors for transvestism have been identified, although the body of evidence from which these risk factors have been identified is limited.

Parental relationships

Various, often contradictory, family theories of transvestism have been proposed. Newcomb (1985) found that transvestite men were more likely than other heterosexual men to characterize their parents as less sex-typed and more sex-reversed in terms of dependence and affiliation. This suggested some form of modelling process may be involved. However, men who become transvestites tend to adopt typical masculine roles as a young child, countering this type of theory. A second theory suggested that the principal maternal influence in transvestism is one of hostility and anger towards males. Zucker and Bradley (1995) noted evidence that boys who develop transvestism have higher separation rates from their mothers than is the norm, suggesting this reflected their mothers' aggressive attitudes towards men.

Behavioural models

One school of thought suggests that transvestism results from being cross-dressed during childhood, particularly by mothers or other female figures, as a form of punishment – a process known as 'petticoat punishment'. A number of case examples have been published (Stoller 1968), although it is not clear why an adult should choose to adopt a behaviour used to punish them as a child as a sexual fetish. Stoller argued that this may represent a form of mastery over the punishment. However, a number of clinicians have claimed that incidences of forced cross-dressing are rare, and that it is usually the child who initiates such behaviour. More conventional reinforcement models (Crawford et al. 1993) suggest that if a child is exposed to women's clothing and enjoys the feel of them or masturbates while wearing them, this may establish a reinforcement process that results in the continuation of this behaviour.

Psychoanalytical models

Ovesey and Person (1973) suggested that the psychoanalytic processes that lead to transvestism occur after an individual has consolidated their sense of maleness. Their mother is typically warm and supportive, their father distant and threatening, even verbally or physically abusive. As a result, the mother turns towards her son for gratification not forthcoming from her marriage. She is seductive in her closeness to the boy, but at the same time encourages his cross-dressing either overtly or covertly. In doing so, she is thought to be gratifying herself sexually, but repressing her real (sexual) interest by denying his masculinity. The child is gratified by her intimacy, but also feels guilty. He assumes that his mother wishes to dress him as a girl in order to placate his father. The intimacy of his mother and the perceived rivalry of his father prevent a successful resolution of the oedipal complex (see Chapter 2).

After childhood, the individual seeks to preserve the mother as a dependency object, and is attracted to women like his mother who will accept or even encourage cross-dressing. Adult transvestites resort to cross-dressing under periods of stress and wear female underclothing as a protective device. Female clothes provide protection in three ways:

- they symbolize the mother and perpetuate dependency and continued need for her protection
- they symbolize auto-castration, a token submission to male competitors, which wards off their retaliation
- they disguise masculinity to disarm rivals.

The clothes conceal the penis, the symbol of masculine power, and deny hostile intent. They allow the individual to avoid detection by their rivals, which not only allays anxiety, but even confers on the individual an inflated sense of masculinity. Ovesey and Person (1973: 69) went as far to suggest that 'the transvestite is Superman in drag!'

Treatment of transvestic fetishism

Transvestism is not a condition that requires treatment. Nevertheless, people whose behaviour is affecting their relationships or who find their behaviour unacceptable may seek treatment. Marital problems often lead to attempts at behavioural change and the initiation of therapy. Wives often have negative feelings towards their husband's behaviour even when they know about it early in their relationship (Bullough and Weinberg 1988).

Treatment usually focuses on the sexual elements of transvestite behaviour, and includes aversion therapy and modification of sexual fantasy. Some aversion programmes have proven moderately successful. Marks et al. (1970) reported that two-thirds of participants in electrical aversion therapy improved with treatment, up to a follow-up period of two years. This compared to one-quarter of a control group who did not receive the intervention. A second approach to the treatment of transvestism involves masturbatory retraining. Here, the individual masturbates using his preferred sexual object, including female props worn either by the individual or his partner, before reverting to images of more 'normal' sex objects immediately before and at orgasm. Again, a number of case descriptions and uncontrolled studies have shown this method to have been used with good effect (Laws and Marshall 1991).

Gender identity disorder

In contrast to transvestism, where men dress as women, but accept their male identity, individuals with gender identity disorder (GID) believe themselves to have been born the wrong sex. DSM-IV-TR defines GID as:

- a strong and persistent cross-gender identification
- persistent discomfort with one's sex, or a sense of inappropriate-ness in the gender role of that sex
- clinically significant distress or impairment in social, occupational or other important areas of functioning.

In adolescents and adults, GID is manifest by a preoccupation with the belief that he or she is born 'the wrong sex' and a desire for the removal of primary and secondary sex characteristics. Many people with this disorder opt for surgery to change their body to what they consider to be their appropriate sex. They become transsexuals. Others do not take such a radical step, but dress and try to pass themselves off as a member of their desired sex. People with GID are often sexually attracted to people of the same sex, which they interpret as conventional hetero-sexual preference. There are no prevalence data of the condition within the general population.

Most adults with GID report a history of consistent cross-gender beha-viour in childhood. Boys may reject the rough-and-tumble play and pre-fer the company of girls. They frequently dress in women's clothing and insist they will grow up to be a girl. Some claim their penis and testes are disgusting and hope they will somehow change into female genitalia as they grow older. Girls may reject urinating in the sitting position, and assert that they do not want to grow breasts or menstruate. They may reject typical girls' clothing. Green and Blanchard (1995) reported that these behaviours and attitudes are usually detected before the age of 3. These characteristics are not static, however, and many children adopt more gender-appropriate behaviours and identities over time.

Aetiology of gender identity disorder

Biological factors

No genetic cause of GID has yet been identified. In addition, studies of sex hormonal disturbance are surprisingly difficult to conduct, because many people with GID take hormones of the opposite sex either as part of a treatment programme or by purchasing them on the black market. Despite these interpretive difficulties, what evidence there is does not support a hormonal explanation. Summarizing the evidence, Gladue (1985) reported few if any hormonal differences between men with GID, male heterosexuals and male homosexuals. Similarly negative results have been found in women. Meyer-Bahlung (1979) found some women with GID had elevated levels of male hormones, but most did not.

A second potential hormonal explanation is that abnormal levels of prenatal hormones may influence behaviour, and possibly gender identity. This may affect both sexes. The female children of women who have taken precursors to male hormones during pregnancy to prevent uterine bleeding tend to express high levels of tomboyish behaviour in preschool years (Ehrhardt and Money 1967). Boys whose mothers have taken female hormones while pregnant tend to be less boyish than their peers and to engage less in rough-and-tumble play (Yalom et al. 1973). However, there is no evidence that either group of children dislike their gender.

Although a number of studies have failed to find any differences between the brains of people with and without GID, one study has shown evidence to suggest a neurological substrate to this disorder. Zhou et al. (1995) conducted autopsies on the brains of six people who had changed their sex from male to female. They found an area of the brain, known as the bed nucleus of stria terminalis (BST), to be much smaller than is typically found in men. Indeed, the size of the BST matched that typically found in women, which is usually about half the size of that found in men. What this difference actually means is not really understood, although the BST is known to regulate sexual activity in male rats. It is possible, therefore, that this may contribute in some way to GID.

Psychoanalytical explanations

Psychoanalytic explanations suggest that male transsexuals have an ambiguous core gender identity. According to Ovesey and Person (1973), male transsexualism originates from extreme separation anxiety early in life before the individual has fully established his own sexual identity. To alleviate this anxiety, the individual resorts to fantasy of symbiotic fusion with the mother. In this way, mother and child become one and the danger of separation is nullified. In the transsexual's mind he literally becomes the mother, and to sustain this fantasy attempts to revert his core identity from male to female.

To explain the desire for the removal of the penis, Ovesey and Person (1973) noted that the transsexual does not experience castration anxiety, as do most boys. Instead, they experience anxiety that continues until they *are* castrated. The penis is clear evidence that they have failed to psychically fuse with the mother. For the same reason, they reject the act of homosexuality, as this would also acknowledge them as male. They prefer to reject any sexual experience, and generally have little or no experience of sex, even masturbation. In sum, the motivation for security takes priority over motivation for sexuality, as a result of fear of early maternal abandonment.

Early life conditioning

Perhaps the most widely accepted theory of GID is that of early life conditioning. Parents of people with GID frequently report that they encouraged and gave attention to their child when he or she cross-dressed. This appears to be particularly relevant in boys, where they may be taught how to wear make-up and other feminine behaviours (Green 1987). More subtle factors may also be at play. Girls who exhibit high levels of tomboy behaviour tend to have parents who do the same, and to choose their father as their favourite parent. This allows the possibility of learning such behaviours from their parents and being rewarded for expressing them (Zucker et al. 1994).

Conditioning experiences may also explain why more children than adults are identified as having GID. Early life experiences are dominated by family. However, as an individual grows up, they are subject to influences of a wider range of people: peers, school teachers and so on. It is possible that such exposure results in differing reinforcement processes in which the individual is punished for behaving in 'inappropriate' ways. The competing strengths of each reinforcement system may determine whether or not the individual does or does not behave in gender-discrepant ways. While this approach can explain the development of non-gender-typical behaviours, it has more difficulty in explaining the extremely strongly held beliefs about their gender that such people hold, and their resistance to any form of psychological therapy.

Treatment of gender identity disorder

Psychological therapies

Most people with GID are resistant to psychotherapy. As a result, there are no clinical trials reporting attempts to change gender identity. However, a number of case reports indicate that behaviour and attitudes can be changed should the individual wish, or even when they do not seek help. Barlow et al. (1973) reported an intervention with a 17-year-old boy who chose not to proceed with sex reassignment surgery. The intervention included teaching 'male' behaviours, mannerisms, and social skills. It proved successful: by the end of therapy, the individual felt no discrepancy between his biological and psychological sexual identity. A second intervention involved a 5-year-old boy, who had been cross-dressing for a period of two years before the beginning of therapy (Rekers and Lovaas 1974). The parents were required to initiate a behavioural programme in which they encouraged masculine behaviour, including playing with masculine toys and rough-and-tumble. They also actively discouraged female behaviours such as playing with dolls. The programme was successful in changing the boy's behaviour up to a two-year follow-up. This suggests that there is some malleability in the development of behaviours associated with GID.

Surgery

Many people with GID request sex reassignment surgery. This involves a complex, staged process. For male to female transitions, treatment starts at least a year before surgery (see Box 10.2). First, the individual starts taking the female hormone oestrogen that results in a number of physical changes, including the development of breasts and a softening of the skin. Fat may shift from the shoulders to the hips in feminine fashion.

Box 10.2 Problems of gender identity disorder

Access to sex change surgery in Britain is limited. At times of inadequate resources for health care, this type of surgery is given a low priority, and many people with GID can find it extremely difficult, if not impossible, to obtain this treatment from the National Health Service. Many people who choose to have surgery do so by paying privately for it, through specialist private companies such as TRANSFORM, who provide an assessment of the individual's suitability for gender reassignment, hormone therapy, support for a year while they await surgery and try to live as someone of the opposite sex, and then surgery and post-surgery support.

Simon was a 30-year-old man just beginning this process. He had been to the initial assessment and accepted as a possible 'case', and had begun hormone therapy at the time of the interview in which he described what led him to seek gender and reassignment and the frustrations he had experienced on the way:

> I am so angry. I know I have the wrong body, and no one can convince me that I am wrong. As long as I can remember, I have felt this way. I wanted breasts, to be a girl, to have a

period – to get rid of my penis. I envy them so much . . . I have tried to go along with things, not to be as I am. It's really pretty frightening admitting it and having to go the whole way like I want to. But it's what I want . . .

I married someone just to try and conform. I love her as well. Not in a physical way, though. We don't have sex . . . she isn't really a sexual person so that's all right. That's why I began to see her. She isn't very attractive, but she's a good person, so it feels good that she's with someone like me, where sex isn't a big deal. It doesn't feel right, but we are good friends and we get on well. I tried to keep things a secret. I have – had – a place in my wardrobe where I keep women's clothing. I put it on when she is at work. It feels so natural and fantastic. It's the only time I felt was really me, and how I wanted to be. I had a wig, make-up and stuff so I could really feel like a woman. It was secret, but she came home when I was wearing it one day, and so I had to explain some of how I feel and what I want. She knows I want to change my sex. We're going to live together until I do, even though my body is going to change with the hormones. But she wants to live with me despite it. I don't know what will happen and how we'll feel in time, though . . . I wear the clothing and the wig at home all the time now, now she knows. She's OK about it . . . I'm not a 'trannie' [transvestite] though, because I want more – just dressing up isn't enough. They are just men playing at being women. I want and have always wanted to be a proper woman.

It has been so frustrating getting so far. I went for an interview at Charing Cross Hospital and they agreed to put me on their programme, but the local health people wouldn't pay for it, even though I had letters from my GP and a psychiatrist saying I needed it. So I had to go to TRANSFORM. I went to see them and they agreed to give me an assessment by a psychologist, and he agreed to put me on the programme. And that was great . . . but I had no money, so I couldn't do it straight away. I felt so low at the time . . . very depressed. I really needed it, but no one would let me get on with things. I was pretty close to suicidal . . . I thought things would never change . . . and I couldn't tell my wife why I was so low . . . I'm still on antidepressants now . . . I think they're the only thing keeping me going . . . I still don't know how I'm going to pay for surgery . . . I would sell the house but that's not fair on my wife, so I'm happy I'm on the hormones and beginning to see changes, but I can't see how I will go the whole way . . . but I won't be happy unless I do, because emotionally it all feels so right. . . .

Once initiated, hormones are taken indefinitely. At the same time, the person will undergo electrolysis to rid them of masculine hair patterns. They are also trained to raise the timbre of their voice. At this early stage, some people may also have cosmetic surgery to alter facial features such as their chin or larynx to make them appear more feminine. Most of these changes are reversible. More enduring changes are usually held back for at least a year during which the individual is required to live as a woman. Only if this 'trial period' is completed successfully will the final surgery be conducted. This involves amputation of the penis and construction of an artificial vagina. This will permit normal sexual intercourse.

For female–male reassignment a similar process is followed. Hormone therapy changes body shape, redistributing fat, as well as deepening the voice. However, surgery is more arduous and the end-results are less successful. The penis that can be constructed is generally small and not capable of a normal erection. Accordingly, sexual intercourse is not possible without the use of artificial supports. Surgery may also include bilateral mastectomy and hysterectomy.

The social and psychological outcomes of surgery are generally good. Summarizing the data to date, the Wessex Institute for Health Research and Development (1998) reported that two years after surgery, people who received sex reassignment surgery engaged in more visits to family and friends, eating out, sport and sexual activity than those who did not receive surgery. They also made modest gains on outcomes including social drinking, work record, and cinema/theatre attendance. Y.L.S. Smith et al. (2001) followed a cohort of adolescents, who either did or did not receive sex reassignment surgery, for a period of four years. By this time, none of those who received surgery regretted their choice and were considered to be functioning psychologically and socially 'quite well'. Those who did not receive surgery generally did less well, although they showed modest improvements on measures as diverse as gender dysphoria and body dissatisfaction. These gains, however, were of a different order of magnitude to those made in the group treated with surgery. Positive outcomes in uncontrolled studies have been reported in domains such as cosmetic appearance, sexual functioning, self-esteem, body image, family life, social relationships, psychological status and satisfaction. The small number of serious postoperative incidents includes requests for reversal, hospitalization and suicide. New problems may also emerge following reassignment surgery. Some individuals may need to come to terms with painful loss, including jobs, families, partners, children and friends, as a result of their gender change. Many people are forced to move away from a familiar environment and, despite being confident in their gender role, may have difficulties with social adaptation and acceptance by others.

Of interest is that the changes following hormonal treatment are not only physical, but also include cognitive changes. Van Goozen et al.

(1995), for example, reported on the effects of sex-hormone therapy on behaviour and cognitive processes. Among women transforming to men, administration of androgens was associated with significant increases in aggressiveness, sexual arousability and spatial ability, and reduced scores on verbal fluency tasks. For the male-to-female group, the opposite constellation of outcomes was observed: anger and aggression proneness, sexual arousability and visuospatial ability decreased, while verbal fluency improved. Men transforming to women undergoing oestrogen therapy have also shown improved paired associate learning scores compared to a similar group not receiving oestrogens (Miles et al. 1998).

Chapter summary

1 There are two broad categories of sexual disorder: disorders of response (including erectile dysfunction and vaginismus) and disorders of desire, the paraphilias.

2 Erectile dysfunction can be the result of physical factors, but is frequently the result of psychological ones. Common factors include anxiety, often as a result of distorted beliefs about sexual performance, and 'spectating'.

3 Vaginismus is also triggered by anxiety.

4 Treatment using sensate focus and graded exposure methods is effective in both disorders.

5 Paraphilias are generally considered to be the result of conditioning processes in childhood, although specific paraphilias may have multiple casual factors.

6 Paedophilia may result from conditioning processes, poor adult attachment and sexual relationships, an emotional congruence with children, and processes such as justifying cognitions that support the behaviour.

7 Many people imprisoned as a result of paedophile behaviour do not enter treatment programmes. For those that do, cognitive behavioural programmes that address the cognitions supporting the behaviour and develop strategies for dealing with high-risk situations appear the most effective treatment. Masturbatory reconditioning may also alter the object of sexual pleasure. Hormonal therapies may be effective as long as the drug is taken, but compliance is low and relapse once stopped is high.

8 Transvestic fetishism is not a 'disorder' that requires treatment, but some people chose to seek treatment due to social and marital pressures.

9 Transvestism is usually considered to be the consequence of conditioning processes, and treatment involves reconditioning using masturbatory retraining techniques. Aversive approaches are rarely used for ethical reasons.

10 Gender identity disorder occurs when an individual feels that they are the incorrect gender, and wish to change it.

11 GID is poorly understood. No evidence of biological determinants has been found, and psychological models struggle to provide adequate explanations of the condition.

12 People with GID are generally resistant to psychological therapy and most eventually seek surgery and hormonal treatments, following which most enjoy a better quality of life.

For discussion

1 Is transvestism a true sexual 'disorder'?

2 Given the difficulties of treating people who engage in paedophilic behaviour, should they remain in hospital or some other institution to protect society from them? If they are released into society, should the public be made aware of where they live?

3 Consider the argument that applying behaviour modification principles to make a young person's behaviour more gender appropriate is simply reinforcing cultural stereotypes, is unethical, and is against the best wishes of the child, who should be free to express his or her own sexuality and behave in a way that they choose.

4 Could enforced celibacy as an adult increase risk for paedophilia? If so, how?

Further reading

Green, R. and Blanchard, R. (1995) Gender identity disorders, in H.I. Kaplan and B.J. Sadock (eds) *Comprehensive Textbook of Psychiatry*. Baltimore, MD: Williams and Wilkins.

Hall, G.C.N. (1995) Sexual offender recidivism revisited: a meta-analysis of recent treatment studies, *Journal of Consulting and Clinical Psychology*, 63: 802–9.

Laws, D.R. and O'Donohue, W. (eds) (1997) *Sexual Deviance: Theory, Assessment, and Treatment.* New York: Guilford.

Murray, J.B. (2000) Psychological profile of pedophiles and child molesters, *Journal of Psychology*, 134: 211–24.

Tierney, D.W. and McCabe, M. (2002) Motivation for behavior change among sex offenders: a review of the literature, *Clinical Psychology Review*, 22: 113–29.

Personality disorders

Personality disorders affect an individual for much of their life. A number of these disorders have been identified, some of which, such as the schizoid or schizotypal disorders, have some of the features of other conditions, but not to such a degree that a formal diagnosis can be assigned. Others, including borderline personality or psychopathy, differ markedly from any other DSM diagnoses. This chapter starts by outlining a general theory of personality disorders, before questioning the view of them as a distinct diagnostic category. A thorough review of all the personality types is not possible within a text such as this. Accordingly, the chapter focuses on two key personality disorders where perhaps the most relevant research has been conducted: borderline and antisocial/psychopathic personalities. By the end of the chapter, you should have an understanding of:

- A general theory of personality disorders
- Challenges to the diagnostic category of personality disorder
- The aetiology of borderline personality and its treatment
- Differing definitions of antisocial behaviour, psychopathy, their aetiology and potential interventions.

Personality disorders

DSM-IV-TR defines a personality disorder as an enduring pattern of inner experience and behaviour that deviates markedly from the expectations of the individual's culture in at least two of the following: cognition, mood, interpersonal functioning or impulse control. The pattern is inflexible and pervasive across a range of personal or social situations and is long lasting. Its onset can be traced back to adolescence or early childhood. It is usually associated with significant distress or impairment.

DSM-IV-TR identified ten personality disorders in three clusters, although the overlap between the disorders is so great that it can be difficult to distinguish one from another, raising concerns about the reliability and validity of such diagnoses:

- Cluster 1: '*Odd or eccentric*' – paranoid, schizoid and schizotypal
- Cluster 2: '*Flamboyant or dramatic*' – antisocial, histrionic, narcissistic, borderline
- Cluster 3: '*Fearful or anxious*' – avoidant, dependent, obsessive-compulsive.

The key characteristics of each condition are sketched out in Table 11.1. Community prevalence levels of the various disorders vary between 0.4 per cent of the population for the paranoid and narcissistic personality disorders and 4.6 per cent for borderline personality disorders (Davidson 2000). Personality disorders are often accompanied by other disorders of mood. Depending on the study, between 24 and 74 per cent of people with personality disorder also have major depression, and between 4 and 20 per cent have bipolar depression. The frequency of the co-occurrence of anxiety disorders is not known, but the prevalence of these disorders among people with personality disorders is thought to be greater than population levels (Davidson 2000). Antisocial and narcissistic disorders are generally thought to be more prevalent in men, and histrionic and borderline disorders more prevalent among women (APA 2000).

By definition, personality disorders are traits that are relatively stable over time. However, Loranger et al. (1994) found that many of these disorders appear to be less stable than first thought. Dependent and schizotypal 'personalities', for example, appear to be quite unstable even over relatively short time periods, while prevalence levels of antisocial personality fall as age increases, suggesting some moderation of behaviour over time. In the longest follow-up yet reported, Paris and Zweig-Frank (2001) reported the 27-year outcomes of a cohort of individuals diagnosed with borderline personality disorder. By this time, only 5 out of 64 individuals in the cohort met the criteria for the diagnosis: 10 per cent had committed suicide over the follow-up period.

Diagnosis of personality disorders has, until recently, been somewhat arbitrary. Widiger et al. (1987), for example, reported that 55 per cent of people diagnosed as having borderline personality using DSM-III criteria could also have been diagnosed as having schizotypal disorder. The change to DSM-IV-TR has reduced, but not obviated, this problem. The development of structured clinical interviews has also improved levels of diagnostic agreement, which now match those of the major diagnostic categories of depression, anxiety, schizophrenia, and so on. Loranger et al. (1994) reported inter-rater agreements to vary between 75 per cent for diagnoses of paranoid personality to 89 per cent for borderline and dependent personality types.

Table 11.1 Key characteristics of the various personality disorders

Disorder	Key diagnostic features include	
Paranoid	• Preoccupied with doubts of trustworthiness of others • Reads hidden demeaning or threatening meaning into benign events	• Suspicious of others • Reluctant or fearful of confiding
Schizoid	• Avoids close relationships • Few pleasurable activities	• Chooses solitary activities • Emotionally 'cold'
Schizotypal	• Ideas of reference • Odd beliefs or magical thinking • Unusual perceptual experiences • Suspicious	• Inappropriate or restricted affect • High anxiety in social situations associated with paranoid fears
Antisocial	• Failure to conform to social norms with repeated unlawful behaviour • Impulsive • Aggressive or irritable	• Disregard for safety of self or others • Lack of remorse • Deceitfulness
Histrionic	• Needs to be centre of attention • Inappropriate sexually seductive behaviour • Physical appearance is attention seeking	• Shallow expression of emotion • Misjudges closeness in relationships
Borderline	• Fear of abandonment • Identity disturbance • Feelings of emptiness	• Unstable and intense personal relationships • Recurrent deliberate self-harm
Narcissistic	• Grandiose self-importance • Fantasies of success, power • Need for excessive admiration	• Exploitative interpersonally • Lacks empathy • Envious and arrogant
Dependent	• Requires excessive reassurance in everyday decisions • Fears disagreeing with others	• Fears of being alone • Excessive need for nurturance
Obsessive-compulsive	• Preoccupation with rules and detail • Perfectionism • Hoards objects	• Unable to delegate • Miserliness

A dimensional view challenging DSM

Despite these improvements in identification and classification, some (e.g. Widiger and Costa 1994) have argued that people with these traits should not be assigned a categorical diagnosis identifying them as 'disordered' or mentally ill (see Chapter 1). The characteristics and experiences of people with these 'disorders' are not distinct from those of 'normal' individuals. They may therefore better be considered as at the extreme of the distribution of personality characteristics rather than categorically different to the norm. Here is a hypothetical profile, suggested by the *five-factor model of personality* (Costa and McRae 1995) for antisocial personality disorder:

- *Low neuroticism:* lack of appropriate concern for potential problems in health or social adjustment; emotional blandness.
- *Low extraversion:* social isolation, interpersonal detachment and lack of support networks; flattened affect; lack of joy and zest for life; reluctance to assert self or assume leadership roles, even when qualified; social inhibition and shyness.
- *Low openness:* difficulty adapting to social or personal change; low tolerance or understanding of different points of view or lifestyles; emotional blandness and inability to understand and verbalize own feelings; alexithymia; constricted range of interests; insensitivity to art and beauty; excessive conformity to authority.
- *Low agreeableness:* cynicism and paranoid thinking; inability to trust even friends or family; quarrelsomeness; too ready to pick fights; exploitive and manipulative; lying; rude and inconsiderate manner alienates friends, limits social support; lack of respect for social conventions can lead to troubles with the law; inflated and grandiose sense of self; arrogance.
- *Low conscientiousness:* underachievement: not fulfilling intellectual or artistic potential; poor academic performance relative to ability; disregard of rules and responsibilities can lead to trouble with the law; unable to discipline self (such as stick to diet or exercise plan) even when required for medical reasons; personal and occupational aimlessness.

Not only can the dimensional view be argued on theoretical and philosophical grounds, but also it may be better at predicting outcome than the DSM categorical approach. Ullrich et al. (2001), for example, found that scores on personality tests were better able to predict subsequent offending behaviour than categorical diagnoses of antisocial personality disorder. Heumann and Morey (1990) also found dimensional scores to be more reliable across clinicians than categorical diagnoses following DSM criteria.

A cognitive model

Beck et al. (1990) adopted an evolutionary perspective in their explanation of personality disorders. They suggested that key neuro-cognitive responses, including those affecting perception, mood and behaviour, are genetically pre-programmed and that these responses may be adaptive in some evolutionary stages, but less adaptive in others. Competitive behaviour, for example, may be of benefit at times of scarcity but not at times of social cohesion and mutual cooperation.

According to Beck and colleagues, what we term personality disorders are the inappropriate expression of these pre-programmed responses. They suggested that it is not the behaviour per se that is problematic, but the individual's lack of adaptability and responsiveness to the environment. Most of us learn to adapt our behaviour as a result of life experiences, particularly those in childhood. For some people, however, childhood experiences may maintain or reinforce inappropriate pre-programmed responses. The naturally shy child, for example, who is rewarded by his or her parents being over-protective, may not experience any other way of dealing with the world. As a result, they may fail to develop alternative coping skills and come to believe that the only way to survive in the adult world is to be dependent and subservient. Adult personality is the combined result of these pre-programmed responses and childhood experiences. Rigid cognitive schemata develop over time, each of which govern behaviour. Beliefs of 'being bad', for example, will lead to self-punishment; beliefs of 'not being worthy of love' will result in the avoidance of closeness, and so on.

As in his model of depression, Beck considered the core schema that drive personality disorders to be the cognitive triad concerning the self, others and the future. Instead of being episodically activated, as in the case of depression, those underlying schemata are more chronically activated in people with personality disorders. By placing these schemata as the central driving factor in all personality disorders, the cognitive model of personality disorders provides an explanation for an apparently diverse set of attributes and behaviours. The content of the schema may vary, as a result of different child and adult experiences (and perhaps the pre-programmed neuro-cognitive responses), but the underlying structures are the same. Some of the key beliefs for the different personality 'types' include:

- Avoidant personality
  - self: socially inept and incompetent
  - others: potentially critical, uninterested and demeaning
  - beliefs: the self as worthless and unlovable: 'If people get close to me, they will discover the real me and would reject me – that would be intolerable'.

- Dependent personality
  - self: needy, weak, helpless and incompetent
  - others: need a strong 'caretaker' in an idealized way; can function well in their presence, but not without them
  - beliefs: 'I need other people – specifically a strong person – in order to survive'.

- Schizoid personality disorder
  - self: self-sufficient and a loner
  - others: intrusive; closeness provides an opportunity for others to fence the individual in
  - beliefs: 'I am basically alone'; 'I can do things better when I am unencumbered by other people'.

According to Young and Lindemann (1992), the schemata most involved in personality disorders are those that relate to the need for security, autonomy, desirability, self-expression, gratification and self-control. Once formed, they become self-fulfilling, and are maintained through three different processes: schema maintenance, schema avoidance and schema compensation. Schema maintenance involves resistance to information or evidence that would disconfirm the schema through cognitive distortions and self-defeating behavioural patterns. Avoidance involves avoiding situations that may test or provide information counter to the schema. Finally, schema compensation involves over-compensating for a negative schema by acting in the direction opposite to the schema's content. This may reinforce the initial schema, as the outcome of such actions may not be positive. A shy woman, who believes herself unattractive to men, yet acts flirtatiously, for example, may find herself in situations in which she feels unsafe, or hurt by men drawn to her flirtatiousness who reject her when they find her withdrawn and quiet, thus supporting her schema of being unattractive.

Borderline personality disorder

DSM-IV-TR defines borderline personality disorder as a pervasive pattern of instability of interpersonal relationships, self-image and affect, and marked impulsivity. It begins in early childhood and its key characteristics include five of the following:

- frantic efforts to avoid real or imagined abandonment
- a pattern of unstable and intense personal relationships characterized by alternating between idealization and devaluation
- identity disturbance: markedly and persistently unstable self-image
- impulsivity in at least two areas that are potentially self-damaging (such as substance abuse, reckless driving)
- recurrent suicidal behaviour or self-mutilating behaviour; may involve repeated threats or gestures
- chronic feelings of emptiness
- inappropriate intense anger or difficulty in controlling anger
- transient stress-related paranoid ideation or severe dissociative symptoms.

About 2 per cent of the US population, of whom about 75 per cent are thought to be women, are thought to have this disorder (APA 2000). It typically begins in adolescence and continues through adulthood. Thoughts of suicide and suicide attempts are common: up to 9 per cent of people with this disorder eventually commit suicide. Self-harm, in particular cutting of arms, legs or torso, burning or other mutilatory acts, is also common. This is usually in response to experiencing negative emotions such as anger or anxiety, attempts to block painful memories, or as a cry for help. These behaviours may also be used in a manipulative manner, to control relationships or the behaviour of others around them. People with the disorder often have intense, over-involved relationships, and have an intense fear of being rejected. This may result in them becoming panicky at the thought of being isolated, and they may engage in self-destructive behaviour to try and maintain relationships that are disintegrating ('If you leave, I will hurt myself . . .').

Aetiology of borderline personality disorder

Biological factors

Genetic studies suggest that risk for borderline personality disorder may be, in part, a consequence of genetic factors, although the evidence is not strong. It is also methodologically flawed. Dahl (1994), for example, noted that the relevant evidence was based on studies that failed to carry out reliability assessments of diagnoses assigned to relatives of index cases, did not exclude other potential diagnoses, and/or used inappropriately low cut-off scores on a diagnostic scale. No single brain system or neurotransmitter has been associated with a diagnosis of personality disorder, although impulsivity, one of the diagnostic criteria, has been associated with low levels of serotonin (Gurvits et al. 2000). PET (positron emission tomography) scans have also suggested the possibility of subtle damage to the frontal lobes, which control emotion and planning (Goyer et al. 1994).

Socio-cultural factors

Risk for personality disorder is increased by a number of social factors. People with borderline personality are more likely than the general population to have been neglected by their parents, to have had multiple caregivers and to have experienced parental divorce, death or significant childhood trauma such as sexual abuse or incest (Brown and Anderson 1991). These findings suggest that the prevalence of borderline personality may vary according to differences in social factors that facilitate or inhibit close family relationships. Taking this argument further, Paris (1991) suggested that times of increased fragmentation of families and society are likely to be associated with higher levels of the disorder. As a culture loses its stability, so do the individuals within it, and increasing percentages of the population have feelings of alienation, confused identity, increased anxiety and fears of abandonment. In line with this argument, Paris noted that the prevalence of the disorder does seem to be increasing, but these findings may be confounded by changes in diagnostic criteria and more evidence is required to support this model.

Psychological processes

Psychological processes translate the social factors considered above into individual experiences. Object relations theorists (e.g. Kernberg 1985) suggest that as a result of negative childhood experiences, the individual develops a weak ego and needs constant reassuring. They frequently engage in a defence mechanism known as *splitting*, dichotomizing objects into 'all good' or 'all bad' objects, and fail to integrate the positive and negative aspects of self or other people into a whole (Klein 1927: see Chapter 2 in this volume). This inability to make sense of contradictory elements of self or others causes extreme difficulty in regulating emotions as the world is constantly viewed as either 'perfect' or 'disastrous'.

Cognitive theorists (e.g. Young and Lindemann 1992) argue that negative childhood experiences translate into maladaptive schemata about self-identity and relationships with others. These include beliefs that 'I am bad', leading to self-punishment; 'No one will ever love me', leading to avoidance of closeness; and 'I cannot cope on my own', leading to over-dependence. Self-harm may be maintained by operant processes: successful control of other people's behaviour by threats of self-harm reinforces its use as a means of coping. Lack of alternative coping resources may also mean that people with borderline personality disorder continue to use this type of strategy even in the absence of gain.

Strong negative emotions experienced as a consequence of catastrophic or other negative beliefs may also lead to episodes of self-harm. Many people with borderline personalities feel numbness or dissociation immediately before or while they harm themselves. In this way, self-harm may provide a means of escape from unbearable emotions, and may not be accompanied with feelings of physical pain. Other people, who feel confused and out of control, may actually find any pain they experience a form of self-validation of their own status and self-identity (see Table 11.2). According to the cognitive model, the use of self-harm to avoid emotional pain or manipulate others is indicative of high levels of interpersonal anxiety, low self-esteem and a lack of alternative coping strategies to deal with personal stress.

Treatment of borderline personality disorder

Psychological approaches

Treatment of people with borderline personality is not easy, and there are relatively few controlled trials examining the effects of therapy. Roth

Table 11.2 Example of an episode of self-harm and the development of alternative coping strategies

What happened before self-harm?	Two hours before meal with parents. They were stuck, not talking to each other. I felt stuck in the middle: couldn't eat
Feelings leading up to the self-destructive act	Numbness
Associated thoughts	I feel nothing. I am nothing
Self-destructive behaviour	Cut thighs with a razor blade
Feelings	No one feeling; pain on cutting
Associated thoughts	At least I feel pain: I can feel something
Consequences	More marks on thighs Blood on clothes Feel ashamed Hate self
Alternative to cutting	Go to bed and sleep or listen to loud music Tense my muscles really hard Melt ice cubes in my hand

Source: Davidson (2000)

et al. (1998) tried to establish some overall goals of therapy and some guidelines for who may benefit most from it. They suggested that:

- Psychotherapy is more likely to be effective for less severe personality disorders.
- In individuals under the age of 30 years, the greatest risk comes from suicide. Prevention of this, rather than 'cure', may form a legitimate therapeutic target.
- Individuals with good social support, chronic depression, who are psychologically minded, and with low impulsivity, are most likely to benefit from 'talking therapies'.
- People who have high levels of impulsivity are most likely to benefit from the limit-setting group or a therapist who is supportive of their attempts to struggle with uncontrollable impulses.
- Commitment and enthusiasm of the therapist may be of special significance, and finding the 'right' therapist for the 'right' patient is particularly important.

Because of the complex facets of the disorder, including the very real threat of self-harm, therapy with people with personality disorder is necessarily complex and the approaches used need to be governed by the individual's ability to cope with particular therapeutic issues. Sometimes the severity of symptoms brings people with borderline personality disorders into hospital. It may also be useful for them to spend some time in hospital during the early stages of therapy, as they may find these sessions so stressful they either drop out or harm themselves in some way. The hospital can provide a safe environment, where their behaviour can be observed and controlled, and both therapist and client have the security of knowing that any impulsive self-harming behaviour will be seen and dealt with should it occur.

Cognitive therapy

The core of cognitive therapy is the identification and modification of cognitions and underlying schemata that drive inappropriate behaviours. However, this typically combines with a number of other strategies, including developing problem-focused plans to cope with urges to self-harm, mood disturbances, suicidal feelings, improving relationship problems, and so on. The issues addressed in therapy and the strategies used are dependent on the most pressing and problematic behaviour at the time (Davidson 2000).

One of the most important therapeutic aims is to minimize risk of self-harm. This involves identifying the antecedents to episodes of self-harm, the thoughts and feelings that accompany them, and their consequences (see Table 11.2). Each of these forms a potential point of intervention, including preventing the need to self-harm or engaging in alternative behaviours at times of high risk for self-harm. Alternatives to self-harm often involve a high intensity action, such as listening to loud music or painful, but not personally damaging, behaviours such as squeezing a ball until the muscles ache. Where there is risk that an episode of self-harm will escalate into a serious attempt at suicide, specific strategies may be used to minimize this risk, including problem-solving and identifying reasons for living (see Chapter 8).

A second set of strategies aim to help the person tolerate dysfunctional mood states. One useful technique is known as mindfulness (Kabat-Zinn et al. 1992). This involves teaching the client to focus their concentration on a particular element of the environment or self at times of stress: to be aware of thoughts and feelings, but to observe them in a dispassionate way. They learn to 'stand back' from distressing thoughts and feelings and to become a 'participating observer'. With practice, this can result in the individual being aware of their emotions, accepting them, but not reacting to them. Alternative strategies for coping with adverse emotional states include deliberately provoking an incompatible mood state, for example by listening to music with a different mood or talking to a friend. Other strategies include the individual taking time out to look after themselves. This may involve behaviours as basic as remembering to take regular meals and enough rest and sleep, and as complex as learning to slow down and think before acting in self-destructive ways. It may also be useful to teach clients social skills, to help them be more effective in developing constructive and supportive relationships.

Any intervention using these strategies is likely to take up to nine months or more to be effective (Davidson 2000). Studies of cognitive interventions in this population are limited, and most are case studies. Turner (1989), for example, described a series of four case studies using a combination of drug and psychological interventions. Participants in the study were prescribed alprazolam, a benzodiazepine, for the first six months of therapy, to help protect against the strong emotions likely to be engendered by the psychological therapy, which involved the following:

- *imaginal exposure* to a variety of situations in which participants had previously experienced emotional problems, with the intention of teaching tolerance to high levels of emotional distress
- *cognitive restructuring*, including identification of cognitive distortions and rehearsal of more accurate alternatives and rehearsal of adaptive reactions to real-life problems
- *interpersonal skills training*, including training in reflective listening skills and role play.

The intervention proved effective, achieving significant reductions on measures of anxiety and depression, and frequency of self-harm. These gains were sustained for up to two years by all those involved, and for three years by three participants.

A controlled evaluation of a similar treatment package by Linehan et al. (1993) found that those who received the intervention had fewer episodes of self-harm than a group who received routine outpatient appointments, although levels of self-harm were high in both groups: 63 versus 96 per cent of those in each group self-harmed in the year following therapy. Participants in the active intervention also improved on measures of social adjustment, employment performance, and number of days in hospital relative to those in the control group. People in the control condition spent an average of 33 days in hospital: those in the intervention condition spent an average of 7 days.

Emotional awareness training
According to Farrell and Shaw (1994), people with borderline personality lack the ability to understand and describe their emotional state. Emotional awareness training is a structured programme to try and teach such awareness. Once this is achieved, according to Farrell and Shaw, the individual will have greater emotional stability and be more able to regulate arousal, resulting in more effective problem-solving and interpersonal functioning. The programme works through a hierarchy of emotional awareness, starting at awareness of bodily sensations, through awareness of the body in motion and arousal, awareness of extremes of emotion and differentiation and integration of conflicting emotions, to an understanding of more pervasive and less extreme emotions. A basic exercise would involve the individual standing in the far end of a room,

and then taking slow steps towards the therapist. As they walk, they are asked to describe any physical sensations they experience. Over repetitions of the exercise, they are asked to draw links between their feelings during the exercise and feelings outside the session. More advanced sessions involve monitoring thoughts, behaviours and emotions, and use of distress reduction skills. There are, as yet, no controlled trials of the effectiveness of this intervention (see Box 11.1).

Box 11.1   Sarah's borderline personality disorder

Here is a therapist's view of working with someone identified as having borderline personality disorder, using an interesting 'no-treatment' approach.

Sarah was 31 years old and had just moved back to live with her parents 'for a while'. The referring psychiatrist had judiciously refused to apply the label of borderline personality disorder on the grounds of its future potential for harm – nevertheless the referral letter bore the hallmarks: 'emotionally unstable', 'manipulative', 'potentially aggressive and violent' – an occasional 'self-harmer' with a history of involuntary treatments and involvement from a variety of professions including psychiatry, clinical psychology, social work, housing and the police.

What would you be expecting? Well, the Sarah I met in that initial meeting was so anxious she could hardly speak. She didn't look me in the eye once. At the end of the session, during which we mostly talked about everyday stuff, I asked her if she'd like to meet again next week.

'What do you think?' she said.
'Well, it's up to you.'
'Do you think it'll help?'
'I've really no idea – it might do and it might not.'

Thus started our first negotiation of competence – a central feature of our 'no-therapy' therapy. Sometimes we met in a consulting room, sometimes we went shopping, sometimes we went to an Internet Café – it was her choice. We drank coffee, talked about whatever Sarah wanted to talk about, and throughout that time I tried to refrain from assuming responsibility for her well-being or conduct in any way. One of the things that she decided she wanted to do with our time was to get the hang of email and the Internet. But she was a perfectionist, and when things went wrong, she seemed engulfed by feelings of failure, anxiety and blame ('This f**king computer's shit'). What seemed to work best at these times was to contain, minimize and normalize . . .

'Hey, maybe it's just a glitch – I remember when I first started to use the net . . . [tale of woeful incompetence]'

... and slowly but surely those major setbacks became minor setbacks as her confidence began to grow.

I learned that, for Sarah, the world seemed a black and white place – good or bad, triumph or disaster. Nowhere was this more apparent than in her chaotic personal relationships – a world of angels and devils. Sarah would model herself entirely on new found friend(s), who were invariably seen as the embodiment of wisdom and goodness ... that is until the friend would begin to withdraw from this lopsided, burdensome and exhausting 'godlike' position. Then Sarah, faced with her biggest fear of all – rejection – would wreak a vengeance that had left several ex-friends in hospital.

This was the point of '*no* therapy' – of avoiding that mantle of competence and expertise that invited Sarah, with her negligible self-esteem, to define herself as 'the other' – i.e. incompetent and unknowing. Even an invitation to 'collaboratively work on issues' would have been an example of me defining the overall framework, thus taking an 'expert' role. The point of this intervention was simply to attempt a stable relationship, undistorted by oppositional roles – in other words the focus was on process, *not* content. When this had been achieved then maybe – just maybe – we could entertain the idea of 'therapy'. Yet this stability in itself would be an achievement. Thus I found myself continually, at least in the early stages of our 'no therapy', having to be aware of, and step aside from, assigned roles (e.g. 'expert', 'the competent one', 'rescuer') – because to accept them would be to allow Sarah to play out the opposite (not knowing, incompetent, needing to be rescued).

One of my most valuable resources was variations on '*I don't know*'. This didn't mean avoiding stuff, it meant staying neutral and modelling comfort with uncertainty and shades of grey:

> 'So what do you think of the death penalty?'
> 'It's a complex issue – I really don't know?'
> 'But what about for people who kill children?'
> 'Well, some would say they deserve it, others might say that two wrongs don't make a right – it's a tricky subject. What do you reckon?'

An issue I initially found problematic was giving useful information without falling into the role of 'teacher'. My solution was to offer a range of options:

> 'So if I wanted to be a landscape gardener what should I do?'
> 'Blimey ... well I suppose some people might look in the Job Centre, others might check out courses somewhere like Green College, others might buy a lawnmower and stick a note in the local Post Office. Some folks might do something completely different ... I've no idea what would be the best option.'

'Hmmm, I might check out Green College. What do you think?'
'Who knows, they might have something useful.'

So it went on, with Sarah making steadily more competent decisions about her life. And how did I celebrate this newfound competency? Outwardly, I didn't. Why? Because Sarah was liable to lose herself in aiming to please others – when the only person she'd really benefit from putting first was herself:

'I went to Green College to look at courses the other day – what do you think about that?'
'Crumbs, I've no idea – never been there. Any good?'
'Yeah – I might try and sign up for one ...'

Look again at the conversation above – what was I being invited to say? 'That's great'? 'Nice one Sarah'? 'Go for it'? But then who would she potentially have been pleasing if she signed up? Herself – or me? At first, working in this way felt awkward and counterintuitive because it appears to partly deny the values that bring people into the 'caring' professions: that is, caring, concern, empathy and helping. However, it's the unsophisticated utilization of these qualities that seems most harmful to those who tend to attract the borderline label.

Sarah's life experiences had taught her that she was bad, sick, irresponsible and unlovable – that things she attempted of her own accord would be judged wrong, that she was to blame, she would be punished, and that taking control and responsibility was too dangerous to risk. For me there was initially the sense of a vacuum where her self-belief and confidence should have been and, at first, avoiding being 'sucked in' and used to fill that gap required a constant state of vigilance. Sarah was supremely skilled at subtly handing over the initiative – after all she'd spent her childhood learning, for the sake of her own safety and survival, to do exactly that.

After about nine months of 'no therapy' Sarah informed me that she wouldn't be requiring my services any more, as she was starting a job at the Botanical Gardens and it would be difficult to make the sessions. Additionally, she had started to feel that our work was 'going nowhere'. She was right – she had already got there. She was making competent, responsible decisions about her life of her own accord. And, crucially, I hadn't asked or demanded them (or indeed anything) of her – I had simply refrained from making them for her.

Additionally, she was able to end our relationship without guilt or recrimination, and as far as I knew that was a first. She had come wanting 'to be wrapped up in cotton wool and kept safe', but left appreciating 'you giving *me* the control' in a supportive (rather than hostile – like her childhood) environment. We never got as far as therapy, and that was fine.

Pharmacological treatment

Since the 1980s, there have been relatively few controlled trials of the effectiveness of drug therapy in borderline personality. These have had mixed and contradictory results. Soloff et al. (1993) found that a major tranquillizer, haloperidol, reduced a broad spectrum of symptoms, including anxiety, hostility and paranoid ideation. These benefits were not replicated in a subsequent study by the same group. Tricylics have proven ineffective, even in treating depressive symptoms. Indeed, some people have experienced an increase in suicidal threats, suicidal ideation and aggressive behaviour after taking them (Soloff et al. 1986). Accordingly, while some individuals may be helped by major tranquillizers, including the newer drugs such as reserpine (see Chapter 3), pharmacotherapy has so far not provided a consistently effective treatment for borderline personality disorder.

Antisocial personality and psychopathy

The terms antisocial personality and psychopathy are often used interchangeably. Indeed, the DSM-IV-TR category of antisocial personality disorder was intended to combine diagnoses of antisocial personality and psychopathy, which DSM-III did not. Critics of DSM-IV-TR have argued that it has not succeeded in this attempt, and that the two conditions are not synonymous: they have different characteristics and long-term outcomes. According to Hare et al. (2000), DSM-IV-TR still describes an individual who is criminally antisocial. By contrast, psychopathy refers to an individual who not only has these characteristics, but also experiences a poverty of both positive and negative emotions, and is motivated by thrill-seeking as much as any other gain. Antisocial behaviour tends to reduce with age; psychopathic behaviour does not.

DSM-IV-TR defines antisocial personality as a pervasive pattern of disregard for, and violation of, the rights of others occurring from the age of 15 years. Its core characteristics include:

- repeatedly performing acts that could lead to arrest
- repeated lying, use of aliases, or conning others for personal profit or pleasure
- impulsivity or failure to plan ahead
- reckless disregard for the safety of self or others
- consistent irresponsibility: repeated failure to sustain work or honour financial obligations
- lack of remorse for others.

People with antisocial disorder have been described as having a developmental delay in moral maturity and cognitive functioning (Davidson

2000), and tend to operate at a concrete rather than abstract level of intellectual functioning. As a consequence, they lack problem-solving skills, and tend to act impulsively with little consideration of long-term consequences. They often believe they can do exactly what they want and that other people are there to be exploited for their benefit. Prevalence rates of antisocial personality are as high as 3.7 per cent (Widiger and Corbitt 1995). Antisocial personality appears to remit with age: few if any people over the age of 45 years are diagnosed with the disorder (Swanson et al. 1994).

Without specific DSM diagnostic criteria, those who distinguish between antisocial behaviour and psychopathy generally use Hare's (1991) diagnostic criteria to define psychopathy. This identified two major clusters of behaviours characteristic of people with psychopathy: emotional detachment and an antisocial lifestyle. Emotional detachment involves a lack of capacity to process emotional information, and a consequent lack of understanding and disregard for the emotions of others. It is Hare's defining characteristic of psychopathy. Using this definition of psychopathology, Hare found that up to 80 per cent of criminals could be categorized as having antisocial personality disorder: only between 15 and 25 per cent met the criteria for psychopathy (Hare et al. 2000). A finding that supported his argument of clinical differences between the two conditions.

Aetiology of antisocial personality and psychopathy

The apparent confusion between antisocial personality and psychopathy has meant that the relevant literature often confuses the two concepts. Some studies of antisocial personality include within them what Hare and others would consider to be psychopathy. Other studies specifically focus on psychopathy as defined by Hare. As psychopathy is linked to an 'antisocial lifestyle', it is perhaps not surprising that many of the factors that predispose to antisocial behaviour are also associated with psychopathy. What distinguishes psychopathy from the antisocial personality are distinct neurological factors that are uniquely associated with the emotional detachment and limited range or depth of emotions central to the condition. Accordingly, this section first considers factors that increase risk for antisocial behaviour or personality, before considering the neurological factors that contribute uniquely to the development of psychopathy.

Genetic factors

Genetic studies of families have found it difficult to discriminate between genes for problem drinking, criminality and antisocial behaviour, all of which seem to be closely related. Nevertheless, at least two adoptee studies have implicated genetic factors in moderating risk of antisocial behaviour. Crowe (1974) reported that adopted-away children of women prisoners with antisocial personality disorder had higher rates of antisocial personality than control adoptees without this family history. Similarly, Cadoret (1982) found that rates of antisocial behaviour were higher among adopted adolescent females with a biological relative who engaged in antisocial behaviour than a matched group of adolescents without this family history. Risk for engaging in antisocial behaviour was further increased if the environment of the adoptive family was 'adverse', indicating an interaction between social and genetic factors in the development of antisocial behaviour. The behaviour of children of antisocial parents may itself provoke negative reactions from foster parents, exacerbating the child's behaviour pattern (O'Connor et al. 1998).

Biological mechanisms

High levels of impulsivity, irritability, aggression and sensation seeking are associated with low levels of serotonin. Low levels of sympathetic activity at times of stress may also be implicated in antisocial behaviour (Raine et al. 1998), perhaps because they predispose the individual to fearlessness and thrill seeking as a means of increasing arousal levels. High levels of testosterone may also be implicated in criminality (see Dolan 1994).

Some evidence of neural underpinnings of the disorder has also been found. Raine et al. (2000), for example, found an 11 per cent reduction in prefrontal grey matter volume among adolescents who engaged in antisocial behaviour compared to control groups. These neurological findings complement findings of psychometric studies such as that of Chretien and Persinger (2000) which show people diagnosed with antisocial personality disorder to perform less well on psychometric tests that assess prefrontal skills including critical thinking, conceptual flexibility, and spatial association than people without the diagnosis.

Socio-cultural factors

Social factors clearly influence the probability of an individual engaging in antisocial behaviour and being diagnosed with antisocial personality. Henry et al. (2001), for example, found that lack of emotional closeness within the family and poor parenting at the age of 12 years was predictive of both violence and delinquency at the age of 17 years. Having violent peers at this time was also predictive of later violent and non-violent delinquency. Perhaps the longest longitudinal study is the Cambridge Study in Delinquent Development (Farrington 2000). This was able to identify childhood factors that were predictive of antisocial personality and adult convictions up to the age of 40 years. The most important childhood predictors were similar to those of Henry et al. (2001): a convicted parent, large family size, low intelligence or school attainment, a young mother and disrupted family. Family factors may also contribute to the lack of emotion associated with psychopathy. It has been suggested that the sustained experience of negative emotional events during childhood results in the individual learning to 'switch off' their emotions both in response to negative events that occur to them and to their behaviours that affect others.

Borduin (1999) summarized the non-family antecedents of antisocial behaviour as:

- *peer relations:* high involvement with deviant peers, poor social skills, low involvement with pro-social peers
- *school factors:* poor academic performance, dropout, low commitment to education, poor academic quality and weak structure of school
- *neighbourhood and community:* criminal subculture, low organizational participation among residents, low social support and high mobility.

In an attempt to quantify the degree to which family and peer factors contribute to antisocial behaviour, Eddy and Chamberlain (2000) followed a group of offenders over a two-year period. Family management skills and deviant peer association accounted for 32 per cent of the variance in antisocial behaviour over this period.

The prevalence of antisocial behaviour is increasing over time in many countries, virtually doubling over a period of 15 years in the USA to about 3.6 per cent of the general population. There are also marked differences in its prevalence across countries, ranging from about 0.14 per cent in Taiwan to over 3 per cent in countries such as New Zealand. These various findings led Paris (1996) to speculate that Asian cultures are protective against antisocial personality as a result of their family structure, which is typically highly cohesive with clear limits on acceptable behaviour – the opposite constellation of characteristics to those implicated in the development of antisocial behaviour.

Cognitive models

Children within family systems that increase risk of antisocial behaviour do not have clear limits set to their behaviour. As a result, they frequently fail to internalize the controls on their behaviour that other children adopt. This environment may also foster beliefs about the individual and the world that support antisocial behaviour. Dodge and Frame (1982) suggested that all children develop routine responses that guide their behaviour: antisocial children develop aggressive and antisocial scripts and few pro-social ones. Lopez and Emmer (2002), for example, found that adolescents who engaged in crime believed aggression to be an effective and appropriate response to threat. Similarly, Vernberg et al. (1999) found that aggression among teenagers was associated with three key beliefs:

- aggression is legitimate and warranted
- aggression enhances power and esteem
- one should not intervene in fights.

Finally, Liau et al. (1998) found that specific beliefs led to specific behaviours. Beliefs concerning overt antisocial behaviour ('People need to be roughed up once in a while') were associated with overt but not covert antisocial behaviour. Conversely, beliefs related to covert behaviour ('If someone is careless enough to lose a wallet, they deserve to have it stolen') led to covert but not overt antisocial behaviour.

Similar scripts may underpin adult behaviour of psychopaths. Beck et al. (1990), for example, identified their core beliefs as 'people are there to be taken', and the strategy derived from this to be one of attack. Other core beliefs included:

- Force or cunning is the best way to get things done.
- We live in a jungle and the strong person is the one who survives.
- People will get at me if I don't get them first.
- I have been unfairly treated and am entitled to get my fair share by whatever means I can.
- If people can't take care of themselves, that's their problem.

Neurological mechanisms

Converging evidence suggests that the deficits in emotional processing associated with psychopathy are linked to damage to the limbic system, which inhibits the processing of emotional information. Laakso et al. (2001), for example, used brain imaging techniques to gain accurate data on the brain anatomy of 18 habitually violent psychopathic offenders. They found a strong negative association between the size of hippocampus and scores on the Hare Psychopathy Checklist, suggesting that damage in this area, which is involved in the acquisition of conditioned fear, may explain the lack of fear associated with psychopathic behaviour.

These data are added to by the findings of Kiehl et al. (2001) who used brain imaging to study activity within the limbic system in response to an 'affective memory task'. In it, three groups of participants (criminal psychopaths, criminal non-psychopaths and 'normal' controls) were asked to rehearse and remember lists of either neutral words or words describing negative emotions, and to identify these words in a subsequent recognition task. Psychopaths had significantly less activity within their limbic systems and greater activation of the frontal lobes while processing negative emotional words than the other groups, suggesting that the psychopaths and non-psychopaths used quite different brain systems to process emotional information. These data are similar to those of Intrator et al. (1997), who argued that psychopathic individuals have difficulty in processing emotional information and require more cognitive processes to do so than other people. Whether these factors are present from birth, or develop as a consequence of childhood experiences is not known.

Treatment of antisocial personality

Psychological interventions

Although there are a number of potential intervention types and focuses for people labelled as having antisocial personality disorder, treatment trials have almost exclusively focused on criminal behaviour and violence in adolescents. As such, they may be considered better as programmes designed to change criminal behaviour than antisocial personality per se. The consensus of these studies is that the classic 'boot camp' or incarceration does not work. More effective interventions appear to be those targeted at the family. Borduin (1999), for example, described a multisystemic, family-based approach, the goal of which was to provide participants with the skills to help them cope with family and extra-family problems. Family interventions aimed to improve parenting skills, encourage parents to support their child and reduce levels of parental stress within the household. Parents were encouraged to develop strategies to monitor and reward progress at school, and to establish homework routines. Peer-oriented interventions were designed to increase affiliation with pro-social peers through participation in youth group meetings, organized athletics and after-school activities. Sanctions were applied following associations with deviant peers. Cognitive behavioural interventions focused on teaching social and problem-solving skills. Interventions generally lasted up to five months, with initial sessions occurring as frequently as once a day, before tailing off to weekly as therapy progressed.

This approach has achieved significant success rates. Henggeler et al. (1992), for example, compared it with monitoring and general counselling in a group of 'serious juvenile offenders', most of whom had committed some form of violent crime. Immediately following the intervention, participants in the multisystemic intervention had improved their family and peer relationships more than those in the comparison condition. By one-year follow-up, they had also been arrested less frequently and had spent less time in prison: an effect that held up to the two-year follow-up. In a four-year follow-up of a similar trial by the same group, Borduin et al. (1995) reported a halving of the known recidivism rate among those who received the intervention compared to a control group (21 versus 47 per cent) four years after the intervention.

Pharmacological interventions

A number of pharmacological interventions have been used to treat individuals who present with delinquent or antisocial behaviour. Some have proven effective, particularly in the treatment of aggression. Lithium, for example, has been shown to reduce the number of impulsive aggressive episodes among offenders in an American correction centre, although only a quarter of the young offenders treated evidenced more than modest behavioural changes. By contrast, chronic aggressive behaviour among the older inmates was completely suppressed by lithium treatment, returning to baseline levels on placebo (Sheard 1971). SSRIs have also been suggested as a means of controlling impulsive aggression, but there are as yet no controlled trials of their efficacy. How these interventions would compare with psychological programmes in which individuals are taught to control their anger is not known.

Treatment of psychopathy

Psychopathic individuals do not seek treatment, and most interventions have occurred within prison or other custodial settings. As a result of their lack of motivation to change, psychopathy has often been considered an untreatable condition, although there have been some voices of dissent from this somewhat negative viewpoint. Of interest are three review papers of the treatment of psychopathy published within two years of each other and reviewing essentially the same literature. Salekin (2002) conducted a meta-analysis on data from 42 treatment studies, and concluded that while ECT and therapeutic communities were relatively ineffective interventions, good results could be achieved following psychoanalytic and cognitive therapy. Evaluating much the same literature, Reid and Gacono (2000) were more pessimistic in their conclusions and could find no evidence of consistent therapeutic gain following any form of treatment. Similarly, Wong and Hare (2002) concluded that of the 74 empirical studies they could identify, only 2 were adequately conducted, and that the evidence was so weak that it remained unclear whether any intervention can be effective.

Measuring the effectiveness of programmes to treat psychopathy is problematic. A defining characteristic of psychopathic individuals is that they tell lies and are manipulative. Self-report measures should therefore be treated with considerable caution. Even behavioural measures cannot be relied on. The results of a study by Seto and Barbaree (1999) illustrate the problem. Their study examined the impact of a relapse prevention programme for sexual offenders similar to those described in Chapter 9. Participants included a range of people, not just psychopathic individuals.

Their report focused on the relationship between apparent progress made within therapy as a function of in-session behaviour, homework quality, and therapist ratings of motivation and 'progress', and the frequency of reoffending following treatment. Among non-psychopathic individuals, greater within-therapy improvements were predictive of lower levels of offences following discharge from prison. By contrast, there was a *positive* association between apparent progress in therapy and the frequency of offences committed by the psychopathic individuals who took part in the programme: greater apparent progress was associated with higher offence rates. It seems that these people were able to learn the responses that the therapists considered indicative of progress and were able to simulate them. Those that were best at this simulation were also the most likely to reoffend. Therapy did nothing to change the underlying motivation of their behaviour.

Psychoanalysis

A number of early studies of the treatment of psychopathic individuals involved psychoanalytic methods (Salekin 2002). These were virtually all case studies, and none compared the intervention with any other form of treatment or changes within a control group. Case histories are generally considered with some caution, as clinicians typically report their treatment successes, not their failures, so they represent a biased sample of cases. The successes reported in these studies may therefore not indicate the likely success rates among an unselected group of individuals, and do not provide strong evidence for the effectiveness of psychoanalysis in this population.

Therapeutic communities

Therapeutic communities were first developed under the leadership of Maxwell Jones in the UK in the late 1940s. They provide an intensive 24-hour a day intervention to change psychopathic behaviour. Those within them are made responsible for the physical and emotional care of others within the community. The group itself establishes acceptable and unacceptable behaviours. Members are required to accept the authority of the group, and to submit to its sanctions if they disobey the rules. Communities are loosely based on Rogerian principles (see Chapter 2), and try to inculcate high levels of honesty, sincerity and empathy.

One of the best evaluations of the effectiveness of this approach was reported by Rice et al. (1992). They focused on a therapeutic community situated within a maximum security prison. The programme was led by those within it, and comprised 80 hours of intensive group therapy each week, intended to help participants develop empathy and responsibility for their peers. Those who responded well led therapeutic groups and became involved in administering the programme. All participants were involved in decisions about who was released or transferred from the programme.

Participants had little contact with professional staff. Nor did they have much opportunity for diversion: access to television or even informal social encounters were severely limited. Participation in the programme was compulsory: disruptive behaviour, for example, resulted in entry into a sub-programme in which the individual discussed their reasons for not wanting to be in the programme, but they were ultimately expected to resume participation. The authors noted that some of these programme characteristics would now not be ethically acceptable, but that the programme was well regarded at the time it took place in the 1960s and 1970s.

The programme accepted both psychopaths and non-psychopaths, who were followed up for an average of ten years after discharge. Analyses compared the outcomes on psychopathic individuals, non-psychopathic participants and a matched control group who did not enter the community. Their results were similar to those reported by Seto and Barbaree (1999). Non-psychopathic individuals were less likely to offend following discharge than those in the control group. By contrast, psychopathic individuals who participated in the programme were more likely to engage in violent crime following discharge than those in the control group, with known recidivism rates of 78 versus 55 per cent respectively. The therapeutic community approach may actually have taught psychopathic individuals how to manipulate others more effectively – an unexpected and unwanted result.

Cognitive interventions

Cognitive behavioural interventions may not be immune from this paradoxical outcome. Hare et al. (2000) examined the outcome of a number of short-term, prison-based, cognitive behavioural programmes including anger management and social skills training. Their data revealed that the interventions had little effect on reoffence rates of most psychopathic individuals. However, among offenders with particularly high levels of psychopathy, reoffence rates rose following treatment. Again, it seems that these courses taught these people how to be 'better psychopaths'.

Despite these negative results, a number of research groups have considered how the goals and strategies of cognitive behavioural therapy could be adapted to treat psychopathic individuals. Beck et al. (1990) attempted to define the realistic goals of such interventions. They noted that the individual will continue to act primarily out of self-interest, and that the goal of therapy should therefore be to help them act in ways that are functional and adaptive within these limits. Cognitive challenge, which lies at the heart of the intervention, may therefore not only address core schema such as 'I am always right', or 'Other people should see things my way', but also question whether antisocial behaviour is in the individual's own interest. Participants in therapy may, for example, be encouraged to question whether behaving in a way that assumes 'other people should see things my way' causes interpersonal friction which interferes with their own goals, and to change their behaviour if this is the case. This approach allows client and therapist to work together towards agreed goals.

Wong and Hare (2002) developed a substantial cognitive behavioural approach to the treatment of psychopathy, involving interventions at both an institutional (prison) and individual level. Their intervention was problem-focused and addressed issues specific to psychopathic individuals. Key elements of the programme included the following:

- *Support of pro-social attitudes and behaviour:* many psychopathic individuals within an institution seek out others with similar views who will reinforce their own beliefs. To minimize the risk of this happening, Wong and Hare (2002) suggest that a 'pro-social milieu' is established within the institution. This may be achieved by high-status individuals within the programme modelling positive attitudes and encouraging them in others, and encouraging group reinforcement of pro-social behaviours. Note that the results of Rice et al. (1992) suggest that this may not be easy to establish.
- *Changing dysfunctional behaviours – aggression, manipulation, intimidation:* strategies to achieve change include self-instruction training (Meichenbaum 1985: see Chapter 2 in this volume) to prevent over-reacting to situations in which the individual feels inappropriately threatened or angry, and interpersonal skills training where these are lacking and contributing to the use of intimidation or other dysfunctional behaviours. These may be taught through role play and reinforcement of appropriate behaviour.
- *Learning to take responsibility for one's actions:* the intervention here involves a detailed analysis of the factors that lead up to offences, and identifying where the individual made choices that ultimately lead to offending. This also forms the core of relapse prevention training (see Chapters 9 and 12), as information here both encourages the individual to take responsibility for the actions that led to offending behaviour and to identify strategies to avoid them in the future.

The programme also examined strategies for minimizing substance misuse and helping the individual gain work skills or develop leisure activities to help avoid boredom once discharged, as this may trigger antisocial behaviour. Finally, the programme addressed the social network into which the individual is discharged following their stay in prison. Attempts to maintain or re-establish links with supportive family or other means of social support were recommended, although family contacts may be conducted with some caution, as relationships with family members are frequently poor. Evidence of the effectiveness of these therapeutic approaches has yet to be tested empirically.

Chapter summary

1   DSM identifies ten types of personality disorder in three clusters: odd or eccentric, flamboyant or dramatic, and fearful or anxious.

2   These may be better considered as extremes on a continuum of personality factors rather than distinct 'diagnoses'.

3   Beck's evolutionary model of personality disorders suggests they are the inappropriate maladaptive pre-programmed responses to environmental events, that result from an interaction between genetic and childhood factors.

4   The core elements of borderline personality are an intense fear of abandonment, difficulties in coping with strong emotions and the use of self-harm as means of coping with strong emotions.

5   The origins of the disorder seem largely linked to experiences of childhood rejections and trauma that translate into strong negative self-schemata and dissociation as a means of coping with distress.

6   Borderline personality is difficult to treat, although significant therapeutic gains have been made using cognitive behavioural techniques. The effectiveness of a method known as emotional awareness training has yet to be fully evaluated. It seems resistant to pharmacological therapy.

7   Although DSM tried to combine psychopathy and antisocial behaviour under one diagnostic umbrella, critics such as Hare have argued that they are different conditions. The DSM diagnostic criteria describe someone who is criminally antisocial. Psychopathic individuals experience a poverty of emotions as well as engaging in antisocial behaviour.

8   Antisocial behaviour seems primarily to be the result of adverse social circumstances.

9   Psychopathic individuals also have neurological deficits within the limbic system that inhibit emotional processing.

10 Family or systemic interventions appear to be effective in the treatment of antisocial behaviour.

11 Finding effective treatments of psychopathic behaviour has proven more difficult. Standard interventions may actually increase psychopathic behaviour. Beck and Wong are presently developing cognitive therapeutic interventions that may prove more effective.

For discussion

1 Are the 'personality disorders' categorically different from the personalities of 'normal' people?

2 Should families whose dynamics increase the risk of their children developing personality (or other) disorders be routinely offered some form of therapeutic support?

3 Should psychopaths be treated or punished for their behaviour?

Further reading

Beck, A.T., Freeman, A. and associates (1990) *Cognitive Therapy of Personality Disorders*. New York: Guilford.

Davidson, K. (2000) *Cognitive Therapy for Personality Disorders*. Oxford: Butterworth-Heinemann.

Hare, R.D., Clark, D., Grann, M. and Thornton, D. (2000) Psychopathy and the predictive utility of the PCL-R: an international perspective, *Behavioural Sciences and the Law*, 18: 623–45.

Reid, W.H. and Gacono, C. (2000) Treatment of antisocial personality, psychopathy, and other characterologic antisocial syndromes, *Behavioral Science and Law*, 18: 647–62.

Salekin, R.T. (2002) Psychopathy and therapeutic pessimism: clinical lore or clinical reality?, *Clinical Psychology Review*, 22: 79–112.

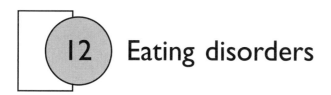

12 Eating disorders

Most of us have 'gone on a diet' at some time in our lives or wished to change our shape. Many of us succeed, at least in the short-term, although we often experience a gradual increase in weight as we get older. For some, the imperative to diet or change shape may be more extreme than the norm. Two eating disorders are considered in this chapter: anorexia nervosa and bulimia nervosa. By the end of the chapter, you should have an understanding of:

- The nature of anorexia and bulimia
- The various aetiological explanations of both disorders, including genetic, social, familial and cognitive factors
- The nature and effectiveness of interventions conducted with people who have eating disorders.

Although both disorders present in quite different ways, they have a number of elements in common, and many people with anorexia may shift into bulimic eating patterns at some time. Both involve prioritizing weight control. There are also significant differences between the conditions. People with bulimia, for example, are rarely underweight and they value being sexually attractive, unlike most people with anorexia. The chapter first describes the two conditions. Then, it discusses the aetiological factors that the conditions have in common and those on which they differ. It finally considers the treatment of the two conditions.

Anorexia nervosa

First identified in the late nineteenth century, anorexia nervosa involves behaviours intended to keep the individual as thin as possible. Indeed, the defining characteristic of anorexia is being significantly underweight. DSM-IV-TR suggested a weight-based cut-off point for a diagnosis of anorexia as being 15 per cent below the normal weight for age and height. Weight loss and control is generally achieved using one of two methods: the classic, Type 1, pattern of self-imposed starvation, and the Type 2 pattern of binging and purging through vomiting or the use of laxatives. Where anorexia is discussed in this chapter it usually refers to the first of these two types.

The DSM-IV-TR criteria for anorexia are

- a refusal to maintain body weight above a minimally normal weight for age and height
- intense fear of gaining weight, even though underweight
- disturbed body perception, undue influence of weight or shape on self-evaluation, or the denial of the seriousness of current low weight
- cessation of menstruation if this has already begun.

Between 80 and 90 per cent of those who develop anorexia nervosa are female, with the typical age of onset being between the ages of 14 and 18 years old (Pike 1998). Rooney et al. (1995) estimated the prevalence of anorexia nervosa to be 0.02 per cent of the total population and 0.1 per cent of young females. For most people with anorexia, weight control is a long-term issue. Loewe et al. (2001), for example, found that 21 years after their initial admission, just over half of a cohort of women identified as anorexic were 'fully recovered', 21 per cent were 'partially recovered' and 10 per cent still met the full diagnostic criteria for anorexia. Few had sought help or any form of treatment, and 16 per cent were dead of causes related to anorexia.

Many people with anorexia go on to develop eating habits typical of bulimia nervosa: that is, maintenance of normal weight while still having abnormal eating and vomiting patterns. In contrast to many mental health disorders, the prevalence of anorexia is highest among women in the higher socio-economic groups, and among those who achieve high academic achievement. People with anorexia tend to score low on measures of assertiveness and self-esteem, and high in self-directed hostility (Williams et al. 1993).

Despite their avoidance of eating, most people with anorexia are preoccupied with thoughts of food. They may spend much of their time thinking about food, preparing it for themselves or others, or watching others eat. They may report dreaming about food, experience hunger pains and retain an appetite for food. High levels of exercise or other behaviours that consume calories are common weight-loss strategies. Most, but not all, people with anorexia have a distorted body image, considerably overestimating their body proportions, and have a low opinion of their body shape (Gupta and Johnson 2000). Psychological problems including mild depression, obsessive-compulsive disorder and anxiety are common among people with anorexia.

The control and reduction in weight associated with anorexia can result in a number of health consequences. The most immediate is the absence of menstruation (or amenorrhoea). Less obvious problems include reduced bone mineral density and low blood pressure, rough and cracked skin, and dry and brittle hair. Health problems may move to crisis in the form of metabolic and electrolyte imbalances that can be life threatening. Across studies, between zero and 21 per cent of people with anorexia die, with the most common causes of death being starvation and suicide (Steinhausen and Glanville 1983).

Bulimia nervosa

The DSM-IV-TR criteria for bulimia are

- recurrent episodes of binge eating
- recurrent inappropriate compensatory behaviour, such as vomiting after eating, in order to prevent weight gain
- compensatory behaviours occur, on average, at least twice a week for three months
- undue influence of weight or shape on self-evaluation.

Many people with bulimia feel unattractive, have a fear of becoming fat, and consider themselves to be heavier than they actually are (McKenzie et al. 1993). Their attempts to avoid being overweight are more chaotic than in anorexia, and periods of controlled eating are frequently interrupted by repeated, relatively short episodes of uncontrollable eating. These are followed by behaviours designed to counteract the consequences of bingeing. The amount of food consumed in binges can be vast: up to and beyond 5000 calories at any one time. Food is not eaten for pleasure; indeed, it is usually eaten secretly, rapidly and barely tasted. Episodes are usually preceded by periods of considerable physical and psychological tension, and eating serves to reduce this tension. While bingeing, the individual may feel out of control; episodes are typically followed by feelings of guilt, self-blame and depression. The weight of people with bulimia usually remains within the normal range, although it may fluctuate considerably over time.

Between 80 and 90 per cent of people with bulimia vomit after eating in an attempt to control their weight, one-third abuse laxatives, while others may exercise excessively (Anderson and Maloney 2001). Compensatory behaviours reduce discomfort and feelings of anxiety, self-disgust or lack of control associated with bingeing. Ironically, however, they frequently fail to prevent the calorific intake from much of the

Table 12.1 Differences between 'classic' anorexia nervosa and bulimia nervosa

Restrictive anorexia	Bulimia nervosa
Body weight significantly below age/height norms	Weight varies: underweight, overweight, close to age/height norms
Less likely to experience intense hunger	More likely to experience intense hunger
Less likely to have been overweight in the past	More likely to have been overweight in the past
More likely to be sexually immature and inexperienced	More likely to be sexually active
Considers behaviour as reasonable and 'normal'	Considers behaviour as abnormal
Less likely to abuse drugs or alcohol	More likely to abuse drugs or alcohol
Less likely to engage in deliberate self-harm	More likely to engage in deliberate self-harm
Tendency to deny family conflict	Acknowledges family conflict
Age of onset between 14 and 18 years	Age of onset between 15 and 21 years
Relatively independent	Seeks the approval of others; wants to be attractive to others
Weight loss is not driven by a wish to look 'feminine'	Accepts social concepts of 'femininity' and wishes to adhere to them
High self-control	Impulsive and emotional instability

ingested food. Bulimia involves some risk to health. Repeated vomiting and laxative abuse can lead to problems including abdominal pain, digestive problems, dehydration, damage to the stomach lining and to the back of the teeth, where regurgitated acid can do permanent damage to the tooth enamel. The most serious outcome can be an electrolyte imbalance leading to renal damage and potentially fatal cardiac arrhythmias.

The prevalence of bulimia varies between 0.5 and 1 per cent of the population across community samples (Fairburn and Beglin 1994). However, among young women, rates are much higher. Up to 50 per cent of female students surveyed by Schwitzer et al. (2001) reported periodic binges; 6 per cent had tried vomiting; 8 per cent had used laxatives on at least one occasion. Few, however, engaged in these behaviours sufficiently frequently for them to be considered a disorder. In a population of slightly older women attending a family planning clinic, Cooper and Fairburn (1983) found that 20 per cent reported at least one bulimic episode; 3 per cent had used it as a means of weight control (see Table 12.1).

Aetiology of anorexia and bulimia

Genetic factors

Genetic factors may contribute to risk for both anorexia and bulimia. Klump et al. (2001), for example, estimated 74 per cent of the variance in anorexic behaviours to be attributable to genetic factors, after a twin study in which they found 50 per cent of MZ twins and no DZ twins to be concordant for anorexia. Similarly, Kendler et al. (1991) found the rate of concordance for bulimia between MZ twins to be higher than that between DZ twins, although the concordance rates for both were relatively low: 23 and 9 per cent respectively.

Biochemical mechanisms

A number of studies have found people with eating disorders to have low levels of serotonin. Whether this is cause or result of the disorders is unclear, and a number of explanations for these findings have been proposed (Kaye et al. 2001a), including the following:

- Low levels of serotonin may be the consequence of other conditions, including obsessive-compulsive disorder or depression, with which eating disorders frequently co-occur, and which are mediated by low serotonin activity.
- Low serotonin levels may contribute directly to eating disorders by causing cravings for carbohydrates and consequent binge eating.
- People with eating disorders may have naturally high levels of serotonin, which they try to reduce by starving and purging. Distorted eating patterns eventually reduce serotonin levels below normal.

No one hypothesis is strongly supported by the available data.

A second biological model, known as the *set-point theory* (Keesey and Corbett 1984), involves the hypothalamus. The lateral hypothalamus produces hunger when stimulated; the ventral hypothalamus triggers feelings of satiation and reduces hunger. The balance between the two controls eating and other metabolic processes, and tries to maintain the body at a weight set-point. Eating excessively results in a variety of metabolic processes that burn calories and reduce hunger. Eating too little results in reductions in metabolic rate and feelings of hunger. According to set-point theory, as an individual tries to diet and their weight begins to fall, hypothalamic activity reduces metabolic rate and increase the urge to eat. This combination of processes makes it difficult to lose weight. Successful dieting involves countering these processes, which remit in time and allow weight loss to occur. Individuals with anorexia learn to control their feelings of hunger and continue to control their diet whatever their symptoms. In doing so, they counter the effects of the hypothalamic control and continue to lose weight. People with bulimia, on the other hand, enter a constant battle against these processes: sometimes winning and sometimes losing. The set-point is not static and can be 'set' either up or down over time.

Socio-cultural factors

'Thin is attractive.' People with both anorexia and bulimia place a prime importance on shape and weight, probably because of a more general cultural emphasis placed on physical appearance within western society. Images of femininity and female attractiveness have shifted since the 1960s to a slimmer, less 'hour glass' shape. The classic 'figure' portrayed in *Playboy* magazine, for example, has slimmed during the 1990s, with smaller hips, waist and bust measurements (Rubinstein and Caballero 2000). Not surprisingly, the prevalence of low body weight and eating disorders are particularly high among those groups where physical attractiveness or performance is placed at a premium, such as models, dancers and athletes. As social groups develop positive attitudes towards thinness, levels of eating disorders rise within them. In the USA, for example, as a high value on thinness has shifted from white upper-class women to those in the lower socio-economic groups and other ethnic groups, so has the prevalence of dieting and eating disorders (Striegal-Moore and Smolak 2000).

Judgements based on weight are not only aesthetic; attributions of a variety of personal attributes can be based on the appearance of the individual. Food, eating and weight are seen by many as moral issues, and body shape can be major criteria of self- and other-evaluation (Wardle and Marsland 1990); many people hold prejudicial views against overweight individuals.

Over half the families in which an individual develops an eating disorder are likely to place a strong emphasis on weight and shape (Haworth-Hoeppner 2000). The mothers in such families are also more likely to diet and to be perfectionist than those in families where these disorders do not develop (Pike and Rodin 1991). Successful dieting may be one way of gaining acceptance from parents with high aspirations, particularly where the child has not 'succeeded' in other life domains. Not eating may make an individual important within the family, and give them some degree of control over other family members ('I'll eat if you . . .'). It may also provide a means of punishing them ('I'm not eating because you . . .'). A second consequence of anorexia is that it can lead the individual to be treated as a child, and allow them to avoid the responsibilities they would otherwise have to face; again, this may be most influential in families where there is a high emphasis on achievement.

A completely different model of anorexia is afforded by some family therapists, in which the person with anorexia is viewed as a symptom of a dysfunctional family. Minuchin et al. (1978) defined the characteristic of 'anorexic families' as being enmeshed, over-protective, rigid and conflict-avoidant. That is, there is conflict between parents, which is controlled and hidden. According to Minuchin et al. (1978) adolescence is a stressful time for such families, as the adolescent's push for their independence within the family increases the risk of the parental conflict being exposed. The development of anorexia prevents total dissension within the family, and may even hold it together as the family unites around the 'identified patient'. The presentation of the young person as weak and in need of family support ensures they become the focus of the family attention and deflects it away from parental conflict. Evidence for this theory is mainly based on the clinical experience of the Minuchin group of family therapists.

A final socio-cultural model suggests that both anorexia and bulimia may occur as a result of sexual abuse (Oppenheimer et al. 1985). According to this model, abuse results in the adolescent girl having strong negative attitudes towards their femininity, resulting in a rejection of the typical feminine shape and attempts to avoid it. This is most likely to occur around puberty. The evidence for this is not strong. Even though rates of sexual abuse are relatively high among people with eating disorders, it is not a defining characteristic, as they are no higher than those among people with mood, anxiety and other psychological disorders.

Psychological explanations

Weight-related schema

Social factors translate into behaviour through cognitive processes. Despite the many differences in presenting problems, Fairburn's (1997) cognitive model proposed a similar cognitive disturbance in both anorexia and bulimia: a set of distorted beliefs and attitudes towards body shape and weight. Thinness and weight loss are prioritized, perhaps because of the high status given to looking thin and attractive, and the individual works to avoid weight gain and becoming fat. The underlying schema involve judging one's self-worth on the basis of achieving a low body weight and being thin – so-called *weight-related self-schema*.

Once weight-related schemas are established, they distort the way the individual perceives and interprets their experiences. Other people are evaluated not on the basis of personal qualities, but in terms of being thinner or fatter than the individual. All activities are assessed in terms of weight control, and any situation that leads to self-evaluation also results in an intensified focus on weight and shape. Any weight fluctuation has a profound effect on thoughts and feelings.

For some people, their concerns and prioritizing control over their weight reflects a wider lack of self-esteem and the desire to gain control over one aspect of their life. They hope to feel better about themselves if they are thinner – a process that leads them to be perpetually dissatisfied with their appearance and to be continually working to lose weight.

Depression that seems to result from anorexic behaviour may intensify feelings of low self-esteem and increase dependence on controlling weight as a means of maintaining self-worth.

Initial attempts at weight loss may be triggered by a variety of factors, including critical comments about weight or appearance, teasing, or role confusion at the time of transition from child to woman. Dietary changes are typically maintained by a number of reinforcement processes. Positive reinforcement may initially be experienced in the form of compliments on looking slim. As these comments turn to concern, they may still provide positive reinforcement as the individual gains attention from their family. One specific form of feedback may be particularly important: the daily or weekly reinforcement of the bathroom scales. These provide unequivocal feedback on performance. For people with low self-esteem, weight loss may provide one element of control and success in their life. Weight loss becomes equated with self-esteem and self-worth, perhaps more so than any other factor in life. Anorexic behaviours may also be driven by negative reinforcement processes. People with anorexia experience an intense fear of gaining weight. Avoidance of this fear, by restrictive eating, provides relief from such fears.

Both anorexia and bulimia may reflect different ways of coping with the same underlying cognitions. According to Fairburn (1997), people with anorexia are more able to sustain long-term control over their eating than those with bulimia, who are more chaotic and less consistent. He suggested that because of their restrictive dietary habits, individuals with both bulimia and anorexia are under significant psychological and physiological pressure to binge eat. To cope with these demands, both groups set a series of rules to govern their eating: when they should eat, what they can and cannot eat, and so on. These rules are typically perfectionist and difficult to achieve. Despite this, people with anorexia have sufficient self-control to be able to follow the rules they have set. By contrast, individuals with bulimia may on occasion fail to do so.

Once an individual with bulimia starts to eat, they typically engage in dichotomous thinking ('I've eaten, so that's the end of my diet. What's the point of even trying to diet . . . ?') and a binge occurs. Binge eating also tends to improve low mood, and is thus in itself reinforcing. This is due to several effects, including drowsiness that follows eating large quantities of food and, in those who vomit, the feeling of relief and release of tension. These initial positive feelings are typically followed by feelings of disgust and shame at overeating, which results in a determined effort to follow the dietary rules set, which places the individual at risk of bingeing, and so the circle continues (see Figure 12.1).

Distorted body image

A second cognitive model, involving a distorted body image, applies only to anorexia. This suggests that people with anorexia feel 'fat'

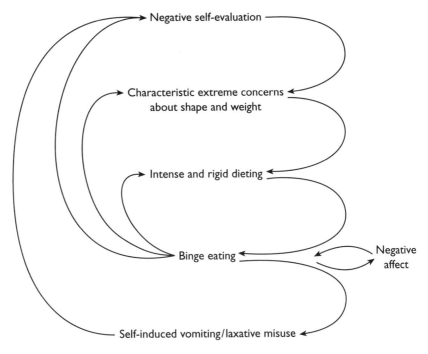

Negative self-evaluation

Characteristic extreme concerns
about shape and weight

Intense and rigid dieting

Binge eating

Negative
affect

Self-induced vomiting/laxative misuse

Figure 12.1   The cycle of bulimic behaviour and cognitions

even when their weight is actually clinically subnormal (Bruch 1982). Summarizing a plethora of research studies, Gupta and Johnson (2000) suggested that many people with anorexia considerably overestimate their body proportions, have a low opinion of their body shape, and consider themselves to be unattractive. By contrast, Slade and Brodie (1994) suggested that many of these reports represent an *emotional* reaction to their body shape rather than a perceptual experience. They suggested that those who experience an eating disorder are uncertain about their body size and shape, and only when they are compelled to make a judgement about these issues do they err on the side of reporting an overestimated body size. Such speculation is supported by the work of, among others, Epstein et al. (2001), who were able to show experimentally that people with anorexia do not have long-term perceptual distortions of their body size.

The restricted food intake achieved by people with anorexia may have biological effects unrelated to body size or shape that serves to perpetuate cognitive distortions. Starvation affects a number of cognitive processes, resulting in poor concentration, concrete thinking, rigidity, withdrawal, obsessive-compulsive behaviour and depression. As a result, starvation may lead to a positive feedback loop in which people with anorexia become increasingly rigid in their beliefs and are unable to consider other ways of looking at their problem (Whittal and Zaretsky 1996).

Psychoanalytic explanations

Classic psychoanalytic theory provides a number of explanations for anorexia (Zerbe 2001). One explanation is that it stems from an unconscious confusion between eating and the sexual instinct. Some women may avoid eating as a means of, symbolically, avoiding sex. Another interpretation suggests that women with anorexia have fantasies of oral impregnation, and confuse fatness with pregnancy. Starvation reduces the risk of pregnancy. Yet another explanation is that anorexia reflects a regression to an earlier stage of development. The individual literally 'shrinks' in size. This, and the cessation of menstruation, is an unconscious rejection of adulthood and a wish to revert to a childhood state. Finally, anorexia is considered the result of an arrested psychosexual development. If the child is fixated in the oral stage, sexual anxieties and obsessions are likely to be expressed as disturbances of eating.

Integrating psychoanalytical and cognitive processes, Bruch (1982) argued that anorexia is the result of disturbed mother–child interactions that lead to ego deficiencies including a poor sense of autonomy and control, manifest through disordered eating patterns. According to Bruch (1982), some mothers fail to attend appropriately to their young children's needs, perhaps as a result of prioritizing their own needs over those of the child or misunderstanding their behaviour. They may, for example, provide food and intimacy at times that suits them rather than the child, or misinterpret the child's emotions or needs. As a result, the child may grow up confused and unaware of their own internal needs, not knowing for themselves when they are hungry or full, and unable to identify their own emotions. As a consequence of their confusion, they turn to external guides such as their parents, and appear to be 'model children'. However, they fail to develop genuine self-reliance and the experience of being in control of their behaviour, needs and impulses. They feel as if they do not own their own bodies. Adolescence increases their innate need to establish autonomy, but they feel unable to achieve this. To overcome their sense of helplessness, they seek excessive control over their body size and shape and eating habits. A number of studies have provided some support for Bruch's assertions. Steiner et al. (1991), for example, reported that many parents of young girls with anorexia tended to have fed them as a baby on their schedule rather than that of child. Fukunishi (1997) reported that many people with bulimia mistake emotions such as anxiety or upset as signs of hunger and respond to them by eating. Finally, Walters and Kendler (1995) reported that people with eating disorders tend to rely excessively on the opinions of others, and worry about how other people view them (see Box 12.1).

Box 12.1 Bulimia and anorexia

Here are two accounts of people with bulimia and anorexia. Despite both being eating-related disorders, their discourse is completely different. The account of the person with bulimia centres on the drive to eat and the guilt and discomfort associated with it. That of the person with anorexia focuses on wider issues, in particular issues of revenge and control. The pathways to each disorder differ across people, so although these may be considered 'typical' accounts in some ways, the accounts of other people with the same disorder may differ markedly.

Bulimia

I think it's easier not to drink or take drugs than to eat normally. You can either take them or not. If you don't want to – you just avoid them. But eating is so different. You have to eat . . . and once you – well, I – start it's so difficult to stop. I want to be slim and look good. And I like my food. So I say to myself OK. Today you will not eat till 6 o'clock and you will eat a healthy meal. So I start the day with good intentions.

But then I live for food. I can avoid eating at lunchtime – it's almost easy with people around me. But as the day goes on, I want food!! I don't feel hungry. But what happens when I get home, I just want to eat. It's on my mind, and I know there's food in the fridge – lovely ice cream . . . chocolate. God, I love chocolate! Why can't I like something healthy and low calorie?! I sit and watch the TV, but I'm thinking of food. I am now! Anyway, some nights I can get by, cook myself something reasonable – nights when I'm busy or interested in what's on TV or something. But other nights, I just go straight to the fridge and have a snack. Unfortunately, it's never a small one – what does that do to you? A couple of biscuits just doesn't work for me. So, I tend to snack on something big and calorific. Even that would be OK if I could stop there. But I tend to think, 'I've blown it now . . . I've begun to eat, so what's the point of stopping now. Once I've blown away my good intentions, then I just give in to eating I suppose. So I eat and eat. I don't stop when I am full. I eat till I am bursting. I feel uncomfortable, and I know I'm bound to put on weight. I feel really guilty – another day when I haven't kept my good intentions. So, I make myself sick. I'm good at it. It's not difficult now. Then I feel better. At least I can relax and know that I won't put on weight. It feels such a relief. But I also know that I shouldn't have had to do it, so I feel guilty and vow that tomorrow I will control my eating and not need to do it. But, of course, tomorrow never comes . . .

Anorexia

My anorexia kicked in at age 13. I battled food issues for years before that. Mum was always on a diet – and I was often hooked into being her dieting partner, and sometimes competitor. Both our food struggles – I see now – only diverted our and the family's attention from the emotional turmoil permeating our household. I became the convenient whipping post of my parents' outbursts of anger, insecurities . . . I was hit a lot and verbally abused.

At age 13, my parents cracked down and tried to totally control my life – friends, boyfriends – everything. That control pushed me over the edge . . . Dieting became an obsession for me. I dropped two stone in a month! The hunger was still there. Some days, all I thought about was food. But I was determined to conquer it. I strove for complete control – perhaps the only control I had. I felt repulsed if I ate – I had let myself down, lost control.

I wanted to look good, to fit the ideal of womanhood. But a large part of the drive was revenge! I loved to see my parents' reactions to me starving. Dieting was no longer good, something to do with my mother . . . it was a weapon. Turning her own behaviour on her. They were partly angry because they could not control this part of me, and partly fear and worry. But I had control. They ranted, they shouted, and tried to get me to eat. But I wouldn't – not for them.

I began to lose contact with my feelings. I wanted to starve to be in control, to prove I could do it, but also because I deserved to . . . because I hated myself.

Interventions in anorexia

Given the multiple routes to anorexia, the optimal emphasis of treatment may vary considerably across individuals. Potential interventions include cognitive behaviour therapy, family therapy, insight-oriented psychotherapy, with each being complimentary rather than competitive interventions. Interventions can be considered in two stages: first, initial treatment, usually in hospital, focusing on weight gain, and second, longer-term outpatient treatment focusing on sustained cognitive and behavioural change.

Promoting weight gain

Inpatient care may be necessary where an individual's weight is seriously compromised, that is less than 75 per cent of 'normal'. Interventions in hospital usually focus on providing extrinsic rewards for weight gain. This operant-based process involves gaining pre-specified rewards for pre-specified gains in weight, the most valued of which may be discharge from hospital on achieving a target weight. This avoids the danger of rewarding food intake, which may be subsequently vomited up and is therefore ineffective.

Some years ago, the nature of these rewards included access to a telephone or television. These are now considered to be basic rights, and removal of them would infringe such rights. Accordingly, the 'rewards' for eating are now typically defined by the individual and are more than the basic elements available to all inpatients. They may include increased social privileges, access to visitors, and exercise privileges. Calorific intake is gradually increased over time: too high an initial calorie intake may result in refusal to consume the calories. Nurses may also educate the individual about anorexia and provide more informal support and encouragement. Critical here is the reassurance that weight gains made at this time will not be translated into becoming overweight in the long run. Schwartz and Thompson (1981) reviewed the outcome of inpatient programmes such as this and found that at follow-up, there was a 6 per cent mortality rate from self-starvation, 49 per cent of people had recovered, 31 per cent had improved but still had an eating disorder, and 18 per cent showed no change from their original state.

While a majority of people gain weight in this first phase of treatment, some continue to lose weight, possibly to the stage that this becomes life-threatening. This presents a significant clinical and ethical challenge to those involved in the care of such people. A key issue at this time is whether nutrition should be given against the affected individual's wishes. This debate has focused, in particular, on the competence or otherwise of people with anorexia to make what are truly life and death decisions. Some clinicians (e.g. Russon and Alison 1998) have argued that the majority of people with anorexia are mentally competent to make decisions about whether or not to eat. As a result, they suggest that it is inappropriate to treat them against their wishes, even if this leads to their death. Others (e.g. Treasure 2001), while accepting that force-feeding is inhumane and unacceptable, have pointed out that both it and other active treatments can be legally used with people with anorexia in extremis, as they are not mentally competent to make decisions that may result in their death.

Treasure (2001) identified four general principles that define whether an individual is competent under the law to make therapeutic choices or to refuse treatment. They must be able to

- take in and retain information relevant to their decision and understand the likely consequences of having or not having the treatment
- believe the information

- weigh the information in the balance as part of the processes of arriving at a decision
- recognize they have a health problem and take action to remedy their condition.

According to Treasure (2001), individuals with anorexia do not conform to these criteria and are therefore deemed, under law, incompetent to make medical decisions that may endanger their life. Accordingly, doctors have the right to treat the individual without their consent. This argument is in accord with previous legal precedents (Dyer 1997) which have stated that compulsory treatment of people with anorexia, including forced feeding, is both legal and may be necessary on occasion.

Cognitive behavioural approaches

The second phase of treatment involves interventions aimed at achieving and maintaining long-term behavioural change. Perhaps the most widely used cognitive behavioural approach was developed by Garner and Bemis (1985). This was divided into a number of phases, the first of which was intended to establish a working alliance with the individual. Garner and Bemis stated that at this time, it is critical that the individual's core beliefs are not directly challenged, as this is likely to result in a withdrawal from therapy. Instead, the therapist needs to align with the individual, recognize how their weight-control strategies are intended to fulfil important functions for them, and appreciate that these strategies have been partly successful. This may be linked to questioning whether they have achieved everything the individual intended, and evaluating the emotional and physical costs of extreme dieting. The first few sessions may be spent developing a list of the advantages and costs of their anorexic behaviour. There may also be exploration of the deeper schemata underlying this behaviour. Homework assignments may be used to gather data on how events influence thoughts and feelings, and to provide opportunities to practice different ways of interpreting weight- and eating-related events. Only once a working alliance has been achieved and the individual is motivated to at least consider change, can cognitive therapy begin.

Cognitive interventions may have multiple targets, including modifying inappropriate cognitions and developing autonomy. Emphasis may be placed on challenging perceptual/attitudinal distortions. While these may never change to perceptions of being thin, an awareness of distortions and an acceptance that they have some degree of exaggeration may help change the individual's willingness to eat. Autonomy may be encouraged by challenging negative cognitions and encouraging the individual to trust their own intuitions and feelings. Cognitive challenges encourage the individual to consider the high emotional cost of their behaviour, and help them to explore some of the more entrenched schemata that underpin this behaviour, such as the belief that body weight or shape can serve as the sole criterion for self-worth and that complete control of one's body is necessary. Participants in therapy may also be taught problem-solving techniques to help them deal with any crises that might occur more effectively.

Despite the life-threatening nature and chronicity of the problem, there are remarkably few controlled trials of the effectiveness of cognitive behavioural interventions in anorexia (Pike 1998). This may be because the chronic nature of the condition means that many people could take part in several treatment programmes over the course of their condition, making it difficult to ascribe changes in their behaviour to any one intervention. The long-term risk of serious harm if individuals are assigned to a no-treatment condition and high dropout of most interventions also makes it difficult to conduct standard trials.

What data there are, nevertheless, suggest that cognitive behavioural therapy may be an effective intervention. In an early trial, Channon et al. (1989) compared behavioural and cognitive behavioural approaches. Behaviour therapy involved a gradual exposure to avoided foods: cognitive behavioural therapy identified challenging dysfunctional beliefs about eating. There were few differences between the two interventions at both six- and twelve-month follow-up, although the authors suggested that the greater acceptability of cognitive procedures and the lower attrition rate associated with them made this the better of the two interventions. The study had no 'no-treatment' control as this was considered unethical, so the benefits of intervention over no intervention could not be determined. In a similar comparison, Treasure et al. (1995) compared the effectiveness of a cognitive and combined cognitive/psychoanalytical therapy. By the end of the one-year intervention, both therapies proved equally effective, with 63 per cent of participants having achieved a 'good' or 'intermediate' recovery.

Family therapy approaches

A number of different family therapies have been used to treat anorexia, although all seek to change the power structure within the family by empowering parents, preventing alliances that cross generations, and reducing tensions and problems between parents. Note that this approach contrasts markedly with the cognitive behavioural interventions described above which encourage autonomy and personal control over eating.

Structural family therapy

One of the first family approaches to treating anorexia was reported by Minuchin et al. 1978: see Chapter 4 of this volume. They reported an 85 per cent success rate, although this has been viewed with some caution as it was based on a series of case reports with relatively young and 'intact' families rather than data from controlled trials. More recently, Russell et al. (1987) followed a similar therapeutic approach which focused on the underlying stresses within the family. The approach had three tasks. The first involved engaging the family in the therapy process. They termed the second part the refeeding phase. In this, the family was observed eating together to identify relationships, communication of support, and rules about food and eating. At this time, the 'identified patient' and their siblings were encouraged to align, in order to reinforce appropriate boundaries within the family. The final stage involved changes in the family system, including return of control over eating to parents, working to support cooperation between parents, and stopping alignments or collusion between one or other parent and the person with the eating disorder.

Russell et al. (1987) compared the effectiveness of this approach with that of individual supportive therapy in the treatment of people with both anorexia and bulimia. Their findings were somewhat disappointing. Although many of the people with anorexia achieved significant weight gain, most participants achieved only modest gains on more general measures of outcome. At one-year follow-up, 23 per cent of the participants were rated as having a 'good' outcome, 16 per cent had a 'moderate' outcome and 61 per cent had a 'poor' outcome. Family therapy proved more effective than individual therapy on measures of weight, menstrual functioning and psychosocial adjustment for participants whose problems began before the age of 19 years and where the duration of problems was less than three years. Individual therapy proved marginally more effective than family therapy for older participants.

Behavioural family therapy

Behavioural family therapy (Robin et al. 1995) combines systemic and behavioural therapy approaches. The goals of therapy begin with restoration of weight. Strategies to achieve this include changing eating habits and cognitive therapy to minimize body image distortions, fear of fatness, and feelings of ineffectiveness. Family interaction patterns such as conflict avoidance, enmeshment and over-protectiveness are also targeted. Therapy follows three phases. First, control over eating is taken away from the individual and given to the parents, to restore the family hierarchy. Parents are taught and encouraged to implement a behavioural weight-gain programme for their child, including making meals, regulating exercise and establishing consequences for following or not following the plan. Once weight gain has been achieved, therapy moves to the second stage. This combines three elements:

- cognitive restructuring of distorted body image and unrealistic food beliefs
- working with the family to alter enmeshment, coalitions and inappropriate family hierarchies (see Chapter 4)
- gradually giving control over eating to the person with the eating disorder.

Finally, the family may be taught problem-solving and communication skills. Robin et al. (1995) evaluated the effectiveness of their approach, comparing it with supportive individual therapy, in a group of female adolescents aged between 12 and 19 years. At one-year follow-up, both forms of treatment had positive effects, although there were no between group differences.

Psychoanalytic therapy

A number of case studies and uncontrolled studies have shown psycho-analytic approaches to the treatment of anorexia to be effective with adolescents with relatively minor problems. However, studies of the effectiveness of this approach compared to others are limited. Dare et al. (2001) provided one such comparison. Their psychoanalytic intervention was relatively time-limited, averaging 24 sessions over a one-year period. In it, the therapist took a non-directive stance, gave no advice about eating or other problems of symptom management. Instead, he or she addressed the conscious and unconscious meanings of the symptom (that is, not eating) in terms of the individual's history, the effects of the symptom and its influence on their current relationships, and the manifestations of these influences in their relationship with the therapist. Dare et al. (2001) compared the effectiveness of this approach with family therapy similar to that provided by Russell et al. (1987), an individually based intervention with elements of both analytic and cognitive approaches, and a low-contact support condition in which participants received no systematic therapeutic approach. Participants in the study had a relatively poor prognosis. They had a late age of onset, a long duration of problems, and had not improved with other therapies. Nevertheless, by the end of the year-long interventions, about one-third of the women in the active interventions no longer met the criteria for a diagnosis of anorexia. Only 5 per cent of those in the control group had shown such improvements. No one intervention proved more effective than the others.

Pharmacological interventions

Pharmacological interventions do not appear to be particularly effective in the treatment of anorexia. Jimerson et al. (1993) conducted a meta-analysis of all the controlled studies of the treatment of anorexia using antidepressants and neuroleptics then available. They found little evidence of any benefit. Results of trials since this review have not changed the general picture. Although treatment with SSRIs may prove effective in the treatment of depression that may coexist with anorexia, there is no evidence of consistent changes in 'core' anorexic symptoms (Ferguson et al. 1999). There are some exceptions to this finding, however. Kaye et al. (2001b) reported an intervention in which women with anorexia were treated either with fluoxetine or placebo control. Of those on fluoxetine

63 per cent achieved a 'good' response as a result of gains in 'appropriate weight maintenance', obsessionality, 'core eating disorder symptoms' and mood. Only 16 per cent of those in the placebo group achieved comparable gains. The effectiveness of pharmacological interventions may well depend on the willingness of patients to remain on medication, as compliance is generally low. In a meta-analysis of comparisons between psychological and pharmacological therapies, Bacaltchuk et al. (2002) found overall remission rates of 20 per cent for following treatment with antidepressants compared to 39 per cent following psychotherapy. Dropout rates were higher for antidepressants than for psychotherapy.

Interventions in bulimia

Cognitive behavioural therapy

In contrast to interventions in anorexia, those in bulimia are more structured, and have a better prognosis (Anderson and Maloney 2001). One of the pioneers of cognitive behavioural interventions in bulimia developed a three-stage approach (Fairburn 1997). The first stage has two aims: first, to provide a rationale for the treatment, and second, to replace binge-eating with a pattern of more regular eating. Eating is restricted to three planned meals a day, plus two or three planned snacks, none of which are followed by vomiting or other compensatory behaviours. This is not usually accompanied by weight gain. Indeed, reductions in the frequency of binge-eating should result in weight loss. Distracting activities, such as having a bath or contacting friends, can be used to minimize the risk of bingeing. Once regular meals are established, the desire to vomit may reduce naturally. However, where this remains problematic, continued use of these inhibitory behaviours for an hour or so after eating may be necessary. Laxative and diuretic use should also be stopped at this time, with a phased withdrawal programme established for those who are unable to do so immediately. Knowledge that these strategies do not prevent food absorption aids this process. Towards the end of this phase, therapy sessions may involve both the client and key friends or relatives, with the intention of establishing an environment that will support behavioural change.

The second stage involves the using of both behavioural and cognitive procedures to counter concerns about shape and weight, and other cognitive distortions. Behavioural interventions may involve eating previously avoided types of food and, where necessary, increasing energy intake. This may be achieved by working up a hierarchy from relatively acceptable foods to those that initially invoke high levels of anxiety or desires to binge or purge. At the same time, clients are encouraged to identify negative assumptions about their shape and weight, and to find evidence in support or against them using cognitive challenge techniques.

Fairburn (1997) noted that many clients have a limited repertoire of such thoughts, triggered by a range of different circumstances. By repeatedly examining these thoughts and the circumstances that trigger them, their potency and automacity gradually declines. Further behavioural hypothesis testing may involve a gradual introduction of previously avoided and feared behaviours, including exposing body shape through wearing tight clothing, undressing at swimming baths, or even no longer undressing in the dark.

The third stage involves maintenance of progress achieved in the first two stages and consideration of strategies to prevent relapse once therapy is terminated.

Cognitive behavioural therapy is considered the psychological treatment of choice for bulimia (Anderson and Maloney 2001), achieving good results both in the short- and long-term. Wilson (1996), for example, reported that an average of 55 per cent of participants in cognitive behaviour therapy programmes no longer purged at the end of therapy, and those who continued to purge did so much less: an average of an 86 per cent reduction in purging. Long-term follow-up data are also encouraging. Fairburn et al. (1995) reported that 63 per cent of their sample had not relapsed at an average of nearly six-year follow-up. Comparisons of behaviour therapy and cognitive behaviour therapy suggest that both are equally effective in reducing binge–purging immediately following treatment. However, cognitive behaviour therapy is superior in reducing the 'core psychopathology' of distorted weight and shape and in maintaining long-term changes (Fairburn 1997).

Interpersonal psychotherapy

One other psychological approach appears to be particularly effective in the treatment of bulimia. Interpersonal psychotherapy (IPT) focuses exclusively on strategies for improving interpersonal relationships to the exclusion of any other therapeutic issues. Fairburn et al. (1993) found it to be less effective than cognitive therapy in the short-term. However, by one-year follow-up the differences between the two conditions were not significant, as a result of continuing improvements among those who received IPT. Remission rates at this time were 46 per cent for IPT and 39 per cent for cognitive behaviour therapy. The authors speculated that these gains in the IPT condition resulted from an improvement in self-worth and relationships, which made weight and shape much less important to the individual. As the effects of IPT are more indirect than cognitive methods, they took longer to become apparent.

Pharmacological interventions

Overall, antidepressant medications for bulimia decrease binge frequency by an average of 56 per cent, compared with an average decrease of

11 per cent following treatment with placebo (Jimerson et al. 1993). However, many people treated with antidepressants drop out of treatment due to drug side-effects. In addition, a significant relapse rate of between 30 and 45 per cent is typical in patients between four and six months following cessation of medication. Jimerson et al. (1993) summarized the data, suggesting that most people show at least a 50 per cent improvement following prescription of antidepressants, although only one-third will experience a sustained remission.

Three of the five studies that have compared cognitive behavioural and pharmacological interventions found no differences in their effectiveness (Bacaltchuk et al. 1999). Two found cognitive behavioural interventions to be superior. Overall, long-term remission rates were 20 per cent for antidepressants and 39 per cent for cognitive approaches. Dropout rates were also higher among those receiving antidepressants than cognitive therapy: 40 versus 18 per cent. In one of the studies reported in this analysis, Agras et al. (1994) randomly allocated women with bulimia into a number of conditions, including a short-term course of anti-depressants, cognitive behaviour therapy or a combined treatment. At four-month follow-up, both cognitive behavioural therapy and the combined treatment were superior to medication alone on measures of binge eating and purging. These advantages were maintained up to one-year follow-up. At this time, 18 per cent of those receiving antidepressant treatment were free of binge eating and purging, in comparison to 78 per cent of those receiving the combined treatment.

Chapter summary

1   Anorexia is defined by the desire to achieve a body weight significantly below normal. This can be achieved in two ways: self-imposed starvation, or bingeing and purging.

2   Anorexia has a relatively poor prognosis, with long-term mortality rates of up to 16 per cent, and complete 'recovery' in just over half the cases.

3   Bulimia has a better prognosis, with most people achieving something like normal eating patterns.

4   Cognitive models suggest that both conditions are driven by cognitions which prioritize control over eating and weight control. The behaviour of people with each condition varies as a result of their abilities to control their responses to hunger. People who engage in Type 1 anorexic behaviour are able to control their hunger; those who are bulimic occasionally give in to urges to eat, and compensate by purging.

5 Psychoanalytic models of anorexia suggest that it forms a rejection of sexual instincts and risk of pregnancy.

6 Bruch contested that anorexia arose out of chaotic parent–child interactions that leave the child confused about their own emotional and physical needs. They turn to their parents to provide feedback on their own feelings. At the time of adolescence, they seek but fail to achieve autonomy from their parents. As a response, they seek excessive control over their size and shape.

7 Socio-cultural models emphasize the role of social pressures in shaping young women's striving for thinness and the perfect body.

8 Family models suggest anorexia results from aberrant family dynamics. Minuchin, for example, suggested that the person with anorexia serves to maintain family cohesion as the family focuses on them and their needs, and ignores the dysfunctional relationship between their parents.

9 There appears to be a genetic risk for anorexia, possibly mediated through disorders of serotonin metabolism.

10 Interventions in anorexia usually involve two stages: first, weight gain to safe levels, and second, longer-term interventions involving cognitive behaviour therapy, family therapy, psychotherapy or drug therapy. The best intervention for each individual may depend on the specific factors that led to their problems, with each of the psychological approaches being of benefit to some. The long-term prognosis, however, is not good.

11 Cognitive behavioural interventions are acknowledged as the treatment of choice in bulimia, with most people making significant long-term gains.

For discussion

1 Should we actively treat people with anorexia who are close to dying as a result of their restrained eating, or should we respect their desire not to eat whatever the consequences?

2 Anorexia is perhaps one of the most difficult psychological conditions to treat. Given the success of cognitive behavioural techniques in other conditions, why should this not be the case in anorexia?

3 Bulimic behaviour could be considered a highly functional way of controlling weight. If this is the case, should it be treated only where the affected individual is distressed by their way of controlling their weight?

Further reading

Bowers, W.A. (2001) Basic principles for applying cognitive-behavioral therapy to anorexia nervosa, *Psychiatric Clinics of North America*, 24: 293–303.

Clark, D.M. and Fairburn, C.G. (eds) *Science and Practice of Cognitive Behaviour Therapy*. Oxford: Oxford University Press.

Haworth-Hoeppner, S. (2000) The critical shapes of body image: the role of culture and family in the production of eating disorders, *Journal of Marriage and the Family*, 62: 212–27.

Russell, G.F. (2001) Involuntary treatment in anorexia nervosa, *Psychiatric Clinics of North America*, 24: 337–49.

Slade, P. and Brodie, D. (1994) Body-image distortion and eating disorder: a reconceptualization based on the recent literature, *European Eating Disorders Review*, 2: 32–46.

Whittal, M.L., Agras, W.S. and Gould, R.A. (1999) Bulimia nervosa: a meta-analysis of psychosocial and pharmacological treatments, *Behavior Therapy*, 30: 117–35.

13 Developmental disorders

This chapter looks at three disorders within the diagnostic category of pervasive developmental difficulties. It describes three conditions in which difficulties in childhood are predictive of subsequent adult problems. It considers the problems associated with a variety of disorders grouped under the broad category of learning difficulties. It then discusses the aetiology and treatment of more specific conditions: autism and attention-deficit/hyperactivity disorder (ADHD). By the end of the chapter, you should have an understanding of:

◆ Definitions and some of the causes of learning difficulties

◆ Aspects of the social and psychological care of people with learning difficulties

◆ The biological and psychological bases of autism

◆ The MMR vaccination and autism controversy

◆ Treatment of autism and autistic behaviours

◆ Factors that contribute to ADHD

◆ Biological and psychological treatments of ADHD.

Learning difficulties

Learning difficulties is a broad term that encompasses a variety of conditions whose defining characteristic is a significant impairment of intellectual functioning. The terms used to describe people with this condition differ across the world and in time. In the UK, they have in the past been referred to as 'handicapped', 'subnormal' or 'retarded'. Now, all people with intellectual deficits, however profound, are referred to as having learning difficulties. The reasons for these changing terms are not trivial:

they reflect attempts to minimize the prejudice often expressed in relation to this group of people. In the USA, people with mild learning difficulties are referred to as having learning difficulties, those with more profound deficits are still referred to as having mental retardation.

The first criterion for a diagnosis of having a learning disability is that its onset is before the age of 18 years, to exclude the affects of trauma or other neurological illness later in life. In addition, the individual needs to score significantly below the norm on intelligence tests. The usual cut-off score for this diagnosis is between 70 and 75 on the standard IQ test: two standard deviations below the population mean of 100. About 3 per cent of the population fall into this category. Within this category are a number of subcategories.

- IQ 50/55 to 70 *Mild learning difficulties:* includes about 85 per cent of people with learning difficulties. As children, they may be superficially indistinguishable from children with normal IQs, although their school performance shows they have clear learning difficulties. As adults, they are likely to be able to hold down unskilled jobs, although they may need help with social and financial issues.
- IQ 35/40 to 50/55 *Moderate learning difficulties:* includes about 10 per cent of people with learning difficulties. Within this group of people, learning difficulties are often combined with other neurological deficits, including problems with motor skills such as walking, holding implements and so on. People in this group usually live independently within families or in group homes. Many have obvious brain damage and other pathologies.
- IQ 20/25 to 35/40 *Severe learning difficulties:* usually associated with genetically mediated physical abnormalities and limited sensorimotor control. Most people with severe learning difficulties live in institutions and require constant aid and supervision. As adults, they are typically lethargic and lack motivation. They may, nevertheless, communicate at a simple and concrete level.
- IQ < 20/25 *Profound learning difficulties:* profound mental and physical problems mean that people with this degree of difficulty require total supervision and nursing care all their lives. They cannot communicate using language and cannot get around on their own.

Although performance on IQ tests is frequently used to define the degree of learning disability an individual has, a critical issue is how this affects their ability to adapt to their environment. The third criterion for being identified as having learning difficulties is, therefore, evidence of a failure to develop the skills necessary to cope with the increasing demands placed on the individual as they grow older. Problems here may be the first sign of more pervasive problems.

Severe learning difficulties are more common among males than females. Mild learning difficulties are most common among males and those
from economically deprived or adverse family backgrounds (Roeleveld
et al. 1997). As the medical care of people with learning disabilities
improves, the prevalence of older people with learning disabilities within
society is increasing, at the same time as there are reductions in childhood
prevalence resulting from increased prenatal screening and better child
health care.

Aetiology of learning difficulties

Only about 25 per cent of cases of learning difficulty have an identified
cause. These include:

- *genetic conditions:* for example Down syndrome and Fragile X
  syndrome (see pp. 306–7)
- *infectious diseases:* for example rubella, parental syphilis and
  encephalitis
- *environmental hazards:* for example lead paint and exhaust fumes
  in leaded petrol
- *antenatal events:* for example parental infections (including
  rubella), endocrine disorders such as hypothyroidism
- *perinatal trauma:* for example asphyxia during birth.

For many people, there is no known biological cause. This is unsurprising,
as IQ like all other natural phenomena follows a normal distribution
within the population, with the exception of the so-called 'hump' within
the lower end of the distribution that occurs as a consequence of biological causes (see Figure 13.1).

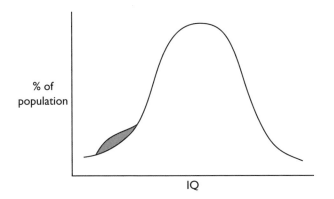

Figure 13.1   The genetic 'hump' within the distribution of IQ scores

This does not mean that poor performance on IQ tests is totally bio-logically determined. Environmental factors, including quality of parental care, education and the social environment, can markedly influence IQ scores, academic performance and the development of adaptive skills, particularly for people with mild–moderate learning difficulties. Birch et al. (1970), for example, identified all children born with learning difficulties in Aberdeen between the years 1951 and 1955. Some 20 years later, they collected information from health and social services, and conducted interviews with their parents and the individuals themselves. Mild learning difficulties were significantly more prevalent in families from the lower socio-economic groups and families classed as unstable, defined by high levels of multiple carers, abuse and child neglect. No such relationship was found for more severe learning difficulties.

Down syndrome

People affected by Down syndrome are short and stocky in stature, and have typical facial characteristics, including upward-slanting eyes, sparse, fine straight hair, and a large furrowed tongue which protrudes as the result of a small mouth. They may also have a number of other less obvi-ous characteristics including serious heart malformations. All people with this condition have some degree of learning difficulty. Autopsy reveals brain tissue very similar to that found in Alzheimer's disease.

Down syndrome is found in about one of 500–600 live births and has been detected in about 3 per cent of foetuses that spontaneously abort before 20 weeks' gestation. It occurs sporadically. People with the disorder are generally the children of parents without it, precluding an obvious genetic linkage. Because the risk of having a child with Down syndrome increases with the age of the mother, rising significantly in women giving birth over the age of 32 years, it was originally thought to be the result of an 'unfavourable' interaction between mother and foetus during pregnancy. However, it is now known to result from a chromo-somal abnormality. People with Down syndrome have three, instead of two, chromosomes-21, leading to the more technical name of the dis-order, trisomy-21.

This is the result of a process that occurs during the first few cell divisions that occur prior to fertilization. In trisomy-21, as the female egg cells duplicate, they fail to do so properly and some sex cells receive two chromosomes-21; some receive none. If these eggs are fertilized by a normal sperm, the resultant cells contain either three or one chromosome-21. The latter is not a viable combination and the developing cells are aborted. However, in the case of trisomy-21, the embryo and then the foetus remain viable and survive. The age-related risk is thought to be the result of some kind of metabolic or physical damage ac-cumulated by the egg cells while lying in the ovaries for decades before ovulating.

Fragile X syndrome

Fragile X syndrome affects approximately 1 in 1000 male and 1 in 2500 female births. This syndrome is caused by a defect within the FMR-1 (Fragile X mental retardation) gene located on the X chromosome. In Fragile X syndrome, a small region of the gene undergoes repeated, unnecessary duplications of a number of amino acids that result in a longer gene. When the number of repeats is small (fewer than 200) the individual often has no signs of the disorder. Where there are a larger number of repeats, the learning disabilities associated with Fragile X syndrome are observed. In families that show evidence of Fragile X syndrome, both the number of repeats and the length of the chromosome increase with succeeding generations, with a proportional increase in the severity of symptoms.

Because of the X-linkage, the frequency of the syndrome is greater in males than in females. This is because females typically have two X chromosomes, and males have one X and one Y chromosome. A female who inherits a chromosome carrying the Fragile X gene from either parent is likely to inherit a normal X chromosome from the other parent. This masks the presence of the Fragile X gene in a female. However, she may carry the gene and be capable of passing it on to her children. By contrast, because a male has only one X chromosome, if he inherits an affected X chromosome he will inevitably inherit the condition. This simple genetic model does not always hold, however: about 20 per cent of males who carry mutated forms of FMR-1 are either unaffected or only mildly affected. In addition, a single copy of the Fragile X gene can be sufficient to cause the syndrome in some females. Why this happens is not understood.

Social interventions in learning difficulties

Care of people with learning disabilities is partly social and educational, and partly psychological. The lives of people with learning difficulties have been affected by socio-political factors as well as psychological and social interventions. One ideological movement, known as *normalization* (Wolfensberger 1972), has been particularly influential. This began in the 1960s in response to the poor institutional conditions in which many people with learning difficulties then lived. The movement called for people with learning difficulties to live a life as close to normal living conditions as possible, to have normal rhythms to their lives, and the means to establish and maintain behaviour as close to the cultural norms as possible. Under the rubric of *social role valorization* (Wolfensberger 1983), the movement subsequently called for the creation, support and defence of valued social roles for people with learning disabilities. These have led to five key aims of any service provided for people with learning disabilities:

- *Community presence:* people with learning difficulties live in the community, in normal houses, not institutions. To avoid 'pockets' of disability, housing is distributed through the community.
- *Choice:* people have the choices of accommodation, care and day-to-day routine, available to the 'normal' population.
- *Competence:* the competences of people with learning disabilities are acknowledged and maximized.
- *Respect:* people with learning difficulties are afforded the respect due to all other people within the population.
- *Participation:* people with learning difficulties have equal rights of participation in society, including access to work, leisure facilities, political activities and sexual relationships, as the rest of the population.

In the spirit of this integrated approach, children with learning disabilities are increasingly being taught in mainstream classes, and most adults with learning disabilities live in the community following the closure of large institutions. However, these changes fall short of the goals of normalization, and there is still work to do. About 63 per cent of British adults with learning difficulties, for example, continue to live with their family of birth – a significantly higher proportion than among the 'normal' population.

Schooling

Government policy during the 1990s within most western countries is that all children should be educated in ordinary schools, although in the UK at least, education authorities are left with substantial discretion, and many 'special schools' still operate. However, the number of children taught in them is gradually reducing: only 1.35 per cent of all British 5–15-year-olds were enrolled in special schools in 1998 (Emerson et al. 2001). This political and social policy is supported by the empirical evidence: educating children with learning disabilities in mainstream schools with additional support seems to be at least as effective as placing them in segregated 'special' schools (Emerson et al. 2001).

Preparing for adulthood

The transition from school to adult life requires planning, as many people require some sort of social support in adulthood. Children leaving school are assessed and a care plan drawn up, setting out how services will meet their continuing needs. Individual circumstances differ, but this process includes consideration of

- future daytime activities: including possible further education, supported employment and attendance at day services

- living arrangements: choices may include remaining in the family home or moving to more independent living
- leisure opportunities
- physical health care needs.

Occupation and employment

Support in adulthood is usually provided through some form of day care or employment. In the UK, this has involved attendance at adult training centres. In them, the individual takes part in a number of 'productive' activities, including simple contract work for which they received a token 'wage', simple skills training, sports, and arts and craft activities. These centres also provide day care for people with severe or complex disabilities.

More recently, significant effort has been given to placing people with learning disabilities into real working environments. One of the best models of this approach, known as the *supported employment model*, originated in the USA. It assumes that almost anyone can be employed if given sufficient support. It is colloquially known as a 'place, train and maintain' model, because the process involves identifying a job suitable to the individual, training them to do the job effectively, and then supporting them in the job, with decreasing levels of support as appropriate. This can be effective in increasing integration into the workplace, particularly where co-workers are prepared and receive appropriate training (Farris and Stancliffe 2001).

Living away from institutions

Most adults with learning disabilities continue to live in their family of origin. Others may live independently in rented accommodation. A number of other options are available, each providing differing levels of support, including the following:

- *Registered care homes:* have up to twenty residents, though between three and six are more typical; 24-hours a day support is provided. All personal care and meals are provided.
- *Shared housing:* usually for groups of three or four people; levels of support vary from staff visiting once or twice a week to 24-hours a day support. Residents may do their own shopping, cooking, budgeting and housework, with some support from staff.
- *Cluster of flats or bedsitters:* self-contained units, usually on a single site but occasionally dispersed across a neighbourhood. Support staff are available, but residents are more independent than in other settings.

Psychological interventions in learning difficulties

Psychological interventions for people with learning disabilities usually have one of two goals: either to train people in the skills necessary to maximize their abilities or to reduce inappropriate behaviours. Both approaches are frequently based on the principles of operant conditioning, in which behaviour is shaped by a series of rewards and, less frequently, punishments. The remaining part of this section focuses on three interventions relevant to people with learning disabilities, starting with a programme targeted at preschool children. More programmes, developed for people with a combination of autism and learning difficulties, are described in the next section of the chapter.

Preschool behavioural programmes

Most children with learning disabilities live in their family home. Preschool programmes provide opportunities for teaching age-dependent skills necessary for when the child starts to attend school. One of the most widely used systems through which this is provided is known as *Portage*.

First established in the town of Portage, USA, this home-visiting service for preschool children who have special needs is now used in countries as far spread as India, Britain, Japan, as well as the USA. The teaching process first involves assessment of the child's abilities. Therapists and parents then work together to develop a training programme addressing six domains: infant stimulation, social development, communication speech and language, self-help, cognitive development and motor development. Once the programme is designed, the parent works with the child on a planned programme of skills training, with weekly visits by health professionals providing support and assessment of progress. Parental interventions are facilitated by the provision of cards describing in detail how to teach 580 behaviours. Each card includes a behavioural description of a skill (such as 'Mary will place 6 pieces in puzzle with verbal prompt'), suggested teaching materials and the type of reinforcement to be used in its development. Despite its widespread use, there are relatively few formal evaluations of the approach. However, what evidence there is suggests it works. Revill and Blunden (1977), for example, reported significant acceleration in achieving skills and scores on a measure of mental development in a group of 19 children aged from 8 months to 4 years following implementation of the Portage programme.

Cognitive behavioural interventions

Older children and adults may also benefit from interventions designed to teach age-appropriate skills or to help them cope with the learning demands being placed upon them. People with learning disabilities may benefit, for example, from learning social skills involving complex social behaviours and how to respond appropriately to social cues. Corrigan (1991), for example, reported outcomes of studies of the effects of this type of training in people with learning disabilities, psychosis and offenders. People with learning difficulties gained significantly from the intervention. They performed best on measures of skill during role play and maintenance of skills over time. They were, however, less successful in transferring these skills to situations beyond the training setting.

Self-instruction training (Meichenbaum 1985) can be used to help children cope more effectively with the learning process. Used in this way, it typically involves a five-stage procedure, in which the child learns to talk themselves through the procedures necessary to learn a new skill or solve a problem: first, the teacher performs the task speaking instructions aloud as they do so, second, the child performs the task following instructions from the teacher, third and fourth, the child performs the task twice more, once while talking through the instructions and then whispering them, fifth, the child performs the task while thinking the instructions only.

This approach can also be used to help reduce anxiety by including self-instructions that focus on anxiety-reducing statements as well as task-oriented ones. Kamann and Wong (1993), for example, used self-instruction to reduce maths-anxiety in children, 20 of who had learning difficulties and 20 of whom were normally achieving children. Before the intervention, the latter group produced substantially more self-instructions aimed at reducing anxiety than children with learning disabilities. Following training in the use of self-instructions, the children with learning disabilities produced levels comparable to the group of more able children. They also gained in their ability to work through mathematical problems.

Coping with challenging behaviour

Between 10 and 15 per cent of people with learning disabilities engage in challenging behaviours, that is, behaviours that transgress social rules, and usually involve violence either towards themselves or others, destructive behaviours, or place the individual or others at risk of harm. These are now considered to be operantly conditioned behaviours, through which people with restricted abilities try to achieve some degree of control over their environment and the people around them: for example, by attracting attention or getting someone to stop an unwanted action. Emerson (1998) identified a number of principles that can be applied in interventions to reduce levels of challenging behaviour.

Enrich the environment
Reinforcement theory suggests that the rate of behaviours maintained by positive reinforcement should reduce as the background level of

reinforcement increases. Enriching environments by increasing social interaction or providing more things to engage and interest the individual
should therefore reduce challenging behaviours. This seems to be the
case for **stereotypic behaviours**, which seem to be self-reinforcing, but
less so for other challenging behaviours.

Reduce exposure to the triggers to challenging behaviour

One simple way in which challenging behaviour can be prevented is to
minimize or obviate its triggers. Touchette et al. (1985), for example, identified that one woman's outbursts were associated with her attendance at
pre-vocational and community living classes. Rescheduling them resulted
in an almost total cessation in the frequency of aggressive behaviour.

Teach or support alternative behaviours

Most challenging behaviour is considered to be functional: that is, it is
engaged in order to gain some end-point. A key intervention, therefore,
involves teaching people how to gain these outcomes without engaging
in challenging behaviour. To be effective, the new behaviour has to achieve
exactly the same outcome as the original behaviour and be a more
'efficient' way of achieving this goal. An example of this approach was
reported by Steege et al. (1990), who taught two young children with
severe multiple disabilities to press a micro-switch to activate a tape-
recording of a request for a break from self-care activities, a process that
led to marked reductions in self-injurious behaviour previously used to
stop such activities.

Note that this list does not include the use of punishments, which
would essentially punish the individual for attempting to gain some
control over an aspect of their life.

Autism

Autism was first identified in 1943, and was differentiated from schizophrenia only in 1971. For a DSM diagnosis of autism to be made, a total
of at least six symptoms must be present, with at least two from the first
section and at least one from each of the second and third sections, with
onset prior to age 3 years.

    1 Impairment in social interaction:
- impairment in the use of non-verbal behaviours such as eye-
  to-eye gaze, facial expression, and gestures to regulate social
  interaction
- failure to develop peer relationships
- lack of spontaneous seeking to share enjoyment, interests or
  achievements with other people
- lack of social or emotional reciprocity.

2 Abnormalities in communication:
- delay in, or total lack of, the development of spoken language
- in individuals with adequate speech, marked impairment in the ability to initiate or sustain a conversation
- stereotyped and repetitive use of language or idiosyncratic language
- lack of spontaneous make-believe play or social imitative play.

3 Restricted, repetitive and stereotyped patterns of behaviour, interests and activities:
- inflexible adherence to specific, non-functional routines or rituals
- stereotyped and repetitive motor mannerisms
- persistent preoccupation with parts of objects.

In its severest form, autism occurs in about 4–15 individuals per 10,000 population. There may, in addition, be a wider spectrum of milder problems that are more widespread through the population (Bailey et al. 1995). The abilities and difficulties of people with autism vary considerably. Some people are able to take an active part in society, with no deficits apparent to the casual observer, although the individual may have significant problems in establishing and maintaining relationships. About 80 per cent of children with autism score less than 70 on intelligence tests, placing them in the learning disabilities range. These deficits are quite specific, and relate to abstract thought, symbolism and sequential logic. Some people may have isolated skills that reflect great talent, including prodigious mathematical or memory skills, in a condition known as *'idiot savant'*.

Core limitations of autism

The core limitations associated with autism are social isolation, communication deficits and obsessive-compulsive or ritual behaviours.

Social isolation

Many children with autism act as if people have no special characteristics that distinguish them from inanimate objects. As babies, they do not respond to their mothers when being touched or fed, and may reject attempts at cuddling by arching their back. By the age of 2 or 3, they may form a weak emotional bond with their parents. Few will initiate play with other children, and they are usually unresponsive to attempts by other children to engage them in play. Attempts at achieving eye contact are usually met with avoidance or movement away. By contrast, children with autism may develop strong bonds with inanimate objects, and carry them around with them if possible.

Communication deficits

About 50 per cent of children with autism never learn to speak. Those that do have a number of common abnormalities. One frequent speech characteristic is known as *echolalia*: the repetition of words or phrases spoken to the child immediately, hours or even days earlier. This is now thought to be an attempt at communication, and may be associated with an event or stimulus. Repetition of the phrase, 'Do you want a sweet?', for example, may indicate a learned association between the phrase and being given a sweet. A second common characteristic is known as *pronoun reversal*. In this, children refer to themselves in the third person. This may be associated with echolalia, and reflect how they have heard others speak about them (e.g. 'How are you Mary?' – 'She's here . . .'). This is highly resistant to change, even after substantial training programmes.

Obsessive-compulsive and ritualistic acts

Children with autism rarely engage in symbolic play. More frequently, they engage in repetitive, stereotypical and seemingly meaningless behaviour. These include ritualistic hand movements, such as flicking fingers across their face, or repetitive body movements, including rocking or walking on tip-toe. They may become upset if prevented from doing these behaviours or when minor elements of their daily routine are changed. Their play often has an obsessive flavour to it, lining up toys or constructing complex patterns with household objects.

Growing up

The prognosis of children with autism is mixed. Those with learning difficulties often make a poor adjustment to adulthood, and most need some level of supervised care. By contrast, those without learning disabilities frequently go on to achieve an independent life, gain employment and live independently. Some go on to make significant contributions in their lives. However, most continue to have significantly impaired social relationships and little understanding of social and emotional aspects of life. For a powerful description of the feelings and development of a 'high functioning autistic' (her phrase), it may be useful to go to a chapter by Temple Grandin, a professor at Colorado State University (available at www.autism.org/temple/inside.html). Here are some of her fascinating insights into her own condition, starting with her childhood frustration at not being able to speak:

> Not being able to speak was utter frustration. If adults spoke
> directly to me I could understand everything they said, but I could
> not get my words out. It was like a big stutter . . . My speech

therapist knew how to intrude into my world. She would hold me by my chin and made me look in her eyes and say 'ball.' At age 3, 'ball' came out 'bah,' said with great stress. If the therapist pushed too hard I threw a tantrum, and if she did not intrude far enough no progress was made. My mother and teachers wondered why I screamed. Screaming was the only way I could communicate . . .

I wanted to feel the good feeling of being hugged, but when people hugged me the stimuli washed over me like a tidal wave . . . I pulled away to avoid the all-engulfing tidal wave of stimulation. The stiffening up and flinching was like a wild animal pulling away. At age 18 I built a squeezing machine. This device is completely lined with foam rubber, and the user has complete control over the duration and amount of pressure applied. The machine provides comforting pressure to large areas of the body. It took me a long time to learn to accept the feeling of being held and not try to pull away from it . . . I almost never feel aggressive after using it. In order to learn to relate to people better, I first had to learn how to receive comfort from the soothing pressure of the squeeze machine . . .

Shortly after my first menstrual period, the anxiety attacks started. The feeling was like a constant feeling of stage fright all the time. The 'nerves' were almost like hypersensitivity rather than anxiety. It was like my brain was running at 200 miles an hour . . . The 'nerves' were worse in the late afternoon and early evening. They subsided late at night and early in the morning. There are two . . . ways to fight the nerves: fixate on an intense activity, or withdraw and try to minimize outside stimulation. Fixating on one thing had a calming effect. I used to write three articles in one night. While I was typing furiously I felt calmer. I was the most nervous when I had nothing to do.

Aetiology of autism

Genetic factors

Genetic studies of autism are difficult to conduct as the condition is so rare. Nevertheless, what evidence there is suggests a significant genetic component to the risk for autism. McBride et al. (1996), for example, reported that the siblings of people with the disorder are about 75 times more likely to develop the disorder than those without an affected sibling. Further data have been reported in twin studies, where concordance rates of between 60 and 91 per cent for MZ and 20 per cent for DZ twins have been reported (e.g. Bailey et al. 1995). Any genetic model is likely to be polygenic. Six 'potential sites' for these genes are on chromosomes

7q and 16p (International Molecular Genetic Study of Autism Consortium 1998), although these data are far from definitive.

Biological mechanisms

The opioid theory

It has proven difficult to find a biochemical model of autism. The most widely supported theory, known as the opioid theory, suggests that the condition is the result of an early overload of the central nervous system by opioids. This is based on findings that certain behaviours found in autism, including stereotyped behaviour, can be artificially induced in animals following injection with opioid agonists. The excess opioids are thought to be the result of incompletely digested dietary gluten and/or casein found in barely, rye, oats and milk products (Reichelt et al. 1991). These result from a lack of chemicals within the gut known as peptidases which break down natural opioids found in these foodstuffs into innocuous metabolites. A number of studies have used drugs or dietary restrictions to inhibit uptake of opioids from the gut as a treatment of autism. These have met with limited success (see p. 319). However, treatment studies may provide only a tangential test of the opioid theory, as it is not clear whether any neurological changes resulting from this excess of opioids are reversible.

Any damage to the brain may affect serotinergic mechanisms (see Chapter 3), which appear to be involved in the restricted interests and compulsive behaviours in autism. The anterior cingulated area of the brain, which is involved in face recognition, social, cognitive and affective functions relevant to autism, may also be particularly damaged.

MMR and autism

An excess of opioids may also result from inflammation of the bowel wall. Here may be a link between the MMR (measles, mumps, rubella) vaccine and autism. Wakefield et al. (1998) examined 12 children referred to hospital with a normal developmental history followed by an apparently sudden loss of cognitive skills accompanied by a number of abdominal symptoms. Symptom onset was reported to have followed MMR vaccination in 8 of the children; 9 were diagnosed as having autism. Each of these 9 children was found to suffer from an inflammation of the bowel wall, known as lymphoid hyperplasia. Wakefield et al. (1998) suggested that this may have resulted in a failure to break down dietary gluten and/or casein and, hence, triggered the onset of autism. This finding, and the subsequent public fears of MMR, sparked a widespread controversy and significant reductions in the uptake of the MMR vaccination.

A number of subsequent reports have both supported and challenged Wakefield's conclusions. The same research group (Uhlmann et al. 2001) compared 91 patients with lymphoid hyperplasia and 70 controls without the condition. Of those with lymphoid hyperplasia, 75 were found to have the measles virus in their gut; only 5 of the control group had the virus. They concluded that this was evidence of a plausible link between measles, MMR and lymphoid hyperplasia – with its potential link to the onset of autism. More negative findings were reported by Taylor et al. (1999), who examined trends in births and any subsequent registration of children with special needs and disabilities since 1979 in the UK. They noted a gradual increase in the numbers of children with autism since this time, but no sudden increase coinciding with the introduction of the MMR vaccine, nor any evidence of a cluster of children with developmental regression occurring within two to four months of MMR vaccination.

These two methods, looking at highly specific and selected cases or whole populations, both have weaknesses. About 600,000 children receive the MMR vaccine in any year, mostly at the time that autism first becomes evident. It is possible that among these children, the identification of a small number of cases of autism will coincide with vaccination. This apparent association could have been exaggerated by the highly selective way in which children were identified and assessed in the Wakefield et al. (1998) study. In addition, it is possible that the link between receiving the MMR vaccine and the onset of symptoms made by parents may be inaccurate. It is usually difficult to identify the time of onset of symptoms of autism, and most people search for a 'cause' of such problems. If parents were to attribute their child's problems to the vaccination, this may result in unconscious memory biases and inappropriate linkages of behaviour with the timing of the MMR vaccination. Epidemiological evidence may also be biased. This involves the study of whole populations, and provides a very 'blunt instrument' which may fail to identify any relationship between MMR and the very small number of children that according to Wakefield are sensitive to the vaccine. More research is needed before this complex issue can be fully understood.

Psychodynamic explanations

Early theories of autism focused on psychodynamic processes. Autism was seen as a form of escape from environments that lacked warmth and care. Bettelheim (1967), for example, suggested that children who develop autism have rejecting parents and are able to perceive their negative feelings. The infants learn that their actions have little or no impact on their parents' emotions or behaviour. They come to believe they have no power to influence the world, and so choose not to enter it. Instead, they build an 'empty fortress' of autism against this pain and disappointment. Unfortunately, from Bettelheim's perspective, there is no evidence that the parents of children who develop autism differ from those of children who develop normally. Cox et al. (1975), for example, found that the parents of children with autism and those of children with problems in understanding speech did not differ in terms of emotional demonstrativeness, responsiveness to their children, or sociability.

A biopsychosocial model

A similar explanation is found in the psychobiological theory of Koegel et al. (2001). They suggested that children who develop autism lack motivation to engage with other people and, as a result, withdraw from social interactions. This may begin early in life as a result of neurological dysfunction. However, it can be exacerbated by carers' efforts to 'help' affected children by doing things for them regardless of their behaviour. Whatever the child does, they receive the same response from their environment. As a result of this, and because social interactions and communication are inherently difficult, they revert to early forms of communication such as crying or tantrums to get their needs met and avoid social interactions.

Treatment of autism

Pharmacological approaches

A number of psychoactive drugs have been used to treat the symptoms of autism. Perhaps the most commonly used drugs are neuroleptics, which block the effects of dopamine (see Chapter 3). Campbell et al. (1988), for example, found haloperidol to be more effective than placebo in decreasing levels of stereotyped behaviour and withdrawal. In addition, it enhanced the effects of behavioural techniques used in developing the use of language, perhaps because it allowed the children to focus more on the learning process than previously. To avoid the long-term adverse effects of neuroleptics, including tardive dyskinesia and Parkinsonism, they may be used at relatively low levels and episodically (five days on, two days off) and still maintain their therapeutic effectiveness.

Tricyclics and SSRIs have also proved effective in reducing repetitive behaviours and aggression. McDougle et al. (1994), for example, found that half those treated with fluvoxamine (an SSRI) were rated as 'clinical responders' and evidenced significant reductions in repetitive behaviours. The National Institute of Mental Health study (Gordon et al. 1993) compared the effectiveness of two SSRIs, clomipramine and desipramine, with placebo in a group of children and adolescents with autism. Treatment with clomipramine resulted in more improvements on measures of repetitive behaviours, self-injury and aggression than placebo.

Opiate antagonists, such as naltrexone, have been used with only modest effect. Perhaps the most consistent effect of naltrexone is a reduction in activity levels. It did not aid a behavioural programme conducted by Campbell et al. (1993), nor did it reduce self-injurious behaviour in a study reported by Willemsen-Swinkels et al. (1995). Indeed, in this study treatment with naltrexone actually increased levels of stereotypic behaviour.

An alternative biological approach has been to reduce levels of dietary casein and gluten in order to reduce the extent to which opiates continue to be absorbed from the gut. Evidence of the effectiveness of this approach is not yet convincing. Knivsberg et al. (1998), for example, reported on the outcomes in a group of 20 children who either received or did not receive this restricted diet for a period of one year. They reported significant success, with improvements in the treated group relative to those who did not receive the diet on a combined measure of behaviour and communication. However, the relatively small number of children in the trial, together with the lack of statistical analyses and measures of the diet given to the children, makes these results somewhat preliminary.

Behavioural approaches

Many programmes to change behaviours associated with autism have involved direct reinforcement of behaviours such as speech or pro-social behaviours. In these, the therapist/trainer typically provides a cue, usually a question or command, to evoke a specific response. This may be physically prompted if necessary, and performance of the behaviour is reinforced by a tangible reward such as a sweet: 'Look at me' – move head to face therapist if necessary – reward with sweet. In some programmes, inappropriate behaviours such as self-injury may be followed by an aversive response, including mild electric shocks or exposure to the smell of ammonia (Koegel et al. 2001). Other programmes have implemented non-aversive procedures even in response to challenging behaviour (see p. 311). This type of approach has resulted in reductions in self-injury, aggressive behaviour and echolalia, and gains on measures of eye contact, vocalizations and toileting.

One of the key researchers in this area is Ivar Lovaas, who developed a highly intensive operant programme for children. In his initial study (Lovaas 1987) therapy continued for much of the children's waking hours both at home and in school, for a period of two years. Children were rewarded for being less aggressive and more socially appropriate: talking, playing with other children, and so on. They were also punished, on occasion, for engaging in challenging behaviour. They were taught with their peers, not in special groups. This intensive intervention was compared with a similar treatment maintained for only ten hours a week. The differences between the two groups were dramatic. By the end of the two-year programme, the average IQ of the intervention group was 83 points, compared to 55 in the less intense intervention; 12 of the 19 children in the intensive intervention group had IQs at or above the norm, compared to 2 out of 40 in the less intensive intervention. These findings translated to school performance, with 9 children in the intensive therapy group being accepted in the same age class as their peers: only 1 child in the less intensive therapy group achieved this. Four years later, the relative gains made by the children in the intensive therapy had been maintained.

These findings created considerable controversy and have been criticized on methodological grounds (e.g. Gresham and MacMillan 1998). One criticism was that assignment of subjects to treatment and control groups was not random, allowing the possibility that the groups differed on potentially important variables that may have been left uncontrolled. A second criticism is that the pre- and post-treatment measures were not the same for all children. A third criticism is that the study results have not been reliably replicated, nor has a more recently developed non-aversive version of Lovaas's treatment been shown to be effective (Gresham and MacMillan 1998). These criticisms have been strongly refuted by Lovaas (www.feat.org/lovaas). In addition, some studies (e.g. T. Smith et al. 2000) have achieved similar gains to those made in the original Lovaas study. Accordingly, while this approach may not always achieve the therapeutic gains achieved by Lovaas, it does form a potentially effective approach to the treatment of children with autism.

Koegel et al. (2001) further refined the operant approach by targeting a number of what they termed primary factors, which they considered to precede a number of consequent or secondary factors: poor communication skills, for example, typically precede severe behaviour problems. Interventions to improve language and communication skills could, therefore, prevent the need for interventions to deal with disruptive behaviour. Koegel and colleagues argued for targeting a variety of pro-social behaviours that facilitate communication, including improving eye contact, head positioning, reducing stereotypical movements and unusual facial expressions, as well as encouraging children to initiate social interactions.

A second innovation was based on the idea that the goal of any behavioural programme should not just be to modify one particular behaviour, but to increase the individual's motivation to engage in a number of similar behaviours. A key element of their behavioural programmes, therefore, was to provide rewards for behaviours similar to the target one. An example of the difference between this and previous conditioning approaches was reported by Koegel et al. (1988). In this, the traditional operant approach reinforced specified phonetic sounds, as they became increasingly word-like over time. To obtain reinforcement, the child had to produce responses that were at least as good as their previous responses. The newer approach reinforced any attempts to verbalize, however accurate or inaccurate the noise made. In a direct comparison between the two approaches, Koegel et al. (1988) found the newer method to result in more rapid gains in the use of appropriate speech and greater levels of pro-social behaviours than the traditional method.

A final innovation of their approach was to allow the child control over the reward they were given for engaging in the targeted behaviours. Perhaps the most extreme, and ultimately most rewarding, examples of this allowed the child to engage in stereotypical or ritualistic behaviours, which are intrinsically highly rewarding, as a reward for completion of other tasks. This strategy has been shown to reduce the incidence of aggressive tantrums and other 'off-task' behaviours (Charlop-Christy and Haymes 1998).

Attention-deficit/hyperactivity disorder

DSM-IV-TR identified three categories of attention-deficit/hyperactivity disorder (ADHD): problems of poor attention, hyperactive-impulsive behaviour and a combination of both. Most children with the disorder have both sets of problems. Criteria for each diagnosis are engaging in at least six of the behaviours in Table 13.1 over a period of at least six months.

For a diagnosis to be given, problem behaviours need to have begun before the age of 7 years, be present in school and home, and significantly impair functioning. Many children with ADHD have difficulty in getting on with their peers and establishing friendships. They fail to recognize when their behaviour is annoying others, and may make significant social mistakes. They can usually understand such issues in

Table 13.1   Key features of the ADHD diagnostic categories

Inattention	Hyperactivity-impulsivity
• Fails to pay close attention to details or makes careless errors in schoolwork, work or other activities	• Squirms in seat or fidgets
• Has trouble keeping attention on tasks or play	• Inappropriately leaves seat
• Doesn't appear to listen when being told something	• Has trouble playing quietly or engaging in leisure activity
• Neither follows through on instructions nor completes tasks, schoolwork or jobs (not due to oppositional behaviour or failure to understand)	• Runs or climbs inappropriately; in adolescents or adults, there may be only a subjective feeling of restlessness
• Has trouble organizing activities and tasks	• Appears driven or 'on the go'
• Dislikes or avoids tasks that involve sustained mental effort (e.g. homework, schoolwork)	• Talks excessively
• Loses materials needed for activities: books, pencils, tools, toys, and so on	• Answers questions before they have been completely asked
• Easily distracted by extraneous stimuli	• Has trouble waiting turn
• Forgetful	• Interrupts or intrudes on others

hypothetical scenarios, but have trouble translating this understanding into the 'real world' (Whalen et al. 1985). About 25 per cent of children with ADHD have some form of learning difficulty, and many are placed in special education units as a consequence of their disruptive behaviour. Children with ADHD are more likely to drop out of school than those without the disorder.

An estimated 3–5 per cent of children in the USA could be diagnosed as having ADHD (APA 1994). Some but not all problems abate as the individual grows older. Of children identified with ADHD, 40 per cent continue to have these problems in late adolescence, and about 10 per cent have some level of symptoms in adulthood (Mannuzza and Klein 2000). Between 1 and 6 per cent of adults meet the criteria for ADHD (Murphy and Barkley 1996). By this time, most people have learned to adapt to their symptoms and can hold down jobs.

Diagnostic versus categorical understandings of ADHD

Many children exhibit some of the characteristics of those diagnosed as having ADHD. This indistinct line between what is 'ordinary' and 'pathological' behaviour, and the potential abuse of the diagnosis of ADHD as a justification for medicating disruptive children (see p. 325), has led to strong arguments as to whether ADHD exists as a separate 'condition' or whether the behaviours that comprise ADHD are better thought of as being at the extreme end of the normal distribution of behaviour. That is, the condition may best be considered in dimensional rather than categorical terms (see Chapter 1).

Arguments favouring the dimensional approach are both clinical and empirical. Clinicians note that a child may have significant problems in one particular area, but may not receive help because they do not fulfil the 'diagnostic requirements' for ADHD and therefore may not be considered to have a 'problem'. Similarly, a diagnosis of ADHD may justify drug treatments where other approaches may be more beneficial to the child. Empirical evidence suggests that dimensional scores of behaviours subsumed within ADHD appear to be more predictive of outcome than categorical diagnostic judgements. Fergusson and Horwood (1995), for example, compared the predictive validity of dimensional and categorical ratings/diagnoses of ADHD to predict levels of substance abuse, juvenile offending and school dropout in a cohort of New Zealand school children. They found a dose–response relationship between the number and severity of behaviours associated with ADHD and risk of each of these outcomes. Dimensional scores were more predictive of outcome than diagnostic category. These various findings suggest that the behaviours that comprise ADHD are better thought of as the end of a distribution of behaviours rather than categorically different to the norm.

Aetiology of attention-deficit/hyperactivity disorder

Genetic factors

Genetic factors appear to contribute to risk of developing ADHD. One early genetic study (Goodman and Stevenson 1989) found a 51 per cent concordance for ADHD between MZ twins and a 31 per cent concordance between DZ twins. More recent studies have found concordance between MZ twins to vary between 58 and 83 per cent compared to between 31 and 47 per cent for DZ twins, with heritability estimates for attention problems varying between 60 and 80 per cent (Wender et al. 2001).

Biological mechanisms

The main characteristics of ADHD are thought to reflect problems with behavioural control and management. Impulsivity is not thought to result from an inability to attend, but is the result of problems in executive function: a failure to decide when actions should be taken and how they should be executed. This implicates dysfunction of the frontal lobe as central to the disorder, a hypothesis supported by findings of smaller frontal lobes among children with ADHD than among a 'normal' comparison group reported by Castellanos et al. (1996).

The neurotransmitter involved in ADHD seems to be dopamine. Data to support this hypothesis mainly stems from studies that have found drugs that increase dopamine levels to be most effective in reducing or even eliminating the symptoms of ADHD. These include various types of amphetamines, and indirect dopamine agonists (see p. 325). In addition, administration of l-dopa and tyrosine, which are precursors to dopamine, results in moderate to marked reductions in ADHD symptoms in about half the people with ADHD given them (Reimherr et al. 1987). It seems paradoxical that an amphetamine actually reduces levels of physical activity, but it appears to do so by increasing frontal activity and control over executive dysfunctions that underpin the behaviour.

Another biological explanation has focused on the role of environmental toxins. Feingold (1979) suggested that salicylates, artificial colours and artificial flavours contribute to ADHD, although treatment using the Feingold diet, which is free from such additives, has proved effective only for a few children, and less so than medication (Hill 1998).

Psychological explanations

As noted above, ADHD is characterized not by hyperactivity, but by high levels of impulsivity. According to Barkley (1997), children with ADHD do things other children think of doing, but don't actually do. The urge to act is not inhibited. The first response to a situation is the response that is taken. The core of ADHD is a failure to inhibit inappropriate responses to environmental events. In addition to this, children with ADHD are more emotionally responsive to events than most children. They are poor at controlling feelings, and less able to tolerate negative emotions. Their emotions are driven by the moment and the object of their attention at that time. As a consequence, they have difficulties in maintaining goal-oriented behaviour, particularly when this is associated with some type of negative emotion. They have difficulty in sticking to a task in the expectation of future rewards or satisfaction on its completion. Schoolwork or other demanding and sometimes boring or frustrating tasks do not hold their attention and they move rapidly to other more immediately rewarding activities.

Barkley (1997) noted that as children grow older they use an internal dialogue as a means of self-control. This internalized language develops around the age of 3–4 years, the time that ADHD is often first identified. This is not coincidental: Barkley suggests that children with ADHD have disorganized internal speech, which contributes to their disorganized responses to external events. Barkley noted that children with ADHD often appear 'chatty', but their conversation usually deals with the present rather than the future: thoughts do not lead to planning and future expectations. This disorganization also means that children with ADHD have difficulties in dealing with abstract issues. They find it hard to explain things: they don't get to the point, they talk around it. Of interest is that while Barkley (1997) provides a psychological perspective on ADHD, he considers it to have a biological basis, and to be largely the result of biochemical and neurological factors. He describes people with ADHD as *biochemical outliers* acknowledging a dimensional view of their behaviour rather than a categorical one.

A biopsychosocial model

Bettelheim (1973) integrated biochemical models with social and psychological factors in a biopsychosocial model of ADHD. He suggested that ADHD develops when children with a biological predisposition to hyperactivity are raised in an environment with a strong authoritarian ethos or one where there is evident resentfulness at inappropriate behaviour. According to Bettelheim, if a child with a predisposition to hyperactivity is responded to with obvious frustration or impatience by their parents, they may feel unable to respond effectively to their parents' need for controlled behaviour and obedience. As both react to each other in negative ways, this may spiral into a continuous battle between child and parents, that spills over to other settings and eventually results in what may be termed ADHD.

Evidence of a role of family dynamics as a causal factor for ADHD is mixed. A.J. Smith et al. (2002), for example, found significant associations between conflictual child–mother relationships and the presence of

ADHD. By contrast, although Rey et al. (2000) found an adverse family environment was associated with conduct disorder and oppositional defiant disorder, it was not associated with ADHD. In addition, although family relationships may be strained in families with a child who has ADHD, there is some evidence that parent–child relationships improve once treatment is initiated, suggesting that adverse or conflictual family environments are at least in part a response to the child's behaviour, not simply the originating cause (Tallmadge and Barkley 1983).

Treatment of attention-deficit/hyperactivity disorder

Pharmacological interventions

Perhaps the best known pharmacological treatment of ADHD involves methylphenidate, better known as Ritalin. The combined results of studies investigating its efficacy suggests it achieves significant improvements in about 60 per cent of those prescribed it, compared to about 10 per cent of those prescribed placebo (Wender et al. 2001). The key benefit of Ritalin is that it moderates the symptoms of both inattention and hyperactivity, allowing the individual to focus more on educational, social and family issues. Pelham et al. (1993), for example, compared an eight-week school-based behaviour modification programme combined with Ritalin and the same programme combined with placebo in the treatment of a group of 8-year-old boys with ADHD. The behavioural programme involved a points system with both rewards for appropriate behaviour and 'costs' for inappropriate classroom behaviours. Acquisition of a fixed number of points could be exchanged for a variety of items chosen by the child. The effect of the behavioural intervention combined with Ritalin was significantly greater than when it was combined with placebo on measures of both class behaviour and academic performance.

The benefits of Ritalin can be dramatic. Here, a teacher describes the impact of Ritalin on one child and his classmates:

> He just came to us in Year 7, with a real history of paperwork behind him . . . poor behaviour, learning difficulties. He came to the school in September. We thought he had ADHD because he was beyond control, reason. He couldn't stay seated – or wouldn't – he wandered round the classroom, started wandering about the school. He was a powerful lad, and just pushed people out of the way that tried to stop him. By the end of November he had been seen by the doctor. He was given a diagnosis of ADHD and prescribed Ritalin. He stayed at home a couple of days, because he was pretty zonked out on it. Then he came back to school. The change was instantaneous. He was a difficult child, and he still

had behavioural problems . . . but you could reason with him.
You could sit him down and talk to him. He decided he liked
learning, as for the first time he could understand what he was
being taught. He started reading . . . which boosted his self-
esteem . . . lots of these kids with ADHD have low self-esteem as
they fail in school . . .

Ritalin does allow them to access the curriculum. For the first
time, they can concentrate on something and make progress. But
when the medicine wears off you know about it. We start to
give the mid-day dose at about a quarter to twelve. By this time,
they [children with ADHD] have got more 'edgy', more loud.
Lots of walking, winding people up: 'loud' is the predominant
word . . .

Sometimes you think the poor kids don't have a chance. It's
difficult at home – and they may trash their room. But you
think sometimes it's a response to real problems they have with
their parents. Some of them are like their child: they go from
'down here' to sky high in seconds. It's got to be bad for the
kids.

Ritalin is now widely used: so much so that some have argued that it is
now over-prescribed, and used to control unruly or unwanted behaviour
– not just ADHD. This has led to concern by pressure groups such
as Parents Against Ritalin and legal action. Class action suits for fraud
and conspiracy against the drug company that produces Ritalin have
been filed in various US states. These alleged that Ritalin has been over-
promoted, and that the defendants 'wilfully failed to address or provide
adequate information to consumers, doctors, and/or schools concerning
[its] significant hazards'. Some suits have been rejected, but some remain
pending at the time of writing (www.attention-deficit-disorder.org).
   Ritalin's side-effects include loss of appetite, abdominal pain, weight
loss, insomnia and increased heart rate. Retardation of growth may also
occur during prolonged therapy in children. Of more concern may be
the triggering of psychotic symptoms. Cherland and Fitzpatrick (1999)
reported a 9 per cent prevalence of psychotic symptoms, including hallucinations and paranoia, among their sample of 192 children treated with
Ritalin for ADHD, which ceased immediately on withdrawal of the drug.
No psychotic symptoms were reported among children with ADHD who
did not receive the drug. A final risk associated with Ritalin is its use
as a drug of abuse, which is becoming increasingly common in the USA.
As an amphetamine, it suppresses appetite, increases wakefulness and
produces an emotional high. When abused, tablets are either taken orally
or crushed and snorted. Some abusers dissolve the tablets in water and
inject the mixture, which can cause complications as insoluble fillers in
the tablets can block small blood vessels.

Operant approaches

The behavioural intervention used by Pelham et al. (1993) is typical of operant-conditioning based interventions. These usually take the form of a token economy, in which the child is rewarded for engaging in specific pre-specified behaviours by receiving a token. Tokens can be collected and, when enough have been accrued, exchanged for a desired item. This approach has a number of variants, including charts on which stars are placed as a reward for appropriate behaviours and, again, exchanged for tangible rewards when enough are displayed. Although this type of intervention can be effective on its own, the results of studies such as that of Pelham and colleagues suggest that operant procedures may be most effective when used in conjunction with treatment by Ritalin.

Training attention

The attention training tasks used to treat head injuries described in Chapter 14 (p. 344) can also be used to help children with ADHD. Semrud-Clikeman et al. (1999), for example, examined the effectiveness of the APT programme combined with training in problem-solving in a school setting with children identified as having problems in attention and not completing work. As a result of the training programme, the children improved on the training tasks, completed more tasks in class, and their teachers reported that they seemed more attentive. Using materials specifically developed for young children, Kerns et al. (1999) reported improvements in a group of 7–11-year-old children following a similar attention training programme. By the end of the training period, participants achieved better scores on untrained cognitive tasks, academic performance and on teacher reports of impulsiveness.

Environmental manipulation

As many of the behaviours associated with ADHD are seen as immediate responses to the environment, one way in which they may be influenced is by environmental manipulation. The ERIC (Educational Resources Information Center) Clearinghouse on Disabilities and Gifted Education (www.ericec.org) set out some clear guidelines, including the nature of the learning environment, to help teachers work with children with ADHD. These included:

- seat students with ADHD at the front of the class with their backs to the rest of the class to keep other students out of view
- surround students with ADHD with good role models
- avoid distracting stimuli

- produce a stimuli-reduced study area for teaching (which other children can access to avoid isolation.

In addition to these environmental factors, they considered a number of other factors including guidelines for maintaining and enhancing self-esteem, responding to inappropriate behaviour, and the process of teaching, all of which contribute to best practice when teaching children with ADHD.

Working with families

As noted above, the families of children with ADHD experience significant levels of stress and upset. A number of studies have attempted to reduce family problems by working with the whole family. Barkley et al. (2001), for example, compared the effectiveness of problem-solving communication training alone or following training behavioural management skills in an attempt to minimize conflict within families. Problem-solving communication training involved teaching a five-stage process through which the family combined to deal with problems: defining the problem, brainstorming potential solutions, negotiating and deciding within the family which solutions to implement, and then implementing the solution. The behavioural skills management involved learning to change triggers or responses to disruptive behaviour using operant procedures. Both interventions proved equally effective in those that completed them. However, three times as many people dropped out of training where the problem-solving approach was used alone than when the combined intervention was used, suggesting that some form of combined intervention is the treatment of choice.

Working with adults who have ADHD

Self-management strategies

Adults with ADHD can be taught a number of self-management strategies to help them manage their attentional problems (Sohlberg and Mateer 2001). These include *orienting procedures* in which they regularly monitor their activities to ensure they focus on planned activities. An example of this approach may be the use of a watch that beeps every hour, reminding the individual to ask themselves, 'What am I currently doing? What was I doing before doing this? What am I supposed to do next?' An example of another orienting task, used for people who set off to drive somewhere and then forget their destination, is to routinely write down their destination, expected time of arrival, and the time at which it may be useful to ask for help if lost, at the beginning of every trip.

A second approach involves *pacing*. People with attention problems often experience fatigue or problems in maintaining concentration over extended periods of time. To combat this, they may benefit from pacing the demands they place upon themselves, by not setting too high standards of productivity and taking breaks at regular intervals. They can also be taught to monitor fatigue levels and take breaks at appropriate times rather than fighting through the fatigue and being unproductive. People with attention problems also find that they have difficulty in switching from one task to another. The *key ideas log* minimizes the problems associated with this by encouraging people with attention problems to quickly write down or tape-record ideas that spring to mind so they do not disrupt their ongoing task.

Environmental strategies

A final intervention involves thinking through the impact environmental factors have on attention, and consider ways in which it can be modified to maximize cognitive performance (Sohlberg and Mateer 2001). Central to this approach is avoiding 'busy' or distracting environments and making use of 'quiet' environments when attention is required. This may involve, for example, shopping in quiet local shops rather than attempting to shop in bustling supermarkets. Further strategies may include minimizing the demand on attentional or organizational abilities, by setting up standing orders to pay bills or labelling cupboards to ensure maximum organization. The use of 'Do not disturb' signs both at home and work may also help minimize distraction from ongoing tasks. While these types of approaches would seem logical and likely to be effective, their highly individual nature has meant that their effectiveness has largely been explored through individual case reports rather than controlled trials (Sohlberg and Mateer 2001).

Chapter summary

1 About 3 per cent of the population have learning difficulties.

2 Only about 25 per cent of cases of learning difficulty have an identified cause. These include genetic conditions, infectious diseases, environmental hazards and several perinatal factors.

3 Social factors contribute strongly to mild learning difficulties; less so to more severe problems.

4 Down syndrome and Fragile X syndrome are two common conditions resulting from differing genetic factors.

5 The principles of normalization and social role valorization ensure that people with learning difficulties achieve the same respect and rights as the rest of the population.

6 Care of people with learning difficulties includes both social and psychological interventions.

7 Psychological interventions are frequently based on operant conditioning approaches to skills learning or behavioural change, although cognitive behavioural interventions may also prove effective.

8 People with autism have difficulties in three areas: social interaction, communication, and obsessive-compulsive or ritualistic acts.

9 When combined with learning disabilities these may profoundly affect the outcome of affected individuals.

10 The opioid theory of autism suggests that it results from an overdose of opioids as a result of a failure to metabolize gluten and casein from the gut. The MMR vaccine may contribute to this problem.

11 Bettelheim's psychodynamic model suggests that autism is an escape from an adverse family environment.

12 The biopsychosocial model of autism proposes that it results from a combination of lack of motivation to engage in social interactions combined with a lack of appropriate responses from the environment.

13 Lovaas's controversial behavioural treatment has proven moderately effective in the treatment of autism. Koegel and colleagues have developed a more strategic approach to such interventions.

14 Pharmacological interventions have also been shown to reduce a number of negative behaviours.

15 An estimated 3–5 per cent of children in the USA have ADHD.

16 It seems to be driven by low levels of dopamine and can be treated with drugs that increase these levels.

17 ADHD is driven by high levels of impulsivity, or lack of 'executive control'.

18 Family factors may also increase risk for ADHD, although relevant data are surprisingly sparse.

19 Treatment by Ritalin has been shown to facilitate behavioural interventions and education in children.

20 A variety of self-management programmes may be effective in treating adult ADHD.

For discussion

1 Do changes in technology and society help or hinder people with learning disabilities to cope with everyday living?

2 What are the implications for a family that has a child with a significant learning disorder?

3 What limits should there be to health professionals' responses to 'challenging behaviour'?

4 What are the implications for a family that has a child with ADHD?

5 Should all families of children with ADHD be encouraged to take part in family therapy to minimize the negative impact of an adverse family environment?

Further reading

Emerson, E., Hatton, C., Bromley, J. et al. (eds) (1998) *Clinical Psychology and People with Intellectual Disabilities*. Chichester: Wiley.

Emerson, E.C., Hatton, J., Felce, D. et al. (2001) *Learning Disabilities: The Fundamental Facts*. London: Mental Health Foundation.

Grandin, T. and Scariano, M.M. (1996) *Emergence: Labeled Autistic*. New York: Warner.

Jordan, R. (2001) *Autism with Severe Learning Difficulties*. London: Souvenir Press.

Teeter, P.A. (2000) *Interventions for ADHD*. New York: Guilford.

14 Neurological disorders

Neurological disorders are the result of damage or degeneration of the brain following the onset of disease or trauma. This chapter focuses on the consequences of three types of disorder arising from two disease processes, Alzheimer's disease (AD) and multiple sclerosis (MS), and from head injury. In the case of AD and MS, therapy is targeted at maintaining cognitive function and well-being in the face of a progressive deterioration of cognitive processes. Cognitive processes may be markedly impaired following head injury, but recover to some extent over time. Interventions here focus on maximizing the process of recovery and helping the individual cope with any residual cognitive deficits. By the end of the chapter, you should have an understanding of:

- The neurological processes that result in AD and MS

- The psychological consequences of these diseases

- Interventions targeted at both improving or maintaining cognitive functioning and well-being as the diseases progress

- The immediate and long-term cognitive consequences of head injury

- Interventions used to maximize recovery following head injury.

Alzheimer's disease

Alzheimer's disease is the most common type of dementia, affecting between 5 and 10 per cent of those aged over 65 years, and at least 20 per cent of those aged over 80 years (Roca et al. 1998). Although generally a condition found in elderly people, this is not always the case. Indeed, Alois Alzheimer's first description of the condition in the early years of the twentieth century was of a middle-aged woman. DSM-IV-TR defined AD as a progressive disease having the following characteristics (often summarized as the 4As):

- *amnesia:* loss of memory
- *aphasia:* language disturbance
- *apraxia:* impaired ability to carry out motor activities despite intact motor function
- *agnosia:* failure to recognize or identify objects despite intact sensory function
- *disturbance in executive functioning:* (that is, planning, organizing, sequencing, abstracting).

To achieve a diagnosis of AD, these deficits should cause significant impairment in social or occupational functioning and represent a significant decline from previous levels of functioning. Memory loss is progressive, with recent memories typically lost before remote ones, which are thought to be preserved as a consequence of rehearsal over life. However, as the disease progresses even remote and emotionally charged memories are lost. Early forgetfulness becomes a pathologically poor memory for present events, daily routine, and even family members. Word-finding difficulties are common. In its final stages, AD destroys the ability to communicate in any way.

In the early stages of AD, levels of insight are high and most people are aware of their deficits. However, as the disease progresses, insight is lost, all sense of self seems to vanish, and the individual becomes completely dependent on others for care. Suspiciousness, paranoia and delusions are common. The individual may experience spontaneous changes in mood, including anger and irritability, as well as restlessness and agitation. Confusion is common, and may be worse at night when cues that may orient the individual in time and place are less obvious, and oxygen supply to the brain is at its least. Although most health care services aim to maximize the independence of the individual and maintain them in their own home, there may come a time when they are hospitalized. By this time, they may be confused for much of the time, incontinent, and respond only vaguely to their environment.

The duration of AD from time of diagnosis to death can be 20 years or more: the typical duration is between 4 and 8 years. Over this time the individual will progress through the following stages:

- *Questionable dementia:* the individual begins to behave 'oddly' and relatives suspect there is a problem
- *Mild dementia:* there is no question that there is a problem, but the affected individual is able to maintain independence
- *Moderate dementia:* help is required for routine tasks; 'problem' behaviours such as wandering or aggression may be evident
- *Severe dementia:* the individual becomes increasingly frail and eventually chair- or bed-bound.

Alzheimer's disease does not just impact on the individual with the disorder. Many elderly people, the preponderance of them women (Parker and Lawton 1990), care for people with dementia in their own home, often until the disease is far progressed. These people typically experience significant stress (see Box 14.1).

Aetiology of Alzheimer's disease

Genetic factors

Up to 50 per cent of first degree relatives of a person with AD will develop the disorder (Korten et al. 1993). Genes on chromosomes 14, 21 and in particular the *apoE4* gene on chromosome 19 have been implicated in AD. ApoE4 is one of several forms, or alleles, of the apoE gene, the others being apoE2 and apoE3. People who carry two apoE4 genes are about eight times more likely to develop AD than those who have two of the E3 allele. The aopE4 gene may bring forward the onset of AD by as much as 17 years (Warwick Daw et al. 2000). However, it is found in only 40 per cent of people who develop AD and many people who carry the gene do not develop the condition. It may therefore be a risk factor for AD, but not a definitive one. It is also important to note that the prevalence of known genes for risk of AD is relatively low: familial AD accounts for less than 1 per cent of all cases of the disorder,

---

Box 14.1   Focus groups for mild–moderate dementia

Recently, one of my colleagues ran some focus groups exploring the factors that contributed to the quality of life of people with mild–moderate dementia. The results were of interest, not just because of what the people in the groups said, but also because of what they didn't say. Below are some quotes taken from the focus groups, with people telling us what added to or took away from their quality of life. The quotes are actually quite unremarkable, and could be made by virtually anyone of any age. Importantly, what the participants did not say was that their failing memory made their quality of life any worse. Some said that it might in the future. In fact, this became the theme related to this issue. However bad people's cognitive abilities were, they were always not affecting their quality of life at the time, but might in the future. This is not to say that loss of memory is not an issue and concern for people with dementia – and some people may become profoundly depressed as a result of their failing abilities. But many other things contributed to their quality of life – this did not just hinge on their cognitive abilities.

Husband/wife/partner

- Like I said, my husband is still there and so I'm all right.
- All I want is to be with my husband that I've been with practically since I left school.
- I think the majority would say if anything happens to the partner, there's nothing worse could happen, nothing worse could happen.

Children/grandchildren

- You got the love of a family and the grandchildren, like me.
- If I lost one of my children, I would be devastated.

Family

- Lack of friends or relations [would make the quality of life worse].
- I've got a good father and I had a good mother, but I'm afraid I've just lost my mum and dad, you know.

Your friends

- Lack of friends or relations, loneliness, all these things take away the quality of life.
- Friendship, that's very important, isn't it?

Feeling happy

- If you are happy, you are fair enough. Sometimes people are not happy and that must be awful.

Feeling that you are useful

- If you could do a good turn for anybody, do it, that makes the quality of life, don't it?
- If you see a dirty cup there, what's stopping you picking it up and just giving it a swirl, helping that poor lady there? . . . but people walk past . . . and I like [gestures angrily], that's my way.

Feeling content/satisfied

- Well, I could say nothing [could make the quality of life worse], I'm quite contented as I am.
- Whatever I do I am contented with.

Feeling that you have had a good life

- I'm an extremely lucky person, I think.
- I suppose you don't know me, but over the years I've really enjoyed my life.

and less than half of all people with the disease have a family history (Owen et al. 1994).

Neurological processes

Alzheimer's disease is the result of premature degeneration of brain systems. Degeneration is progressive, and the course of AD can be mapped against the geography of the brain affected. Problems typically initiate in the entorhinal cortex before proceeding to the hippocampus, and then gradually spreading to other regions, particularly the cerebral cortex. As the hippocampal neurons degenerate, short-term memory falters, as does the ability to perform routine tasks. As the disease spreads through the cerebral cortex, it begins to take away language.

The nature of the changes that occur appear to be both structural, including the development of beta amyloid plaques and neurofibrillary tangles, and involve a number of neurotransmitters. Beta amyloid results from damage to amyloid precursor protein (APT), which lies within the neuron cell membranes. It is a member of a larger family of proteins which enclose cells and act as a barrier to control which substances go in and out of them. Damage to APT results in the formation of beta amyloid fragments, which may clump together to form amyloid plaques and cause neuronal death, perhaps because they form tiny channels in neuron membranes through which uncontrolled amounts of calcium can flow (Sinha et al. 2000). Neurofibrillary tangles comprise abnormal collections of twisted threads inside nerve cells. The chief component of these tangles is a protein called tau. In healthy individuals, this binds and stabilizes the microtubules that carry nutrients and molecules from the bodies of the cells to the ends of the axon. In AD, tau is changed chemically, and this altered tau twists the microfilaments around each other to form tangles. The resultant collapse of the transport system causes errors in communication between nerve cells and neuronal death.

The most important neurotransmitter implicated in AD is acetylcholine: levels decline moderately in normal ageing but drop by about 90 per cent in people with AD (Whitehouse et al. 1982). Acetylcholine is involved in memory formation and influences neuronal activity in the hippocampus and cerebral cortex. Other neurotransmitters may also be involved. Serotonin and noradrenaline levels are lower than normal in some people with AD, which may contribute to sensory disturbances and aggressive behaviour. They may also be linked to other psychological conditions associated with the early stages of AD, including depression and anxiety.

Environmental factors

Risk for AD is also determined in part by environmental factors, although their exact roles in its aetiology are little understood. One consistent risk factor appears to be a history of head injury (McDowell 2001). A previous hypothesis that exposure to high levels of aluminium may result in AD has generally not been supported, although exposure to water massively polluted by aluminium in the UK may have resulted in a measurable decline in cognitive performance in a small number of people (Altmann et al. 1999). Smoking seems to be protective, even among those with a family history of dementia. Other protective factors include high levels of physical activity, moderate levels of red wine, and a diet high in vitamins B6, B12 and folic acid. A number of medications may also be protective, including non-steroidal anti-inflammatory drugs and oestrogen replacement therapy in post-menopausal women.

Treatment of Alzheimer's disease

Pharmacological interventions

Increasing levels of acetylcholine

If reductions in acetylcholine cause AD, increasing available acetylcholine levels may reverse its symptoms. Drugs that do so prevent its breakdown in the synaptic cleft by acetylcholinesterase and increase uptake in the postsynaptic receptor (see Chapter 3). Acetylcholinesterase inhibitors such as Donepizil (Aracept) generally achieve short-term cognitive improvements, although they delay rather than prevent cognitive decline (Rogers et al. 1998). Unfortunately, many people experience significant side-effects, most notably gastrointestinal tract disturbances, and up to 35 per cent of participants have been withdrawn from medication in clinical trials (Rogers et al. 1998). In addition, not all people respond to the treatment, although why this happens is unclear (Forette and Rockwood 1999).

A second method of increasing acetylcholine levels is through ingestion of nicotine, which triggers the release of acetylcholine, and has been shown to improve memory in aged monkeys (Buccafusco and Jackson 1991). People with AD have also shown short-term gains on a number of cognitive tasks and mood following injections of nicotine. However, there are, as yet, insufficient data to decide whether or not nicotine can prove effective in the treatment of AD.

Inhibiting the development of amyloid

A completely different pharmacological approach has involved attempts to block the production of beta amyloid within the brain, through the use of vaccines. Some degree of protection against plaques has been achieved in mice (Schenk et al. 1999) and preliminary safety studies in humans have shown injections of one vaccine to be potentially safe. In addition, Weiner et al. (2000) have found a smaller, but still significant, response using nasal administration in rats: an approach that may be more tolerated in the long-term (perhaps lifelong) administration of such a treatment.

Psychological approaches

Psychological interventions aim to maximize quality of life and functional ability as the disease progresses. Support groups, involving other people with similar problems, may provide support or coping strategies in the early stages of AD (Yale 1995). Three more formal therapeutic approaches are frequently used in its later stages.

Reality orientation

Reality orientation (RO: Holden and Woods 1995) involves providing confused elderly people with relevant information to help them maintain an accurate understanding of the world. There are two types of RO: *24-hour RO* involves establishing an environment with multiple cues to orient the individual in time, place and person: large clocks and calendars, reminders of the name of an institution or ward, name badges and so on. Social interactions with the person are also designed to provide relevant information ('Hello, Mr Jones. It's Tom here . . . It's really cold outside, like it usually is in January . . .'). Sentences are simple and specific, repeating information throughout the day and even within conversations. *Classroom RO* involves small groups of people meeting for between 30 and 60 minutes. Despite its name, these are held in comfortable rooms, with easy chairs and a relaxed atmosphere. Attenders are matched according to ability, and sessions involve discussion and information provision, with memory triggered by multiple cues and modes of information: newspapers, pictures, talking and so on.

In their review of 21 controlled trials of RO, Holden and Woods (1995) concluded that it achieved small but significant gains on measures of verbal orientation in comparison to no treatment or unstructured therapy. There appears to be limited generalization to other cognitive or behavioural skills, although Reeve and Ivison (1985) did report some improvements on measures of incontinence following a combination of classroom and 24-hour RO.

Whatever its outcome, RO can present difficulties for those trying to implement it, particularly when it may be necessary to remind people of distressing information. Many people with AD, for example, forget about the death of a loved one, and in their confusion may start looking for them or demanding they come and see them. Proper adherence to RO involves a carer telling them that their loved one is dead. This can be devastating news and cause significant distress. Unfortunately, they may forget this information after a period of time and once more start looking for their loved one, requiring the carer to once more break the news of their loved one's death: a cycle that can be distressing for both the individual and carer.

Validation therapy

As a consequence of this negative aspect of RO, Feil (1990) introduced a very different form of therapy. Validation therapy involves listening to the fears and concerns of the affected individual, taking time to fully understand their problems and to 'validate' them by valuing what they have to say. These conversations can provide opportunities to identify and modify any false beliefs, but this is not a core element of this approach. The focus is listening and responding to the emotional rather than the factual content of what is said.

In group therapy, small groups of individuals may engage in discussions designed to elicit 'universal' feelings of anger, separation or loss (Bleathman and Morton 1992). Feil (1990) suggested that by verbalizing memories and thoughts and having them validated by the group, the person gains a feeling of being accepted. This emphasis on the need to deal with unresolved conflicts has elements of psychodynamic therapy, while the therapeutic use of empathy and acceptance of the individual's personal view of the world provide a strong humanistic element. Evaluation of the effectiveness of this approach is largely anecdotal or based on uncontrolled case histories. In one such study, Feil (1990) reported a reduction in crying, pounding and pacing following validation therapy, but there is no evidence of persisting effects or greater benefits than other approaches.

Reminiscence therapy

There are three forms of reminiscence therapy (McMahon and Rhudick 1964). *Story-type reminiscence* involves remembering factual memories for pleasure. *Life-review* involves remembering and discussing memories, both good and bad, which come naturally to consciousness. Finally, *halo reminiscence* involves the repeated recollection of a particular situation involving guilt or despair. Life-review and halo reminiscence are thought to help resolve past conflicts.

Reminiscence therapy is based on Erikson's (1980) developmental model in which life-review is considered to occur naturally towards the end of life. This review may be generally positive or negative, with a resultant outcome of ego integrity or despair. In individual therapy, the therapist aids the individual through this already occurring self-analysis in order to make it more conscious and efficient. In group therapy, small groups review participants' lives through the use of prompts including old photographs, television and radio broadcasts, and so on. As with validation therapy, there are few studies of the effectiveness of reminiscence therapy. Participants typically enjoy their involvement in reminiscence groups, and there are reports of increased self-esteem and life satisfaction following group attendance (e.g. Kovach 1990). However, there is little evidence that it is more effective than other group activities.

Behaviour modification

Despite considerable interest in operant approaches to modifying the behaviour of confused elderly people, there are relatively few reports of its use and effectiveness. However, studies that have used these procedures have generally been effective. Burgio et al. (1988), for example, initiated a programme to increase appropriate toilet use and reduce incontinence which involved asking residents on a regular schedule whether they wished to go to the toilet and then reinforcing its use. This proved successful, although levels of self-initiated toileting actually fell, presumably as participants in the programme grew used to the system of prompts. Other programmes have reduced wandering, stereotyped behaviours, and increased social interaction and mobility (see Woods and Roth 1997). According to Woods and Roth, the critical element to the success of operant procedures in elderly people may not be the 'reward' for engaging in a particular behaviour. The use of prompts or cues to initiate behaviour may be more important.

One superordinate factor in providing care for confused elderly people is that the cognitive demands made of them are as minimal as possible (Woods and Bird 1999). Conversations should include short sentences, with repetition. Other relevant cues, such as pictures, may add to verbal information, but distraction with irrelevant information should be avoided. Cues should be simple and direct: an obvious line leading to the toilets and a picture of a toilet on the door, for example, may be more effective than the typical cue of a silhouette of a man or woman. Even people with mild–moderate dementia may find such socially based cues too subtle to interpret. Any cues may require training and repetition to enhance acquisition of relevant information. When taking an individual to the toilet, for example, the carer can talk the person through the process, and show the cues each time. In the home, safety can be maximized by a number of strategies that minimize the need for active planning, including installing storage heaters rather than gas fires, and so on.

Helping the carers

Caring for people with AD at home places enormous strain on the carers, who are usually elderly themselves, and often in poor health. Many benefit from some form of support and help. This can be provided by voluntary bodies such as the Alzheimer's Disease Society in the UK, and short periods in which the affected person stays in hospital to provide a break for the carer. They may also benefit from other, more formal interventions.

In a meta-analysis of nine studies designed to help carers cope more effectively with their stress, Knight et al. (1992) concluded that both group and individual interventions reduced both perceptions of burden and feelings of depression. Gallagher-Thompson and Steffen (1994) subsequently contrasted cognitive-behavioural and psychodynamic interventions in the treatment of depressed carers of elderly relatives. By the end of the intervention phase, both interventions proved equally effective: 71 per cent of participants no longer met the criteria for depression. However, those who had been in the caring role for a relatively short-time benefited most from dynamic therapy. Those who had cared for their relative for a longer period gained most from the cognitive behavioural intervention. It may be that people relatively new to the caring role benefit from exploration of their new role and its implications, while those who have been involved for longer benefit from learning more practical techniques for coping with their day-to-day stress.

A second way of helping carers cope is to provide them with strategies to help them manage the behaviour of their relative more effectively. Pinkston et al. (1988), for example, showed carers how to manage a number of behaviours, including self-care, aggression and wandering. Over 75 per cent of the relatives showed some improvement in their behaviour following their carer's training, reducing the strain experienced by their carers.

Head injury

Closed head injury occurs when an individual is struck on the head with no resultant damage to the skull or specific brain injury. This type of trauma usually results in the whole brain shifting within the skull at the time of the incident, resulting in diffuse damage. About half the cases of closed head injury result from road traffic accidents. The second highest cause is falls, particularly among frail elderly people and young children. Violence accounts for a further 20 per cent of cases, while sports injuries account for about 3 per cent. Alcohol consumption also adds to risk. People aged between 15 and 25 years old are most at risk. In the UK, there are up to 150 cases of closed head injury requiring hospitalization for every 100,000 people each year (Jennett 1996).

One simple index of the severity of injury is that of 'time to follow commands': that is, the time after trauma it takes the head-injured person to be able to respond to simple commands. Mild head injury is indicated by a time to follow commands of less than one hour; for moderate head injury this time is between one hour and 13 days; for severe head injury it is 14 days or more. Between 30 and 50 per cent of people will die as a result of severe head injury. About 10 per cent will still be in a 'vegetative' (non-responsive) state three months after the trauma, decreasing to about 4 per cent at six-month follow-up, and 2–3 per cent one year following injury.

For those who survive their injury and recover consciousness, recovery follows a typical pattern. The first phase involves a period of acute confusion and disorientation during which they are unable to form and retain new memories: *post-traumatic amnesia*. The longer the period of amnesia, the poorer the outcome. However, even a fairly long period of post-traumatic amnesia may not necessarily predict poor recovery. Jennett et al. (1981), for example, reported 'good' outcomes in 71 per cent of people who had post-traumatic amnesia lasting between one and two weeks.

Following resolution of post-traumatic amnesia, the majority of people with moderate or severe head injuries experience significant physical, cognitive and behavioural impairment. Most physical problems eventually resolve, although a minority of people continue to experience a wide range of symptoms including persistent muscle spasticity, impaired swallowing, and balance disturbances. About 5 per cent of those with moderate to severe closed head injury develop epileptic seizures: this compares with 35–50 per cent of people with penetrating head injuries. Risk for developing epilepsy continues to be higher than the population norm for as long as five years after the original trauma.

Cognitive and neuro-behavioural deficits are the most common residual symptoms of closed head injury. Diffuse brain injury results in a typical pattern of cognitive deficits, including slowed cognitive speed, decreased attention plus impaired memory, complex language skills and 'executive function' (Levin 1993). The latter includes problems in working memory, problem-solving, monitoring performance and organizing behaviour. Most recovery occurs in the first six months following injury, although recovery may continue more slowly for a further year. One month following injury, almost all people with moderate to severe injury have detectable cognitive impairments. Six months following injury about 8 per cent of those with moderate injury and 16 per cent of those with severe injury will require hospital care as a result of cognitive disabilities. The corresponding rates one year following injury are zero and 10 per cent. Only about a quarter of people with a severe head injury will ever return to work (Sherer et al. 2000).

Neuro-behavioural symptoms experienced by people with head injuries include increased irritability, headaches, anxiety, difficulty in concentrating, fatigue, restlessness and depression (Satz et al. 1998). These are more common than either physical or cognitive deficits and may have a greater impact on long-term outcome. One important feature of long-term recovery from head injury is a lack of self-awareness. Perhaps for this reason, relatives of people who have sustained a head injury frequently report more psychological changes than the affected individual. Relative reports include problems of slowness, irritability, fatigue, depression, rapid mood shifts and anxiety (Brooks et al. 1986). The long-term deficits of head injury can be profound and result in increased risk for divorce, chronic unemployment, economic strain, and substance abuse. Perhaps not surprisingly, depression and suicide rates are higher among people with significant head trauma than population levels (Teasdale and Engberg 2001).

Cognitive rehabilitation following head injury

Rehabilitation following moderate to severe head injury involves a number of treatment approaches provided by a variety of health professionals. Medical treatments include pain control for headaches, drug treatment of epilepsy and surgical treatment for **hydrocephalus**. Physiotherapy may maintain muscle flexibility and strength, occupational therapy teach skills necessary for self-care or return to some form of work. Speech therapists may work with the individual to improve their understanding and articulation of speech. From a psychological perspective, the main intervention is targeted at the cognitive and behavioural consequences of the trauma. The rest of this section will focus on some of the techniques used to improve cognitive function or help the individual cope with enduring cognitive deficits.

Coping with memory problems

A number of general techniques can improve memory, including memory drills, combining imagery with words to improve subsequent recall, and so on. Specific techniques have also been developed for use with people with head trauma. These have frequently involved very specific learning tasks. Wilson (1989), for example, used a preview, question, read, state and test (PQRST) model to improve encoding and recall of lists of words. This involved the participant examining the task, thinking about its requirements, and then reading a list of words over a number of trials both aloud and silently, before testing. The additional cognitive processing required in this approach was thought to enhance learning in comparison to simple repetition of lists of words. Unfortunately, memory gains made in such sessions frequently do not generalize beyond the specific memory task. In addition, as many people with head injuries underestimate their memory loss, attempts to implement such programmes are not always acceptable. Dobkin (1996) concluded that memory aids rather than memory 'treatments' may be the best approach to use (just as with people with MS and AD). His list of possible memory aids included use of a tape-recorder or hand-written notes, palmtop computers, time reminders such as alarm clocks, phone calls or radio pagers, and the use of a personal organizer or orientation boards within the home.

People with significant impairment may need training in the use of memory aids. Sohlberg and Mateer (1989), for example, used a three-stage process of training to use a memory notebook. The first stage involved systematic training in the contents and purpose of the notebook. This was reinforced by a question and answer approach ('What are the five sections of your notebook?'). During the application phase, individuals practised using the book through role play. Finally, they used the book 'in real life'. Using this approach, it took one participant in their programme as long as 17 days to acquire the skills necessary to use the notebook.

Memory aids can be particularly helpful in reminding the individual to do various tasks they otherwise may have forgotten to do. Wilson et al. (2001), for example, evaluated the use of a paging system that reminded people with head injuries to do various tasks through the day. Most of those given the pager benefited both when they had it and during the seven weeks after returning it. Its use seems to have established behavioural patterns that were self-sustaining.

Improving 'executive functions'

A second problem that people face following head injury is a decrement in problem-solving skills. Interventions designed to compensate for this have focused on breaking down problem-solving into specific stages. One such model, which utilized a simple acronym, *IDEAL*, to trigger each phase, was developed by Bransford and Stein (1984). *I* involved identification of the problem, *D* involved defining the problem (its specific nature and causes), *E* involved exploring alternative approaches to dealing with the problem, *A* involved acting on the plan developed in stage E. Finally, *L* involved checking on the effectiveness of any chosen plan. People with head injuries may also be taught not to try to deal with multiple problems simultaneously, but to try to identify and deal with specific problems one-at-a-time.

Where people lose the attention required for problem-solving and other tasks, attention compensation training may be used. This involves the individual first identifying when they are losing concentration, and then using strategies such as self-instruction (Meichenbaum 1985: 'Come on now, pay attention here . . .') to help remain focused. External cues can also be useful in initiating behaviour (Wilson et al. 2001).

A number of standardized programmes have also been developed to remediate attention problems. The *Attention Process Training programme (APT)* of Park et al. (1999) did so by using a number of differing strategies. Sustained attention was trained by exercises including attention tapes that required listening for target words or word/number sequences and pressing a buzzer when identified, listening to a paragraph and testing comprehension, and mental arithmetic exercises. Shifting attention was trained by exercises including tapes that required identification of one type of target word followed by identification of another. Tasks were presented in order of difficulty and repeated until the individual was able to cope effectively with the task demands. If necessary they were practised at home with the help of relatives as well as in the clinic. This type of approach has proven moderately effective. Most studies have shown gains on psychometric measures of memory or attention following such interventions. Less have looked at 'real world' improvements, although there is some evidence that improvements can be made on measures as diverse as driving skills, independent living and return to work (Sohlberg and Mateer 2001). Some other strategies to increase attention or prevent distraction are discussed in the context of attention deficit disorder in Chapter 13.

Coping with negative emotions

Given the high levels of depression and suicide among people who have sustained a significant head injury, there is little doubt that many would benefit from some form of psychological or pharmacological intervention to help moderate their mood. The American National Institutes of Health (NIH Consensus Development Panel 1991), for example, noted that psychotherapy could be an important aid to emotional recovery, reducing depression and improving the low self-esteem associated with cognitive dysfunction. They suggested that such interventions should provide emotional support, explanations of the injury and its likely outcome, help achieve increased self-esteem by maximizing gains towards achievable goals, reduce denial, and increase the individual's ability to relate to family and society. Despite this optimism, they noted that the use of psychotherapy has not been studied systematically in people with head injury, and its benefits therefore remain unproven. They also noted that while antidepressants may be of value in this population, people who have sustained head injuries are likely to experience more adverse side-effects from these drugs than the norm. This necessitates careful observation of those receiving such medication, and indicates that other therapeutic approaches should be selected where appropriate.

Helping the carers

People living with, and caring for, a person who has sustained a head injury may themselves experience significant stress and distress (Harris et al. 2001). While there is some evidence that strain on the family reduces as a consequence of improvements in cognitive deficits and health service input, there is a strong argument for the provision of services to help the family cope with the stress of caring for a person with a head injury more directly. Despite this, just as with studies to help people cope emotionally with the trauma and consequences of head injury, there are few studies of the effectiveness of such programmes, and most of these are uncontrolled and naturalistic studies. As a result, the impact of family or partner support programmes is difficult to judge (Sinnakaruppan and Williams 2001).

Multiple sclerosis

Multiple sclerosis is a neurological condition resulting from the destruction of the myelin sheath that surrounds all nerve cells within the brain and central nervous system. Where this destruction occurs, sclerotic plaques develop, which block or distort the normal transmission of nerve impulses. As this may occur in any part of the brain or spinal cord, the symptoms they cause differ markedly across individuals, and include loss of limb function, loss of bowel and/or bladder control, blindness due to inflammation of the optic nerve, and cognitive impairment. Muscular spasticity is a common feature, particularly in the upper limbs; 95 per cent of people with MS experience debilitating fatigue, which prevents any sustained physical activity in about 40 per cent of people. Nearly half the people with MS consider this to be their most serious symptom (Lechtenberg 1988). Between 30 and 50 per cent of people with the condition require walking aids or a wheelchair for mobility.

The course of MS differs across individuals. Onset before the age of 15 years is rare; 20 per cent of those who have MS have a benign form of the disease in which symptoms show little or no progression after the initial attack. A few people experience malignant MS, resulting in a swift and relentless decline and significant disability or even death shortly after disease onset. Onset of this type of MS is usually after the age of 40 years. The majority of people have an episodic condition, with acute flare-ups followed by periods of remission. Each flare-up is usually followed by a failure to recover to previous levels of function, resulting in a slowly deteriorating condition. Death is usually due to complications of MS including choking, pneumonia and renal failure. Suicide rates are significantly higher among people with MS than in the general population (Sadnovick et al. 1991).

Susan provides a glimpse of what it feels like to have MS. At the time of our talk she was taking antidepressants for her depression and, as you will read, was having problems coming to terms with her disorder:

> I developed MS about four years ago. It was odd to start with.
> I didn't think I had anything serious, although you do worry
> about symptoms you don't understand. It started when I had
> some problems with my sight. I couldn't see as well as I used to
> be able to – it came on suddenly so I didn't think it was age or
> anything normal. I think at the time I was also a bit more clumsy
> than I had been – nothing obvious, but I dropped things a bit
> more than before. Nothing really that you'd notice unless other
> things were happening as well. I went to my GP about my eyes
> and he sent me to see a neurologist. He tried to reassure me that
> there was nothing too badly wrong and that he wanted to check
> out a few symptoms. But I began to worry then . . . you don't get
> sent on to see the hospital doctors unless there is anything really
> wrong with you. He suggested that he thought it might be MS,
> which was why he was not sending me to an eye specialist.

I got to see the neurologist pretty quickly and she ran a few tests over a few weeks – testing my muscle strength, coordination, scans and so on . . . sticking needles into me at various times. The upshot of this was that I was diagnosed as having MS. My consultant told me and my husband together, and allowed us to ask questions about things. We also got to speak to a specialist nurse who has helped us over the years. She was able to take the time to tell us more than the doctor about what to expect and what support we could have. Although I think it was nice to hear the diagnosis from the doctor.

I must admit that I found it really hard to deal with things at the beginning – you don't know what to expect and perhaps you expect the worst. You hear all sorts of horror stories about people dying with MS and that. And no one can really reassure you that you won't have problems . . . Over the last few years, I've got to know my body and seen things getting worse. But it happens gradually and a lot of the time there are no changes. So that is reassuring that things aren't going to collapse too quickly and I won't be left incontinent and unable to feed myself for a long time – hopefully not ever!

The worse thing is the tiredness and clumsiness. My eyes have actually got better, thank goodness. I use sticks to get around the house. Sometimes I can walk a little out of the house. Often I have to take the wheelchair. I just get exhausted too quickly, there isn't a lot of point trying to walk, because I cannot go far . . .

I hate having MS. I used to take part in sports, go out, be lively. Now I can't do any of that. I'm tired . . . down a lot of the time. I think the two often go together. My memory was never that good, but now it seems to be worse than ever. I can hold conversations, but keeping my concentration up for a long time is difficult. So, people find you difficult to deal with. I know my husband feels that way. He married a lively, sporty, slim woman . . . now I'm lethargic, down, putting on weight because I eat and don't exercise – even though they tell me not to, so I can keep mobile and not develop skin problems. I don't go out very much because it's such a hassle in my wheelchair . . . cities were not designed for people in wheelchairs . . . and people don't like people in wheelchairs. You are ignored . . . and just want to say, 'Hey, I'm here. I have a brain you know . . .' I know this sounds sorry for myself. And sometimes I feel more positive. But I find living with uncertainty difficult. Will I have a bad day today? Will I have a flare up – have to go to hospital, take mega-steroids, come out worse than when I went in? I guess you have to live for the day . . . but it can be difficult.

Aetiology of multiple sclerosis

Genetic factors

The lifetime risk of developing MS for the general population is 1 in 800. This increases to 1 in 50 for the children of affected individuals and 1 in 20 for their siblings. However, increased concordance among family members may not exclusively indicate a genetic aetiology. Siblings who both develop MS usually do so in the same calendar year rather than the same age, indicating the possibility of common environmental factors impacting on risk for MS (Haines and Pericak-Vance 1999).

Biological mechanisms

The aetiology of MS is still not fully understood, although the favoured hypotheses are that it is the result of errors in the immune system or viral infection.

One chemical within the immune system, called *gamma-interferon*, is particularly implicated in MS: high levels of gamma-interferon co-occur with high levels of MS activity. How gamma-interferon affects the disease process is not yet fully understood, but it is likely that it stimulates production of Cytotoxic T cells by the immune system that are responsible for attacking and destroying diseased or damaged body cells. These cells can attack cells directly and are usually able to discriminate between 'self' cells (those of the body) and 'non-self' cells (damaged or cancerous cells, or pathogens). In MS, it seems to be that the activated Cytotoxic T cells wrongly identify the myelin sheath of nerve cells within the brain and spinal column as 'non-self', and attempt to destroy it. Viral infections may act as a trigger to the production of gamma-interferon: hence, the link between viral infections and MS.

Stress and MS

There is good evidence that stress can influence activity within the immune system. Given the possible role of the immune system in the aetiology of MS, it is possible therefore that stress may influence the onset and course of the condition. Evidence for the former was provided by Palumbo et al. (1998). They interviewed a group of people with MS and a healthy control group about the frequency and types of stress they had experienced in the year preceding the onset of disease or an equivalent time period. People with MS reported more stressful life-events than those in the control group, suggesting that these may have triggered its onset. Unfortunately, while these data are indicative of a stress–MS link, they cannot be considered definitive. Many people with serious physical illnesses try to find reasons why they have developed the disease at any particular time, a process known as 'the search for meaning'. As many people consider stress to be an important trigger to disease, this may make them more aware of stresses they have experienced or more likely to label events as stressful than people without the disease. Accordingly, any between-group differences in pre-disease stress may have been more apparent than real.

Longitudinal studies of the impact of stress on the progression of MS are easier to interpret and also indicate that stress may have a role in MS. In one such study, Mohr et al. (2000a) took various measures of stress and disease progression every 4 weeks over periods of up to 100 weeks in a group of people with MS. They found that increases in personal conflict or disruption to routine typically preceded increases in disease activity. These data supported the findings of Schwartz et al. (1999) who found a bidirectional relationship between stress and MS: risk of disease progression increased as a consequence of stress, and increases in disease progression contributed to reported levels of stress – a vicious cycle between stress and disease progression.

Psychological sequelae of multiple sclerosis

Cognitive problems

As well as physical problems, people with MS frequently experience a number of cognitive deficits in memory, attention, conceptual reasoning, verbal fluency and abstracting abilities. Nearly half the people with MS complain of some degree of cognitive impairment and memory problems. The latter do not follow a distinct progression, but usually involve problems in retrieval from long-term memory storage: short-term and recognition memory is seldom impaired. Speed of information processing is also slowed in comparison to people without the condition, partly due to slowed psychomotor performance as a result of slowed neuronal activity (Brassington and Marsh 1999). Visual and auditory attention may also be impaired.

Increasing cognitive deficits can be charted against progressive brain damage. Feinstein et al. (1993) conducted two-weekly cognitive assessments and magnetic resonance imaging (MRI) scans of brain lesions over a six-month period in a group of people with MS. Performance on the cognitive tasks varied as a function of disease progression. The test performance of participants whose MRI scans showed increasing lesions deteriorated over time, despite the practice effects of repeated administration. By contrast, those people whose MS did not progress either maintained or improved their scores. Damage to the corpus callosum, the bundle of fibres connecting both hemispheres of the cortex, appears implicated in a variety of cognitive impairments including visuo-spatial ability, and speed of problem-solving. Left parietal lesions are associated with impaired memory and learning (Huber et al. 1992).

Depression

The reported prevalence of depression among people with MS varies between 14 and 57 per cent, higher than among people with other neurological conditions (Schubert and Foliart 1993). Whether this is a direct result of neuronal damage or a psychological reaction to the experience of the disease is not clear. It may, of course, be both.

Perhaps the strongest indicator that depression is the result of neurological changes is that depression can be the first sign of MS, preceding obvious neuro-cognitive symptoms by months or years (Berrios and Quemada 1990). Proponents of the neurological model have suggested that this is the result of sclerotic plaques in brain areas that mediate mood such as the limbic system, prior to any obvious disorder to which the individual will react. An alternative explanation could be that depression provides a trigger to the onset of MS (as may stress) rather than being an early indicator of its presence.

The findings of Dalos et al. (1983) also suggested a psychological causation. They reported a prospective study of the relationship between mood and disease progression, following 64 patients for a one-year period. Over this time, 90 per cent of people with progressive or relapsing MS developed depression, compared to 39 per cent of those with stable MS, and 12 per cent of a matched group of people with spinal cord injury. This pattern of results is consistent with a model of depression as a reaction to increasing and uncontrollable disability. Aronson (1997) provided further evidence of depression as a reaction to the physical and social consequences of disease: in their sample of people with MS, low mood was associated with unemployment, mobility limitations, fatigue, episodic exacerbations and interference with social activities.

The relationship between mood and neurological disease is further complicated by the findings of Lyon-Caen et al. (1986). They noted that some people with neurological diseases, including MS, experience a dissociation between the mood they feel and their expressive behaviour: they may cry without feeling sad, laugh without feeling happy, and so on. People with this syndrome lack control over and rapidly switch between emotions, and are over-sensitive to emotional stimuli. Lyon-Caen and colleagues reported this dissociation in 9 of 19 non-depressed, and 5 of 11 depressed people with MS they interviewed.

Depression is not just a problem in itself. It may bring with it a number of negative health consequences. Johnston et al. (1999) reported a six-month longitudinal study of 38 people newly diagnosed with MS; 10 people died over the course of the study. Depressed mood at baseline was predictive of death, more rapid disease progression, and more severe disability at six-month follow-up. There was no association between severity of symptoms and depression at baseline, suggesting that depression predicted these outcomes independently of illness severity.

That depression predicts the degree of disability resulting from MS is not surprising. Depressed individuals are less likely to 'push' themselves to maintain independence or follow exercise regimes. Its impact on mortality is more difficult to explain. However, Johnston and colleagues provided three potential explanations for their findings. First, depressed people may behave differently than non-depressed people in ways that increase risk for disease progression: smoking more, eating less adequately or taking less care of themselves. They are also less likely to adhere to recommended treatments as closely as non-depressed people (Mohr et al. 2000b). Second, depressed individuals may differentially influence the behaviour of those around them, resulting in carers or health professionals giving less attention to their needs or restricting entry to aggressive treatments that may prolong life, as they may be considered too emotionally weak to cope with them. Finally, depression is associated with impaired immune functioning, which may directly affect disease progression. Which of these (or other) explanations is most appropriate is not yet understood.

In sharp contrast to the previous discussion, some people with MS experience periods of euphoria. This is found in people with advanced disease and is thought to be a consequence of scarring in the limbic system isolating it from frontal control, although this has not been confirmed by MRI studies (Minden and Schiffer 1990). Steroids used to treat MS during acute flare-ups may also trigger such episodes.

Treatment of multiple sclerosis

Psychological interventions in MS have two primary foci: first, to help people manage the cognitive and other symptoms of MS, and second, to help people cope emotionally with the impact of the disease.

Coping with cognitive deterioration

Many of the memory aids used in dementia and head injury can also be used to help people with MS who have memory problems or problems of executive function. One additional strategy has been developed specifically for people with MS. Goldstein et al. (1992) suggested that *gist recall* can be a powerful aid to memory for people with MS. They noted that while people with MS may have trouble remembering specific details of events, they are able to remember the gist or basic elements of what occurred. According to this model, rehabilitation should focus on teaching people to encode and retrieve information according to its overall meaning rather than trying to remember the details of what may have occurred. How effective this is has yet to be fully evaluated.

Coping with emotional problems

A number of interventions can be used to help people cope with the symptoms of MS. One relatively simple method involves providing information about the likely course of the disease, as uncertainty is associated with lower mood. There is consistent evidence that more sophisticated interventions can also alleviate depressive symptoms experienced by people with MS. In a meta-analysis of the evidence, Mohr and Goodkin (1999) found both psychological and pharmacological treatments to be effective in treating depression, with no difference in benefits following either approach. Only five studies had been reported at this time, so any conclusions should be viewed with some caution. However, brief cognitive behavioural interventions appeared superior to both waiting list control and standard outpatient appointments. Larcombe and Wilson (1984), for example, randomly allocated 20 depressed people with MS into a cognitive behavioural or waiting list condition. The cognitive behavioural programme was based on Beck's depression treatment programme, and involved increased social interaction, pleasant event scheduling, and challenging cognitive distortions. People who took part in the intervention evidenced greater improvements in mood than those in a waiting list control group, both at the end of therapy and at one-month follow-up. The magnitude of reductions in depression reported were similar to those found in general psychiatric populations, suggesting there is nothing about depression in MS that makes it harder to treat than in people without MS.

Fatigue and poor mobility may make it difficult for many people with MS to attend outpatient therapy appointments. With this in mind, Mohr et al. (2000b) examined the effectiveness of a cognitive behavioural programme for the treatment of depression delivered by telephone. The intervention lasted eight weeks and involved a workbook with standardized assignments combined with telephone contacts. Assignments focused on identifying and modifying dysfunctional thoughts, increasing pleasant events, and developing strategies to manage fatigue. The latter included scheduling achievable amounts of exercise, scheduling breaks, and learning to identify physical cues to determine when to take breaks. The usual care control involved routine outpatient appointments. By the end of the intervention, participants in the cognitive behavioural programme reported lower levels of depression and were more likely to adhere to their interferon therapy than those in the normal care condition.

The one pharmacological intervention published at this time of the review was reported in Minden and Shiffer (1990). This found desipramine (a tricyclic) to be superior to placebo. However, nearly half those in the trial experienced significant side-effects, even at less than optimum treatment levels of the drug. This sensitivity to medication has also been found in the treatment of depression following head injury, and may make psychological interventions the therapy of choice in such cases.

Chapter summary

1 Alzheimer's disease affects a significant proportion of elderly people.

2 It is characterized by a progressive process of cognitive and behavioural degeneration following a regular pattern as differing brain systems become involved.

3 The neurological processes underpinning the disorder appear to be neurofibrillary tangles and beta amyloid plaques. Reductions in levels of the neurotransmitter acetylcholine also appear to be implicated.

4 There is, as yet, no cure for AD. In its early stages, interventions are targeted at maximizing cognitive abilities. As the illness progresses, interventions focus on minimizing cognitive load and maintaining independence.

5 Closed head injuries can result in profound and long-lasting cognitive deficits.

6 Psychological interventions in this population focus on cognitive retraining, although any gains often fail to generalize beyond the training context. Accordingly, many interventions incorporate the use of external aids to trigger routine behaviours as well as cognitive strategies for maintaining concentration.

7 Multiple sclerosis is a degenerative disease of varying course.

8 It impacts on both the cognitive and emotional life of people with the disease.

9 Interventions are therefore targeted at both developing strategies for coping with cognitive impairments as well as depression. Both appear to be effective.

For discussion

1 Many frail and elderly people act as carers for people with AD. How may their stress be minimized?

2 Does cognitive retraining really provide meaningful benefit to people who have had a head injury, or are its effects too limited?

3 How may people with MS be helped to cope effectively with their disease?

Further reading

Brassington, J.C. and Marsh, N.V. (1999) Neuropsychological aspects of multiple sclerosis, *Neuropsychology Review*, 8: 43–77.

Holden, U.P. and Woods, R.T. (1995) *Positive Approaches to Dementia Care.* Edinburgh: Churchill Livingstone.

NIH Consensus Development Panel on Rehabilitation of Persons with Traumatic Brain Injury (1999) Rehabilitation of persons with traumatic brain injury, *Journal of the American Medical Association*, 282: 974–83.

Wilcock, G.K., Bucks, R.S. and Rockwood, K. (eds) (1999) *Diagnosis and Management of Dementia: A Manual for Memory Disorders Teams.* Oxford: Oxford University Press.

Addictions

Ask someone to describe an addict, and they will usually give a stereotypical description of someone addicted to 'hard' drugs such as heroin or cocaine. However, most chemical addictions are to legal drugs such as coffee, cigarettes and alcohol. People may also be addicted to a variety of behaviours, including exercise or gambling. For these people, the neurochemical reaction to their behaviour is similar to that induced by drugs. After a brief introduction to drugs and drug dependence, this chapter considers the aetiology, implications and treatment of three types of addiction: to alcohol, heroin and gambling. By the end of the chapter, you should have an understanding of:

♦ Why people take drugs, and the nature of dependence

♦ Factors leading to alcohol and opiate abuse, and gambling disorders

♦ The types of interventions used to treat each disorder, and their relative effectiveness.

Drugs and drug dependence

Many people take drugs, and start taking them at a relatively young age. In the UK 41 per cent of 16-year-olds report having used cannabis, in comparison to 34 per cent of US, 10 per cent of Italian and 2 per cent of Greek teenagers (Hibell et al. 1997). Participants in the rave culture typically report having used over ten drugs including alcohol, cannabis, ecstasy, tobacco, LSD, amphetamine and cocaine (Forsythe 1996). Use of drugs among the wider population is considerably less, although about 25 per cent of the population report having used an illegal drug, most frequently cannabis, at some time in their life. Only 3 per cent of the drug-using population injects.

Table 15.1 The neurotransmitters involved and 'addictiveness' of various drugs

Drug class	Neurotransmitter involved	Physical withdrawal problems	Psychological withdrawal problems
Mimic natural transmitters			
Opiates	Endorphins	+++	+++
Cannabis	Anandamide	+	+
Alcohol	GABA	+++	++
Nicotine	Acetylcholine	+	+++
Release transmitters			
Cocaine	Dopamine	++	+++
Amphetamines	Dopamine	+	++
Nicotine	Dopamine	+	+++
Ecstasy	Dopamine; serotonin	+	0
Block transmitters			
Barbiturates	Glutamate	+++	++
Psychedelics (incl. LSD)	Serotonin	+	0

Source: adapted from Nutt and Law (2000)

Drugs impact through changes in neurotransmitters within brain systems (see Table 15.1). With few exceptions, the quicker a drug's action, the more addictive it is. Cocaine, for example, was originally ingested by chewing coca leaves. This produced an increase in vigour and resistance to fatigue but little pleasure. More recently, it has been made into cocaine hydrochloride powder which, when taken nasally, impacts on the brain within 4–10 minutes of ingestion. Crack cocaine is a further refinement that allows it to be smoked and to impact on the brain in seconds. Each form of cocaine is thought to be increasingly addictive.

Problems arising from drug use defy simple categorization. They may be social, physical, legal, interpersonal or psychological. DSM-IV-TR (APA 2000) acknowledged these factors in its definition of 'abuse or harmful use of substances' as a maladaptive pattern of substance use leading to clinically significant impairment or distress and one or more of the following:

• failure to fulfil major role obligations at work, school or home
• use in situations in which it is physically hazardous
• legal problems
• social or interpersonal problems.

DSM-IV-TR also identified a more problematic level of dependency, in which the individual becomes psychologically or physically dependent on a particular drug. The key factor here is the development of a tolerance to the drug, involving a need for more of it to achieve the desired experience and withdrawal symptoms if use of the drug is ceased. Other criteria include social impairment, devoting substantial time and effort to obtaining the drug, and a history of repeated, unsuccessful attempts to stop using.

Excess alcohol consumption

Alcohol is a socially sanctioned drug. Drunk at moderate levels, certain types of alcohol, such as red wine, may benefit health. Excess consumption may be harmful. Defining what is meant by excess alcohol consumption has proven far from simple. This confusion is illustrated by changes to health advice made by the UK government in 1995. Between 1986 and 1995 the recommended limits for weekly consumption were 21 units of alcohol or less for men, and 14 units or less for women. In 1995, a government committee established to review these guidelines recommended they be increased to 28 and 21 units per week respectively. These changes caused a furore and much criticism among alcohol experts, particularly as they were not based on any new evidence (see, for example, *British Medical Journal*, volume 293). Consequently, a number of health promotion and alcohol agencies have been reluctant to adopt these guidelines and there is a lack of clear advice concerning the recommended limits to consumption.

Acute intoxication can result in risk-taking or other behaviours that may damage both the individual or others. About 20 per cent of psychiatric admissions, 60 per cent of suicide attempts, 40 per cent of incidences of domestic violence and 15 per cent of all traffic deaths in the UK are associated with alcohol consumption (Royal College of Psychiatrists 1986; Edwards et al. 1994). Long-term dangers include physical health problems such as liver cirrhosis, hypertension and various cancers. Long-term excess consumption may also result in significant neurological problems. Wernicke's encephalopathy is caused by thiamine deficiencies common in heavy drinkers as a consequence of poor diet, and results from degenerative changes and small bleeds in the brain. Its symptoms include memory deficits, **ataxia** and confusion. If not treated, it may progress to a more problematic disorder, known as Korsakoff's syndrome. This irreversible condition affects about 5 per cent of heavy drinkers and involves significant **retrograde amnesia** and **anterograde amnesia**. Anterograde memory deficits are usually the most marked problems, and individuals with the condition live a very 'minute by minute' existence, frequently **confabulating** in an effort to replace the memories they fail to sustain.

Problem drinking is usually the end-point of a progression from social drinking to drinking at times of stress or difficulty, through to an increasing 'need' to drink to cope with social or psychological problems or prevent the onset of withdrawal symptoms. In the early stages of dependence, individuals may need a drink at lunchtime to alleviate discomfort. As they become more dependent, they may need an early morning drink or one during the night to avoid withdrawal. Periods of abstinence of three to four hours may be difficult. Withdrawal results in a variety of symptoms, including tremor, nausea, sweating and mood disturbance. Delirium Tremens ('the DTs') is the most extreme element of withdrawal. It usually begins within three to four days of abstinence and lasts between two and three days. It involves reductions in consciousness, impairment of memory, insomnia and frightening auditory and/or visual hallucinations.

The story of Anne is typical of many women who drink to excess:

First started drinking when I was 18. I was at college at the time – a part of the norm – drinking cider or lager at weekends. I met my first partner out drinking when I was about 22. We got into a crowd who were wine drinkers and so we started drinking more wine. He'd always been a heavy drinker – more than I ever did. And often as a result of his drinking he'd become quite violent towards me and arguments would follow after drinking. As a result of this, I began to drink more – to join him, to keep up. My violent marriage made me think about my childhood – which had been very unstable and unhappy for various reasons – and the more I brooded on that, the more I drank. I was drinking about two bottles of wine a night at this time. Drinking helped me cope with my marriage and memories of my childhood. It also made things in the relationship worse, of course.

By the time I was 28–29, the relationship had broken down, and my drinking fell a little – but not that much. Then one night, I was followed home by a man from a nightclub and sexually assaulted by him. My drinking escalated again. I felt I couldn't go out of the house. I was scared and felt trapped. I lost my job as a care worker with children and then I had nothing to keep me going, so I just drank through the day. I was drinking a couple of bottles of wine and perhaps a flagon of cider a day at this time.

I did this for about six months or so, when I met my next partner, and I began to drink less. I managed to get another job. But the drinking was always there. I managed to get another job – as a health care assistant in an old people's home. I had a child – but things were never good in the relationship I suppose.

For the last 20 years, things have pretty much been the same.
I drink all the time – sometimes more, sometimes less. Drinking
helps me forget my problems and go into oblivion – it blocks
things out. And there's a lot to block out. I thought I had been an
OK mother – perhaps not the best, but OK. But my son doesn't
want to know me anymore. My partner has long gone. I've had
jobs on and off over this time – that last one, about eight years
ago.

I feel guilty about my drinking. I've never really been there for my
family – I've always been the drunk that doesn't fit in. I suppose if
you are always drunk – quietly not loudly – you still can't do
your best. Now, I stay in – I don't go out much. I'm ashamed
when I go to the shops – people looking at me, talking about me.
I feel they are looking at me – judging me. I don't feel good when
I'm drunk, but I do feel in oblivion. I just sit there – or lie in bed
all day. I'm drinking from the moment I get up – I have to control
the tremors.

I want to stop drinking. I feel despair at the circle I'm caught
up in – there's no way out. I try – I do all the right things from
pouring the drink down the sink, going to the GP for help and
so on. But when I stop drinking I get violent stomach cramps.
I shake. I get headaches. I feel paranoid, that people are talking
about me. I can't cope with these withdrawals, so I end up
drinking again.

Since telling her story, Anne has been going through inpatient detoxification and a six-month programme in a residential setting involving both
exploratory psychotherapy and a cognitive behavioural relapse prevention
programme. At the time of writing all is going well.

Aetiology of excess alcohol consumption

Many people drink excessively for years without becoming dependent
on alcohol. Most reduce their consumption as they grow older. Young
men who drink excessively while single, for example, may moderate
their consumption as they marry, have children and so on. Any explanation of alcohol-related problems needs therefore to explain factors that
contribute to the early stages of alcohol use as well as why some people
continue to use and then abuse alcohol. The biopsychosocial model
appears to be the most appropriate model, as it may explain why some
people are more prone to alcohol dependency than others, as well as the
social and psychological factors that may independently and together
lead to this state.

Genetic factors

There is some evidence of a genetic predisposition to alcohol problems. Prescott and Kendler (1999), for example, reported concordance for 'high lifetime alcohol consumption' of 47 per cent in MZ and 32 per cent in DZ twins. Adoption studies have also shown the adopted children of parents with alcohol problems to have higher rates of alcohol problems than those of parents without this history (e.g. Cadoret et al. 1995).

This evidence does not necessarily point to a gene for alcoholism: alcohol problems may be secondary to other genetically mediated traits including poor impulse control or emotional problems. However, there is also indirect evidence implicating a specific gene or genes related to alcohol dependence. Schuckit et al. (1996) found that individuals from families in which there were high levels of problem drinking had a lower physiological response to alcohol than matched controls. This may lead to heavy, and then problem, drinking. Similarly, men with family histories of problem drinking typically experience a greater reduction in anxiety after drinking alcohol than the norm (Finn et al. 1992). Again, this is thought to reinforce drinking. One potential genetic process is through the dopamine D2 receptor gene. A variant of the D2 dopamine receptor DRD2, D2A1, has been found to be more prevalent in individuals with a dependence on alcohol (Lawford et al. 1997). This may confer a general risk for dependence, as it has been also found in people with an addiction to gambling and opiates (see below).

Biological factors

The biological factors associated with alcohol dependence are generally thought to be a consequence of long-term alcohol use. Alcohol enhances the action of GABA within the hypothalamus and sympathetic nervous system (see Chapter 3), helping calm mood and behaviour. Over time, this results in a reduction in the natural production of GABA, leading to a dependency on alcohol to maintain desired emotional states. Abstinence results in sub-optimal levels of GABA, increases in anxiety and agitation, and the onset of physical withdrawal symptoms. These are relieved by continued drinking or, in time, the body's resumption of normal levels of GABA.

Consumption of alcohol also triggers a cascade of chemical events resulting in the release of dopamine within the reward or 'pleasure centre' of the brain: a complex of structures that includes the basal ganglia, thalamus, frontal cortex, amygdala and hypothalamus. The ability of more everyday events to activate this system is reduced in people who chronically stimulate it through alcohol consumption, again leading to continued dependence on alcohol to maintain a desired mood state.

Socio-cultural factors

Alcohol is a socially sanctioned drug, and consumption is markedly influenced by social and environmental factors. Beginning to drink alcohol is seen as one of the transitions from childhood to adulthood, although this may happen relatively early in life: about one-third of British 13–14-year-olds report having been drunk on more than one occasion (Sutherland and Wilner 1998). The early consumption of alcohol by young people is associated with positive attitudes to alcohol use, some of which are linked to family and peer attitudes and behaviours, and may result from the positive images of consumption seen on television, films, and so on (see Bennett and Murphy 1997). Social factors influence consumption once initiated. Round buying, for example, may increase consumption among young social drinkers, for whom alcohol is frequently linked to social and group activities. Life transitions, both good and bad, may also influence consumption: developing relationships and families, or getting and maintaining a job, may inhibit consumption. Adverse life-events may increase consumption, particularly among people who use alcohol as a means of coping with stress (Perreira and Sloan 2001).

The prevalence of alcohol problems varies markedly across differing social and cultural groups. Men are more likely to drink heavily than women. Blue-collar workers are more likely than white-collar workers to report problem drinking, as are workers with access to alcohol as part of their job. Binge drinking is most frequent among the young, male, lower-income and lower-educated groups (e.g. Hemmingsson et al. 1997).

Psychological factors

Behavioural explanations of alcohol consumption consider it to be the consequence of both operant and classical conditioning. Consumption is rewarded by both the pleasure associated with drinking, which may be physiological or social, or relief from stress. Once an individual has developed a dependence on alcohol, a further motivator to drink is the avoidance of withdrawal symptoms. Classical conditioning may occur as drinking becomes associated with particular cues or events, subsequent exposure to which may trigger episodes of drinking (e.g. Wilson 1988).

Beliefs about alcohol, known as *addictive beliefs* (Beck et al. 1993), are important determinants of consumption at all stages in a drinking career. At the beginning of a history of alcohol use, positive beliefs such as 'It will be fun to get drunk' predominate. As the individual begins to rely on alcohol to counteract feelings of distress, relief-oriented thoughts ('I need a drink to get through the day') may predominate. Addictive beliefs are frequently accompanied by a wider set of negative core beliefs, including a negative view of oneself, one's circumstances and environment, which may contribute to depression or anxiety. Both addictive and negative beliefs may be triggered by external cues, including walking past a bar, or internal ones, such as adverse mood states.

Interventions in excess alcohol consumption

Prevention: the socio-cultural approach

Approaches to preventing excess alcohol consumption have generally assumed that controls over drinking that affect the whole population will also impact on heavy or problem drinkers. As a result, preventive approaches have typically focused on all drinkers rather than just those who drink to excess (see also Chapter 4). These have generally attempted to change the context or rules surrounding consumption. Many have met with success. Drink-drive laws and related advertising, for example, have markedly decreased the number of alcohol-related accidents and appear to have made drink-driving much less acceptable than was previously the case (see Wagenaar et al. 1995). An apparent contrast to attempts to control drinking can be found in laws that liberated the consumption of alcohol by extending the drinking hours. These, however, do not seem to have resulted in increased consumption, and may have even decreased binge drinking, because the pressure to drink rapidly before closing time was lessened (Bruce 1980).

Alcoholism versus problem drinking

A sharp divide can be found between the beliefs that different practitioners hold about the nature and treatment of alcohol-associated problems, and the terminology they use. Some consider what they term 'alcoholism' to be a biological disease. Interventions based on this approach usually involve medical treatments or programmes of complete abstinence, such as that followed by Alcoholics Anonymous (AA). Others consider what they term 'problem drinking' to be the result of psychological and social factors, and argue that most people can learn to drink alcohol in moderation and appropriately. Interestingly, there is a substantial transatlantic split on this issue. A majority of US practitioners subscribe to the medical, abstinence model; most Europeans subscribe to the psychosocial, controlled drinking model (Peele 1992). Advocates of the latter (e.g. Heather 1995) contend that many problem drinkers can moderate their consumption while others may refuse to consider abstinence. Attempts at abstinence by these people may result in more problems, not fewer. Trials that have offered dependent drinkers a choice between controlled drinking or abstinence (e.g. Booth et al.

1992) have resulted in similar gains in both conditions. The best treatment goal may therefore be the choice of the client, not the therapist.

Withdrawal

The initial treatment of people with alcohol problems may involve a period of withdrawal. This may take three to four days, and is usually aided by the use of sedatives such as valium which moderate the severity of any withdrawal symptoms. Once they have withdrawn from alcohol, many people will receive one or more of the interventions described below.

Drug therapy

Antidipstrotrophics deter consumption by causing the drinker to feel ill if they consume alcohol while taking them. The most commonly used drug of this type is Disulfram (Antabuse). It prevents alcohol being broken down further than its intermediate metabolite acetaldehyde. This accumulates in the body and causes a number of symptoms, including flushing, headache, pounding in the head or chest, nausea and occasional vomiting, about 15–20 minutes after consumption of alcohol. Patients may be given a test reaction to alcohol to alert them to the consequences of consumption. The benefits of Disulfram depend on its regular consumption. Where this is enforced, it appears an effective barrier to consumption. It is less effective when taken voluntarily (Hughes and Cook 1997). Its use clearly follows a biological, abstinence model. However, some studies have evaluated the effectiveness of similar drugs in programmes that accept that participants may choose to drink on occasion. In these, it may be used as an occasional control to consumption, particularly when users feel they are losing control over their drinking (Sinclair 2001).

The 12-step approach

The 12-step approach is the treatment programme of AA. It is based on a belief that alcoholism is a physical, psychological and spiritual illness that cannot be cured, but can be controlled by total abstinence from alcohol. The organization provides a strong social support network that encourages emotional expression and the admission of failure. Attenders at group meetings are encouraged to accept that they are powerless to control their drinking, to cease their struggle and to allow a 'higher power' to take control (Gorski 1989).

The millions of attenders of AA meetings across the world attest to the potential benefits of this approach. More empirical data provide mixed support. In a meta-analysis of research prior to the mid-1990s, Kownacki and Shadish (1999) concluded that attendance at AA meetings resulted in minimal gains on measures of abstinence, and that some studies found it to be less effective than no treatment or alternative treatments. However, the particularly poor outcomes in their review were among people whose attendance at AA was compulsory. More positive results were reported by Timko et al. (2000), who compared outcomes on people who self-selected either into AA or a variety of formal treatment programmes including residential, psychological or psychiatric treatments. At one-year follow-up, 56 per cent of the participants in AA had a 'benign' drinking pattern in comparison to 33 per cent of those who received other formal interventions. At three-year follow-up, the figures were 64 and 43 per cent respectively. Note that while AA follows a model of abstinence, many of the people who engaged in this approach seemingly learned to drink within reasonable limits.

Cognitive behavioural approaches

A number of aversive approaches have been used in the treatment of alcohol-related problems, including presenting alcohol-related stimuli at the same time as mild electrical shocks or inducing feelings of suffocation by injection of succinylcholine. These have proven, at best, moderately effective in the short- but not long-term, and are now considered ethically questionable. More recent cognitive behavioural programmes have involved training in social skills and strategies for preventing relapse (see Longabough and Morgenstern 2000). Social skills training involves teaching interpersonal and assertive skills to help participants cope more effectively with stressful situations, refuse drinks and so on. In relapse prevention programmes, high-risk situations are identified, and the individual develops and rehearses specific strategies to help them cope with them should they arise. These may include specific strategies to challenge addictive beliefs and to cope with cravings to drink.

Relapse is frequently associated with marital problems and prevented by strong marital cohesion. For this reason, some programmes involve the problem drinker's partner where this is possible. O'Farrell and Fals-Stewart (2000), for example, described an intervention intended to increase the communication and problem-solving skills of couples rather than just the individual. Both the problem drinker and their partner learned strategies to reduce consumption, including the partner changing behaviours that may trigger alcohol use, finding new ways to discuss drinking and situations involved with it, and new responses to their partner's drinking. A further strand of therapy focused on the type and quality of communication between the partners. In their review of the effectiveness of this approach, O'Farrell and Fals-Stewart (2000) concluded that it was consistently more effective than individual therapy on measures of alcohol consumption, abstinence, alcohol-related problems and the quality of marital relationships.

Brief therapies

Some problem drinkers may be helped by relatively brief interventions. Chick (1991), for example, considered that hospital patients may be particularly motivated to improve their general health, and screened medical patients for high levels of alcohol consumption. Those who reported alcohol-related problems were randomly allocated into either a single counselling session with a booklet detailing how to reduce consumption or no treatment. One year later, consumption was lower among those in the intervention group than those who received no intervention. A similar opportunistic intervention was reported by Monti et al. (1999), who evaluated the effect of an intervention designed to enhance motivation to reduce consumption among adolescents treated in a casualty department following an alcohol-related incident. Those who received the intervention had a significantly lower incidence of drinking and driving, traffic violations, alcohol-related injuries and alcohol-related problems over the following year than those who received no intervention.

The intervention used by Monti et al. (1999) is known as motivational interviewing (Miller and Rollnick 2002). Its primary goal is to encourage individuals to explore both their positive and negative beliefs about a particular behaviour or behavioural change. This process is intended to trigger a state of cognitive dissonance in which the individual actively considers two sets of opposing beliefs and attitudes towards a particular issue (in this case, the 'good' and 'not so good' things about drinking). According to cognitive dissonance theory, this is an aversive state and motivates cognitive work to reduce the discomfort. It may result in a rejection of the newly considered arguments, or the adoption of new beliefs or behaviours – in this case, a reduction in alcohol consumption.

This approach, either as a one-off interview or as part of an extended intervention, has proven effective in reducing consumption in problem drinkers. Sellman et al. (2001), for example, compared the effects of motivational therapy, non-directive reflective listening, and a no-treatment control among problem drinkers. The goal of therapy was controlled drinking, and the key outcome was the frequency of binge drinking. In the six months following the interventions, 43 per cent of people who received the motivational intervention had engaged in binge drinking, in comparison to over 63 per cent of those in the other conditions.

Project MATCH

Despite the differences in philosophy and strategies of the treatment approaches, their effectiveness appears to be very similar. The largest ever alcohol-treatment trial, involving over 1500 participants (Project MATCH Research Group 1998), found few differences in the effectiveness of a number of interventions, including motivational, cognitive behavioural and 12-step approaches. By one-year follow-up, 35 per cent of all participants reported complete abstinence over the previous year; a further 25 per cent reported having not having drunk heavily on more than two consecutive days in this time, a measure considered to reflect some degree of control over their alcohol consumption. At one-year and three-year follow-ups, there were, again, no differences between the three intervention groups. However, those who came from a social milieu where they mixed with many drinkers did best if they received the 12-step intervention. Why the therapies seem equally effective is not clear. However, they may work by influencing similar mechanisms. The 12-step intervention, for example, may change addictive beliefs and increase drink refusal skills as a result of group work and discussion within AA meetings: skills that are taught more directly in cognitive behavioural interventions.

Heroin use

Opiates are a group of drugs derived from the opium poppy. The key derivatives, in order of strength and addictiveness, are opium, morphine and heroin. The most widely used form of the drug is heroin. Initially widely used as a sedative, the non-medical use of all opiates is now illegal across the world. Taking heroin results in profound feelings of warmth, relaxation and euphoria. Worries, fears and concerns are forgotten, and self-confidence increases. These effects last for between 4 and 6 hours, before the individual 'comes down' from the drug. Once dependent on the drug, withdrawal usually begins about 8 hours after an injection, and results in muscle pain, sweats, sneezes and uncontrollable yawning. Within 36 hours, the symptoms become increasingly severe, and include uncontrollable muscle twitching, cramps, chills, sweats, and a rise in heart rate. The person is unable to sleep, vomits and has diarrhoea. These symptoms typically last for about 72 hours, and then gradually reduce over a period of between 5 and 10 days.

In the 1960s to the early 1990s, heroin was taken predominantly through intravenous injection. Now it is more frequently smoked, a practice known as 'chasing the dragon'. In Dublin, for example, Smyth et al. (2000) reported a 330 per cent increase in the number of new attenders of drug clinics between 1991 and 1996. Over this time, the age of initiating heroin use fell, and users were more likely to smoke than inject it. Chasers were more likely to be employed, younger, use fewer other drugs, and to be more educated and have a shorter history of use than people who injected. Most heroin users, however, do use other drugs. Beswick et al. (2001) reported that 60 per cent of their sample of attenders at a London clinic also used crack cocaine, 58 per cent used alcohol, 11 per cent diazepam, 9 per cent methadone and 8 per cent used cocaine powder at the same time as taking heroin.

Aetiology of heroin use

Genetic factors

Although environmental factors predominate in the development of drug addiction, there is evidence of a genetic vulnerability to drug abuse involving two pathways (Cadoret et al. 1995). The first involves a direct pathway of drug dependency. Cadoret and colleagues found that the adopted children of parents who evidenced alcohol abuse or dependency were three times more likely to develop drug dependency than those from non-alcohol dependent parents, suggesting the potential of a gene for an 'addictive personality' rather than one for opiate addiction in particular. The second, indirect route identified by Cadoret involved genetic linkages of antisocial behaviour (see Chapter 11) that led to aggression, conduct disorder, antisocial personality and eventually drug or alcohol abuse. As with addiction to alcohol, the D2 dopamine gene may be involved in determining risk for opiate dependence.

Biological factors

Just as with alcohol, the action of opiates results from their impact on dopamine systems within the 'pleasure centre' (see p. 360). A second mechanism through which they influence mood and well-being is through their chemical similarity to chemicals known as endorphins and enkephalins. These moderate pain and produce feelings of well-being, contributing, for example, to the 'runner's high' that can accompany intense prolonged physical exercise. Opiates bind to the same receptor sites as endorphins and enkaphalins, resulting in a state of well-being, as well as having a sedating effect. Both chemicals are found throughout the brain, although there are high concentrations in the midbrain, hypothalamus and thalamus, as well as the spinal cord.

Socio-cultural factors

Only about 20 per cent of those who initiate drug use do so with the primary goal of pleasure seeking (Nutt and Law 2000). Other reasons include self-medication, social pressure and the search for 'meaning' or mystical experiences. Evidence of the use of heroin as a means of self-medication or as a means of reducing stress can be found in studies that show higher rates of heroin use in populations who live in stressful environments. Perhaps the most dramatic evidence of this is the estimated 40 per cent of American soldiers who used heroin during the Vietnam War, and the approximately 1 per cent who continued to use it when back in the USA (Grinspoon and Bakalar 1986). Further support for this hypothesis can be found in the high use of heroin and other drugs among people with conditions as varied as post-traumatic stress, eating disorders and schizophrenia (Najavitis et al. 1998).

A second route to the use of heroin is as a progression from the use of other drugs, as users seek a greater 'high' or different experience to those already achieved. Use can escalate to abuse, and then to dependence, involving increased tolerance of the drug, compulsive drug taking and withdrawal symptoms if the drug is not taken regularly. Sharing needles is relatively common and may contain a social or ritual element. For many addicts, maintaining a drug habit can be expensive, and potentially beyond their financial resources, particularly where they find it difficult or choose not to hold down a job. As a result, use is often maintained by stealing: more than 95 per cent of American opiate-dependent individuals reported committing crimes to maintain their drug use (NIH Consensus Development Panel on Effective Treatment of Opiate Addiction 1998). Many users cannot maintain jobs, as much of their day is spent seeking and then taking drugs. The 'addiction career' often involves cycles of cessation and relapse, often over many years. Between one-quarter and one-third of users will die of a drug-related cause, generally an overdose. An example of this history is afforded by Dai, a 29-year-old brought up in an economically marginalized council estate in south Wales. Here is the story of his drug taking, its associated problems, and how it was at least partly maintained by the social world which he inhabited:

> Started smoking ciggies when I was 9 . . . bunk off school – hang around with me mates – some of the older kids – just hang around all day – no worries – just wander the streets all day. Soon got into sniffing glue – did it for about a year, year and a half. Didn't start as a regular thing – every now and then – but did it most days after a while. Used to be one of us would have a bag and some glue. Gave us a buzz. Yeah!

> Move on to dope at about 12. Did it with my mates. Spend a day in someone's house shitless on dope. F . . . cking good! Still smoke. Mellows me out. But then went on to speed. Took it about when I was 12 and something. Only took it at weekends, washed down with lager. Billy whiz . . . keeps you going, going, going. Good for dancing . . . After a while, taking the stuff everyday – starts getting expensive, so start lifting things, nicking, TWOCing [Taking without consent: stealing cars]. Problems with the police – in front of the bench a few times. Got a fine, so have to nick again!

> Parents found out once got to police. Went ballistic when they found out. First time they knew I was taking drugs. Beaten shitless by my father. Grounded – not that that did much good. Old man's a hypocrite anyway – drinks loads, but dead against drugs.

Anyway, tried loads of other shit after that – LSD, tabs [benzodiazepines], Temazies, E's, uppers, downers. Sixteen. Stoned out of my mind on dope, one of my mates asked if I wanted some smack. So I said, 'Yeah!' Anything for a buzz. He injected me. That did it. What a rush! I felt I was superman! I could do anything. That was it. Hooked. Stopped taking speed – smack was it.

Left school at 16. Parents knew I taking smack. Took me to loads of docs, but didn't do anything. So, they washed their hands of me – didn't want to know – chucked me out. Crashed on my mates' floors for a while. Got a council house pretty quickly. Got chucked out pretty quickly too – didn't pay the rent! Not good at paying rent!

Smack had me hooked. The more I used, the more money I needed. So, I got into breaking and entering – always getting caught. Fines, probation, then time in prison. But that didn't stop me taking the stuff. You can get anything you want inside if you know the right people. Went to prison for the first time just before my 18th birthday – four months for burglary.

Cut a long story short – been in and out of prison for the last 12 years. Had girlfriends. Lived with one woman for about three years. Got a daughter with her – see her sometimes, but not a lot. They don't come and see me when I'm inside . . .

Smack has a hold on me and I can't let go. My mates all take the stuff. I don't know anyone that doesn't use. So, I've nothing else. Did give up once. Went on a programme in prison. Came out clean – stayed clean for about three months. They put me up in a hostel when I came out – so I could stay away from my mates . . . Stop using in the 'real world' . . . But then I had to leave as they didn't have money to keep me there. So, I went back to my old haunts. Soon back to jacking up . . .

Don't enjoy the dope now. I'm pissed with the routine – take drugs, steal, go to prison, take drugs . . . Don't get the buzz from using. I've got to take it so it doesn't do my head in. I'm trying to get out of it – stop using. I'm on methadone [see p. 370], so I can stop taking the stuff. But they don't give enough . . . still get withdrawals – heart pounding, sweats, cramps. So I'm still using – but less than I was – was using about three bags a day, now it's a bag, bag and a half. I'll try to get more methadone – try to keep off the smack altogether, but they don't like to give you too much.

Psychological factors

The psychological factors associated with opiate use are similar to those involved in alcohol use (discussed earlier in the chapter). That is, the pleasure of taking the drug establishes an operant conditioning process in which the individual is rewarded for taking the drug by the pleasant effects and reductions in tension associated with its use, and then the avoidance of withdrawal symptoms. Classical conditioning triggers cravings for heroin when a user encounters conditions similar to its previous use. These conditioned responses may be both powerful and sustained over time. Meyer (1995), for example, reported that the sight of a needle may decrease the severity of withdrawal symptoms while coming off heroin. Conversely, cues conditioned to withdrawal may trigger its symptoms, even years after heroin use has been stopped. Cognitive factors are also involved in expectancies of both pleasure and ultimately, fear of withdrawal.

Solomon's (1980) *opponent-process theory* suggested that the neurological mechanisms that result in pleasurable emotions have a rebound effect in which a drug-induced 'high' is inevitably followed by some negative after-effects (the opponent element), in which the individual feels worse than usual. As a result they become increasingly motivated to avoid these negative consequences, and less so by the initial pleasure associated with the drug. There is certainly evidence that many drug users do become increasing anxious and depressed over time (Roggla and Uhl 1995), although specific evidence of the neural mechanisms suggested by Solomon (1980) has not been systematically examined.

Treatment of heroin use

Harm minimization approaches: the socio-cultural approach

Harm minimization strategies do not attempt to 'treat' addiction. Instead, they reduce the harm associated with the continued use of drugs either by substituting the use of heroin with a safer oral medication, known as methadone, or reducing risk of infection by ensuring those who continue to inject do so using clean needles.

Methadone maintenance
Methadone is an opiate agonist. Methadone replacement programmes provide opiate users with an orally taken drug that does not give them the high associated with opiate use, but does prevent withdrawal symptoms when opiates are not taken. Its use is intended to prevent the risks of needle sharing and overdose, and to prevent withdrawal when individuals initially seek help: a time that may be particularly

chaotic in their lives. Methadone can be prescribed for periods of a year or more, during which time the recipient is expected to 'stabilize' their life and prepare for subsequent withdrawal from it. Users typically have to report to a drug centre on a daily basis, where they are given sufficient methadone to get them through to the next day, to try to maintain contact with support services and to stop them selling it on the black market.

This approach appears to be moderately successful. In the largest study of its use, the Drug Abuse Treatment Outcome Study (Hubbard et al. 1997) followed nearly 3000 people receiving outpatient methadone treatment. In the year following its prescription, the percentage of people to use heroin weekly or daily fell from 90 to 30 per cent. Only 17 per cent of those who remained in the programme for a year were still using heroin at follow-up. Reasons given for continued use of heroin included being maintained on too low a dose of methadone, the desire for the 'high' achieved with opiates, the strength of self-identity as an 'addict', and living with a partner or continued social relationships with people who took intravenous drugs (Avants et al. 1999).

Needle-exchange schemes

Needle-exchange schemes exchange old for new needles and prevent the need for sharing, reducing risk of cross-infection of various blood-borne viruses including HIV and hepatitis. Some right-wing and church groups in the USA have condemned this approach, claiming that it maintains, or even encourages, the use of drugs. As a result, needle-exchange schemes are legal in some US states and illegal in others. A report by the North American Syringe Exchange Network (in Yoast et al. 2001), for example, found that of a sample of 100 US programmes, 52 were legal, 16 were illegal but 'tolerated', while 32 were 'underground'. Longitudinal studies suggest that where syringes cannot legally be obtained elsewhere, needle-exchange programmes are effective in reducing use of shared needles (Gibson et al. 2001). Most studies have also found lower rates of HIV infection among intravenous drug users who use needle-exchange schemes than those who do not. The failure to find consistent gains in levels of HIV should, perhaps, be expected, as most people continue to share needles at a reduced rate and may still engage in other risky behaviours, such as unprotected sex.

One final and perhaps important study published since Gibson and colleagues' review (Taylor et al. 2001) reported the prevalence of shared needle use between 1990 and 1999 in Scotland. These data showed a reduction in the use of shared needles between 1990 and 1992 following the introduction of needle-exchange schemes, but then a gradual increase in sharing whether from a partner or 'casual acquaintance' in the following years despite their continued provision. These data mirror some of the changes in risk behaviours in other populations at risk for HIV, where initial changes towards safer behaviours have dwindled and more risky behaviours have returned over time. The reasons for this are unclear, but may relate to the relatively low profile given to HIV/AIDS awareness in the UK and increasing beliefs that AIDS can be 'cured'.

Withdrawal

Most of the interventions described below follow a period of withdrawal. This often involves levels of methadone being gradually reduced over a period of weeks, to minimize withdrawal symptoms. A shorter-term withdrawal involves rapid detoxification, with withdrawal symptoms controlled by other opiate agonists such as clonidine. This reduces, but does not totally prevent, many of the symptoms of withdrawal. These strategies can be used in both inpatient and outpatient settings, and can achieve total withdrawal within three days.

Drug therapy

One longer-term use of drug therapy involves the use of drugs that negate the effects of heroin. Naltrexone is an opiate antagonist that binds with opioid receptors in the brain and blocks the effect of opiate drugs. It is taken on a regular basis and prevents the 'high' associated with opiates if taken. As few as 3 per cent of people offered this form of intervention chose to take it up, and many fail to take the drug regularly. This may be the consequence of an inability to withdraw from opiates, fear of a new drug and residual dependence, or a lack of genuine motivation to remain drug free (Tucker and Ritter 2000). Among highly motivated individuals who actually use naltrexone, outcomes are relatively good. It results in lower cravings for opiates, longer periods of abstinence, and greater improvements in psychosocial functioning than placebo. Despite these successes, many people will restart or continue using opiates following treatment. Abstinence rates as high as 64 per cent have been found in well-supported and 'high coping' individuals at 18-month follow-up, although rates between 31 and 53 per cent are more typical (Tucker and Ritter 2000).

Psychological approaches

Operant programmes

Many people who take methadone also continue to use opiates (see the case of Dai, pp. 368–9). In an attempt to minimize this, Gruber et al. (2000) investigated whether providing extrinsic rewards to people attending methadone clinics could increase attendance and drug abstinence. Their incentives to attend counselling sessions included bus tokens and vouchers to be spent on activities or items agreed by their counsellor. As incentives for abstinence, participants received free weekend recreational activities, lunches, a modest financial sum per week in vouchers and rent payment. This approach was compared with a standard treatment approach in which clients were encouraged to attend routine methadone clinics but were not rewarded for doing so. One month after entry, 61 per cent of participants in this condition, compared to 17 per cent of those in the standard treatment, were enrolled in treatment; 50 per cent of participants compared to 21 per cent of controls had achieved 30 days of abstinence from heroin.

Cognitive behaviour therapy

Despite their effectiveness in the treatment of alcohol problems, there are relatively few studies of the effectiveness of cognitive behavioural programmes in injecting drug users. One of the few such interventions (Woody et al. 1983), examined whether the addition of either supportive psychodynamic counselling or cognitive behaviour therapy enhanced the effectiveness of methadone maintenance and standard drug counselling. Psychodynamic counselling involved supportive techniques to foster a safe therapeutic environment in which the individual explored their relationship patterns and 'worked through' relationship themes. Special attention was given to themes that involved drug dependence, the role of drugs in relation to problem feelings and behaviours, and how these could be resolved without the use of drugs. Cognitive behavioural therapy followed the relapse prevention model described above in relation to alcohol. Standard drug counselling involved support, monitoring of drug usage and exploration of current problems. Both additional treatments added to the effect of counselling up to one-year follow-up on measures as diverse as employment status, legal problems, psychiatric symptoms and opiate-negative urine specimens. Neither was more effective than the other.

Couples therapy

Just as for alcohol problems, couples therapy may be more effective in the treatment of drug dependence than individual therapy. In their review of interventions with over 1500 drug users, Stanton and Shadish (1997) reported that those people who received couples therapy had improved relationships and used fewer drugs, both in the short- and long-term, than comparative groups in either no treatment or individual therapy conditions. In addition, dropout rates were significantly lower than for any other treatment approaches. This has important implications, as it means that more people received a beneficial 'level' of intervention, some of whom may have been 'less motivated' individuals who would have dropped out of other forms of intervention. That couples therapy still appears more effective than the other treatment approaches, while including a 'harder to treat' group of clients, reinforces its high success levels.

Pathological gambling

Most of us gamble at some time. However, for some, gambling becomes addictive and is as difficult to stop as the use of drugs. Although it is identified as an impulse disorder in DSM-IV-TR (APA 2000), pathological gambling is considered in the same behavioural terms as an addiction. Its diagnosis requires five or more of the following:

- a preoccupation with gambling
- a need to gamble with increasing amounts of money in order to achieve the desired excitement
- repeated, unsuccessful efforts to control, cut back or stop gambling
- its use as a way of escaping from problems or relieving **dysphoric** mood states
- a return to gambling following losses in the hope of 'getting even' ('chasing')
- lying to family members or others to conceal the extent of gambling
- committing illegal acts such as forgery or fraud to continue gambling
- jeopardizing or losing significant relationships as a result of gambling.

Pathological gambling is usually the end-point of a gradual shift through social, frequent, problem and finally pathological gambling. Each 'stage' involves a greater psychological and financial commitment to gambling, and an increase in associated problems. A survey commissioned by the British gambling charity GamCare reported that 0.8 per cent of British gamblers could be classified as 'problem gamblers': lower than the USA (1.1 per cent), Australia (2.3 per cent) and Spain (1.4 per cent).

Pathological gambling can result in the individual jeopardizing or losing a significant relationship or job. When they can no longer raise the money needed, they may turn to criminal activity to obtain money: an estimated 60 per cent of pathological gamblers have committed criminal offences in order to continue gambling (Blaszczynski 1995). It has been linked to antisocial, narcissistic and borderline personality disorders. In addition, up to 30 per cent of pathological gamblers may have alcohol-related problems. The relationship with alcohol is important, as some have taken it to suggest that both alcohol and gambling problems are indicative of a more general 'addictive' personality. About 20 per cent of individuals in treatment for pathological gambling are reported to have attempted suicide (APA 1994).

Aetiology of pathological gambling

Genetic factors

Some studies (e.g. Eisen et al. 1998–99) involving large numbers of twin pairs have found shared environmental and genetic factors to account for between 35 and 54 per cent of the vulnerability to pathological gambling, with much of the vulnerability thought to be accounted for by genetic factors. One potential genetic process is through the dopamine D2 receptor gene (Comings et al. 1996). A variant of the D2 dopamine receptor, D2A1, has been found to be more prevalent in individuals with pathological gambling than in normal populations (Potenza 2001: see also its relationship with alcohol and opiate dependence).

Biological factors

One of the factors thought to be associated with gambling is the 'buzz' of winning or coming close to winning, which has been equated with the 'high' achieved through taking drugs. A number of neurotransmitters seem to mediate this response. Dopamine levels have been found to rise after a winning streak (Shinohara et al. 1999), with activation of the reward system common to other addictions. Raised levels of norepinephrine have also been found following episodes of gambling. These may impact on activity both within the brain and the sympathetic nervous system (see Chapter 3). In social gamblers, these neurochemical processes typically occur while gambling. Among pathological gamblers, they occur while anticipating gambling or as a classically conditioned response to gambling-related stimuli (Sharpe et al. 1995). There is some evidence that endorphin levels may rise during gambling, although more evidence is required to substantiate this finding (Shinohara et al. 1999).

Socio-cultural factors

In general, greater access to gambling opportunities seems to increase both social or problem gambling. Ladouceur et al. (1999), for example, found that as availability of gambling increased over time in a number of countries, so too did rates of pathological gambling. In Australia, the Productivity Commission (1999), however, found little difference in levels of gambling-related expenditure and problem gambling as a consequence of significant differences in access to gambling across various Australian states. The one exception to this was access to gaming machines. In this case, greater availability was associated with higher rates of problem gambling. These data led the Commission to suggest that if gaming machine availability were to increase in the states where access was restricted to the same level as the more liberal ones, there would be a 110 per cent increase in problem gamblers in these states. In the UK, despite some concerns, the introduction of a national lottery in 1994 did not result in widespread gambling problems. A 1998 survey by GamCare, for example, found that 65 per cent of the UK population had played the national lottery in the previous year, a figure below the 90 per cent of adults in Sweden and New Zealand who played their national equivalent over the same period.

Once in a gambling context, a number of factors may influence the extent of gambling. Alcohol consumption, in particular, seems to increase gambling. Pols and Hawks (1991), for example, found that young game machine players persisted for twice as long when losing after drinking moderate amounts of alcohol than they did when sober. The increasing location of gaming machines in drinking areas suggests that some of those who drink regularly may also come to gamble regularly (Sharpe 2002). It is perhaps noteworthy, that many regular casino gamblers drink less while gambling than they usually do: a finding that led Dickerson and Baron (2000) to challenge the notion that gambling and alcohol consumption share a common genetic risk.

Psychological factors

Impulsivity

High levels of impulsivity in childhood, at its most extreme evident as childhood attention deficit/hyperactivity disorder (ADHD: see Chapter 13), may be a risk factor for pathological gambling. Carlton and Manowicz (1994), for example, found that adult pathological gamblers reported a higher rate of ADHD as children than is found within the general population. Prospective longitudinal studies have supported this retrospective evidence. Vitaro et al. (1999), for example, investigated the predictive strength of four measures of impulsivity in 13–14-year-olds: teacher ratings, self-report and performance on a card-playing task and a 'delay in gratification task'. Gambling was subsequently measured at the age of 17 years. Among the factors that predicted gambling at this time were perseveration on the card-playing task and an inability to delay gratification. These findings were considered indicative of a tendency to respond excessively to positive outcomes, to require immediate reinforcement and insensitivity to negative consequences: characteristics of the pathological gambler. Sharpe (2002) noted that whether these are biologically driven or a consequence of environmental factors is not clear.

Learning history

As with other addictions, operant and classical conditioning serve to maintain gambling behaviour. Early models of gambling assumed that gambling was essentially maintained by the intermittent reinforcement

– both biological and economic – inherent in gambling. Losses would be sustained in the hope of later gains. Variable and intermittent reinforcement schedules lead to the rapid acquisition of behaviour and render it resistant to extinction. Sharpe (2002) suggested that while these undoubtedly contribute to high levels of social gambling, they do not fully explain pathological gambling, where consistent and significant losses do not result in a cessation of gambling. Sharpe (2002) suggested that large pay-outs, and in particular a 'big win' early in a gambling career, establish and sustain pathological gambling. These presumably distort expectations of the outcomes of gambling, and support losses in the expectation of future 'big wins'.

Cognitive processes

Differing cognitive processes instigate and maintain gambling. Pro-gambling attitudes appear to lead to participation in gambling activities, but do not sustain gambling once initiated (Sharpe 2002). Other forms of cognitive self-talk may be important at this time. Delffabbro and Winefield (1999), for example, found that 75 per cent of all game-related cognitions during gambling were irrational in nature and supportive of continued gambling. Such thoughts may stimulate impulsivity, discount losses, and even lead the individual to feel that they have some degree over their fate. This type of self-talk may also sustain arousal while gambling: a number of studies (e.g. Sharpe et al. 1995) have found a relationship between the frequency of irrational verbalizations and arousal levels.

Negative emotions

Low mood or anxiety also appear to be triggers to gambling among some pathological gamblers. Dickerson et al. (1996), for example, reported that 9 per cent of a sample of regular gamblers did so as an escape from feeling depressed; 30 per cent were more likely to gamble following a 'frustrating day'. Dysphoric mood before gambling may also result in more persistent gambling following losses. As a partial explanation for this phenomenon, Dickerson and Baron (2000) suggested that low mood may reduce perceptions of control over gambling, and hence reduced attempts to curtail the activity even when losing.

A biopsychosocial model of gambling

These various findings each contributed to Sharpe's (2002) biopsychosocial model of gambling. She suggested that this may involve three early risk factors:

* a biological vulnerability involving the dopaminergic and serotinergic systems

- family attitudes that support gambling
- high levels of impulsivity.

These factors may lead to a number of gambling experiences as a relatively young individual. In these, the individual becomes socialized into a gambling culture. A pattern of early wins may also reinforce gambling and distort beliefs about, and attitudes towards, it. More attention may be paid, for example, to success than failures. At the same time, the individual may become pleasantly physiologically aroused while gambling. All of these factors serve to maintain an interest. As a gambling career progresses, episodes may be triggered by hopes of avoiding stress, boredom or improving mood. Gambling is used to increase arousal and as a means of escape from reality. Once in the gambling situation, cognitive biases and the arousal experienced serve to maintain the behaviour, whether winning or losing.

Treatment of pathological gambling

Empirical evaluations of treatments for pathological gambling are still relatively rare, although what evidence there is, is encouraging. Self-help programmes such as the Gamblers Anonymous 12-step programme have achieved abstinence rates of about 8 per cent over a one-year period and 7 per cent over two years (Stewart and Brown 1988). More formal interventions have succeeded in achieving one-year abstinence rates as high as 55 per cent.

Behavioural approaches

One of the earliest treatment studies, reported by McConaghy et al. (1983), compared the effectiveness of aversion therapy and imaginal desensitization. Aversion therapy involved participants reading aloud words on a series of cards, some of which were related to gambling activities and some of which described alternative actions such as 'went straight home'. Each time they read out a gambling-related phrase they received a mild electric shock described as 'unpleasant but not emotionally upsetting' (McConaghy et al. 1983: 367) for two seconds. Imaginal desensitization involved participants imagining a variety of gambling-related scenarios at the same time as using relaxation procedures to reduce arousal. The latter approach proved the most effective on measures of gambling urge and behaviour over the year following treatment. Long-term follow-up, conducted between two and nine years after the end of therapy, found that 79 per cent of those who took part in the desensitization programme reported control over or having stopped gambling. Just over 50 per cent of the aversion therapy group reported the same outcomes (McConaghy et al. 1991).

Cognitive behavioural approaches

A small number of studies have reported positive results following cognitive behavioural procedures. Ladouceur et al. (2001), for example, randomly allocated pathological gamblers into either cognitive therapy or waiting list control group. The cognitive intervention had two elements. The first involved cognitive correction, in which participants' misconceptions on randomness were challenged. This involved both an educational component on the nature of randomness and the identification and challenge of erroneous cognitions made while gambling. This was achieved by tape-recording verbalizations ('. . . if I lose four times in a row, I will definitely win the next time . . .') made during a session of imaginal gambling followed by the therapist 'correcting' them within the therapy session. The second element involved training in relapse prevention. In this, participants identified high-risk situations and planned how to cope with them should they arise. The intervention was successful: 54 per cent of participants in the cognitive intervention improved by at least 50 per cent on a composite measure of recovery which included frequency of gambling and perceived control over gambling behaviour, compared to only 7 per cent of those in the control group. Furthermore, 85 per cent of participants in the treatment programme compared to only 14 per cent of those in the control group achieved 50 per cent improvements on at least three of the four measures. These gains were generally maintained at six-month and twelve-month follow-up.

Pharmacological therapies

In one of the few evaluations of drug therapies in the treatment of pathological gambling, Hollander et al. (2000) evaluated the effectiveness of fluvoxamine, an SSRI, in a small study involving 15 people. They were first treated with a placebo drug before entering an eight-week period of active treatment. Only 10 people completed the study, but the drug showed a significant benefit, with greater reductions in gambling and urges to gamble than in the placebo treatment phase. More trials are clearly needed before any strong conclusions about the effectiveness of drug therapies are required.

Chapter summary

1 Drug use is relatively common throughout most social groups, although some groups use more than others do.

2 Excess alcohol consumption results in a number of negative short-term social consequences, including risky or dangerous behaviours,

and long-term health consequences, such as cirrhosis and Korsakoff's syndrome.

3 Genetic factors may influence risk for high levels of alcohol.

4 Alcohol influences mood through its impact on levels of GABA and dopamine.

5 Social factors, including ease of access, peer influence, cost and advertising, influence levels of consumption.

6 Psychological explanations of drinking include operant and classical conditioning experiences and cognitions that support consumption.

7 Legal and social interventions impact on drinking levels throughout the population.

8 Treatment of alcohol-dependent individuals usually begins with a period of withdrawal.

9 Antidipstrotrophics can help maintain abstinence in highly motivated groups or where its use is compulsory.

10 Both the 12-step model which advocates abstinence and cognitive behavioural interventions that can support abstinence or controlled drinking appear equally effective in maintaining abstinence or appropriate drinking levels.

11 Couples therapy is particularly effective for people with drinking problems.

12 Opiates exert their action through dopamine levels, endorphins and enkephalins.

13 Harm reduction strategies including methadone maintenance and needle-exchange schemes can be successful in reducing opiate-use related harm.

14 As with alcohol, behaviour therapy and social approaches can be effective in the treatment of opiate dependence: couples therapy may be the most effective intervention where appropriate.

15 Gambling results in similar neurochemical changes to those associated with drug use.

16 The biopsychosocial model implicates biological, family, psychological and learning history factors in the aetiology of problem gambling.

17 Cognitive behavioural and antidepressants may both prove effective in reducing gambling-related problems.

For discussion

1 Why might the differing approaches to the treatment of alcohol-related problems differ little in their effectiveness?

2 Switzerland intends to legalize opiate use in 2004. What are the costs and benefits of this approach for the individual and society?

3 Many people receiving treatment for addictions continue to engage in their addiction. Is this an acceptable behaviour within therapy?

4 Should access to gaming machines be controlled?

Further reading

Heather, N. (1995) The great controlled drinking consensus: is it premature?, *Addiction*, 90: 1160–3.

Heather, N., Peters, T.J. and Stockwell, T.R. (eds) (2001) *International Handbook of Alcohol Dependence*. Chichester: Wiley.

Longabaugh, R. and Morgenstern, J. (2000) Cognitive-behavioral coping skills therapy for alcohol dependence: current status and future directions, *Alcohol Research and Health*, 23: 78–87.

Lopez-Viets, V.C. and Miller, W.R. (1997) Treatment approaches for pathological gamblers, *Clinical Psychology Review*, 17: 689–702.

NIH Consensus Development Panel on Effective Treatment of Opiate Addiction (1998) Effective medical treatment of opiate addiction, *Journal of the American Medical Association*, 280: 1936–43.

O'Farrell, T.J. and Fals-Stewart, W. (2000) Behavioral couples therapy for alcoholism and drug abuse, *Journal of Drug Abuse Treatment*, 18: 51–4.

Sharpe, L. (2002) A reformulated cognitive-behavioral model of problem gambling: a biopsychosocial perspective, *Clinical Psychology Review*, 22: 1–25.

Wilk, A.I., Jensen, N.M. and Havighurst, T.C. (1997) Meta-analysis of randomized control trials addressing brief interventions in heavy alcohol drinkers, *Journal of General Internal Medicine*, 12: 274–83.

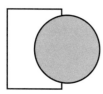

Glossary

Aetiology: explanations of the causes of disease.

Agonist: drugs that increase the action of a neurotransmitter.

Alexithymia: a paucity of emotional experience and awareness, with an associated poverty of imagination and a tendency to focus upon the tangible and mundane.

Alogia: poverty of speech; literally, 'no words'.

Alzheimer's disease: the most common cause of dementia in old age.

Antagonist: drugs that inhibit the action of a neurotransmitter.

Anterograde amnesia: lack of memory for events that occur after an event that causes amnesia.

Ataxia: an incoordination and unsteadiness due to brain's failure to regulate posture and strength and direction of limb movement.

Avolition: lack of volition, or voluntary motivation.

Behaviour therapy: form of therapy that targets behavioural change by changing the triggers or consequences of behaviour using operant or classical conditioning-based interventions.

Benzodiazepines: group of commonly used tranquillizers; includes valium and Librium. They act on the GABA system.

Catatonic behaviour: behaviour found in one form of schizophrenia; includes posturing, or 'waxy flexibility', mutism and stupor.

Catharsis: reliving past repressed emotions in order to come to terms with past conflicts.

Chromosome: structures within a cell that contain genes.

Classical conditioning: the learned association between two co-occurring stimuli, such that a similar response is evoked by either.

Client: a term often used to denote an individual in therapy. In contrast to words such as patient or subject, it is used to indicate the helping, non-hierarchical nature of the therapeutic relationship between therapist and individual.

Clinical supervision: discussion and feedback on therapy by peers or experts intended to improve therapeutic formulation and treatment.

Cognitive challenge: the identification and disputation of maladaptive cognitions.

Cognitive schema: a consistent set of beliefs that influence mood and behaviour.

Confabulate: to make up 'facts', usually to hide confusion or poor memory.

Defence mechanism: an unconscious mental act that prevents the individual from psychological harm.

Delusion: a strongly held inappropriate belief; usually a belief that is normally considered impossible.

Depot injection: injection of a slow release drug that will provide a therapeutic dose for days or weeks.

Disorganized symptoms (of schizophrenia): include confused thinking and speech and behaviour that do not make sense.

DSM-IV-TR: the *Diagnostic and Statistical Manual* (fourth edition with text revision: APA 2000) – US system of classification of mental health disorders.

Dysphoric: unhappy, but not sufficiently so to warrant a diagnosis of depression.

Dyzygotic (DZ) twins: non-identical twins.

Electroconvulsive therapy (ECT): treatment involving passing a brief electric current through the temporal lobe(s) as a treatment for depression and schizophrenia.

Effect size: provides a measure of the effect of an intervention; 0.2 is considered small, above 0.6 is a large effect, and between is moderate.

Ego: according to Freud, the part of the personality that operates under the reality principle and works to maximize gratification within the constraints of the 'real world'.

Executive function: neurological coordination of a number of complex processes, including speech, motor coordination and behavioural planning.

Extrapyramidal symptoms: symptoms that result from low levels of dopamine in the extrapyramidal regions of the brain, often as a result of long-term phenothiazine use. Include Parkinsonism and tardive dyskinesia.

Flattened mood: lack of emotional response, either positive or negative, to events.

GABA: a neurotransmitter involved in the anxiety response, otherwise known as gamma-aminobutyric acid.

Hallucination: the experience of touch, visions or sounds in the absence of external stimuli.

Heritability coefficient: the degree to which individual differences are due to genetic factors.

Hydrocephalus: retention of cerebrospinal fluid within the ventricles of the brain. The fluid is often under increased pressure and can compress and damage the brain.

Hyperventilation: short rapid breaths that lead to low levels of carbon dioxide in the blood and physical sensations including tingling in the arms, dizziness and feelings of an inability to breathe.

Hysterical disorder: physical symptoms in the absence of physical pathology.

Id: according to Freud, the personality component driven by the basic instincts of sex and aggression.

Incidence: the frequency with which new cases of a condition arise within the population.

Interpersonal psychotherapy: a form of therapy focusing exclusively on changing interpersonal problems that contribute to mental health problems.

Learned helplessness: a belief that one has no control over events; results in a cessation of attempts at control.

Lobotomy: an early form of psychosurgery.

Major tranquillizers: see **phenothiazines.**

MAOI (monoamine oxydase inhibitor): a form of antidepressant, whose action is on the norepinephrine system.

Mental Health Act Commission: established by the British government to keep under review the operation of the UK Mental Health Act 1983 with respect to patients liable to be detained under the Act.

Meta-analysis: a statistical method of combining the data from several studies using similar measures that allows a more powerful analysis of the effect of the intervention than that provided by single, relatively small studies.

Monozygotic (MZ) twins: identical twins, with identical genetic structure.

Negative symptoms (of schizophrenia): include absence of activation, and include apathy, lack of motivation, or poverty of speech.

Neologism: making up new words.

Neuroleptics: a broad class of drugs used to treat psychotic condition such as schizophrenia; otherwise known as major tranquillizers or phenothiazines.

Neurotransmitter: chemical involved in maintaining neuronal activity; transmits information across the synaptic cleft.

NMDA: a neurotransmitter, with the full name N-methyl-D-aspartate.

Operant (Skinnerian) conditioning: manipulation of behaviour through the use of reinforcement and punishment schedules.

Perseveration: inability to shift from a cognitive set, resulting in inappropriate repetitive behaviour including speech.

Pharmacotherapy: treatment with drugs.

Phenothiazines: major tranquillizers used to treat schizophrenia, of which the best known is chlorpromazine; their action is usually on the dopaminergic system.

Phobia: persistent irrational fear of an object or situation.

Placebo: inactive treatments (either pharmacological or psychological) against which active treatment trials are often evaluated. These allow the assessment of the general effects of receiving some form of attention or 'treatment'. Differences in outcomes between placebo conditions and active interventions are considered to show the specific effects of the therapy against which it is compared.

Polygenic: caused by multiple genes.

Positive symptoms (of schizophrenia): include hallucinations, delusions, disorganized speech or positive thought disorder.

Prevalence: the frequency with which a particular condition is found within the population at any one time.

Psychoanalysis: there are a number of different psychoanalytic therapies. Most share a number of therapeutic goals including gaining insight into the nature of the original trauma, and bringing troubling material to consciousness so the individual can cope with it without the use of ego defence mechanisms.

Psychodynamic: theory or therapy based on the assumption that mental health problems arise from unconscious conflicts. Here, used synonymously with psychoanalytic.

Psycho-educational programme: a treatment usually combining elements of education about a problem or means of coping with it with cognitive behavioural strategies of change.

Psychomotor: movements involving both mental and motor processes.

Psychosis: includes a number of mental health conditions, such as schizophrenia, each of which have the common symptom of a loss of contact with reality.

Psychotherapist: a generic term for someone who provides some form of therapy. In this book, it does not denote any particular therapeutic orientation, and may include therapists as diverse as cognitive and psychoanalytical in practice.

Psychotic: the presence of a mental health condition, such as schizophrenia, of which the main symptom is a loss of contact with reality.

Psychotropic medication: drugs used to treat mental health problems by their action on neurotransmitter levels.

Retrograde amnesia: lack of memory for events that occurred before an event that causes amnesia.

Self-actualization: described by the humanists as the experience of fulfilling one's potential for growth.

Self-instruction training: developed by Meichenbaum, involves the use of coping self-statements at times of stress.

Social learning theory: developed by Bandura, one of the first theories to consider the relationship between cognitive factors and behaviour. Key factors include self-efficacy and vicarious learning.

Spillover: here, a failure to separate work and home life, such that both intrude on the other.

SSRIs (selective serotonin re-uptake inhibitors): a form of antidepressant, whose action is on the serotinergic system.

Stereotypic behaviours: repetitive, non-spontaneous, apparently non-functional behaviours.

Stress management: a specialist cognitive behavioural intervention focusing on teaching people to cope with stress; includes the usual elements of this approach, including relaxation, self-instruction and cognitive challenge.

Superego: according to Freud, contains the individual's morals and societal values; the psychoanalytical equivalent of the conscience.

Transference: the unconscious transfer of experience from one interpersonal context to another: i.e. the reliving of past interpersonal relationships in current situations, including therapies.

Tricyclic: a form of antidepressant, whose action is the serotonin and norepinephrine systems.

Vicarious learning: learning the outcomes of therapy from observation of others.

Waiting list control: used in randomized controlled trial; provides a group whose treatment is delayed, so comparisons can be made between treatment and no treatment conditions without withholding treatment to some people.

Waxy flexibility: a condition found in schizophrenia in which individuals maintain posture in which they are placed for prolonged periods of time.

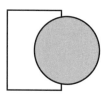

References

Abela, J.R.Z. and Seligman, M.E.P. (2000) The hopelessness theory of depression: a test of the diathesis-stress component in the interpersonal and achievement domains, *Cognitive Therapy and Research*, 23: 361–78.

Abraham, H.C. (1956) Therapeutic and psychological approach to cases of unconsummated marriage, *British Medical Journal*, 1: 837–9.

Abramson, L.Y., Seligman, M.E. and Teasdale, J.D. (1978) Learned helplessness in humans: critique and reformulation, *Journal of Abnormal Psychology*, 87: 49–74.

Agras, W.S., Rossiter, E.M. and Arnow, B. (1994) One-year follow-up of psychosocial and pharmacologic treatments for bulimia nervosa, *Journal of Clinical Psychiatry*, 55: 179–83.

Allen, M.G. (1976) Twin studies of affective illness, *Archives of General Psychiatry*, 33: 1476–8.

Allison, R.B. and Schwarz, T. (1980) *Minds in Many Pieces*. New York: Rawson Wade.

Alloy, L.B. and Abramson, L.Y. (1979) Judgement of contingency in depressed and nondepressed students: sadder but wiser?, *Journal of Experimental Psychology: General*, 108: 441–85.

Altmann, P., Cunningham, J., Dhanesha, U. et al. (1999) Disturbance of cerebral function in people exposed to drinking water contaminated with aluminium sulphate: retrospective study of the Camelford water incident, *British Medical Journal*, 319: 807–11.

American Psychiatric Association (APA) (1987) *Diagnostic and Statistical Manual of Mental Disorders*, 3rd edn, text revision. Washington, DC: APA.

American Psychiatric Association (APA) (1994) *Diagnostic and Statistical Manual of Mental Disorders*, 4th edn. Washington, DC: APA.

American Psychiatric Association (APA) (2000) *Diagnostic and Statistical Manual of Mental Disorders*, 4th edn, text revision (DSM-IV-TR). Washington, DC: APA.

Anderson, D.A. and Maloney, K.C. (2001) The efficacy of cognitive-behavioral therapy on the core symptoms of bulimia nervosa, *Clinical Psychology Review*, 21: 971–88.

Anderson, I.M. (1998) SSRIS versus tricyclic antidepressants in depressed inpatients: a meta-analysis of efficacy and tolerability, *Depression and Anxiety*, 7: 11–17.

Andreasson, S., Allebeck, P. and Engstrom, A. (1987) Cannabis and schizophrenia: a longitudinal study of Swedish conscripts, *Lancet*, 2: 1483–6.

Andrews, G., Stewart, G., Allen, R. et al. (1990) The genetics of six neurotic disorders: a twin study, *Journal of Affective Disorders*, 19: 23–9.

Angst, J. (1999) The epidemiology of depressive disorders, *European Neuropharmacology* (suppl.): 95–8.

Aronson, K.J. (1997) Quality of life among persons with multiple sclerosis and their caregivers, *Neurology*, 48: 74–80.

Avants, S.K., Margolin, A. and McKee, S. (1999) A path analysis of cognitive, affective, and behavioral predictors of treatment response in a methadone maintenance program, *Journal of Substance Abuse*, 11: 215–30.

Awad, A.D. and Vorungati, L.N. (1999) Quality of life and new antipsychotics in schizophrenia: are patients better off?, *International Journal of Social Psychiatry*, 45: 268–75.

Bacaltchuk, J., Trefiglio, R., Lima, M.S. et al. (1999) Antidepressants versus psychotherapy for bulimia nervosa: a systematic review, *Journal of Clinical Pharmacy and Therapeutics*, 24: 23–31.

Bacaltchuk, J., Hay, P. and Trefiglio, R. (2002) Antidepressants versus psychological treatments and their combination for bulimia nervosa, *Cochrane Database of Systematic Reviews*, issue 1.

Bailey, A., Le Couteur, A., Gottesman, I. et al. (1995) Autism as a strongly genetic disorder: evidence from a British twin study, *Psychological Medicine*, 25: 63–77.

Bakker, A., van Dyck, R., Spinhoven, P. et al. (1999) Paroxetine, clomipramine, and cognitive therapy in the treatment of panic disorder, *Journal of Clinical Psychiatry*, 60: 831–8.

Ballenger, J.C. (2000) Panic disorder and agoraphobia, in M.G. Gelder, J.J. Lopez-Ibor Jr and N.C. Andreasen (eds) *New Oxford Textbook of Psychiatry*. Oxford: Oxford University Press.

Bancroft, J. (1999) Central inhibition of sexual response in the male: a theoretical perspective, *Neuroscience Biobehavioral Review*, 23: 763–84.

Bandura, A. (1977) Self-efficacy: toward a unifying theory of behavioural change, *Psychological Review*, 84: 191–215.

Barbaree, H.E. (1990) Stimulus control of sexual arousal, in W.L. Marshall, D.R. Laws and H.E. Barbaree (eds) *Handbook of Sexual Assault: Issues, Theories, and Treatment of the Offender*. New York: Plenum.

Barbaree, H.E. (1991) Denial and minimization among sex offenders: assessment and treatment outcome, *Forum on Corrections Research*, 3: 30–3.

Barbaree, H.E. and Marshall, W.L. (1989) Erectile responses among heterosexual child molesters, father–daughter incest offenders and matched nonoffenders: five distinct age preference profiles, *Canadian Journal of Behavioural Science*, 21: 70–82.

Barbaree, H.E. and Seto, M.C. (1997) Pedophila: assessment and treatment, in D.R. Laws and W. O'Donohue (eds) *Sexual Deviance: Theory, Assessment, and Treatment*. New York: Guilford.

Barker, C., Pistrang, N., Shapiro, D.A. et al. (1993) You in Mind: a preventive mental health television series, *British Journal of Clinical Psychology*, 32: 281–93.

Barkley, A. (1997) Behavioral inhibition, sustained attention and executive functions. Contructing a unifying theory of ADHD, *Psychological Bulletin*, 121: 65–94.

Barkley, R.A., Edwards, G., Laneri, M. et al. (2001) The efficacy of problem-solving communication training alone, behavior management training alone, and their combination for parent-adolescent conflict in teenagers with ADHD and ODD, *Journal of Consulting and Clinical Psychology*, 69: 926–41.

Barlow, D.H., Reynolds, E.J. and Agras, W.S. (1973) Gender identity change in a transsexual, *Archives of General Psychiatry*, 29: 569–76.

Barlow, D.H., Bruce, T.J., Gregg, M.K. et al. (2000) Cognitive-behavioral therapy, imipramine, or their combination for panic disorder: a randomized controlled trial, *Journal of the American Medical Association*, 283: 2529–36.

Barrett, M.S. and Berman, J.S. (2001) Is psychotherapy more effective when therapists disclose information about themselves, *Journal of Consulting and Clinical Psychology*, 69: 597–603.

Bass, E. and Davis, L. (1988) *The Courage to Heal: A Guide for Women Survivors of Sexual Abuse*. New York: Harper & Row.

Basso, M.R., Nasrallah, H.A., Olson, S.C. et al. (1998) Neuropsychological correlates of negative, disorganized and psychotic symptoms in schizophrenia, *Schizophrenia Research*, 25: 99–111.

Bateson, G., Jackson, D., Haley, J. et al. (1956) Toward a theory of schizophrenia, *Behavioural Science*, 1: 251–64.

Battle, Y.L., Martin, B.C., Dorfman, J.H. et al. (1999) Seasonality and infectious disease in schizophrenia: the birth hypothesis revisited, *Journal of Psychiatric Research*, 33: 501–9.

Bebbington, P. and Ramana, R. (1995) The epidemiology of bipolar affective disorder, *Social Psychiatry and Psychiatric Epidemiology*, 30: 279–92.

Beck, A.T. (1977) *Cognitive Therapy of Depression*. New York: Guilford.

Beck, A.T. (1997) Cognitive therapy: reflections, in J.K. Zeig (ed.) *The Evolution of Psychotherapy: The Third Conference*. New York: Brunner/Mazel.

Beck, A.T., Mendelson, M., Mock, J. et al. (1961) Inventory for measuring depression, *Archives of General Psychiatry*, 4: 561–71.

Beck, A.T., Rush, A.J., Shaw, B.F. and Emery, G. (1979) *Cognitive Therapy for Depression*. New York: Guilford.

Beck, A.T., Ward, C.H., Mendelson, M. et al. (1962) Reliability of psychiatric diagnoses: 2. A study of consistency of clinical judgements and ratings, *American Journal of Psychiatry*, 119: 351–7.

Beck, A.T., Freeman, A. and associates (1990) *Cognitive Therapy of Personality Disorders*. New York: Guilford.

Beck, A.T., Wright, F.D., Newman, C.F. et al. (1993) *Cognitive Therapy of Substance Abuse*. New York: Guilford.

Beidel, D.C. and Turner, S.M. (1986) A critique of the theoretical bases of cognitive-behavioral theories and therapy, *Clinical Psychology Review*, 6: 177–97.

Bennett, P. and Murphy, S. (1997) *Psychology and Health Promotion*. Buckingham: Open University Press.

Bennett, P., Smith, C., Nugent, Z. et al. (1991) 'Pssst . . . the really useful guide to alcohol': evaluation of an alcohol education television series, *Health Education Research, Theory and Practice*, 6: 57–64.

Bennett, P., Conway, M. and Clatworthy, J. (2001) Predicting post-traumatic symptoms in cardiac patients, *Heart and Lung*, 30: 458–65.

Bennett, P., Lowe, R. and Honey, K. (2002) Appraisals and emotions: a test of the consistency of reporting and their associations, *Cognition and Emotion*.

Bentall, R.P. (1993) Deconstructing the concept of 'Schizophrenia', *Journal of Mental Health*, 2: 223–38.

Bentall, R.P., Corcoran, R., Howard, R. et al. (2001) Persecutory delusions: a review and theoretical integration, *Clinical Psychology Review*, 21: 1143–92.

Bergin, A.E. (1971) The evaluation of therapeutic outcomes, in A.E. Bergin and S.L. Garfield (eds) *Handbook of Psychotherapy and Behavioral Change*. New York: Wiley.

Berlin, F.S. and Meinecke, C.F. (1981) Treatment of sex offenders with antiandrogenic medication: conceptualization, review of treatment modalities and preliminary findings, *American Journal of Psychiatry*, 138: 601–8.

Berretini, W.H. (2000) Susceptibility loci for bipolar disorder: overlap with inherited vulnerability to schizophrenia, *Biological Psychiatry*, 47: 245–51.

Berrios, G.E. and Quemada, J.I. (1990) Depressive illness in multiple sclerosis: clinical and theoretical aspects of the association, *British Journal of Psychiatry*, 156: 10–16.

Berrios, R.P. (1991) Delusions as 'wrong beliefs': a conceptual history, *British Journal of Psychiatry*, 159: 6–13.

Beswick, T., Best, D., Rees, S. et al. (2001) Multiple drug use: patterns and practices of heroin and crack use in a population of opiate addicts in treatment, *Drug and Alcohol Review*, 20: 201–4.

Bettelheim, B. (1967) *The Empty Fortress*. New York: Free Press.

Bettelheim, B. (1973) Bringing up children, *Ladies Home Journal*, 90: 28.

Beutler, L. and Consoli, A. (1993) Matching the therapist's interpersonal stance to clients' characteristics: contributions from systemic eclectic psychotherapy, *Psychotherapy: Theory, Research and Practice*, 30: 417–22.

Beutler, L.E., Clarkin, J.F. and Bongar, B. (2000) *Guidelines for the Systematic Treatment of the Depressed Patient*. New York: Oxford University Press.

Birch, H., Richardson, S.A., Baird, D. et al. (1970) *Mental Subnormality in the Community: A Clinical and Epidemiological Study*. Baltimore, MD: Williams & Wilkins.

Birchwood, M., Fowler, D. and Jackson, C. (eds) (2000) *Early Intervention in Psychosis*. London: Wiley.

Bird, C.E. and Rieker, P.P. (1999) Gender matters: an integrated model for understanding men's and women's health, *Social Science and Medicine*, 48: 745–55.

Black, D.W., Noyes, R. Jr, Goldstein, R.B. et al. (1992) A family study of obsessive-compulsive disorder, *Archives of General Psychiatry*, 49: 362–8.

Blaszczynski, A. (1995) Criminal offences in pathological gamblers, *Psychiatry, Psychology and Law*, 1: 129–38.

Blazer, D.G., Hughes, D., George, L.K. et al. (1991) Generalized anxiety disorder, in L.N. Robins and D.A. Regier (eds) *Psychiatric Disorders in America: The Epidemiologic Catchment Area Study*. New York: Maxwell Macmillan International.

Blazer, R.C., Hughes, W.D. and George, L.K. (1987) Stressful life events and the onset of a generalized anxiety disorder, *American Journal of Psychiatry*, 114: 1178–83.

Bleathman, C. and Morton, I. (1992) Validation therapy: extracts from 20 groups with dementia sufferers, *Journal of Advanced Nursing*, 17: 658–66.

Blehar, M.C. and Rosenthal, N.E. (1989) Seasonal affective disorders and phototherapy, Report of a National Institute of Mental Health-sponsored workshop, *Archives of General Psychiatry*, 46: 469–74.

Bleuler, E. (1908) Die prognose der Dementia praecox – Schizophreniegruppe, *Prager Medicinische Wochenshrift*, 16: 321–5.

Bliss, E.L. (1986) *Multiple Personality, Allied Disorders and Hypnosis*. New York: Oxford University Press.

Booth, P.G., Dale, B., Slade, P.D. et al. (1992) A follow-up study of problem drinkers offered a goal choice option, *Journal of Studies on Alcohol*, 53: 594–600.

Borduin, C.M. (1999) Multisystemic treatment of criminality and violence in adolescents, *Journal of the Academy of Child and Adolescent Psychiatry*, 38: 242–9.

Borduin, C.M., Mann, B.J., Cone, L.T. et al. (1995) Multisystemic treatment of serious juvenile offenders: long-term prevention of criminality and violence, *Journal of Consulting and Clinical Psychology*, 63: 569–78.

Borkovec, T.D. and Costello, E. (1993) Efficacy of applied relaxation and cognitive behavioral therapy in the treatment of generalized anxiety disorder, *Journal of Consulting and Clinical Psychology*, 51: 611–19.

Boyle, M. (1990) Is schizophrenia what it was? A re-analysis of Kraepelin's and Bleuler's population, *Journal of the History of the Behavioral Sciences*, 26: 323–33.

Brain, K., Norman, P., Gray, J. et al. (2002) A randomized trial of specialist genetic assessment: psychological impact on women at different levels of familial breast cancer risk, *British Journal of Cancer*, 86: 233–8.

Bransford, J.D. and Stein, B.S. (1984) *The Ideal Problem Solver: A Guide for Improving Thinking, Learning, and Creativity*. New York: W.H. Freeman.

Brassington, J.C. and Marsh, N.V. (1999) Neuropsychological aspects of multiple sclerosis, *Neuropsychology Review*, 8: 43–77.

Brewin, C.R. (2001) A cognitive neuroscience account of posttraumatic stress disorder and its treatment, *Behaviour Research and Therapy*, 39: 373–93.

Brewin, C.R. and Andrews, B. (1998) Recovered memories of trauma: phenomenology and cognitive mechanisms, *Clinical Psychology Review*, 18: 949–70.

Bronisch, T. (1996) The relationship between suicidality and depression, *Archives of Suicide Research*, 2: 235–54.

Bronisch, T. and Wittchen, H.U. (1994) Suicidal ideation and suicide attempts: comorbidity with depression, anxiety disorders, and substance abuse disorder, *European Archives of Psychiatry and Clinical Neuroscience*, 244: 93–8.

Brooks, N., Campsie, L., Symington, C. et al. (1986) The five year outcome of severe blunt head injury: a relative's view, *Journal of Neurology, Neurosurgery, and Psychiatry*, 49: 764–70.

Brown, G.R. and Anderson, B. (1991) Psychiatric morbidity in adult clients with childhood histories of sexual and physical abuse, *American Journal of Psychiatry*, 148: 55–61.

Brown, G.W. and Harris, T.O. (1978) *Social Origins of Depression: A Study of Psychiatric Disorder in Women*. London: Tavistock.

Brown, G.W., Birley, J.L.T. and Wing, J.K. (1972) The influence of family life on the course of schizophrenic disorders: a relocation, *British Journal of Psychiatry*, 121: 241–58.

Brown, J.S.L., Cochrane, R. and Hancox, T. (2000) Large-scale health promotion stress workshops for the general public: a controlled evaluation, *Behavioural and Cognitive Psychotherapy*, 28: 139–51.

Bruce, D. (1980) Changes in Scottish drinking habits and behaviour following the extension of permitted evening opening hours, *Health Bulletin*, 38: 133–7.

Bruch, H. (1982) Anorexia nervosa: therapy and theory, *American Journal of Psychiatry*, 139: 1531–8.

Bryant, M.J., Simons, A.D. and Thase, M.E. (1999) Therapist skill and patient variables in homework compliance: controlling an uncontrolled variable in cognitive therapy outcome research, *Cognitive Therapy and Research*, 23: 381–99.

Buccafusco, J.J. and Jackson, W.J. (1991) Beneficial effects of nicotine administered prior to a delayed matching-to-sample task in young and aged monkeys, *Neurobiology of Aging*, 12: 233–8.

Bullough, V. and Weinberg, T. (1988) Women married to transvestites; problems and adjustments, *Journal of Psychology and Human Sexuality*, 1: 83–6.

Burgio, L., Engel, B.T., McCormick, K. et al. (1988) Behavioral treatment for urinary incontinence in elderly inpatients: initial attempts to modify prompting and toileting procedures, *Behavior Therapy*, 19: 345–57.

Burns, D.D. and Noen-Heoksema, S. (1992) Therapeutic empathy and recovery from depression in cognitive-behavioral therapy: a structural equation model, *Journal of Consulting and Clinical Psychology*, 60: 441–9.

Butler, G., Fennell, M., Robson, P. et al. (1991) A comparison of behavior therapy and cognitive behavior therapy in the treatment of generalized anxiety disorder, *Journal of Consulting and Clinical Psychology*, 59: 167–75.

Cadoret, R.J. (1982) Genotype–environment interaction in antisocial behavior, *Psychological Medicine*, 12: 235–9.

Cadoret, R.J., Yates, G.A., Geyer, M.A. et al. (1995) Adoption study demonstrating two genetic pathways to drug abuse, *Archives of General Psychiatry*, 52: 45–52.

Campbell, M., Adams, P., Perry, R. et al. (1988) Tardive and withdrawal dyskinesias in autistic children: a prospective study, *Psychopharmacology Bulletin*, 24: 251–5.

Campbell, M., Anderson, L.T., Small, A.M. et al. (1993) Naltrexone in autistic children: behavioral symptoms and attentional learning, *Journal of the American Academy of Child and Adolescent Psychiatry*, 32: 1283–91.

Carey, G. and Gottesman, I.I. (1981) Twin and family studies of anxiety, phobic and obsessive disorders, in D.F. Klein and J. Rabkin (eds) *Anxiety: New Research and Changing Concepts*. New York: Raven.

Carlton, P.L. and Manowicz, P. (1994) Factors determining the severity of pathological gambling in males, *Journal of Gambling Studies*, 10: 147–57.

Carr, A.T. (1974) Compulsive neurosis: a review of the literature, *Psychological Bulletin*, 81: 311–18.

Castellanos, F.X., Giedd, J.N., Marsh, W.L. et al. (1996) Quantitative brain magnetic resonance imaging in attention-deficit hyperactivity disorder, *Archives of General Psychiatry*, 53: 607–16.

Channon, S., deSilva, P., Helmsley, D. et al. (1989) A controlled trial of cognitive-behavioural and behavioural treatments of anorexia nervosa, *Behaviour Research and Therapy*, 27: 529–35.

Charlop-Christy, M.H. and Haymes, L.K. (1998) Using obsessions as reinforcers with and without mild reductive procedures to decrease inappropriate behaviors of children with autism, *Journal of Autism and Developmental Disorders*, 26: 527–46.

Chen, D. (1995) Cultural and psychological influences on mental health issues for Chinese Americans, in L.L. Adler and R.R. Mukherji (eds) *Spirit versus Scalpel: Traditional Healing and Modern Psychotherapy*. Westport, CT: Bergin & Garvey.

Cherland, E. and Fitzpatrick, R. (1999) Psychotic side effects of psychostimulants: a 5-year review, *Canadian Journal of Psychiatry*, 44: 811–13.

Chick, J. (1991) Early intervention for hazardous drinking in the general hospital, *Alcohol and Alcoholism*, 1: 477–9.

Chorpita, B.F. and Barlow, D.H. (1998) The development of anxiety: the role of control in the early environment, *Psychological Bulletin*, 124: 3–21.

Chretien, R.D. and Persinger, M.A. (2000) 'Prefrontal deficits' discriminate young offenders from age-matched cohorts: juvenile delinquency as an expected feature of the normal distribution of prefrontal cerebral development, *Psychological Reports*, 87: 1196–202.

Clark, D.M. (1986) A cognitive approach to panic disorder, *Behaviour Research and Therapy*, 24: 461–70.

Clark, D.M., Salkovskis, P.M., Gelder, M. et al. (1988) Tests of a cognitive model of panic, in I. Hand and U. Wittchen (eds) *Panic and Phobias*, Vol. 2. Berlin: Springer Verlag.

Clark, D.M., Salkovskis, P.M., Hackmann, A. et al. (1994) A comparison of cognitive therapy, applied relaxation and imipramine in the treatment of panic disorder, *British Journal of Psychiatry*, 164: 759–69.

Clark, L.A., Watson, D. and Reynolds, S. (1995) Diagnosis and classification of psychopathology: challenges to the current system and future directions, *Annual Review of Psychology*, 46: 121–53.

Clarke, R. (2000) Perceptions of interethnic group racism predict increased vascular reactivity to a laboratory challenge in college women, *Annals of Behavioral Medicine*, 22: 214–22.

Clomipramine Collaborative Study Group (1991) Clomipramine in the treatment of patients with OCD, *Archives of General Psychiatry*, 48: 730–8.

Cloutier, S., Martin, S.L. and Poole, C. (2002) Sexual assault among North Carolina women: prevalence and health risk factors, *Journal of Epidemiology and Community Health*, 56: 265–71.

Coffey, M. (1999) Psychosis and medication: strategies for improving adherence, *British Journal of Nursing*, 8: 225–30.

Cole, S.W., Kemeny, M.E., Taylor, S.E. and Visscher, B.R. (1996) Elevated physical health risk among gay men who conceal their homosexual identity, *Health Psychology*, 15: 243–51.

Comings, D.E., Rosenthal, R.J., Lesieur, H.R. et al. (1996) A study of the dopamine D2 receptor gene in pathological gambling, *Pharmacogenetics*, 6: 223–34.

Compton, W.M., Helzer, J.E., Hwu, H. et al. (1991) New methods in cross-cultural psychiatry: psychiatric illness in Taiwan and the United States, *American Journal of Psychiatry*, 148: 1697–704.

Coons, P.M., Bowman, E.S. and Milstein, V. (1988) Multiple personality disorder: a clinical investigation of 50 cases, *Journal of Nervous and Mental Disease*, 176: 519–27.

Cooper, P.J. and Fairburn, C.G. (1983) Binge-eating and self-induced vomiting in the community, *British Journal of Psychiatry*, 142: 139–44.

Corrigan, P.W. (1991) Social skills training in adult psychiatric populations: a meta-analysis, *Journal of Behavior Therapy and Experimental Psychiatry*, 22: 203–10.

Corsico, A. and McGuffin, P. (2001) Psychiatric genetics: recent advances and clinical implications, *Epidemiologia e Psichiatria Sociale*, 10: 253–9.

Costa, P.T. and McCrae, R.R. (1995) Domains and facets: hierarchical personality assessment using the Revised NEO Personality Inventory, *Journal of Personal Assessment*, 64: 21–50.

Costello, E.J., Edelbrock, C.S. and Costello, A.J. (1985) Validity of the NIMH Diagnostic Interview Schedule for Children: a comparison between psychiatric and pediatric referrals, *Journal of Abnormal Child Psychology*, 13: 579–95.

Cottraux, J., Note, I., Yao, S.N. et al. (2001) A randomized controlled trial of cognitive therapy versus intensive behavior therapy in obsessive compulsive disorder, *Psychotherapy and Psychosomatics*, 70: 288–97.

Cox, A., Rutter, M., Newman, S. et al. (1975) A comparative study of infantile autism and specific developmental language disorders: 2. Parental characteristics, *British Journal of Psychiatry*, 126: 146–59.

Craddock, N. and Jones, I. (1999) Genetics of bipolar disorder, *Journal of Medical Ethics*, 36: 585–94.

Cranston-Cuebas, M.A. and Barlow, D.H. (1990) Cognitive and affective contributions to sexual functioning, *Annual Review of Sexual Research*, 1: 119–61.

Crawford, L.L., Holloway, K.S. and Domjan, M. (1993) The nature of sexual reinforcement, *Journal of Experimental Analysis of Behaviour*, 60: 55–66.

Crits-Cristoph, P., Cooper, A. and Luborsky, L. (1988) The accuracy of therapists' interpretations and the outcome of dynamic psychotherapy, *Journal of Consulting and Clinical Psychology*, 56: 490–5.

Crowe, R. (1974) An adoption study of antisocial personality disorder, *Archives of General Psychiatry*, 31: 785–91.

Curran, H.V. (1991) Benzodiazepines, memory and mood: a review, *Psychopharmacology*, 105: 1–8.

Dahl, A.A. (1994) Heritability in personality disorders – an overview, *Clinical Genetics*, 46: 138–43.

Dalgleish, T., Rosen, K. and Marks, M. (1996) Rhythm and blues: the theory and treatment of seasonal affective disorder, *British Journal of Clinical Psychology*, 35: 163–82.

Dalos, N.P., Rabins, P.V., Brooks, B.R. et al. (1983) Disease activity and emotional state in multiple sclerosis, *Annals of Neurology*, 13: 573–7.

Dare, C., Eisler, I., Russell, G. et al. (2001) Psychological therapies for adults with anorexia nervosa, *British Journal of Psychiatry*, 178: 216–21.

Davey Smith, G., Dorling, D., Gordon, D. et al. (1999) The widening health gap: what are the solutions?, *Critical Public Health*, 9: 151–70.

Davidson, J.R.T. (2001) Pharmacotherapy of Generalised Anxiety Disorder, *Journal of Clinical Psychiatry*, 62 (suppl. 11): 46–50.

Davidson, K. (2000) *Cognitive Therapy for Personality Disorders*. Oxford: Butterworth-Heinemann.

Davidson, P.R. and Parker, K.C.H. (2001) Eye movement desensitization and reprocessing (EMDR): a meta-analysis, *Journal of Consulting and Clinical Psychology*, 69: 305–16.

Delffabbro, P.H. and Winefield, A.H. (1999) Poker machine gambling: an analysis of within session characteristics, *British Journal of Psychology*, 90: 425–32.

DeRubeis, R.J., Gelfand, L.A., Tang, T.Z. et al. (1999) Medications versus cognitive behavior therapy for severely depressed outpatients: mega-analysis of four randomized comparisons, *American Journal of Psychiatry*, 156: 1007–13.

Demyttenaere, K., van Ganse, E., Gregoirre, J. et al. (1998) Compliance in depressed patients treated with fluoxetine or amitriptyline. Belgian Compliance Study Group, *International Clinical Psychopharmacology*, 13: 11–17.

Desai, N. (1999) Switching from depot antipsychotics to respiridone: results of a study of chronic schizophrenics, *Advances in Therapy*, 16: 78–88.

Devanand, D.P., Dwork, A.J., Hutchinson, E.R. et al. (1994) Does ECT alter brain structure?, *American Journal of Psychiatry*, 151: 957–70.

Devilly, G.J. and Spence, S.H. (1999) The relative efficacy and treatment distress of EMDR and a cognitive-behavior trauma treatment protocol in the amelioration of posttraumatic stress disorder, *Journal of Anxiety Disorders*, 13: 131–57.

Dhawan, S. and Marshall, W.L. (1996) Sexual abuse histories of sexual offenders, *Sexual Abuse: A Journal of Research and Treatment*, 8: 7–15.

Dickerson, M. and Baron, E. (2000) Contemporary issues and future directions for research into pathological gambling, *Addiction*, 95: 1145–59.

Dickerson, M.G., Baron, E., Hong, S-M. et al. (1996) Estimating the extent and degree of gambling related problems in the Australian population: a national survey, *Journal of Gambling Studies*, 12: 161–78.

Dobkin, B.H. (1996) *Neurologic Rehabilitation*. Philadelphia, PA: F.A. Davis.

Docter, R.F. and Prince, V. (1997) Transvestism: a survey of 1032 crossdressers, *Archives of Sexual Behavior*, 26: 589–605.

Dodge, K.A. and Frame, C.L. (1982) Social cognitive biases and deficits in aggressive boys, *Child Development*, 53: 620–35.

Dolan, M. (1994) Psychopathy – a neurobiological perspective, *British Journal of Psychiatry*, 165: 151–9.

Dollard, J. and Miller, N.E. (1950) *Personality and Psychotherapy*. New York: McGraw-Hill.

Donohoe, G., Owens, N., O'Donnell, C. et al. (2001) Predictors of compliance with neuroleptic medication among inpatients with schizophrenia: a discriminant function analysis, *European Psychiatry*, 16: 293–8.

Drury, V., Birchwood, M. and Cochrane, R. (2000) Cognitive therapy and recovery from acute psychosis: a controlled trial. 3. Five-year follow-up, *British Journal of Psychiatry*, 177: 8–14.

Duncan, G.E., Sheitman, B.B. and Lieberman, J.A. (1999) An integrated view of pathophysiological models of schizophrenia, *Brain Research Reviews*, 29: 250–64.

Durham, R.C., Murphy, T., Allan, T. et al. (1994) Cognitive therapy, analytic psychotherapy and anxiety management training for generalised anxiety disorder, *British Journal of Psychiatry*, 16: 315–23.

Durkheim, E. ([1897] 1951) *Suicide*. New York: Free Press.

Dyer, C. (1997) High court detains girl with anorexia, *British Medical Journal*, 314: 845.

Eagles, J.M., Wileman, S.M., Cameron, I.M. et al. (1999) Seasonal affective disorder among primary care attenders and a community sample in Aberdeen, *British Journal of Psychiatry*, 175: 472–5.

Eaton, W.W., Kramer, M., Anthony, J.C. et al. (1989) The incidence of specific DIS/DSM-III mental disorders: data from the NIMH Epidemiologic Catchment Area Program, *Acta Psychiatrica Scandinavica*, 79: 163–78.

Eddy, J.M. and Chamberlain, P. (2000) Family management and deviant peer associations as mediators of the impact of treatment condition on youth antisocial behavior, *Journal of Consulting and Clinical Psychology*, 68: 857–63.

Edwards, G., Anderson, P., Babor, T.F. et al. (1994) *Alcohol Policy and the Public Good*. Oxford: Oxford University Press.

Ehlers, A., Mayou, R.A. and Bryant, B. (1998) Psychological predictors of chronic posttraumatic stress disorder after motor vehicle accidents, *Journal of Abnormal Psychology*, 107: 508–19.

Ehrhardt, A. and Money, J. (1967) Progestin-induced hermaphroditism: IQ and psychosexual identity in a study of ten girls, *Journal of Sex Research*, 3: 83–100.

Eisen, S.A., Lin, N., Lyons, M.J. et al. (1998–99) Familial influences on gambling behavior: an analysis of 3,359 twin pairs, *Addiction*, 93: 1375–84.

Elkin, I., Shea, T., Watkins, J.T. et al. (1989) National Institute of Mental Health Treatment of depression collaborative research program: general effectiveness of treatments, *Archives of General Psychiatry*, 46: 971–82.

Elliott, M. (2000) Gender differences in the causes of depression, *Women and Health*, 33: 163–77.

Ellis, A. (1977) The basic clinical theory of rational-emotive therapy, in A. Ellis and R. Grieger (eds) *Handbook of Rational-Emotive Therapy*. New York: Springer.

Emerson, E. (1998) Working with people with challenging behaviour, in E. Emerson, C. Hatton, J. Bromley et al. (eds) *Clinical Psychology and People with Intellectual Disabilities*. Chichester: Wiley.

Emerson, E., Hatton, C., Felce, D. et al. (2001) *Learning Disabilities: The Fundamental Facts*. London: Mental Health Foundation.

Epstein, J., Wiseman, C.V., Sunday, S.R. et al. (2001) Neurocognitive evidence favors 'top down' over 'bottom up' mechanisms in the pathogenesis of body size distortions in anorexia nervosa, *Eating and Weight Disorders*, 6: 140–7.

Erikson, E. (1980) *Growth and Crisis of the Healthy Personality: Identity and the Life Cycle*. New York: W.W. Norton.

Evans, E., Kupfer, D.J., Perel, J.M. et al. (1992) Three-year outcomes for maintenance therapies in recurrent depression, *Archives of General Psychiatry*, 47: 1093–9.

Fairburn, C.G. (1997) Eating disorders, in D.M. Clark and C.G. Fairburn (eds) *Science and Practice of Cognitive Behaviour Therapy*. Oxford: Oxford University Press.

Fairburn, C.G. and Beglin, S.J. (1994) Assessment of eating disorders: interview or self-report questionnaire?, *International Journal of Eating Disorders*, 16: 363–70.

Fairburn, C.G., Jones, R., Peveler, R.C. et al. (1993) Psychotherapy and bulimia nervosa: the longer-term effects of interpersonal psychotherapy, behaviour therapy and cognitive behaviour therapy, *Archives of General Psychiatry*, 50: 419–28.

Fairburn, C.G., Norman, P.A. and Welch, S.L. (1995) A prospective study of outcome in bulimia nervosa and the long-term effects of three psychological treatments, *Archives of General Psychiatry*, 52: 304–12.

Falloon, I.R., Boyd, J.L., McGill, C.W. et al. (1982) Family management in the prevention of exacerbations of schizophrenia: a controlled study, *New England Journal of Medicine*, 306: 1437–40.

Farber, S. (1990) Institutional mental health and social control: the ravages of epistemological hubris, *Journal of Mind and Behavior*, 11: 285–300.

Farrell, J.M. and Shaw, I.A. (1994) Emotional awareness training: a prerequisite to effective cognitive-behavioral treatment of borderline personality disorder, *Cognitive and Behavioral Practice*, 1: 71–91.

Farrington, D.P. (2000) Psychosocial predictors of adult antisocial personality and adult convictions, *Behavioral Sciences and the Law*, 18: 605–22.

Farris, B. and Stancliffe, R.J. (2001) The co-worker training model: outcomes of an open employment pilot project, *Journal of Intellectual and Developmental Disability*, 26: 143–59.

Feil, N. (1990) Validation therapy helps staff reach confused patients, *Nursing*, 16: 33–4.

Feingold, B.F. (1979) *The Feingold Cookbook for Hyperactive Children*. New York: Random House.

Feinstein, A., Ron, M. and Thompson, A. (1993) A serial study of psychometric and magnetic resonance imaging changes in multiple sclerosis, *Brain*, 116: 569–602.

Feldman-Summers, S. and Pope, K.S. (1994) The experience of 'forgetting' childhood abuse: a national survey of psychologists, *Journal of Consulting and Clinical Psychology*, 62: 636–9.

Ferguson, C.P., La Via, M.C., Crossan, P.J. et al. (1999) Are serotonin selective reuptake inhibitors effective in underweight anorexia nervosa?, *International Journal of Eating Disorders*, 25: 7–11.

Fergusson, D.M. and Horwood, L.J. (1995) Predictive validity of categorically and dimensionally scores measures of disruptive childhood behaviors, *Journal of the American Academy of Child and Adolescent Psychiatry*, 34: 477–85.

Ferrie, J.E., Martikainen, P., Shipley, M.J. et al. (2001) Employment status and health after privatisation in white collar civil servants: prospective cohort study, *British Medical Journal*, 322: 647.

Fielding, J.E. and Piserchia, P.V. (1989) Frequency of worksite health promotion activities, *American Journal of Public Health*, 79: 16–20.

Fink, D. and Golinkoff, M. (1990) Multiple personality disorder, borderline personality disorder, and schizophrenia: a comparative study of clinical features, *Dissociation*, 3: 127–34.

Finn, P.R., Earleywine, M. and Pihl, R.O. (1992) Sensation seeking, stress reactivity, and alcohol dampening discriminate the density of a family history of alcoholism, *Alcoholism: Clinical and Experimental Research*, 16: 585–90.

Foa, E.B., Steketee, G. and Rothbaum, B.O. (1989) Behavioural/cognitive conceptualizations of post-traumatic stress disorder, *Behavior Therapy*, 20: 155–76.

Foa, E.B., Rothbaum, B.O., Riggs, D.S. et al. (1991) Treatment of posttraumatic stress disorder in rape victims: a comparison between cognitive and behavioural procedures and counselling, *Journal of Consulting and Clinical Psychology*, 59: 715–23.

Forette, F. and Rockwood, K. (1999) Therapeutic intervention in dementia, in G.K. Wilcock, R.S. Bucks and K. Rockwood (eds) *Diagnosis and Management of Dementia: A Manual for Memory Disorders Teams*. Oxford: Oxford University Press.

Forsythe, A.J.M. (1996) Places and patterns of drug use in the Scottish Dance Scene, *Addiction*, 91: 511–21.

Fox, J.W. (1990) Social class, mental illness, and social mobility: the social selection-drift hypothesis for serious mental illness, *Journal of Health and Social Behavior*, 31: 344–53.

Frank, J.D. (1961) *Persuasion and Healing: A Comparative Study of Psychotherapy*. Baltimore, CA: Johns Hopkins University Press.

Fraser, G.A. (1992) Multiple personality disorder, *British Journal of Psychiatry*, 161: 416–17.

Freeman, C. (1995) *The ECT Handbook*. London: Royal College of Psychiatrists.

Freeman, C.P.L., Trimble, M.R., Deakin, J.F.W. et al. (1994) Fluvoxamine versus clomipramine in the treatment of obsessive compulsive disorder: a multicenter, randomised, double-blind, parallel group comparison, *Journal of Clinical Psychiatry*, 55: 301–5.

Freud, S. (1900) *The Interpretation of Dreams*. New York: Wiley.

Freud, S. (1922) *Introductory Lectures on Psychoanalysis*. London: George Allen and Unwin.

Freud, S. ([1917] 1957) Mourning and melancholia, in J. Strachey (ed. and trans.) *The Standard Edition of Complete Psychological Works*, Vol. 14. London: Hogarth Press.

Freud, S. ([1920] 1990) *Beyond the Pleasure Principle*. New York: Norton.

Friedberg, J. (1977) Shock treatment, brain damage, and memory loss: a neurological perspective, *American Journal of Psychiatry*, 13: 1010–14.

Fromm-Reichman, F. (1948) Notes on the development of treatment of schizophrenia by psycho-analytic psychotherapy, *Psychiatry*, 11: 263–73.

Fukunishi, I. (1997) Alexithymic characteristics of bulimia nervosa in diabetes mellitus with end-stage renal disease, *Psychological Reports*, 81: 627–33.

Fukunishi, I., Sasaki, K., Chisima, Y. et al. (1996) Emotional disturbances in trauma patients during the rehabilitation phase: studies of post-traumatic stress disorder and alexithymia, *General Hospital Psychiatry*, 18: 121–7.

Gaebel, W., Janner, M., Frommann, N. et al. (2002) First vs multiple episode schizophrenia: two-year outcome of intermittent and maintenance medication strategies, *Schizophrenia Research*, 53: 145–59.

Gagné, G.G., Furman, M.J., Carpenter, L.L. et al. (2000) Efficacy of continuation ECT and antidepressant drugs compared to long-term anti-depressants alone in depressed patients, *American Journal of Psychiatry*, 157: 1960–9.

Gallagher-Thompson, D. and Steffen, A.M. (1994) Comparative effects of cognitive-behavioral and brief psychodynamic psychotherapies for depressed family caregivers, *Journal of Consulting and Clinical Psychology*, 62: 543–9.

Garner, D.M. and Bemis, K.M. (1985) Cognitive therapy for anorexia nervosa, in D.M. Garner and P.E. Garfinkel (eds) *Handbook of Psychotherapy for Anorexia Nervosa and Bulimia*. New York: Guilford.

Geddes, J.R., Verdoux, H., Takei, N. et al. (1999) Schizophrenia and complications of pregnancy and labor: an individual patient data meta-analysis, *Schizophrenia Bulletin*, 25: 413–23.

Geoffrey, C. (1991) A Prozac backlash, *Newsweek*, 1 April: 64.

Gibson, D.R., Flynn, N.M. and Perales, D. (2001) Effectiveness of syringe exchange programs in reducing HIV risk behavior and HIV seroconversion among injecting drug users, *AIDS*, 15: 1329–41.

Gillespie, K., Duffy, M., Hackmann, A. et al. (2002) Community based cognitive therapy in the treatment of post-traumatic stress disorder following the Omagh bomb, *Behaviour Research and Therapy*, 40: 345–57.

Gladue, B.A. (1985) Neuroendocrine response to estrogen and sexual orientation, *Science*, 230: 961.

Gleaves, D.H. (1996) The sociocognitive model of dissociative identity disorder: a reexamination of the evidence, *Psychological Bulletin*, 120: 42–59.

Gleaves, D.H., May, M.C. and Cardena, E. (2001) An examination of the diagnostic validity of dissociative identity disorder, *Clinical Psychology Review*, 21: 577–608.

Goddard, A.W., Mason, G.F., Almai, A. et al. (2001) Reductions in occipital cortex GABA levels in panic disorder detected with 1h-magnetic resonance spectroscopy, *Archives of General Psychiatry*, 58: 556–61.

Goldman, A. and Carroll, J.L. (1990) Educational intervention as an adjunct to treatment of erectile dysfunction in older couples, *Journal of Sexual and Marital Therapy*, 16: 127–41.

Goldstein, F.C., McKendall, R.R. and Haut, M.W. (1992) Gist recall in multiple sclerosis, *Archives of Neurology*, 49: 1060–4.

Goldstein, I., Lue, T.F., Padma-Nathan, H. et al. (1998) Oral sildenafil in the treatment of erectile dysfunction: Sildenafil Study Group, *New England Journal of Medicine*, 338: 1397–404.

Goodman, R. and Stevenson, J. (1989) A twin study of hyperactivity – II: the etiological role of genes, family relationships, and perinatal adversity, *Journal of Child Psychology and Psychiatry*, 30: 691–709.

Goodyear-Smith, F.A., Laidlaw, T.M. and Large, R.G. (1997) Memory recovery and repression: what is the evidence?, *Health Care Analysis*, 5: 99–111.

Gordon, C.T., State, R.C., Nelson, J.E. et al. (1993) A double-blind comparison of clomipramine, desipramine, and placebo in the treatment of autistic disorder, *Archives of General Psychiatry*, 50: 441–7.

Gorski, T.T. (1989) *Understanding the Twelve Steps*. New York: Prentice Hall/Parkside.

Gould, R.A., Otto, M.W. and Pollack, M.H. (1995) A meta-analysis of treatment outcome for panic disorder, *Clinical Psychology Review*, 15: 819–44.

Goyer, P., Andreason, P.J., Semple, W.E. et al. (1994) Positron-emission tomography and personality disorders, *Neuropsychopharmacology*, 10: 21–8.

Gray, J.A. (1983) A theory of anxiety: the role of the limbic system, *Encephale*, 9 (suppl 2): 161B–6B.

Green, R. (1987) *The 'Sissy Boy Syndrome' and the Development of Homosexuality*. New Haven, CT: Yale University Press.

Green, R. and Blanchard, R. (1995) Gender identity disorders, in H.I. Kaplan and B.J. Sadock (eds) *Comprehensive Textbook of Psychiatry*. Baltimore, MD: Williams and Wilkins.

Greenberg, D.M., Bradford, J. and Curry, S. (1993) A comparison of sexual victimizations in the childhoods of pedophiles and hebephiles, *Journal of Forensic Sciences*, 38: 432–6.

Gresham, F.M. and MacMillan, D.L. (1998) Early intervention project: can its claims be substantiated and its effects replicated?, *Journal of Autism and Developmental Disorders*, 28: 5–13.

Grinspoon, L. and Bakalar, J.B. (1986) Can drugs be used to enhance the psychotherapeutic process, *American Journal of Psychotherapy*, 40: 393–404.

Gruber, K., Chutuape, M.A. and Stitzer, M.L. (2000) Reinforcement-based intensive outpatient treatment for inner city opiate abusers: a short-term evaluation, *Drug and Alcohol Dependence*, 57: 211–23.

Gupta, M.A. and Johnson, A.M. (2000) Nonweight-related body image concerns among female eating-disordered patients and nonclinical controls: some preliminary observations, *International Journal of Eating Disorders*, 27: 304–9.

Gurvits, I.G., Koenigsberg, H.W. and Siever, L.J. (2000) Neurotransmitter dysfunction in patients with borderline personality disorder, *Psychiatric Clinics of North America*, 23: 27–40.

Guscott, R. and Taylor, L. (1994) Lithium prophylaxis in recurrent affective illness: efficacy, effectiveness and efficiency, *British Journal of Psychiatry*, 164: 741–6.

Haaga, D.A. and Beck, A.T. (1995) Perspectives on depressive realism: implications for cognitive theory of depression, *Behaviour Research and Therapy*, 33: 41–8.

Haddock, G., Slade, P.D., Bentall, R.P. et al. (1998) A comparison of the long-term effectiveness of distreaction and focusing in the treatment of auditory hallucinations, *British Journal of Medical Psychology*, 71: 339–49.

Haines, J.L. and Pericak-Vance, M.A. (1999) Genetics of multiple sclerosis, *Current Directions in Autoimmunology*, 1: 273–88.

Hall, G.C.N. (1995) Sexual offender recidivism revisited: a meta-analysis of recent treatment studies, *Journal of Consulting and Clinical Psychology*, 63: 802–9.

Hanson, R.K. and Slater, S. (1988) Sexual victimization in the history of child sexual abusers: a review, *Annals of Sex Research*, 1: 485–99.

Hardy, G.E., Stiles, W.B., Barkham, M. et al. (1998) Therapist responsiveness to client interpersonal styles during time-limited treatments for depression, *Journal of Consulting and Clinical Psychology*, 66: 304–12.

Hardy, G., Aldridge, J., Davidson, C. et al. (1999) Therapist responsiveness to client attachment styles and issues observed in client-identified significant events in psychodynamic-interpersonal psychotherapy, *Psychotherapy Research*, 9: 36–53.

Hare, R.D. (1991) *The Hare Psychopathy Checklist-Revised (PCL-R)*. Toronto: Multi-Health Systems.

Hare, R.D., Clark, D., Grann, M. and Thornton, D. (2000) Psychopathy and the predictive utility of the PCL-R: an international perspective, *Behavioural Sciences and the Law*, 18: 623–45.

Harris, J.K., Godfrey, H.P., Partridge, F.M. et al. (2001) Caregiver depression following traumatic brain injury (TBI): a consequence of adverse effects on family members?, *Brain Injury*, 15: 223–38.

Haworth-Hoeppner, S. (2000) The critical shapes of body image: the role of culture and family in the production of eating disorders, *Journal of Marriage and the Family*, 62: 212–27.

Hawton, K. (1997) Attempted suicide, in D.M. Clark and C.G. Fairburn (eds) *Science and Practice of Cognitive Behaviour Therapy*. Oxford: Oxford University Press.

Hawton, K., Catalan, J. and Fagg, J. (1992) Sex therapy for erectile dysfunction: characteristics of couples, treatment outcome and prognostic factors, *Archives of Sexual Behavior*, 21: 161–75.

Hawton, K., Catalan, J., Martin, P. et al. (1986) Long-term outcome of sex therapy, *Behaviour Research and Therapy*, 24: 665–75.

Heather, N. (1995) The great controlled drinking consensus: is it premature?, *Addiction*, 90: 1160–3.

Heiman, J.R. and LoPiccolo, J. (1988) *Becoming Orgasmic*. London: Piatkus.

Hemmingsson, T., Lundberg, I., Romelsjo, A. et al. (1997) Alcoholism in social classes and occupations in Sweden, *International Journal of Epidemiology*, 26: 584–91.

Hendin, H. (1992) The psychodynamics of suicide, *International Review of Psychiatry*, 4: 157–67.

Henggeler, S.W., Melton, G.B. and Smith, L.A. (1992) Family preservation using multisystemic therapy: an effective alternative to incarcerating serious juvenile offenders, *Journal of Consulting and Clinical Psychology*, 60: 953–61.

Henry, D.B., Tolan, P.H. and Gorman-Smith, D. (2001) Longitudinal family and peer group effects on violence and nonviolent delinquency, *Journal of Clinical Child Psychology*, 30: 172–86.

Hermann, B.P. and Chabria, S. (1980) Interictal psycho-pathology in patients with ictal fear, *Archives of Neurology*, 37: 667–8.

Herz, M.I. and Melville, C. (1980) Relapse in schizophrenia, *American Journal of Psychiatry*, 137: 801–5.

Hettema, J.M., Neale, M.C. and Kendler, K.S. (2001a) A review and meta-analysis of the genetic epidemiology of anxiety disorders, *American Journal of Psychiatry*, 158: 1568–78.

Hettema, J.M., Prescott, C.A. and Kendler, K.S. (2001b) A population-based twin study of generalized anxiety disorder in men and women, *Journal of Nervous and Mental Disorders*, 189: 413–20.

Heumann, K.A. and Morey, L.C. (1990) Reliability of categorical and dimensional judgements of personality disorders, *American Journal of Psychiatry*, 147: 498–500.

Hibell, B., Andersson, B., Bjarnasson, T. et al. (1997) *The 1995 ESPAD Report: Alcohol and Other Drug Use Among Students in 26 European Countries*. Stockholm: Council of Europe Pompidou Group.

Hill, C.E., Nutt-Williams, E., Heaton, K.J. et al. (1996) Therapist retrospective recall of impasses in long-term psychotherapy: a qualitative analysis, *Journal of Counseling Psychology*, 43: 207–17.

Hill, P. (1998) Attention deficit hyperactivity disorder, *Archives of Diseases of Childhood*, 79: 381–5.

Hirschfeld, R.M.A. (1999) Efficacy of SSRIs and newer antidepressants in severe depression: comparison with TCAs, *Journal of Clinical Psychiatry*, 60: 326–35.

Hobfoll, S.E. (1989) Conservation of resources: a new attempt at conceptualising stress, *American Psychologist*, 44: 513–24.

Holden, U.P. and Woods, R.T. (1995) *Positive Approaches to Dementia Care*. Edinburgh: Churchill Livingstone.

Holen-Hoeksema, S. (1990) *Sex Difference in Depression*. Stanford, CA: Stanford University Press.

Hollander, E., DeCaria, C.M., Finkell, J.N. et al. (2000) A randomized double-blind fluvoxamine/placebo crossover trial in pathologic gambling, *Biological Psychiatry*, 47: 813–17.

Holmes, S. (2000) Treatment of male sexual dysfunction, *British Medical Bulletin*, 56: 798–808.

Horowitz, M.J. (1986) Stress-response syndromes: a review of posttraumatic and adjustment disorders, *Hospital and Community Psychiatry*, 37: 241–9.

Horowitz, M.J., Marmar, C.R., Weiss, D.S. et al. (1984) Brief psychotherapy of bereavement reactions: the relationship of process to outcome, *Archives of General Psychiatry*, 41: 438–48.

Horvath, A.O. and Luborksy, L. (1993) The role of the therapeutic alliance in psychotherapy, *Journal of Consulting and Clinical Psychology*, 61: 561–73.

Horvath, A.O. and Symonds, B.D. (1991) Relation between working alliance and outcome in psychotherapy: a meta-analysis, *Journal of Counseling Psychology*, 38: 139–49.

House, J.S., Kessler, R., Herzog, A.R. et al. (1991) Social stratification, age, and health, in K.W. Scheie, D. Blazer and J.S. House (eds) *Aging, Health Behaviours, and Health Outcomes*. Hillsdale, NJ: Erlbaum.

Hubbard, R.L., Craddock, S.G., Flynn, P.M. et al. (1997) Overview of 1-year follow-up outcomes in the Drug Abuse Treatment Outcome Study (DATOS), *Psychological Addiction and Behavior*, 4: 1303–10.

Huber, S.J., Bornstein, R.A., Rammohan, K.W. et al. (1992) Magnetic resonance imaging and correlates of neuropsychological impairment in multiple sclerosis, *Journal of Neuropsychiatry and Clinical Neurosciences*, 4: 152–8.

Hughes, J.C. and Cook, C. (1997) The efficacy of disulfram – a review of outcome studies, *Addictions*, 92: 381–96.

Hunter, E. (1997) Memory loss for childhood sexual abuse: distinguishing between encoding and retrieval factors, in D. Read and D.S. Lindsay (eds) *Recollections of Trauma: Scientific Research and Clinical Practice*. New York: Plenum.

Huppert, J.D., Bufka, L.F., Barlow, D.H. et al. (2001) Therapists, therapist variables and cognitive-behavioral therapy outcome in a multi-center trial for panic disorder, *Journal of Consulting and Clinical Psychology*, 69: 747–55.

Hyman, I.E., Husband, T.H. and Billings, F.J. (1995) False memories of childhood experiences, *Applied Cognitive Psychology*, 9: 181–97.

International Molecular Genetic Study of Autism Consortium (1998) A full genome screen for autism with evidence for linkage to a region on chromosome 7q, *Human Molecular Genetics*, 7: 571–8.

Intrator, J., Hare, R., Strizke, P. et al. (1997) A brain imaging (single photon emission computerized tomography) study of semantic and affective processing in psychopaths, *Biological Psychiatry*, 42: 96–103.

Ishihara, K. and Sasa, M. (1999) Mechanism underlying the therapeutic effects of electroconvulsive therapy (ECT) on depression, *Japanese Journal of Pharmacology*, 80: 185–9.

Jacobson, N.S. and Hollon, S.D. (1996) Cognitive-behavior therapy versus pharmacotherapy: now that the jury's returned its verdict, it's time to present the rest of the evidence, *Journal of Consulting and Clinical Psychology*, 64: 74–80.

Jaffee, S.R., Moffitt, T.E., Caspi, A. et al. (2002) Differences in early childhood risk factors for juvenile-onset and adult-onset depression, *Archives of General Psychiatry*, 59: 215–22.

Janssen, P.L. (1985) Psychodynamic study of male potency disorders: an overview, *Psychotherapy and Psychosomatics*, 44: 6–17.

Jenike, M.A. (1998) Neurosurgical treatment of obsessive-compulsive disorder, *British Medical Journal*, 163 (suppl. 35): 75–90.

Jenike, M.A., Ballantine, H.T., Martuza, R.L. et al. (1991) Cingulotomy for refractory obsessive-compulsive disorder: a long-term follow-up of 33 patients, *Archives of General Psychiatry*, 48: 548–55.

Jenkins, R.L., Lewis, G., Bebbington, P. et al. (1997) The National Psychiatric Morbidity Surveys of Great Britain: initial findings from the household survey, *Psychology and Medicine*, 27: 775–89.

Jenkins, R., Bebbington, P., Brugha, T.S. et al. (1998) British psychiatric morbidity survey, *British Journal of Psychiatry*, 173: 4–7.

Jennett, B. (1996) Epidemiology of head injury, *International Journal of Neurology, Neurosurgery and Psychiatry*, 60: 362–9.

Jennett, B., Snoek, F.J. and Bond, M.R. (1981) Disability after severe head injury: observations on the use of the Glasgow Outcome Scale, *Journal of Neurology, Neurosurgery and Psychiatry*, 44: 285–93.

Jick, S.S., Dean, A.D. and Jick, H. (1995) Antidepressants and suicide, *British Medical Journal*, 310: 215–18.

Jimerson, D.C., Herzog, D.B. and Brotman, A.W. (1993) Pharmacologic approaches in the treatment of eating disorders, *Harvard Review of Psychiatry*, 1: 82–93.

Johnston, M., Earll, L., Giles, M. et al. (1999) Mood as a predictor of disability and survival in patients newly diagnosed with ALS/MND, *British Journal of Health Psychology*, 4: 127–36.

Johnstone, L. (2000) *Users and Abusers of Psychiatry: A Critical Look at Psychiatric Practice*. London: Routledge.

Jones, C., Cormac, I., Mota, J. et al. (2000) Cognitive behaviour therapy for schizophrenia (Cochrane Review), in *The Cochrane Library*, issue 3. Oxford: Update Software.

Jones, P. and Cannon, M. (1998) The new epidemiology of schizophrenia, *Psychiatric Clinics of North America*, 21: 1–25.

Joseph, S., Dalgleish, T., Thrasher, S. et al. (1996) Crisis support following the Herald of Free-Enterprise disaster: a longitudinal perspective, *Journal of Traumatic Stress*, 9: 833–45.

Joseph, S., Williams, R. and Yule, W. (1995) Psychosocial perspectives on post-traumatic stress, *Clinical Psychology Review*, 15: 515–44.

Jung, C.G. ([1912] 1956) *Symbols of Transformation*. New York: Bollingen, no. 5. (Original edition published in 1912 as *The Psychology of the Unconscious*.)

Kabat-Zinn, J., Massion, A.O., Kristeller, J. et al. (1992) Effectiveness of a meditation-based stress reduction program in the treatment of anxiety disorders, *American Journal of Psychiatry*, 149: 936–43.

Kamann, M.P. and Wong, B.Y. (1993) Inducing adaptive coping self-statements in children with learning disabilities through self-instruction training, *Journal of Learning Disabilities*, 26: 630–8.

Karno, M., Golding, J.M., Sorensen, S.B. et al. (1988) The epidemiology of OCD in five US communities, *Archives of General Psychiatry*, 45: 1094–9.

Katan, M. (1953) Mania and the pleasure principle, in P. Greenacre (ed.) *Affective Disorders*. New York: International University Press.

Kawachi, I. and Berkman, L.F. (2001) Social ties and mental health, *Journal of Urban Health*, 78: 458–67.

Kaye, W.H., Klump, K.L., Frank, G.K. et al. (2001a) Anorexia and bulimia nervosa, *Annual Review of Medicine*, 51: 299–313.

Kaye, W.H., Nagata, T., Weltzin, T.E. et al. (2001b) Double-blind placebo-controlled administration of fluoxetine in restricting- and restricting-purging-type anorexia nervosa, *Biological Psychiatry*, 49: 644–52.

Keane, T.M., Fairbank, J.A., Caddell, J.M. et al. (1989) Implosive (flooding) therapy reduces the symptoms of PTSD in Vietnam combat veterans, *Behavior Therapy*, 20: 245–60.

Keesey, R.E. and Corbett, S.W. (1984) Metabolic defense of the body weight set-point, *Research Publications – Association of Research in Nervous and Mental Disease*, 62: 87–96.

Keijsers, G.P.J., Schaap, C.P.D.R. and Hoogduin, C.A.L. (2000) The impact of interpersonal patient and therapist behavior on outcome in cognitive-behavioral therapy: a review of empirical studies, *Behavior Modification*, 24: 264–97.

Keller, M.B., Klerman, G.L., Lavori, P.W. et al. (1984) Long-term outcome of episodes of major depression: clinical and public health significance, *Journal of the American Medical Association*, 252: 788–92.

Kelly, K.A. (1993) Multiple personality disorders: treatment coordination in a partial hospital setting, *Bulletin of the Menninger Clinic*, 57: 390–8.

Kendler, K.S., MacLean, C., Neale, M. et al. (1991) The genetic epidemiology of bulimia nervosa, *American Journal of Psychiatry*, 148: 1627–37.

Kendler, K.S., Neale, M.C., Kessler, R.C. et al. (1993) Panic disorder in women: a population-based twin study, *Psychological Medicine*, 40: 397–406.

Kernberg, O.F. (1985) *Borderline Conditions and Pathological Narcissism*. Northvale, NJ: Jason Aronson.

Kerns, A., Eso, K., Thomson, J. et al. (1999) Investigation of a direct intervention for improving attention in young children with ADHD, *Developmental Neuropsychology*, 16: 273–95.

Kessler, R.C., Sonnega, A., Bromet, E. et al. (1995) Posttraumatic stress disorder in the national comorbidity survey, *Archives of General Psychiatry*, 52: 1048–60.

Kety, S.S., Rosenthal, D., Wender, P.H. et al. (1975) Mental illness in the biological and adoptive families of adopted individual who become schizophrenic: a preliminary report based on psychiatric interviews, in R.R. Fieve, D. Rosenthal and H. Brill (eds) *Genetic Research in Psychiatry*. Baltimore, MD: Johns Hopkins University Press.

Kiehl, K.A., Smith, A.M., Hare, R.D. et al. (2001) Limbic abnormalities in affective processing by criminal psychopaths as revealed by functional magnetic resonance imaging, *Biological Psychiatry*, 50: 677–84.

Klein, M. (1927) The psychological principles of infant analysis, *International Journal of Psychoanalysis*, 8: 25–37.

Kluft, R.P. (1994) Multiple personality disorder: observations on the etiology, natural history, recognition, and resolution of a long-neglected condition, in R. Klein and B.K. Doane (eds) *Psychological Concepts and Dissociative Disorders*. Hillsdale, NJ: Erlbaum.

Kluft, R.P. (1999) An overview of the psychotherapy of dissociative identity disorder, *American Journal of Psychotherapy*, 53: 289–319.

Klump, K.L., Miller, K.B., Keel, P.K. et al. (2001) Genetic and environmental influences on anorexia nervosa syndromes in a population-based twin sample, *Psychological Medicine*, 31: 737–40.

Knight, B.G., Lutzsky, S.M. and Macofsky-Urban, F. (1992) A meta-analytic review of interventions for care-giver distress: recommendations for future research, *Gerontologist*, 33: 475–8.

Knivsberg, A.M., Reichelt, K.L., Høien, T. et al. (1998) Parents' observations after one year of dietary intervention for children with autistic syndromes, *Psychobiology of Autism: Current Research and Practice*, 13–24.

Koegel, R.L., O'Dell, M.C. and Dunlap, G. (1988) Producing speech use in nonverbal autistic children by reinforcing attempts, *Journal of Autism and Developmental Disorders*, 18: 525–38.

Koegel, R.L., Koegel, L.K. and McNerney, E.K. (2001) Pivotal areas in intervention for autism, *Journal of Clinical Child Psychology*, 30: 19–32.

Korten, A.E., Jorm, A.F., Henderson, A.S. et al. (1993) Assessing the risk of Alzheimer's disease in first-degree relatives of Alzheimer's disease cases, *Psychological Medicine*, 23: 915–23.

Kovach, C. (1990) Promise and problems in reminiscence research, *Journal of Gerontological Nursing*, 16: 10–14.

Kownacki, R.J. and Shadish, W.R. (1999) Does Alcoholics Anonymous work? The results from a meta-analysis of controlled experiments, *Substance Use and Misuse*, 34: 1897–1916.

Kraepelin, E. ([1883] 1981) *Clinical Psychiatry* (trans. A.R. Diefendorf). Delmar, NY: Scholar's Facsimiles and Reprints.

Kringlen, E. (1993) Genes and environment in mental illness: perspectives and ideas for future research, *Acta Psychiatrica Scandinavica*, 370: 79–84.

Kulka, R.A., Schlenger, W.E., Fairbank, J.A. et al. (1990) *Trauma and the Vietnam War Generation: Report of Findings from the National Vietnam Veterans Readjustment Study*. New York: Brunner/Mazel.

Laakso, M.P., Vaurio, O., Koivisto, E. et al. (2001) Psychopathy and the posterior hippocampus, *Behaviour Brain Research*, 118: 187–93.

Ladouceur, R., Jacques, C., Ferland, F. et al. (1999) Prevalence of problem gambling: a replication study 7 years later, *Canadian Journal of Psychiatry*, 44: 802–4.

Ladouceur, R., Sylvain, C., Boutin, C. et al. (2001) Cognitive treatment of pathological gambling, *Journal of Nervous and Mental Disease*, 189: 774–80.

Larcombe, N.A. and Wilson, P.H. (1984) An evaluation of cognitive-behaviour therapy for depression in patients with multiple sclerosis, *British Journal of Psychiatry*, 145: 366–71.

Laumann, E.O., Paik, A. and Rosen, R. (1999) Sexual dysfunction in the United States: prevalence and predictors, *Journal of the American Medical Association*, 21: 537–44.

Lawford, B.R., Young, R., Rowell, J.A. et al. (1997) D2 dopamine receptor A1 allele with alcoholism: medical severity of alcoholism and type of controls, *Biological Psychiatry*, 41: 386–93.

Laws, D.R. and Marshall, W.L. (1991) Masturbatory reconditioning with sexual deviates: an evaluative review, *Advances in Behavior Research and Therapy*, 13: 13–25.

Lechtenberg, R. (1988) *Multiple Sclerosis Fact Book*. Philadelphia, PA: F.A. Davis.

Leff, J. and Vaughn, C. (1985) *Expressed Emotions in Families: Its Significance for Mental Illness*. New York: Guilford.

Lenox, R.H., McNamara, R.F., Papke, R.L. et al. (1998) Neurobiology of lithium: an update, *Journal of Clinical Psychiatry*, 59 (suppl. 6): 37–47.

Leskin, G.A., Kaloupek, D.G. and Keane, T.M. (1998) Treatment for traumatic memories: review and recommendations, *Clinical Psychology Review*, 18: 983–1002.

Levin, H.S. (1993) Neurobehavioral sequelae of closed head injury, in P.R. Cooper (ed.) *Head Injury*. Baltimore, MD: Williams & Wilkins.

Lewinsohn, P.M. (1988) A prospective study of risk factors for unipolar depression, *Journal of Abnormal Psychology*, 97: 251–84.

Lewinsohn, P.M., Youngren, M.A. and Grosscup, S.J. (1979) Reinforcement and depression, in A. Depue (ed.) *The Psychobiology of the Depressive Disorders*. New York: Academic Press.

Lewy, A.J., Bauer, V.K. and Cutler, N.L. (1998) Morning vs evening light treatment of patients with winter depression, *Archives of General Psychiatry*, 55: 890–6.

Ley, P. (1997) Compliance among patients, in A. Baum, S. Newman, J. Weinman et al. (eds) *Cambridge Handbook of Psychology, Health and Medicine*. Cambridge: Cambridge University Press.

Liau, A.K., Barriga, A.Q. and Gibbs, J.C. (1998) Relations between self-serving cognitive distortions and overt vs. covert antisocial behavior in adolescents, *Aggressive Behavior*, 24: 335–46.

Liddle, P., Carpenter, W.T. and Crow, T. (1994) Syndromes of schizophrenia: classic literature, *British Journal of Psychiatry*, 165: 721–7.

Lieberman, J.A., Kinon, B.J. and Loebel, A.D. (1990) Dopaminergic mechanisms in idiopathic and drug-induced psychoses, *Schizophrenia Bulletin*, 16: 97–109.

Linde, K. and Mulrow, C.D. (2002) St John's wort for depression, *Cochrane Database of Systematic Reviews*, issue 1.

Linehan, M.M., Heard, H.L. and Armstrong, H.E. (1993) Naturalistic follow-up of a behavioral treatment for chronically parasuicidal borderline patients, *Archives of General Psychiatry*, 50: 971–4.

Lingjaerde, O., Ahlfors, U.G., Bech, P. et al. (1987) The UKU side effect rating scale: a new comprehensive rating scale for psychotropic drugs and a cross-sectional study of side effects in neuroleptic-treated patients, *Acta Psychiatrica Scandinavica*, 334: 1–100.

Lipinski, J.F., Mallya, G., Zimmerman, P. et al. (1989) Fluoxetine-induced akathisia: clinical and theoretical implications, *Journal of Clinical Psychiatry*, 59: 339–42.

Lipton, A.A. and Simon, F.S. (1985) Psychiatric diagnosis in a state hospital: Manhattan state revisited, *Hospital and Community Psychiatry*, 36: 368–73.

Lisanby, S.H., Maddox, J.H., Prudic, J. et al. (2000) The effects of Electroconvulsive Therapy on memory of autobiographical and public events, *Archives of General Psychiatry*, 57: 581–90.

Lloyd, G.G. and Lishman, W.A. (1975) Effect of depression on the speed of recall of pleasant and unpleasant experiences, *Psychological Medicine*, 5: 173–80.

Loebel, J.P., Loebel, J.S., Dager, S.R. et al. (1991) Anticipation of nursing home placement may be a precipitant of suicide among the elderly, *Journal of the American Geriatric Society*, 39: 407–8.

Loewe, B., Zipfel, S., Buchholz, C. et al. (2001) Long-term outcome of anorexia nervosa in a prospective 21-year follow-up study, *Psychological Medicine*, 31: 881–90.

Loftus, E.F. and Coan, D. (1998) The construction of childhood memories, in D. Peters (ed.) *The Child Witness in Context: Cognitive, Social, and Legal Perspectives*. New York: Kluwer.

Loftus, E.F. and Ketcham, K. (1994) *The Myth of Repressed Memory*. New York: St Martin's Press.

Longabaugh, R. and Morgenstern, J. (2000) Cognitive-behavioral coping skills therapy for alcohol dependence: current status and future directions, *Alcohol Research and Health*, 23: 78–87.

Lopez, V.A. and Emmer, E.T. (2002) Influences of beliefs and values on male adolescents' decision to commit violent offenses, *Psychology of Men and Masculinity*, 3: 28–40.

Loranger, A.W., Sartorius, N., Andreoli, A. et al. (1994) The International Personality Disorders Examination: the World Health Organisation/Alcohol, Drug Abuse and Mental Health Administration international study of personality disorders, *Archives of General Psychiatry*, 51: 215–23.

Lovaas, O.I. (1987) Behavioral treatment and normal educational and intellectual functioning in young autistic children, *Journal of Consulting and Clinical Psychology*, 55: 3–9.

Lundberg, U., de Chateau, P., Weinberg, J. et al. (1981) Catecholamine and cortisol excretion patterns in three year old children and their parents, *Journal of Human Stress*, 7: 3–11.

Lyon, H.M., Startup, M. and Bentall, R.P. (1999) Social cognition and the manic defense: attributions, selective attention, and self-schema in bipolar affective disorder, *Journal of Abnormal Psychology*, 108: 273–82.

Lyon-Caen, O., Jouvent, R., Hauser, S. et al. (1986) Cognitive function in recent-onset demyelinating diseases, *Archives of Neurology*, 43: 1138–41.

McBride, P.A., Anderson, G.M. and Shapiro, T. (1996) Autism research: bringing together approaches to pull apart the disorder, *Archives of General Psychiatry*, 53: 980–3.

McCall, W.V. (2001) Electroconvulsive therapy in the era of modern psychopharmacology, *International Journal of Neuropsychopharmacology*, 4: 315–24.

McClure, G.M. (2000) Changes in suicide in England and Wales, 1960–1997, *British Journal of Psychiatry*, 176: 64–7.

McConaghy, N., Armstrong, M.S., Blaszczynski, A. et al. (1983) Controlled comparison of aversive therapy and imaginal desensitization in compulsive gambling, *British Journal of Psychiatry*, 142: 366–72.

McConaghy, N., Blaszczynski, A. and Frankova, A. (1991) Comparison of imaginal desensitization with other behavioural treatments of pathological gambling: a two to nine year follow-up, *British Journal of Psychiatry*, 159: 390–3.

McDougle, C.J., Naylor, S.T., Volkmar, F.R. et al. (1994) A double-blind, placebo-controlled investigation of fluvoxamine in adults with autism, *Society for Neuroscience Abstracts*, 20: 396.

McDowell, I. (2001) Alzheimer's disease: insights from epidemiology, *Aging*, 13: 143–62.

McGuffin, P., Katz, R., Watkins, S. et al. (1996) A hospital-based twin register of the heritability of DSM-IV unipolar depression, *Archives of General Psychiatry*, 53: 129–36.

McKenzie, S.J., Williamson, D.A. and Cubic, B.A. (1993) Stable and reactive body image disturbances in bulimia nervosa, *Behavior Therapy*, 24: 195–207.

McLean, P.D., Whittal, M.L., Thordarson, D.S. et al. (2001) Cognitive versus behavior therapy in the group treatment of obsessive-compulsive disorder, *Journal of Consulting and Clinical Psychology*, 69: 205–14.

McMahon, A. and Rhudick, P. (1964) Reminiscing, *Archives of General Psychiatry*, 10: 292–8.

Madden, P.A.F., Heath, A.C., Rosenthal, N.E. et al. (1996) Seasonal changes in mood and behavior: the role of genetic factors, *Archives of General Psychiatry*, 53: 47–55.

Maes, S., Verhoeven, C., Kittel, F. et al. (1998) Effects of the Brabantia-project, a Dutch wellness-health programme at the worksite, *American Journal of Public Health*, 88: 1037–41.

Mahmood, T. and Silverstone, T. (2001) Serotonin and bipolar disorder, *Journal of Affective Disorders*, 66: 1–11.

Malizia, A.L. (2000) Neurosurgery for psychiatric disorders, in M.G. Gelder, J.J. Lopez-Ibor Jr and N.C. Andreasen (eds) *New Oxford Textbook of Psychiatry*. Oxford: Oxford University Press.

Malizia, A.L. and Bridges, P.K. (1991) The management of treatment resistant affective disorders: clinical perspectives, *Journal of Psychopharmacology*, 6: 145–55 and 172–5.

Mannuzza, S. and Klein, R.G. (2000) Long-term prognosis in attention-deficit/hyperactivity disorder, *Child and Adolescent Psychiatric Clinics of North America*, 9: 711–26.

Marks, I., Gelder, M. and Bancroft, J. (1970) Sexual deviants two years after electric shock aversion, *British Journal of Psychiatry*, 117: 173–85.

Marks, I., Lovell, K., Noshirvani, H. et al. (1996) Treatment of post-traumatic stress disorder by exposure and/or cognition restructuring, *Archives of General Psychiatry*, 55: 317–25.

Marmar, C.R. (1991) Brief dynamic psychotherapy for post-traumatic stress disorder, *Psychiatric Annals*, 21: 405–14.

Marmot, M.G., Smith, G.D., Stansfeld, S. et al. (1991) Health inequalities among British civil servants: the Whitehall II study, *Lancet*, 337: 1387–93.

Marques, J.K., Nelson, C., Alaarcon, J-M. and Day, D.M. (2000) Preventing relapse in sex offenders: what we learned from SOTEP's experimental treatment program, in D.R. Laws, S.M. Hudson and T. Ward (eds) *Remaking Relapse Prevention with Sex Offenders. A Sourcebook*. Thousand Oaks, CA: Sage.

Marshall, W.L. (1994) Treatment effects on denial and minimization in incarcerated sex offenders, *Behaviour Research and Therapy*, 32: 559–64.

Maslow, A.H. (1970) *Motivation and Personality*, New York: Harper & Row.

Masters, W.H. and Johnson, V.E. (1970) *Human Sexual Inadequacy*. Boston, MA: Little, Brown.

Matano, R.A., Futa, K.T., Wanat, S.F. et al. (2000) The Employee Stress and Alcohol Project: the development of a computer-based alcohol abuse prevention program for employees, *Journal of Behavioral Health Service Research*, 27: 152–65.

Meichenbaum, D. (1985) *Stress Inoculation Training*. New York: Pergamon.

Meltzer, H.Y. (1998) Suicide in schizophrenia: risk factors and clozapine treatment, *Archives of General Psychiatry*, 52: 200–2.

Merskey, H. (1992) The manufacture of personalities: the production of multiple personality disorder, *British Journal of Psychiatry*, 160: 327–40.

Meyer, R.E. (1995) Biology of psychoactive substance dependence disorders: opiates, cocaine, ethanol, in A.F. Schatzberg and C.B. Nemeroff (eds) *The American Psychiatric Press Handbook of Psychopharmacology*. Washington, DC: American Psychiatric Press.

Meyer-Bahlung, H. (1979) Sex hormones and female homosexuality: a critical examination, *Archives of Sexual Behavior*, 8: 101–19.

Miles, C., Green, R., Sanders, G. et al. (1998) Estrogen and memory in a transsexual population, *Hormones and Behavior*, 34: 199–208.

Miller, W.R. and Rollnick, S. (2002) *Motivational Interviewing*, 2nd edn. New York: Guilford.

Minden, S.L. and Schiffer, R.B. (1990) Affective disorders in multiple sclerosis: review and recommendations for clinical research, *Archives of Neurology*, 47: 98–104.

Minuchin, S. (1974) *Families and Family Therapy*. London: Tavistock.

Minuchin, S., Rosman, B. and Baker, L. (1978) *Psychosomatic Families: Anorexia Nervosa in Context*. Cambridge, MA: Harvard University Press.

Miranda, J. and Gross, J.J. (1997) Cognitive vulnerability depression, and the mood-state dependent hypothesis: is it out of sight out of mind? *Cognition and Emotion*, 11: 585–605.

Modestin, J. (1992) Multiple personality disorder in Switzerland, *American Journal of Psychiatry*, 149: 88–92.

Mohr, D.C. and Goodkin, D.E. (1999) Treatment of depression in multiple sclerosis: review and meta-analysis, *Clinical Psychology: Science and Practice*, 6: 1–9.

Mohr, D.C., Goodkin, D.E., Bacchetti, P. et al. (2000a) Psychological stress and the subsequent appearance of new brain MRI lesions in MS, *Neurology*, 55: 55–61.

Mohr, D.C., Likosky, W., Bertagnolli, A. et al. (2000b) Telephone-administered cognitive-behavioral therapy for the treatment of depressive symptoms in multiple sclerosis, *Journal of Consulting and Clinical Psychology*, 68: 356–61.

Montgomery, S.A., Dufour, H., Brion, S. et al. (1993) Guidelines for treatment of depressive illness with antidepressants, *Journal of Psychopharmacology*, 7: 19–23.

Monti, P.M., Colby, S.M., Barnett, N.P. et al. (1999) Brief intervention for harm reduction with alcohol-positive older adolescents in a hospital emergency department, *Journal of Consulting and Clinical Psychology*, 67: 989–94.

Moos, R.H., Cronkite, R.C. and Moos, B.S. (1998) Family and extrafamily resources and the 10-year course of treated depression, *Journal of Abnormal Psychology*, 107: 450–60.

Morton, J., Andrews, B., Bekerian, D. et al. (1995) *Recovered Memories*. Leicester: British Psychological Society.

Mowrer, O.H. (1947) On the dual nature of learning: a reinterpretation of 'conditioning' and 'problem-solving', *Harvard Education Review*, 17: 102–48.

Murphy, K. and Barkley, R.A. (1996) Attention deficit hyperactivity disorder adults: comorbidities and adaptive impairments, *Comprehensive Psychiatry*, 37: 393–401.

Murphy, P.M., Cramer, D. and Lillie, F.J. (1984) The relationship between curative factors perceived by patients in their psychotherapy and treatment outcome: an exploratory study, *British Journal of Medical Psychology*, 57: 187–92.

Murray, J.B. (2000) Psychological profiles of pedophiles and child molesters, *Journal of Psychology*, 134: 211–24.

Myers, E.D. and Branthwaite, A. (1992) Out-patient compliance with anti-depressant medication, *British Journal of Psychiatry*, 160: 83–6.

Najavitis, L.M., Gastfriend, D.R., Barber, J.P. et al. (1998) Cocaine dependence with and without PTSD among subjects in the National Institute on Drug Abuse collaboration cocaine treatment study, *American Journal of Psychiatry*, 155: 214–19.

National Institutes of Health (1985) Electroconvulsive therapy, *NIH Consensus Statement Online*, 5: 1–23.

Nazroo, J.Y. (1998) *Genetic, Cultural or Socio-economic Vulnerability? Explaining Ethnic Inequalities in Health*. Oxford: Blackwell.

Neisser, U. and Harsch, N. (1992) Phantom flashbulbs: false recollections of hearing the news about Challenger, in E. Winograd and U. Neisser (eds) *Affect and Accuracy in Recall: Studies in Flashbulb Memories*. Cambridge: Cambridge University Press.

Neumeister, A., Praschak-Rieder, N., Hesselmann, B. et al. (1997) Rapid tryptophan depletion in drug-free depressed patients with seasonal affective disorder, *American Journal of Psychiatry*, 154: 1153–5.

Newcomb, M.D. (1985) The role of perceived relative parent personality in the development of heterosexuals, homosexuals, and transvestites, *Archives of Sexual Behavior*, 14: 147–64.

NIH Consensus Development Panel (1991) Rehabilitation of persons with traumatic brain injury, *Journal of the American Medical Association*, 282: 974–83.

NIH Consensus Development Panel on Effective Treatment of Opiate Addiction (1998) Effective medical treatment of opiate addiction, *Journal of the American Medical Association*, 280: 1936–43.

NIH Consensus Development Panel on Rehabilitation of Persons with Traumatic Brain Injury (1999) Rehabilitation of persons with traumatic brain injury, *Journal of the American Medical Association*, 282: 974–83.

Nutt, D.J. and Law, F.D. (2000) Pharmacological and psychological aspects of drugs of abuse, in M.G. Gelder, J.J. Lopez-Ibor Jr and N.C. Andreasen (eds) *New Oxford Textbook of Psychiatry*. Oxford: Oxford University Press.

O'Connor, T.G., Deater-Deckard, K., Fulker, D. et al. (1998) Genotype–environment correlations in late childhood and early adolescence: antisocial behavioral problems and coercive parenting, *Developmental Psychology*, 34: 970–81.

O'Farrell, T.J. and Fals-Stewart, W. (2000) Behavioral couples therapy for alcoholism and drug abuse, *Journal of Drug Abuse Treatment*, 18: 51–4.

Oie, T. and Shuttlewood, G.J. (1995) Comparison of specific and non-specific factors in a group cognitive therapy for depression, *Journal of Behaviour Therapy and Experimental Psychiatry*, 28: 221–31.

Oke, S. and Kanigsberg, E. (1991) Occupational therapy in the treatment of individuals with multiple personality disorder, *Canadian Journal of Occupational Therapy*, 58: 234–40.

Oldenburg, B. and Harris, D. (1996) The workplace as a setting for promoting health and preventing disease, *Homeostasis in Health and Disease*, 37: 226–32.

O'Malley, S.S., Foley, S.H., Rounsaville, B.J. et al. (1988) Therapist competence and patient outcome in interpersonal psychotherapy of depression, *Journal of Consulting and Clinical Psychology*, 56: 496–501.

Oppenheimer, R., Howells, K., Palmer, R.L. et al. (1985) Adverse sexual experience in childhood and clinical eating disorders: a preliminary description, *Journal of Psychiatric Research*, 19: 357–61.

Orlinsky, D.E. and Howard, K.I. (1986) Process and outcome in psychotherapy, in A.E. Bergin and S.L. Garfield (eds) *Handbook of Psychotherapy and Behavior Change*, 4th edn. New York: Wiley.

Ovesey, L. and Person, E. (1973) Gender identity and sexual pathology in men: a psychodynamic analysis of heterosexuality, transsexualism, and transvestism, *Journal of the American Academy of Psychoanalysis*, 1: 53–72.

Owen, M., Liddell, M. and McGuffin, P. (1994) Alzheimer's disease, *British Medical Journal*, 308: 672–3.

Palumbo, R., Fontanillas, L., Salmaggi, A. et al. (1998) Stressful life events and multiple sclerosis: a retrospective study, *Italian Journal of Neurological Sciences*, 19: 259–60.

Paris, J. (1991) Personality disorders, parasuicide, and culture, *Transcultural Psychiatric Research*, 28: 25–39.

Paris, J. (1996) Antisocial personality disorder: a biopsychosocial model, *Canadian Journal of Psychiatry*, 41: 75–80.

Paris, J. and Zweig-Frank, H. (2001) A 27-year follow-up of patients with borderline personality disorder, *Comprehensive Psychiatry*, 42: 482–7.

Park, N.W., Proulx, G.B. and Towers, W.M. (1999) Evaluation of the Attention Process Training programme, *Neuropsychological Rehabilitation*, 9: 135–54.

Parker, G. (1981) Parental representations of patients with anxiety neurosis, *Acta Psychiatrica Scandinavica*, 63: 33–6.

Parker, G. and Lawton, D. (1990) *Further Analysis of the 1985 General Household Survey Data on Informal Care. Report 1: A Typology of Caring*, Working Paper DHSS 716, 12.90. York: Social Policy Research Unit, University of York.

Partonen, T. and Lonnqvist, J. (1998) Seasonal affective disorder, *Lancet*, 352: 1369–74.

Pato, M.T., Zohar-Kadouch, R., Zohar, J. et al. (1988) Return of symptoms after discontinuation of clomipramine in patients with obsessive compulsive disorder, *American Journal of Psychiatry*, 145: 1521–5.

Pavlov, I.P. ([1927] 1960) *Conditioned Reflexes* (ed. and trans. G.V. Anrep). New York: Dover.

Paykel, E.S. (1994) Life events, social support and depression, *Acta Psychiatrica Scandinavica*, 377: 50–8.

Peele, S. (1992) Alcoholism, politics, and bureaucracy: the consensus against controlled-drinking therapy in America, *Addictive Behaviors*, 17: 49–62.

Pelham, W.E., Carlson, C., Sams, S.E. et al. (1993) Separate and combined effects of methylphenidate and behavior modification on boys with attention deficit/hyperactivity in the classroom, *Journal of Consulting and Clinical Psychology*, 61: 506–15.

Peralta, V. and Cuesta, M.J. (1992) Influence of cannabis abuse on schizophrenic psychopathology, *Acta Psychiatrica Scandinavica*, 85: 127–30.

Perreira, K.M. and Sloan, F. (2001) Life events and alcohol consumption among mature adults: a longitudinal analysis, *Journal of Studies on Alcohol*, 62: 501–8.

Pharoah, F.M., Mari, J.J. and Streiner, D. (2000) Family intervention for schizophrenia (Cochrane Review), in *The Cochrane Library*, issue 4. Oxford: Update Software.

Piaget, J. (1954) *The Child's Construction of Reality*. London: Routledge & Kegan Paul.

Pike, K.M. (1998) Long-term course of anorexia nervosa: response, relapse, remission, and recovery, *Clinical Psychology Review*, 18: 447–75.

Pike, M.J. and Rodin, J. (1991) Mothers, daughters, and disordered eating, *Journal of Abnormal Psychology*, 100: 198–204.

Pinkston, E.M., Linsk, N.L. and Young, R.N. (1988) Home-based behavioral family therapy treatment of the impaired elderly, *Behavior Therapy*, 19: 331–44.

Piper, W.E., Azim, H.F.A., Joyce, A.S. et al. (1991) Quality of object relations vs interpersonal functioning as a predictor of the therapeutic alliance and psychotherapy outcome, *Journal of Nervous and Mental Disease*, 179: 432–8.

Piper, W.E., Joyce, A.S., McCallum, M. et al. (1993) Concentration and correspondence of transference interpretations in short-term psychotherapy, *Journal of Consulting and Clinical Psychology*, 61: 586–95.

Piper, W.E., McCallum, M., Joyce, A.S. et al. (1999a) Follow-up findings for interpretive and supportive forms of therapy and patient personality variables, *Journal of Consulting and Clinical Psychology*, 67: 267–73.

Piper, W.E., Ogrodniczuk, J.S., Joyce, A.S. et al. (1999b) Prediction of dropping out in time-limited, interpretive individual psychotherapy, *Psychotherapy*, 36: 114–22.

Piper, W.E., McCallum, M. and Joyce, A.S. (2001) Patient personality and time: limited outcome in short-term individual psychotherapy, *International Journal of Group Psychotherapy*, 51: 525–52.

Pithers, W.D. (1990) Relapse prevention with sexual aggressors: a method for maintaining therapeutic gain and enhancing external supervision, in W.L. Marshall, D.R. Laws and H.E. Barbaree (eds) *Handbook of Sexual Assault: Issues, Theories, and Treatment of the Offender*. New York: Plenum.

Pols, R. and Hawks, D. (1991) *Is there a Safe Level of Daily Consumption of Alcohol for Men and Women?* Canberra: Australian Government Publishing Service.

Potenza, M.N. (2001) The neurobiology of pathological gambling, *Seminars in Clinical Neuropsychiatry*, 6: 217–26.

Powell, G.E. and Lindsay, S.J.E. (1994) *The Handbook of Clinical Adult Psychology*. London: Routledge.

Power, K.G., Simpson, R.J., Swanson, V. et al. (1990) A controlled study of cognitive behavior therapy, diazepam, and placebo in the management of generalised anxiety, *Behavioural Psychotherapy*, 17: 10–14.

Prescott, C.A. and Kendler, K.S. (1999) Genetic and environmental contributions to alcohol abuse and dependence in a population-based sample of male twins, *American Journal of Psychiatry*, 156: 34–40.

Price, V.A. (1982) *Type A Behavior Pattern: A Model for Research and Practice*. New York: Academic Press.

Productivity Commission (1999) *Australia's Gambling Industries: Inquiry Report*. Melbourne: Productivity Commission.

Project MATCH Research Group (1998) Matching alcoholism treatments to client heterogeneity: project MATCH three-year drinking outcomes, *Alcoholism: Clinical and Experimental Research*, 22: 1300–11.

Quinsey, V.I., Harris, G.T. and Rice, M.E. (1995) Actuarial prediction of sexual recidivism, *Journal of Interpersonal Violence*, 10: 85–105.

Rachman, S.J. and de Silva, P. (1978) Abnormal and normal obsessions, *Behaviour Research and Therapy*, 16: 233–8.

Raine, A., Reynolds, C. and Venables, P.H. (1998) Fearlessness, stimulation-seeking, and large body size at 3 years as early predispositions to childhood aggression at age 11 years, *Archives of General Psychiatry*, 55: 745–51.

Raine, A., Lencz, T., Bihrle, S. et al. (2000) Reduced prefrontal gray matter volume and reduced autonomic activity in antisocial personality disorder, *Archives of General Psychiatry*, 57: 119–27.

Ralph, D. and McNicholas, T. (2000) UK management guidelines for erectile dysfunction, *British Medical Journal*, 321: 499–503.

Rampello, L., Nicoletti, F. and Nicoletti, F. (2000) Dopamine and depression: therapeutic implications, *CNS Drugs*, 13: 35–45.

Rapee, R., Mattick, R. and Murrell, E. (1986) Cognitive mediation of anxiety and panic: a cognitive account, *Journal of Behavior Therapy and Experimental Psychiatry*, 17: 245–53.

Raskin, M., Peeke, H.Y., Dickman, W. et al. (1982) Panic and generalized anxiety disorders. Developmental antecedents and precipitants, *Archives of General Psychiatry*, 39: 687–9.

Reed, G.F. (1985) *Obsessional Experience and Compulsive Behaviour*. London: Academic Press.

Reeve, W. and Ivison, D. (1985) Use of environmental manipulation and classroom and modified informal reality orientation with institutionalized, confused elderly patients, *Age and Ageing*, 14: 119–21.

Regier, D.A., Rae, D.S., Narrow, W.E. et al. (1998) Prevalence of anxiety disorders and their comorbidity with mood and addictive disorders, *British Journal of Psychiatry*, 173 (suppl. 34): 24–6.

Reichelt, K.L., Knivsberg, A.M., Lind, G. et al. (1991) Probable etiology and possible treatment of childhood autism, *Brain Dysfunction*, 4: 308–19.

Reid, W.H. and Gacono, C. (2000) Treatment of antisocial personality, psychopathy, and other characterologic antisocial syndromes, *Behavioral Science and Law*, 18: 647–62.

Reimers, T.M., Wacker, D.P., Cooper, L.J. et al. (1992) Clinical evaluation of the variables associated with treatment acceptability and their relation to compliance, *Behavioral Disorders*, 18: 67–76.

Reimherr, F.W., Wender, P.H., Wood, D.R. et al. (1987) An open trial of l-tyrosine in the treatment of attention deficit disorder, residual type, *American Journal of Psychiatry*, 144: 1071–3.

Rekers, G.A. and Lovaas, O.I. (1974) Behavioral treatment of deviant sex role behaviours in a male child, *Journal of Applied Behavioral Analysis*, 7: 173–90.

Remafedi, G., French, S., Story, M. et al. (1998) The relationship between suicide risk and sexual orientation: results of a population-based study, *American Journal of Public Health*, 88: 57–60.

Revill, S. and Blunden, R. (1977) *Home Training of Pre-school Children with Developmental Delay: Report of the Development and Evaluation of the Portage Service in South Glamorgan.* Cardiff: Mental Handicap in Wales Applied Research Unit.

Rey, J.M., Walter, G., Plapp, J.M. et al. (2000) Family environment in attention deficit hyperactivity, oppositional defiant and conduct disorders, *Australia and New Zealand Journal of Psychiatry*, 34: 453–7.

Rice, M.E., Quinsey, V.L. and Harris, G.T. (1991) Sexual recidivism among child molesters released from a maximum security psychiatric institution, *Journal of Consulting and Clinical Psychology*, 59: 381–6.

Rice, M.E., Harris, G.T. and Cormier, C.A. (1992) An evaluation of a maximum security therapeutic community for psychopaths and other mentally disordered offenders, *Law and Human Behavior*, 16: 399–412.

Rieker, P.P. and Bird, C.E. (2000) Sociological explanations of gender differences in mental and physical health, in C.E. Bird, P. Conrad and A.M. Fremont (eds) *Handbook of Medical Sociology.* Upper Saddle River, NJ: Prentice Hall.

Ritsher, J.E.B., Warner, V., Johnson, J.G. et al. (2001) Inter-generation longitudinal study of social class and depression: a test of social causation and social selection models, *British Journal of Psychiatry*, 178 (suppl 40): s84–s90.

Roberts, J.S. (2000) Schizophrenia epigenesis?, *Theoretical Medicine and Bioethics*, 21: 191–215.

Robin, A.L., Siegel, P.T. and Moye, A. (1995) Family therapy versus individual therapy for anorexia: impact on family conflict, *International Journal of Eating Disorders*, 17: 313–22.

Robins, L.N., Helzer, J.E., Croughan, J. et al. (1981) National Institute of Mental Health Diagnostic Interview Schedule. Its history, characteristics, and validity. *Archives of General Psychiatry*, 38: 381–9.

Roca, W., Cha, R. and Waring, S. (1998) Incidence of Dementia and Alzheimer's Disease: a reanalysis of data from Rochester, Minnesota, 1975–1984, *American Journal of Epidemiology*, 48: 51–2.

Rocca, P., Fonzo, V., Scotta, M. et al. (1997) Paroxetine efficacy in the treatment of generalized anxiety disorder, *Acta Psychiatrica Scandinavica*, 95: 444–50.

Roeleveld, N., Zielhuis, G.A. and Gabreels, F. (1997) The prevalence of mental retardation: a critical review of recent literature, *Developmental Medicine and Child Neurology*, 39: 125–32.

Rogers, C.R. (1961) *On Becoming a Person*. Boston, MA: Houghton Mifflin.

Rogers, S.L., Farlow, M.R., Doody, R.S. et al. (1998) A 24-week, double-blind, placebo-controlled trial of donepezil in patients with Alzheimer's disease, *Neurology*, 50: 136–45.

Roggla, H. and Uhl, A. (1995) Depression and relapses in treated alcoholic alcoholics, *International Journal of Addictions*, 30: 337–49.

Romme, M.A. and Escher, A.D. (1989) Hearing voices, *Schizophrenia Bulletin*, 15: 209–16.

Rooney, B., McClelland, L., Crisp, A.H. et al. (1995) The incidence and prevalence of anorexia nervosa in three suburban health districts in south west London, U.K., *International Journal of Eating Disorders*, 18: 299–307.

Rose, S., Lewontin, R.C. and Kamin, L.J. (1984) *Not in our Genes: Biology, Ideology, and Human Nature*. New York: Penguin.

Rose, S., Bisson, J. and Wessely, W. (2002) Psychological debriefing for preventing post traumatic stress disorder (PTSD), *Cochrane Database of Systematic Reviews*, issue 1.

Rosen, R.C. (2001) Psychogenic erectile dysfunction: classification and management, *Urologic Clinics of North America*, 28: 269–78.

Rosenhan, D.L. (1973) On being sane in insane places, *Science*, 179: 250–8.

Rosenthal, N.E., Sack, D.A., Gillin, J.C. et al. (1984) Seasonal affective disorder: a description of the syndrome and preliminary findings with light therapy, *Archives of General Psychiatry*, 41: 72–80.

Ross, C.A. and Norton, R. (1989) Effects of hypnosis on the features of multiple personality disorder, *American Journal of Clinical Hypnosis*, 32: 99–106.

Ross, C.A., Norton, R. and Wozney, K. (1989) Multiple personality disorder: an analysis of 236 cases, *Canadian Journal of Psychiatry*, 34: 97–101.

Ross, C.A., Miller, S.D., Reagor, P. et al. (1991) Structured interview data on 102 cases of multiple personality disorder from four centres, *American Journal of Psychiatry*, 147: 596–600.

Rossel, R. (1998) Multiplicity: the challenges of finding place in experience, *Journal of Constructivist Psychology*, 11: 221–40.

Roth, A., Fonagy, P., Kazdin, A.E. et al. (1998) *What Works for Whom?* New York: Guilford.

Rothschild, A.J. and Locke, C.A. (1991) Reexposure to fluoxetine after serious suicide attempts by three patients: the role of akathisia, *Journal of Clinical Psychiatry*, 12: 491–3.

Royal College of Psychiatrists (RCP) (1986) *Alcohol: Our Favourite Drug*. London: RCP.

Ruberman, W., Weinblatt, E., Goldberg, J.D. et al. (1984) Psychosocial influences on mortality after myocardial infarction, *New England Journal of Medicine*, 311: 552–9.

Rubinstein, S. and Caballero, B. (2000) Is Miss America an undernourished role model?, *Journal of the American Medical Association*, 283: 1569.

Rudd, M.D. (2000) The suicidal mode: a cognitive-behavioral model of suicidality, *Suicide and Life Threatening Behavior*, 30: 18–33.

Rush, A.J., Weissenburger, J. and Eaves, G. (1986) Do thinking patterns predict depressive symptoms, *Cognitive Therapy and Research*, 10: 225–35.

Russell, G.F.M., Szmukler, G.I., Dare, C. et al. (1987) An evaluation of family therapy in anorexia nervosa and bulimia nervosa, *Archives of General Psychiatry*, 44: 1047–56.

Russon, L. and Alison, D. (1998) Palliative care does not mean giving up, *British Medical Journal*, 317: 195–7.

Sadnovick, A.D., Eisen, K., Paty, D.W. et al. (1991) Cause of death in patients attending multiple sclerosis clinics, *Neurology*, 41: 1193–6.

Salekin, R.T. (2002) Psychopathy and therapeutic pessimism: clinical lore or clinical reality?, *Clinical Psychology Review*, 22: 79–112.

Salkovskis, P. and Kirk, J. (1997) Obsessive-compulsive disorder, in D.M. Clark and C.G. Fairburn (eds) *Science and Practice of Cognitive Behaviour Therapy*. Oxford: Oxford University Press.

Salkovskis, P.M., Atha, C. and Storer, D. (1990) Cognitive-behavioural problem-solving in the treatment of patients who repeatedly attempt suicide: a controlled trial, *British Journal of Psychiatry*, 157: 871–6.

Sarti, P. and Cournos, F. (1990) Medication and psychotherapy in the treatment of chronic schizophrenia, *Psychiatric Clinics of North America*, 13: 215–28.

Satel, S.L. and Edell, W.S. (1991) Cocaine-induced paranoia and psychosis proneness, *American Journal of Psychiatry*, 141: 1708–11.

Satz, P., Zaucha, K., Forney, D.L. et al. (1998) Neuropsychological, psychosocial, and vocational correlates of the Glasgow Outcome Scale at 6 months post-injury: a study of moderate to severe traumatic brain injury patients, *Brain Injury*, 12: 555–67.

Schenk, D., Barbour, R., Dunn, W. et al. (1999) Immunization with amyloid-beta attenuates Alzheimer-disease-like pathology in the PDAPP mouse, *Nature*, 400: 173–7.

Schofield, W. (1964) *Psychotherapy, the Purchase of Friendship*. Englewood Cliffs, NJ: Prentice Hall.

Schotte, D.E. and Clum, G.A. (1987) Problem-solving skills in suicidal psychiatric patients, *Journal of Consulting and Clinical Psychology*, 55: 49–54.

Schubert, D.S. and Foliart, R.H. (1993) Increased depression in multiple sclerosis patients: a meta-analysis, *Psychosomatics*, 34: 124–30.

Schukit, M.A., Tsuang, J.W., Anthenelli, R.M. et al. (1996) Alcohol challenges in young men from alcoholic pedigrees and control families: a report from the COGA project, *Journal of Studies in Alcohol*, 57: 368–77.

Schwartz, C.E., Foley, F.W., Rao, S.M. et al. (1999) Stress and course of disease in multiple sclerosis, *Behavioral Medicine*, 25: 110–16.

Schwartz, D.M. and Thompson, M.G. (1981) Do anorexics get well? Current research and future needs, *American Journal of Psychiatry*, 138: 319–23.

Schwarz, T. (1981) *The Hillside Strangler: A Murderer's Mind*. New York: New American Library.

Schwitzer, A.M., Rodriguez, L.E., Thomas, C. et al. (2001) The eating disorders NOS diagnostic profile among college women, *Journal of the American College of Health*, 49: 157–66.

Scott, J. (2001) Cognitive-behavioral management of patients with bipolar disorder who relapse while on lithium prophylaxis, *Journal of Clinical Psychiatry*, 62: 556–9.

Scott, J., Garland, A. and Moorhead, S. (2001) A pilot study of cognitive therapy in bipolar disorders, *Psychological Medicine*, 31: 459–67.

Secker, J. (1998) Current conceptualisations of mental health and mental health promotion, *Health Education Research Theory and Practice*, 13: 57–66.

Sel, R. (1997) Dissociation as complex adaptation, *Medical Hypothesis*, 48: 2205–8.

Seligman, M.E.P. (1970) On the generality of the laws of learning, *Psychological Review*, 77: 406–18.

Seligman, M.E.P. (1975) *Helplessness*. San Francisco, CA: Freeman.

Sellman, J.D., Sullivan, P.F., Dore, G.M. et al. (2001) A randomized controlled trial of motivational enhancement therapy (MET) for mild to moderate alcohol dependence, *Journal of Studies in Alcohol*, 62: 389–96.

Semrud-Clikeman, M., Nielsen, K.H., Clinton, A. et al. (1999) An intervention approach for the children with teacher- and parent-identified attentional difficulties, *Journal of Learning Disabilities*, 32: 581–90.

Seto, M.C. and Barbaree, H.E. (1999) Psychopathy, treatment behavior, and sex offender recidivism, *Journal of Interpersonal Violence*, 14: 1235–48.

Shadish, W.R., Montgomery, L.M., Wilson, P. et al. (1993) Effects of family and marital psychotherapies: a meta-analysis. *Journal of Consulting and Clinical Psychology*, 61: 992–1002.

Shapiro, D.A. and Shapiro, D. (1983) Comparative therapy outcome research: methodological implications of meta-analysis, *Journal of Consulting and Clinical Psychology*, 45: 543–51.

Shapiro, F. (1995) *Eye Movement Desensitisation and Reprocessing: Basic Principles*. New York: Guilford.

Sharpe, L. (2002) A reformulated cognitive-behavioral model of problem gambling: a biopsychosocial perspective, *Clinical Psychology Review*, 22: 1–25.

Sharpe, L., Tarrier, N., Schotte, D. et al. (1995) The role of autonomic arousal in problem gambling, *Addiction*, 90: 1529–40.

Shea, M.T., Elkin, I., Imber, S.D. et al. (1992) Course of depressive symptoms over follow-up: findings from the National Institute of Mental Health Treatment of Depression Collaborative Research Program, *Archives of General Psychiatry*, 49: 782–7.

Shea, S.C. (1998) *Psychiatric Interviewing: The Art of Understanding*, 2nd edn. Philadelphia: Saunders.

Sheard, M.H. (1971) Effect of lithium on human aggression, *Nature*, 230: 113–14.

Sherer, M., Madison, C.F. and Hannay, H.J. (2000) A review of outcome after moderate and severe closed head injury with an introduction to life care planning, *Journal of Head Trauma and Rehabilitation*, 15: 767–82.

Shinohara, K., Yanagisawa, A., Kagota, Y. et al. (1999) Physiological changes in Pachinko players: beta-endorphin, catecholamines, immune system substances and heart rate, *Applied Human Science*, 18: 37–42.

Simon, R. (1995) Gender, multiple roles, role meanings, and mental health, *Journal of Health and Social Behavior*, 36: 182–94.

Sinclair, J.D. (2001) Evidence about the use of naltrexone and for different ways of using it in the treatment of alcoholism, *Alcohol and Alcoholism*, 36: 2–10.

Sinha, S., Anderson, J., John, V. et al. (2000) Recent advances in the understanding of the processing of APP to beta amyloid peptide, *Annals of the New York Academy of Science*, 920: 206–8.

Sinnakaruppan, I. and Williams, D.M. (2001) Head injury and family carers: a critical appraisal of case management programmes in the community, *Brain Injury*, 15: 653–72.

Sirey, J.A., Bruce, M.L., Alexopoulos, G.S. et al. (2001) Stigma as a barrier to recovery: perceived stigma and patient-rated severity of illness as predictors of antidepressant drug adherence, *Psychiatric Services*, 52: 1615–20.

Skinner, B.F. (1953) *Science and Human Behavior*. New York: Macmillan.

Slade, P. and Brodie, D. (1994) Body-image distortion and eating disorder: a reconceptualization based on the recent literature, *European Eating Disorders Review*, 2: 32–46.

Smith, A.J., Brown, R.T., Bunke, V. et al. (2002) Psychosocial adjustment and peer competence of siblings of children with Attention-Deficit/Hyperactivity Disorder, *Journal of Attention Disorder*, 5: 165–77.

Smith, C.A. and Lazarus, R.S. (1993) Appraisal components, core relational themes and the emotions, *Cognition and Emotion*, 7: 233–96.

Smith, M.L. and Glass, G.V. (1977) Meta-analysis of psychotherapy outcome studies, *American Psychologist*, 32: 752–60.

Smith, M.L., Glass, G.V. and Miller, T.I. (1980) *The Benefits of Psychotherapy*. Baltimore, MD: Johns Hopkins University Press.

Smith, T., Buch, G.A. and Gamby, T.E. (2000) Parent-directed, intensive early intervention for children with pervasive developmental disorder, *Research in Developmental Disabilities*, 21: 297–309.

Smith, Y.L.S., van Goozen, S.H.M. and Cohen-Kettenis, P.T. (2001) Adolescents with gender identity disorder who were accepted or rejects for sex reassignment surgery: a prospective follow-up study, *Journal of the Academy of Child and Adolescent Psychiatry*, 40: 472–81.

Smyth, B.P., O'Brien, M. and Barry, J. (2000) Trends in treated opiate misuse in Dublin: the emergence of chasing the dragon, *Addiction*, 95: 1217–23.

Sohlberg, M.M. and Mateer, C.A. (1989) Training use of compensatory memory books: a three-stage behavioural approach, *Journal of Clinical and Experimental Neuropsychology*, 11: 871–91.

Sohlberg, M.M. and Mateer, C.A. (2001) Improving attention and managing attentional problems: adapting rehabilitation techniques to adults with ADD, *Annals of the New York Academy of Sciences*, 931: 359–75.

Soloff, P.H., Anselm, G., Nathan, R.S. et al. (1986) Paradoxical effect of amitriptyline on borderline patients, *American Journal of Psychiatry*, 143: 1603–5.

Soloff, P.H., Cornelius, J.R., George, A. et al. (1993) Efficacy of phenelzine and haloperidol in borderline personality disorder, *Archives of General Psychiatry*, 50: 377–85.

Solomon, R.L. (1980) The opponent-process theory of acquired motivation: the costs of pleasure and the benefits of pain, *American Psychologist*, 35: 691–712.

Spanos, N.P. (1994) Multiple identity enactments and multiple personality disorder: a sociocognitive perspective, *Psychological Bulletin*, 116: 143–65.

Spanos, N.P., Weekes, J.R. and Bertrand, L.D. (1985) Multiple personality: a social psychological perspective, *Journal of Abnormal Psychology*, 94: 362–76.

Spiegel, D. (1993) Multiple post-traumatic personality disorder, in R.P. Kluft and C.G. Fine (eds) *Clinical Perspectives on Multiple Personality Disorder*. Washington, DC: American Psychiatric Press.

Spiegel, D. (1999) Commentary: deconstructing self-destruction, *Psychiatry*, 62: 329–30.

Spiegel, D.A. and Barlow, D.H. (2000) Generalized anxiety disorders, in M.G. Gelder, J.J. López-Ibor Jr. and N.C. Andreasen (eds) *New Oxford Textbook of Psychiatry*. Oxford: Oxford University Press.

Spiegel, D.A., Bruce, T.J., Gregg, S.F. et al. (1994) Does cognitive behavior therapy assist slow-taper alprazolam discontinuation in panic disorder?, *American Journal of Psychiatry*, 151: 876–81.

Squire, L.R. and Slater, P.C. (1983) Electroconvulsive therapy and complaints of memory dysfunction: a prospective three-year follow-up, *British Journal of Psychiatry*, 142: 1–8.

Stanton, M.D. and Shadish, W.R. (1997) Outcome, attrition, and family-couples treatment for drug abuse: a meta-analysis and review of the controlled, comparative studies, *Psychological Bulletin*, 122: 170–91.

Steege, M.W., Wacker, D.P., Cigrand, K.C. et al. (1990) Use of negative reinforcement in the treatment of self-injurious behavior, *Journal of Applied Behavior Analysis*, 23: 459–67.

Stein, D.J., Zungu-Dirwayi, N., van der Linden, G.J.H. et al. (2002) Pharmacotherapy for Posttraumatic Stress Disorder, *Cochrane Database of Systematic Reviews*, issue 1.

Stein, D.M. and Lambert, M.J. (1995) Graduate training in psychotherapy: are therapy outcomes enhanced?, *Journal of Consulting and Clinical Psychology*, 63: 182–96.

Steinberg, M., Cichetti, D., Buchanan, J. et al. (1993) Clinical assessment of dissociative symptoms and disorders: the Structured Clinical interview for DSM-III dissociative disorders (SCID-D), *Dissociation*, 6: 3–15.

Steiner, H., Smith, C., Rosenkranz, R.T. et al. (1991) The early care and feeding of anorexics, *Child Psychiatry and Human Development*, 21: 163–7.

Steinhausen, H.C. and Glanville, K. (1983) Follow-up studies of anorexia nervosa: a review of research findings, *Psychological Medicine*, 13: 239–49.

Sterling, R.C., Gottheil, E., Weinstein, S.P. et al. (2001) The effect of therapist/patient race- and sex-matching in individual treatment, *Addiction*, 96: 1015–22.

Stewart, R.M. and Brown, R.I. (1988) An outcome study of Gamblers Anonymous, *British Journal of Psychiatry*, 152: 284–8.

Stoller, R.J. (1968) *Sex and Gender: Vol 1. The Development of Masculinity and Femininity*. New York: Jason Aronson.

Strange, P.G. (1992) *Brain Biochemistry and Brain Disorders*. New York: Oxford University Press.

Strickland, B.R. (1992) Women and depression, *Current Directions in Psychological Science*, 1: 132–5.

Striegal-Moore, R.H. and Smolak, L. (2000) The influence of ethnicity on eating disorders in women, in R.M. Esler and M. Hersen (eds) *Handbook of Gender, Culture, and Health*. Mahwah, NJ: Erlbaum.

Sullivan, H.S. (1953) *The Interpersonal Theory of Psychiatry*. New York: Norton.

Sumaya, I., Rienzi, B.M., Deegan II, J.F. et al. (2001) Bright light treatment decreases depression in institutionalized older adults: a placebo-controlled crossover study, *Journal of Gerontology*, 56A: M356–M360.

Suppes, T., Baldessarini, R.J., Faedda, G.L. et al. (1991) Risk of recurrence following discontinuation of lithium treatment in bipolar disorder, *Archives of General Psychiatry*, 48: 1082–8.

Sutherland, I. and Wilner, P. (1998) Patterns of alcohol, cigarette and illicit drug use in English adolescents, *Addiction*, 93: 1199–208.

Swanson, M.C., Bland, R.C. and Newman, S.C. (1994) Antisocial personality disorders, *Acta Psychiatrica Scandinavica*, suppl. 37: 63–70.

Szasz, T.S. (1971) From the slaughterhouse to the madhouse, *Psychotherapy Theory Research and Practice*, 8: 64–7.

Takei, N., van Os, J. and Murray, R.M. (1995) Maternal exposure to influenza and risk of schizophrenia: a 22-year study from the Netherlands, *Journal of Psychiatric Research*, 29: 435–45.

Tallmadge, J. and Barkley, R.A. (1983) The interactions of hyperactive and normal boys with their fathers and mothers, *Journal of Abnormal Child Psychology*, 11: 565–79.

Tan, E., Marks, I.M. and Marset, P. (1971) Bimedial leucotomy in obsessive-compulsive neurosis: a controlled serial inquiry, *British Journal of Psychiatry*, 118: 155–64.

Tang, T.Z. and DeRubeis, R. (1999) Sudden gains and critical sessions in cognitive-behavioral therapy for depression, *Journal of Consulting and Clinical Psychology*, 67: 1–11.

Tarrier, N., Kinney, C., McCarthy, E. et al. (2000) Two-year follow-up of cognitive–behavioral therapy and supportive counseling in the treatment of persistent symptoms in chronic schizophrenia, *Journal of Consulting and Clinical Psychology*, 68: 917–22.

Taylor, A., Goldberg, D., Hutchinson, S. et al. (2001) High risk injecting behaviour among injectors from Glasgow: cross sectional community wide surveys 1990–1999, *Journal of Epidemiology and Community Health*, 55: 766–7.

Taylor, B., Miller, E., Farringdon, C.P. et al. (1999) MMR vaccine and autism: no epidemiological evidence of a causal association, *Lancet*, 353: 2026–9.

Teasdale, J.D. (1993) Emotion and two kinds of meaning: cognitive therapy and applied cognitive science, *Behaviour Research and Therapy*, 31: 339–54.

Teasdale, J. and Fennell, M. (1982) Immediate effect on depression of cognitive therapy interventions, *Cognitive Therapy and Research*, 6: 342–52.

Teasdale, W. and Engberg, A.W. (2001) Suicide after traumatic brain injury: a population study, *Journal of Neurology, Neurosurgery and Psychiatry*, 71: 436–40.

Terman, M. (1988) On the question of mechanism in phototherapy for seasonal affective disorder: considerations of clinical efficacy and epidemiology, *Journal of Biological Rhythms*, 3: 155–72.

Terman, M., Terman, J.S., Quitkin, F.M. et al. (1989) Light therapy for seasonal affective disorder: a review of efficacy, *Neuropsychopharmacology*, 2: 1–22.

Terr, L.C. (1991) *Unchained Memories*. New York: Basic Books.

Tharyan, P. (2002) Electroconvulsive therapy for schizophrenia, *Cochrane Database of Systematic Reviews*, issue 1.

Tienari, P., Wynne, L.C., Moring, J. et al. (2000) Finnish adoptive family study: sample selection and adoptee DSM-III-R diagnoses, *Acta Psychiatrica Scandinavica*, 101: 433–43.

Timko, C., Moos, R.H., Finney, J.W. et al. (2000) Long-term outcomes of alcohol use disorders: comparing untreated individuals with those in alcoholics anonymous and formal treatment, *Journal of Studies in Alcohol*, 61: 529–40.

Torgersen, S. (1983) Genetic factors in anxiety disorders, *Archives of General Psychiatry*, 40: 1085–90.

Torrey, E.F., Miller, J., Rawlings, R. et al. (1997) Seasonality of births in schizophrenia and bipolar disorders: a review of the literature, *Schizophrenia Research*, 28: 1–38.

Touchette, P.E., McDonald, R.F. and Langer, S.N. (1985) A scatter plot for identifying stimulus control of problem behavior, *Journal of Applied Behavior Analysis*, 18: 343–51.

Treasure, T. (2001) *The Mental Health Act and Eating Disorders*. Institute of Psychiatry, Division of Psychological Medicine, Eating Disorders Research Unit: www.iop.kcl.ac.uk.

Treasure, J., Todd, G., Brolly, M. et al. (1995) A pilot study of a randomised trial of cognitive analytical therapy vs educational behavioural therapy for adult anorexia nervosa, *Behaviour Research and Therapy*, 33: 363–7.

Truax, C.B. (1966) Reinforcement and nonreinforcement in Rogerian psychotherapy, *Journal of Abnormal Psychology*, 71: 1–9.

Tsuang, M.T. (2000) Schizophrenia: genes and environment, *Biological Psychiatry*, 47: 210–20.

Tsuang, M.T., Simpson, S.J.C. and Fleming, J.A. (1986) Diagnostic criteria for subtyping schizoaffective disorder, in A. Marneros and M.T. Tsuang (eds) *Schizoaffective Disorder*. Berlin: Springer-Verlag.

Tucker, T.K. and Ritter, A. (2000) Naltrexone in the treatment of heroin dependence: a literature review, *Drug and Alcohol Review*, 19: 73–82.

Turner, R.J., Lloyd, D.A. and Roszell, P. (1999) Personal resources and the social distribution of depression, *American Journal of Community Psychology*, 27: 643–72.

Turner, R.M. (1989) Case study evaluations of a bio-cognitive-behavioral approach for the treatment of borderline personality disorder, *Behavior Therapy*, 20: 477–89.

Uhlmann, V., Martin, C.M., Sheils, O. et al. (2001) Potential viral pathogenic mechanism for new variant inflammatory bowel disease, *Journal of Clinical Pathology: Molecular Pathology*, 55: 1–6.

Ulbrich, P.M., Warheit, G.J. and Zimmerman, R.S. (1989) Race, socio-economic status, and psychological distress: an examination of differential vulnerability, *Journal of Health and Social Behavior*, 30: 131–46.

Ullrich, S., Borkenau, P. and Marneros, A. (2001) Personality disorders in offenders: categorical versus dimensional approaches, *Journal of Personality Disorders*, 15: 442–9.

Van der Sande, R., Buskens, E., Allart, E. et al. (1997) Psychosocial intervention following suicide attempt: a systematic review of treatment interventions, *Acta Psychiatrica Scandinavica*, 96: 43–50.

Van Goozen, S.H.M., Cohen-Kettenis, P.T., Gooren, L.J.G. et al. (1995) Gender differences in behaviour: activating effects of cross-sex hormones, *Psychoneuroendocrinology*, 20: 343–63.

Van Oppen, P., de Haan, E., van Balkom, A.J. et al. (1995) Cognitive therapy and exposure in vivo in the treatment of obsessive compulsive disorder, *Behaviour Research and Therapy*, 33: 379–90.

Van Os, J. and Selten, J.P. (1998) Prenatal exposure to maternal stress and subsequent schizophrenia: the May 1940 invasion of The Netherlands, *British Journal of Psychiatry*, 172: 324–6.

Vaughn, C.E. and Leff, J.P. (1976) The influence of family and social factors on the course of psychiatric patients, *British Journal of Psychiatry*, 129: 125–37.

Vernberg, E.M., Jacobs, A.K. and Hershberger, S.L. (1999) Peer victimization and attitudes about violence during early adolescence, *Journal of Clinical Child Psychology*, 28: 386–95.

Vitaro, F., Arseneault, L. and Tremblay, R.E. (1999) Impulsivity predicts problem gambling in low SES adolescent males, *Addiction*, 94: 565–75.

Wagenaar, A.C., Zobeck, T.S., Williams, G.D. et al. (1995) Methods used in studies of drink-drive control efforts: a meta-analysis of the literature from 1960 to 1991, *Accident Analysis Review*, 27: 307–16.

Wahlberg, K-E., Jackson, D., Haley, H. et al. (2000a) Gene–environment interaction in vulnerability to schizophrenia: findings from the Finnish Adoptive Family Study of Schizophrenia, *American Journal of Psychiatry*, 154: 355–62.

Wahlberg, K.E., Wynne, L.C., Oja, H. et al. (2000b) Thought disorder index of Finnish adoptees and communication deviance of their adoptive parents, *Psychological Medicine*, 30: 127–36.

Wakefield, A.J., Murch, S.H., Anthony, A. et al. (1998) Ileal-lymphoid-nodular hyperplasia, non-specific colitis, and pervasive developmental disorder in children, *Lancet*, 351: 637–41.

Walker, E.F. and Diforio, D. (1997) Schizophrenia: a neural diathesis-stress model, *Psychological Review*, 4: 667–85.

Walters, E.E. and Kendler, K.S. (1995) Anorexia nervosa and anorexic-like syndromes in a population-based female twin sample, *American Journal of Psychiatry*, 152: 64–71.

Ward, E. and Ogden, J. (1994) Experiencing vaginismus: sufferers' beliefs about causes and effects, *Sexual and Marital Therapy*, 9: 33–45.

Ward, T., Hudson, S.M. and Marshall, W.L. (1996) Attachment style in sex offenders: a preliminary study, *Journal of Sex Research*, 33: 17–26.

Wardle, J. and Marsland, L. (1990) Adolescent concerns about weight and eating: a social-developmental perspective, *Journal of Psychosomatic Research*, 34: 377–91.

Warwick Daw, E., Payami, H., Nemens, E.J. et al. (2000) The number of trait loci in late-onset Alzheimer disease, *American Journal of Human Genetics*, 66: 196–204.

Watson, J.B. and Rayner, R. (1920) Conditioned emotional reaction, *Journal of Experimental Psychology*, 3: 1–14.

Watzlawick, P., Weakland, J.H. and Fisch, R. (1974) *Change: Principles of Problem Formulation and Problem Resolution*. New York: W.W. Norton.

Weich, S., Sloggett, A. and Lewis, G. (1998) Social roles and gender difference in the prevalence of common mental disorders, *British Journal of Psychiatry*, 173: 489–93.

Weiner, H.L., Lemere, C.A., Maron, R. et al. (2000) Nasal administration of amyloid-beta peptide decreases cerebral amyloid burden in a mouse model of Alzheimer's disease, *Annals of Neurology*, 48: 567–79.

Wells, A. (1995) Meta-cognition and worry: a cognitive model of generalized anxiety disorder, *Behavioural and Cognitive Psychotherapy*, 23: 301–20.

Wender, P.H., Kety, S.S., Rosenthal, D. et al. (1986) Psychiatric disorders in the biological and adoptive families of adopted individuals with affective disorders, *Archives of General Psychiatry*, 43: 923–9.

Wender, P.H., Wolf, L.E. and Wasserstein, J. (2001) Adults with ADHD: an overview, *Annals of the New York Academy of Science*, 931: 1–16.

Wessex Institute for Health Research and Development (WIHRD) (1998) *Surgical Gender Reassignment for Male to Female Transsexual People*, Development and Evaluation Committee Report. Southampton: WIHRD.

Westra, H.A. and Stewart, S.H. (1998) Cognitive behavioural therapy and pharmacotherapy: complementary or contradictory approaches to the treatment of anxiety?, *Clinical Psychology Review*, 18: 307–40.

Wetzel, J.W. (1994) Depression: women-at-risk, in M.M. Olsen (ed.) *Women's Health and Social Work*. Stroud: Hawthorn Press.

Whalen, C.K., Henker, B. and Hinshaw, S.P. (1985) Cognitive-behavioral therapies for hyperactive children: premises, problems, and prospects, *Journal of Abnormal Child Psychology*, 13: 391–409.

Whitehouse, P.J., Struble, R.G., Clark, A.W. et al. (1982) Alzheimer disease: plagues, tangles, and the basal forebrain, *Annals of Neurology*, 12: 494.

Whittal, M.L. and Zaretsky, A. (1996) Cognitive-behavioral strategies for the treatment of eating disorders, in M.H. Pollack, M.W. Otto and J.F. Rosenbaum (eds) *Challenges in Clinical Practice: Pharmacologic and Psychosocial Strategies*. New York: Guilford.

Wicki, W., Angst, J. and Merikangas, K.R. (1992) The Zurich Study, XIV: epidemiology of seasonal depression, *European Archives of Psychiatry and Clinical Neuroscience*, 241: 301–6.

Widiger, T.A. and Corbitt, E.M. (1995) Antisocial personality disorder, in W.J. Livesley (ed.) *The DSM-IV Personality Disorders: Diagnosis and Treatment of Mental Disorders*. New York: Guilford.

Widiger, T.A. and Costa, P.T. Jr (1994) Personality and personality disorders, *Journal of Abnormal Psychology*, 95: 43–51.

Widiger, T.A., Frances, A. and Trull, T.J. (1987) A psychometric analysis of the social-interpersonal and cognitive-perceptual items for the schizotypal personality disorder, *Archives of General Psychiatry*, 44: 786–95.

Wiersma, D., Nienhuis, F.J., Slooff, C.J. et al. (1998) Natural course of schizophrenic disorders: a 15-year following of a Dutch incidence cohort, *Schizophrenic Bulletin*, 24: 75–85.

Wileman, S.M., Eagles, J.M., Andrew, J.E. et al. (2001) Light therapy for seasonal affective disorder in primary care, *British Journal of Psychiatry*, 178: 311–16.

Wilkinson, M. (1992) Income distribution and life expectancy, *British Medical Journal*, 304: 165–8.

Willemsen-Swinkels, S.H., Buitlaar, J.K., Nijhof, G.J. et al. (1995) Failure of naltrexone hydrochloride to reduce self-injurious and autistic behavior in mentally retarded adults: double-blind placebo-controlled studies, *Archives of General Psychiatry*, 52: 766–73.

Williams, D.R. (1999) Race, socioeconomic status, and health: the added effects of racism and discrimination, *Annals of the New York Academy of Science*, 896: 173–88.

Williams, G-J., Power, K.G., Millar, H.R. et al. (1993) Comparison of eating disorders and other dietary/weight groups on measures of perceived control, assertiveness, self-esteem, and self-directed hostility, *International Journal of Eating Disorders*, 4: 7–32.

Wilson, B. (1989) Models of cognitive rehabilitation, in R.L. Wood and P.G. Eames (eds) *Models of Brain Injury Rehabilitation*. Baltimore, MD: Johns Hopkins University Press.

Wilson, B.A., Emslie, H.C., Quirk, K. et al. (2001) Reducing everyday memory and planning problems by means of a paging system: a randomised control crossover study, *Journal of Neurology, Neurosurgery and Psychiatry*, 70: 477–82.

Wilson, G.T. (1988) Alcohol use and abuse: a social learning analysis, in C.D. Chaudron and D.A. Wilkinson (eds) *Theories on Alcoholism*. Toronto: Addiction Research Foundation.

Wilson, G.T. (1996) Treatment of bulimia nervosa: when CBT fails, *Behaviour Research and Therapy*, 34: 197–212.

Winters, K.C. and Neale, J.M. (1985) Mania and low self-esteem, *Journal of Abnormal Psychology*, 94: 282–90.

Wiser, S. and Goldfried, M.R. (1998) Therapist interventions and client emotional experiencing in expert psychodynamic-interpersonal and cognitive-behavioral therapies, *Journal of Consulting and Clinical Psychology*, 66: 634–40.

Wittchen, H.U. and Essau, C.A. (1993) Epidemiology of panic disorder: progress and unresolved issues, *Journal of Psychiatric Research*, 27 (suppl 1): 47–68.

Wolfensberger, W. (1972) *The Principle of Normalization in Human Services*. Toronto: National Institutes of Mental Retardation.

Wolfensberger, W. (1983) Social role valorization: a proposed new term for the principle of normalization, *Mental Retardation*, 21: 234–9.

Wolfersdorf, M. (1995) Depression and suicidal behaviour: psychopathological differences between suicidal and non-suicidal depressive patients, *Archives of Suicide Research*, 1: 273–88.

Wolpe, J. (1982) *The Practice of Behavior Therapy*, 3rd edn. New York: Pergamon.

Wong, S. and Hare, R.D. (2002) *Program Guidelines for the Institutional Treatment of Violent Psychopathic Offenders*. Toronto: Multi-Health Systems.

Woods, R. and Bird, M. (1999) Non-pharmacological approaches to treatment, in G.K. Wilcock, R.S. Bucks and K. Rockwood (eds) *Diagnosis and Management of Dementia: A Manual for Memory Disorders Teams*. Oxford: Oxford University Press.

Woods, R. and Roth, A. (1996) Effectiveness of psychological therapy with older people, in A. Roth and P. Fonagy, *What Works for Whom? A Critical Review of Psychotherapy Research*. New York: Guilford.

Woody, G.E., Luborsky, L., McLellan, A.T. et al. (1983) Psychotherapy for opiate addicts. Does it help?, *Archives of General Psychiatry*, 40: 639–45.

World Health Organization (1979) *Schizophrenia: An International Follow-up Study*. Chichester: Wiley.

World Health Organization (WHO) (1992) *Tenth Revision of the International Classification of Diseases*. Geneva: WHO.

World Health Organization (WHO) (1996) *Ottawa Charter for Health Promotion*. Geneva: WHO.

Yale, R. (1995) *Developing Support Groups for Individuals with Early Stage Alzheimer's Disease: Planning, Implementation and Evaluation*. Baltimore, MD: Health Profession Press.

Yalom, I.D., Green, R. and Fisk, N. (1973) Prenatal exposure to female hormones: effect on psychosocial development in boys, *Archives of General Psychiatry*, 28: 554–61.

Yoast, R., Williams, M.A., Deitchman, S.D. et al. (2001) Report of the Council on Scientific Affairs: methadone maintenance and needle-exchange programs to reduce the medical and public health consequences of drug abuse, *Journal of Addictive Diseases*, 20: 15–40.

Young, J.E. and Lindemann, M.D. (1992) An integrative schema-focused model for personality disorders, *Journal of Cognitive Psychotherapy*, 6: 11–23.

Zerbe, K.J. (2001) The crucial role of psychodynamic understanding in the treatment of eating disorders, *Psychiatric Clinics of North America*, 24: 305–13.

Zhou, J-N., Hofman, M.A. and Black, K. (1995) A sex difference in the human brain and its relation to transsexuality, *Nature*, 378: 68–70.

Zilbergeld, B. (1992) *The New Male Sexuality*. New York: Bantam.

Zlotnick, C., Elkin, I., Shea, M.T. et al. (1998) Does the gender of a patient or the gender of a therapist affect the treatment of patients with major depression?, *Journal of Consulting and Clinical Psychology*, 66: 655–9.

Zola, S.M. (1998) Memory, amnesia, and the issue of recovered memory: neurobiological aspects, *Clinical Psychology Review*, 18: 915–32.

Zucker, K.J. and Bradley, S.J. (1995) *Gender Identity Disorder and Psychosexual Problems in Children and Adolescents*. New York: Guilford.

Zucker, K.J., Green, R., Garofano, C. et al. (1994) Prenatal gender preference of mothers of feminine and masculine boys: relation to sibling sex composition and birth order, *Journal of Abnormal Child Psychology*, 22: 1–13.

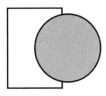

Index

HEALTH PSYCHOLOGY
A TEXTBOOK: 2ND EDITION

Jane Ogden

The additions and updates in this second edition will ensure that it maintains its well deserved position as a leading textbook . . . it provides a clear, comprehensive and up-to-date overview of a wide range of research and theory.

John Weinman, King's College, London

. . . now that Jane Ogden's book has been published I feel that health psychology has finally come of age.

Precilla Choi, Psychology Teaching

. . . a great achievement . . . an excellent textbook.

Journal of Health Psychology

Health Psychology: A Textbook will provide you with an accessible and comprehensive guide to all of the major topics in health psychology.

By reading this book, you will gain a historical and theoretical framework within which to study health psychology. The book focuses on how psychological theory has been applied in the area of health and explores how research can be used to influence and structure practice.

Health Psychology has already become established as a major textbook in the field, not least because it provides a strong coverage of European research as well as the US research which is the exclusive focus of many textbooks. The new edition includes a new chapter on the measurement of health status and new sections on professional issues, recent developments in social cognition models, body dissatisfaction and dieting, causes of obesity and the measurement of pain.

Health Psychology has been designed specifically with the needs of students and teachers in mind. It can form the basis for a complete health psychology course. Each chapter has been designed as the reading for a lecture, and the book contains many special features to aid learning:

- Focus on research sections describe specific studies which test theory
- Questions stimulate discussion and structure revision
- Assumptions in health psychology are highlighted
- Chapter overviews provide outlines of structure, aims and key points
- Figures and diagrams put essential information at your fingertips
- Further reading points to sources of further information and discussion
- Methodology glossary explains key methodological terms

If you are a student or researcher in health psychology, or if you are studying medicine, nursing or any other health-related course, *Health Psychology: A Textbook* is essential reading for you.

Contents
Preface – An introduction to health psychology – Health beliefs – Illness cognitions – Doctor-patient communication and the role of health professionals' health beliefs – Smoking and alcohol use – Obesity and eating behaviour – Exercise – Sex – Screening – Stress – Pain – The interrelationship between beliefs, behaviour and health – The example of placebos – Psychology throughout the course of illness: the examples of HIV, cancer and coronary heart disease – Measuring health status – The assumptions of health psychology – Methodology glossary – References – Index.

416pp   0 335 20596 8 (Paperback)   0 335 20597 6 (Hardback)

THE PSYCHOLOGY OF MEN'S HEALTH

Christina Lee and R. Glynn Owens

- How do traditional concepts of masculinity restrict men's life choices and affect their health?
- Why is it that men die earlier than women?
- Can men find new ways of negotiating masculinity that are not injurious to their physical and emotional health?

This is the first book to provide a comprehensive overview of the psychology of men's health. It represents a wide-ranging introduction, grounded in a thorough review of the international literature in this rapidly developing field, examining the ways in which the social and cultural definitions of appropriate behaviour for men affect their lives and choices in ways that damage their health.

At an individual level, the book covers men's health behaviours and use of health services, emotional expression, risk-taking, sexuality, and men's relationships with their bodies. At a social level, it explores the ways in which social definitions of masculinity affect men's relationships with work and family, and the gendered issues that arise as men age.

The authors seek to place the psychology of men's health in a broad social perspective, and argue that a male centred, patriarchal society does not necessarily benefit all, or indeed any, men. They argue that less restrictive and less gender-typed models of human behaviour would benefit men's physical and emotional health, as well as helping to create a more equitable society.

Contents
Gender and men's health – Health behaviours and health service use – Emotional expression – Risk-taking, violence and criminality – Sexuality and men's health – Men and their bodies – Men and work – Men and family – Men and ageing – The psychology of men's health: a gendered perspective – References – Index.

c192pp   0 335 20705 7 (Paperback)   0 335 20706 5 (Hardback)

INTRODUCTION TO CLINICAL HEALTH PSYCHOLOGY

Paul Bennett

The boundaries between clinical psychology and health psychology are still in the process of being defined. However, it is clear that anyone training to work as a psychologist in medical settings needs to be aware of both health and clinical psychology theory and how it can be applied to maximize the effectiveness of health care delivery. This book provides an introduction to the knowledge base, theory and the practice of health and clinical psychology, in the hospital and in the broader context of health care. It has five key themes:

- the causes of health and illness;
- psychological factors influencing the understandings of health, illness and health-related behaviour choice;
- the theory and application of psychological principles in facilitating individual behavioural and emotional change;
- the role of psychologists within the wider hospital system;
- the role of psychology in population-based health promotion.

Introduction to Clinical Health Psychology addresses the developing curriculum for health psychologists' professional training as well as the more established role of clinical psychologists. It provides essential reading for advanced undergraduates and postgraduates in this increasingly significant and expanding field.

Contents
Part I Behaviour, stress and health – Psychosocial correlates of health – Stress and health – Part II Understanding health-related behaviour – Health-related decision making – Health and illness-related cognitions – Part III Applied health psychology – Hospital issues – Working in the hospital system – Health promotion – Part IV Clinical interventions – Psychological interventions – Assessment issues – Improving quality of life – Risk behaviour change – Notes – Glossary – References – Index.

274pp   0 335 20497 X (Paperback)   0 335 20498 8 (Hardback)

PSYCHOLOGY AND HEALTH PROMOTION
Paul Bennett and Simon Murphy

- What part do behavioural and psychological factors play in the health of an individual?
- Which theories contribute to health promotion at the individual and community level?
- How effective are such interventions in improving people's health?

Psychology and Health Promotion is the first book to set out in clear and authoritative terms the role of psychological theory in health promotion. It adopts both structuralist and social regulation models of health and health promotion, considering the significance of psychological processes in each case. The authors examine how behaviour and the social environment may contribute to health status and how psychological processes may mediate the effect of environmental conditions. They go on to consider the theory underlying interventions that are aimed at individuals and large populations, and the effectiveness of attempts to change both individual behaviour and the environmental factors that may contribute to ill-health.

This highly approachable volume is structured as a textbook and includes a summary and further reading at the end of each chapter, as well as a substantial bibliography. It is designed to provide an invaluable resource for advanced undergraduate and postgraduate courses in health psychology, clinical psychology and social psychology as well as students and practitioners in health and social welfare, including health promotion.

Contents

192pp   0 335 19765 5 (Paperback)   0 335 19766 3 (Hardback)